NEW PERSPECTIVES ON THE
HOUSE OF REPRESENTATIVES

NEW PERSPECTIVES ON THE HOUSE OF REPRESENTATIVES

Edited by:
Robert L. Peabody
The Johns Hopkins University

and

Nelson W. Polsby
Wesleyan University

Rand McNally & Company · Chicago

RAND McNALLY POLITICAL SCIENCE SERIES

Morton Grodzins, Advisory Editor

FROMAN, *Congressmen and Their Constituencies*

GOLDWIN, ED., *The Rand McNally Public Affairs Series: America Armed A Nation of States Why Foreign Aid?*

GOLEMBIEWSKI, *Behavior and Organization: O & M and the Small Group*

LONG, *The Polity*

MILBRATH, *The Washington Lobbyists*

PEABODY AND POLSBY, EDS., *New Perspectives on the House of Representatives*

SCHMIDHAUSER, ED., *Constitutional Law in the Political Process*

STRAUSS AND CROPSEY, EDS., *History of Political Philosophy*

ULMER, ED., *Introductory Readings in Political Behavior*

WILLIAMS AND PRESS, EDS., *Democracy in Urban America: Readings in Government and Politics*

PREFACE

WITH TWO exceptions, the selections in this volume represent what seems to us to be an extraordinary reawakening of scholarly interest in the United States House of Representatives. The awakening is long overdue, for many reasons. The House is a superbly interesting institution, ancient in its customs, intricate in its byways, colorful in its rituals and practices, rich in controversy and in the display of all the arts and crafts of politics. Since 1937, it has been a kind of policy bottleneck in the federal system—the only institution of government which regularly has thwarted the enactment of the major domestic policies of activist Presidents. And yet, aside from exceptions such as the two classic studies which begin and end this book, the scholarly literature on the House—indeed the total amount of all discussion of the House—has, until quite recently, been exceedingly thin.

Although the state of knowledge about the House has improved markedly over the past few years, it has apparently not improved to the point where a summary statement pretending to comprehensiveness and accuracy can be made about its contemporary politics. And so it seems to us that a more preliminary treatment, embodying a variety of perspectives, is appropriate at this time. The rationale for such a procedure was admirably stated by Woodrow Wilson many years ago:

> Like a vast picture thronged with figures of equal prominence and crowded with elaborate and obtrusive details, Congress is hard to see satisfactorily and appreciatively at a single view and from a single stand-point. Its complicated forms and diversified structure confuse the vision, and conceal the system which underlies its composition. It is too complex to be understood without an effort, without a careful and systematic process of analysis. Consequently, very few people do understand it, and its doors are practically shut against the comprehension of the public at large.[1]

Our purpose in presenting this collection is, then, to call the attention of our students, our colleagues, and our neighbors to the

---

[1] *Congressional Government* (New York: Meridian, 1956 [First published, 1885]).

House as a political institution, and to invite their interest. A second purpose is to circulate in a handy form the results of current political research on the House in the hope that other research similarly oriented to the production of middle-range theories and general descriptive statements may be encouraged. And finally, not the least of our hopes is that our long-suffering friends and mentors on Capitol Hill, the congressmen themselves and their staff aides, may observe that their kindness and patience to each of the authors represented here—and to others equally astute and productive not included in this collection—has not been wholly in vain.

A brief word about the principles of selection we employed. We tried to include articles which would give our readers a "feel" for the politics of the House, a sense of its variety and diversity, and which would give as contemporary and accurate a portrait as we could manage in a short compass. The necessity for brevity led us to choose fewer selections than we might have, since we wanted to present them whole and with footnotes intact. To mitigate at least partially our inevitable sins of omission, we have appended a brief bibliography which will bring interested readers into touch with a wider range of materials than could be presented in full here.

RLP
NWP

TABLE OF CONTENTS

PART ONE

Congressmen and their Constituents

THE REPRESENTATIVE AND HIS DISTRICT*

Lewis Anthony Dexter

I

INTRODUCTION

WE TALK frequently of a representative or senator "representing" or "failing to represent" his constituents. This is shorthand. The fact is the congressman represents his image of the district or of his constituents (or fails to represent his, or our, image of them). How does he get this image? Where does it come from?[1]

On numerous important policy matters, he hears nothing from his constituency.[2] But whether he hears anything on an issue, what he hears, whom he hears from, or how he interprets what he hears all *vary* depending upon the kind of person he is, the kind of associations he has had and has in the constituency and in Washington, the public image of his interests and concerns, and the background information or misinformation which he possesses. An editorial summary of an earlier draft of this paper said, "Congressmen make choices about which people communicate with them. . . ."[3]

---

* Reprinted by permission of the author. Part of this article appeared originally in *Human Organization*, 16 (1947), pp. 2–13. Copyright by Lewis Anthony Dexter. An extended discussion of some of this material appears in R. Bauer, L. Dexter, and I. Pool, *American Business and Public Policy* (New York: Atherton, 1963), especially Part V and the chapters on Delaware, Appalachian City, and the 53rd District. Indebtedness to Ithiel Pool is gratefully acknowledged.

[1] The present analysis is based upon 650 interviews, from 1953 to 1957 (420 of them by the author) with politicians, businessmen, trade union leaders, and departmental officials, about the influences impinging upon the formulation of policy. More than 100 interviews were conducted with members of Congress and 40 with executive assistants on Capitol Hill. Four-hundred of the interviews utilized dealt with formation of policy or communication of preference on the Reciprocal Trade Extension Acts of 1953, 1954, and 1955, and it is around these that the analysis is chiefly organized. Considerable use has been made of the writer's own participation in politics, in, for example, the State Government of Massachusetts, September, 1956–August, 1957, the Stevenson primary campaign of 1956, and an effort to arouse public interest in a civil defense bill.

[2] See L. A. Dexter, "Candidates Make the Issues and Give Them Meaning," *Public Opinion Quarterly*, 19 (1955–56), pp. 408–414, for supporting data; and "What Do Congressmen Hear: The Mail," *op. cit.*, 20 (1956–57), pp. 16–27.

[3] Either by consciously providing distracting stimuli or by consciously exposing themselves to countervailing viewpoints.

In large part this is also a manner of speaking. It would be more precise to say that the people in electing a congressman have chosen one sort of recording instrument or another, and that while one instrument may be adjusted to catch or hear one sort of communication, another will hear a different sort, and so on. Although congressmen do, to a small degree, consciously choose what they will hear, it is probably more significant that in large measure their personalities, careers, and public images make them choose what they hear and how they interpret it.

A good many congressmen believe that their districts feel very strongly on this, that, or the other issue, and that they are constrained, therefore, to vote a certain way. The more sophisticated realize, of course, that legislative procedures and processes are so complex that it is more often than not possible to go through the motions of conforming to such views without helping to enact them when they believe the public preference to be wrong.[4] On most issues, out of a desire to serve the district or from indifference, many congressmen do go along with any view which they believe "the district" holds strongly. When the chips are down, and they have to declare themselves, some will vote against their convictions and for their constituents' (presumed) preferences.

This situation has led to a series of classical utterances on the moral problem of the representative: *Should he sacrifice his judgment to his constituents' inclinations as he conceives them or not?* It would be more accurate to emphasize the ways in which representatives' beliefs about constituent preference are functions of the channels of communication and the special processes of transaction between constituents and representatives.

If this is so, more students of representation and representatives would concur with the late Congressman Eberharter's interpretation of the representative-constituent picture. The latter for years was at the center of the legislative issues which provoke the most comment by critics of "pressure," and he told me early in my study of reciprocal trade:

> You know I am sure you will find out a congressman can do pretty much what he decides to do and he doesn't have to

---

[4] See L. A. Dexter, *Congressmen and the People They Listen To* (Cambridge: Center for International Studies, Massachusetts Institute of Technology, Dittoed, 1956), Ch. III, *passim*. M. I. T. has no further copies of this, but it is copyrighted and was also submitted as a doctoral dissertation (Columbia, Sociology, 1960) and therefore is available at the Library of Congress and various libraries.

bother too much about criticism. I've seen plenty of cases since I've been up here where a guy will hold one economic or political position and get along all right; and then he'll die or resign and a guy comes in who holds quite a different economic or political position and he gets along all right too. That's the fact of the matter.

II

The first difference between some congressmen and others is how (consciously or unconsciously) they define their responsibilities.

Many of the congressmen interviewed about both tariff and defense matters referred to a personal conception of what they owe their job, of what in some circles would be called "professional obligation." A few made explicit and many apparently hold implicit theories of representation. These theories of representation were not, except for a few instances, so far as I could tell directly derived from philosophical or academic sources. They resulted from the experiences of men facing the actual moral complexities of a job.

Some members expressed themselves in terms of their obligation to select the right course, regardless of the views of their constituents. For instance, Congressman Stubborn[5] has for a good many years represented a district which (according to interviews with business interests in the district and from an economic analysis of its industrial situation) is inclined to favor the reciprocal trade program. Nevertheless, he says:

> Oh, knowing my stubborn characteristics, no one ever thinks he can change me, you know . . . some of my people say, "You may not agree with this man, 'Stubborn,' but you know where he stands."

Mr. Stubborn agreed that if fate were to select as his successor a Clarence Randall-type "free trader," such a man would be able to vote for a reciprocal trade program without much difficulty, but Stubborn interrupted an effort to probe this point further by declaring:

> That's because they [my constituents] do not really understand the matter. During the twenty-one years reciprocal trade

---

[5] Except for deceased interviewees and (by special permission) Congressman Warburton (R., Del.), the names of all those interviewed and quoted are disguised.

has been in effect, it has had . . . [and he named various alleged or actual consequences which he regards as evil]. . . . There isn't any use trying to change *me!*

Congressman Emphatic on the other hand voted the same way as Mr. Stubborn on the Reciprocal Trade Extension Act of 1955 because of a quite different definition of his responsibility. He said:

> My first duty is to get re-elected. I'm here to represent my district. . . . This is part of my actual belief as to the function of a congressman. . . . What is good for the majority of districts is good for the country. What snarls up the system is these so-called statesmen—congressmen who vote for what they think is the country's interest . . . let the Senators do that. . . . They're paid to be statesmen; we [members of the House] aren't.

(This was said sarcastically, but without humorous intent.)

Mr. Leader, as strong a supporter of reciprocal trade as Mr. Stubborn is an opponent of it, comes fairly close to Mr. Stubborn in his attitude towards constituent opinion. Said Leader:

> You're not identifying me on this, of course? It's strictly con-
> fidential? Always bear in mind there are those in Congress
> who lead their districts and those who are led by them. . . .
> It makes a lot of difference. . . . The "ruanga" growers of my
> district never opposed *me* on reciprocal trade. . . . The answer
> is government stockpiling for them. . . . I think I have con-
> vinced these men that a program of high tariffs would not
> assist them and I think my viewpoint has gained general ac-
> ceptance from them.

Several times he spoke of himself as having "straightened out" people who had seen the matter "wrongly." But Mr. Leader and Mr. Stubborn do not essentially disagree. In another interview during the same session but dealing with an unrelated piece of legislation in which he had also played a prominent part, Mr. Leader showed his conception of his role on this matter to be very similar.

The reciprocal trade issue is so well known, the origin of Mr. Leader's views so deeply based, and his technical knowledge of the field so considerable that he is probably right in his contemptuous dismissal of the possibility that any lobbying or "pressure" could change his position. However, regarding the other legislation, it is entirely probable that a skillful public relations campaign did manipulate *the facts* which came to his attention and to the atten-

tion of some of his colleagues, much as we shall see Mr. Fourth
was influenced on the reciprocal trade issue.

Mr. Fourth represents a district in which there is vociferous anti-
reciprocal trade sentiment. This district also has strong economic
reasons for supporting reciprocal trade and a particularly influential
number of intellectuals predisposed toward reciprocal trade. Mr.
Fourth showed how a portion of the district can influence a man
when he said:

> My impulses when I came down here were in favor of trade
> not aid, until I started to hear all sorts of things from my
> district. . . . So, actually, when you stack all these things to-
> gether, well you're in favor of trade not aid, but, goodness,
> there comes a time . . . if trade means wholesale layoffs in your
> district. . . . I've got any number of letters against it . . . car-
> pets, imported rugs . . . there've been around 300 layoffs in a
> local bicycle plant . . . textiles . . . chemicals . . . electrical
> equipment . . . glass salesmen. It's difficult to get figures. I as-
> sume the Randall Commission report has them. . . . I haven't
> had time to read it. I don't know. . . . I assume that the people
> I hear from exaggerate the seriousness of the situation but still
> that it is serious.

Mr. Fourth ultimately voted against reciprocal trade on the key
votes; the decisive factor appears to have been his unwillingness
to separate himself from several members from his state, also of
junior status, who were definite in their opposition to reciprocal
trade. Mr. Fourth, according to his colleagues was wavering as late
as two hours before the vote. Had the chairman of his state delegation (who strongly supported reciprocal trade) personally requested
his support, he might well have voted the other way. But he was
obviously uncertain, *on the reciprocal trade issue,* whether to adopt
the role of servant of his district (as he conceived its desires) or to
think in terms of the ideology, implied by the phrase "trade not
aid." How he would vote was therefore completely unpredictable.
Had he stumbled into any one of three congressmen with strong
pro-reciprocal trade views in the lobby or the corridors just before
the vote, he might have voted the other way.

Congressman Fourth's vote was unpredictable because on this
particular issue he does not have a clear conception of what his
obligations are. On some issues—flood control or taxes affecting the
major agricultural product of the district—one can predict that he
would see his responsibility as being almost exclusively to the district. On others—particularly those under consideration by the very

important subcommittee of which he is a member—he would be strongly inclined to emphasize national interest in some form as against district concern.

III

Congressmen tend to see their obligations as being either to the nation or to their constituency—other equally possible obligations are seemingly not considered.

Obligation seemed to be conceived as national interest versus district interest (district interest was often, as in the case of Mr. Emphatic, related to re-election and therefore to self-interest). No congressman interviewed indicated any feeling of moral obligation to our allies or to any other country, although our allies are regarded instrumentally as means. This is contrary to a theory sometimes expressed that Americans tend to adopt some favorite foreign country as "theirs." Also, reference to representing a region (the South, the West, New England) was very slight.

The congressman's definition of national interest and responsibility on a particular issue depends in large measure upon his understanding of the facts of a particular issue.

Both Congressman Leader and Congressman Stubborn are quite clear on what they believe are the facts of the reciprocal trade question, and they have no doubt about the effects of the legislation (although their "facts" are to a great extent contradictory, and their conclusions are opposite). Congressman Fourth, on the other hand, was susceptible to influence from either side because he lacked any clear idea of what reciprocal trade legislation means or entails. His sympathy for the phrase "trade not aid" came from a diffuse and generalized acceptance of a *slogan* rather than from an understanding of facts or consequences. He was really uncertain what, if any, difference his vote on reciprocal trade makes to the national welfare. Thus, he much more easily than Mr. Leader or Mr. Stubborn can see the matter as one of simply performing a service for discontented people in his district. It is far less likely that he will —in the absence of external stimuli—feel any strong need to learn the facts. On *service* matters—and much of a congressman's job is service[6]—most congressmen are willing to go along with those con-

---

[6] Cf. J. F. Kennedy, *Profiles in Courage* (New York: Harpers, 1955), esp. pp. 12–21.

stituents who seem to know what service they want performed, and how it is to be performed (provided, of course, nothing irregular is requested). But if, for instance, Mr. Fourth were a New Deal "intellectual"—and his district is one which might easily elect such a person—he would have interpreted the same situation quite differently. And, if he were a politically astute New Deal "intellectual," he would have shown that the major agricultural crop of the district is exported, that several large industries in the area depend on foreign trade, and so forth.

A congressman's conception of his district confirms itself, to a considerable extent, and may constitute a sort of self-fulfilling prophecy.

Within the limits of the morally and sociologically conceivable (no congressman from Alabama in 1942 could have advocated racial integration, for instance!), a congressman has a very wide range of choices on any given issue, *so far as his constituency is concerned.* His relationships in the House or Senate and with party leadership, of course, limit these choices severely. It is a fact, however, that there is no district viewpoint *as such* to be represented on the overwhelming majority of issues. A few will care one way and a few the other, but the issue will be insignificant or unknown to the great majority. Indeed, in many districts, only a fraction of the voters know the name of their congressman, let alone how he voted on a particular issue.

A congressman of my acquaintance took about 100 letters which he received on a particular issue and checked the registration of the writers. He found that almost three-quarters of them were not registered in his district. What difference, then, would their views make with respect to his prospects for re-election?

Mr. Emphatic, who insisted that he was representing his district's desires, was led nevertheless, by my questions, to admit that more than likely none of the workers presumably represented by him actually knew how he had voted. "Not a single one of them," he complained, "wrote in to thank me, though hundreds had written asking me to vote their way." He attributed this in large measure to the allegation that the largest newspaper in the district is "anti-Emphatic." However, since newspapers published outside the district, which gave front page publicity to his stand, have far greater circulation in the district than does the anti-Emphatic "News," this seems an unsound explanation.

Actually, most of the letters Mr. Emphatic received and most of the comments he heard originated in three large plants in the district, and they represented less than 7 per cent of the voters of the district. These plants are organized by national unions which, ironically enough, in chalking up Mr. Emphatic's score in 1956, were inclined to regard his vote against reciprocal trade as an anti-labor vote. Fortunately for him, his stands on other matters and his personal contacts offset this factor. Of the groups in the district, only members of the League of Women Voters wrote to him in favor of reciprocal trade. "They aren't," he averred, "God knows, a potent political force, and all their letters are damn stilted, right out of the same handbook." However, it was likely that the League members *would* remember in 1956, and perhaps again in 1958, how he voted. And, because of the racial and academic composition of the district, League members may have some influence outside their own membership.

It would have been perfectly possible for Mr. Emphatic to take the reverse position favoring reciprocal trade and still regard himself as representing his district—particularly since the area also has a strong port interest.

A congressman has great difficulty in deciding what the viewpoint of the district is even on such an issue as reciprocal trade. Most persons with an interest or belief in the tariff will have interests or beliefs in other issues as well. Thus, the most effective representation of their overall interests may necessitate concessions on some matters, in order to get along with party leadership, colleagues, or prominent committee members in the Congress. "Joe Martin and Charlie Halleck in their heart of hearts," said a prominent Republican, "certainly go along with us, not with the White House on this; and they can swing twenty-five votes, at least, anytime they want; we lost by less than twenty-five votes, so they beat us." Until 1958 Martin was the Republican leader; Halleck became his successor in the 86th Congress. Is a congressman doing a better job of representing his district when he keeps in the good graces of such powerful men (and thereby helps to get a bridge or a new post office or a dam for his district) or when he opposes them on an issue, the details of which few will remember six months later? The Republican who told me about Martin and Halleck is one of the most persistent enemies of reciprocal trade in the party, and he is probably the most effective in a quiet way. He is opposed to reciprocal trade in part because of its "harmful" effect on his district.

However, he cheerfully admitted, "It wouldn't make any difference what my congressman does in this matter," insofar as his reelection is concerned. Afterwards he qualified this by saying that perhaps the incumbent ought not stick his neck out strongly *for* reciprocal trade, but there is no call for activity of any kind.

IV

A congressman hears most often from those who agree with him.
A congressman's relationships with his district tend to be maintained through a small group whom he knew before he was elected or through a group who have since then worked closely with him. Generally speaking, the views of those whom he knew prior to his election tend to be more like his than do the views of the "average" voter. It is a well-known fact that we tend to be like the people with whom we associate and vice-versa. Also, most of the people who have worked closely with the congressman since his election—because he is a congressman—have a particular ax to grind. They will naturally tend to stress agreement with him on issues about which they are not concerned—just as salesmen typically do not disagree with their customers on politics. For several years, I wondered about the unfavorable references congressmen frequently made to the League of Women Voters and several times to delegations from labor unions. Ultimately, it occurred to me that these two groups are probably the only ones which seriously, on a face-to-face basis, year after year, go over with a congressman the issues on which they disagree with him. Because their efforts cannot be entirely discounted as "politics," they make congressmen uncomfortable.

Congressmen may also have a few close supporters upon whom they rely who tend to become "their" men, and who shift as they shift. This is not always just a matter of holding on to a job, but may represent confidence in a man, prestige gained by association with him, or an unwillingness to sacrifice an investment in goodwill which may be utilized for better public or personal purposes in the future. Such supporters are likely to couch any criticism in tactical terms, and ultimately, to follow the leader.[7]

Some men automatically interpret what they hear to support their own viewpoints.

---

[7] Dexter, *Congressmen and the People They Listen To*, Chs. II–III.

Mr. First of New Hungary does not think he hears much about foreign imports. Mr. Second, coming from the same sort of district in the same city, says:

> It's either the first or second most important issue with me. Unemployment is the other. And, of course, they're really the same thing.

The last sentence is the clue to why Mr. Second hears so much more than Mr. First about foreign imports. When Mr. First hears about unemployment, he hears just about unemployment, or just about the declining industries of the area, or just about the invidious differential effect which accelerated amortization and certain other tax provisions have had on industry in the area. In fact, when I talked to him about tariff, he advised me that I really ought to study accelerated amortization. Mr. Second, however, interprets almost any statement about unemployment as a plea for relief from foreign imports. Sometimes it is, but sometimes it isn't. So, seeing the same men and hearing the same things said, Mr. Second will "hear" about tariff matters, Mr. First will not. Mr. Third, their colleague from an adjoining district, is vitally interested in wilderness preservation, hunting, and fishing. He sees many of the same men, but they are likely to talk to him about his interests, and if they do talk to him about unemployment, he is less likely to draw any special conclusions from the talk.

In more general terms, what congressmen hear and how they interpret what they hear depends on who they are.

Conventional discussion of the relationship between congressmen and constituents assumes that the kind of man the congressman is does not influence what he hears from the district and that the question is whether he follows or contravenes district sentiment. The notion of the congressman representing "the" district at least needs restatement *in terms of a particular congressman who represents what he hears from the district as he interprets it.* And his interpretation results from his being the particular kind of person he is and is reputed to be.

Of course, congressmen will hear many of the same things. The similarity is very great since there are common factors in the careers of American politicians, and since Congress is a continuing social group where habits and attitudes are likely to persist. The old hands (staff, lobbyists, and active constituents as well as members) teach the newer ones. Furthermore, and not surprisingly, within any given district the balance of forces may continue so that several successive congressmen will belong to the same politico-social group (sometimes even when they are members of different parties). The real test of how successfully the district exerts an inescapable "pressure" upon the congressman comes when, without any sharp shift in population characteristics in the district, the congressman comes from a different social grouping.

Students of comparative politics have, however, much more manageable ways of exploring this problem than by studying the activities of congressmen from the same district at different times. For instance, even in terms of our foci upon substantive issues, if I had realized the significance of knowing how a congressman's interpretation of what he hears is affected by his perception of the job, the constituency, and the facts, I could have tried to find out how senators of the same party and from the same state (but representing different factions and obviously looking at the world differently) understood the reciprocal trade question. It is almost incredible that Wiley, Republican of Wisconsin, and McCarthy, Republican of Wisconsin, could have heard the same messages on domestic security and international relations. It would have been interesting, therefore, to find out whether Wiley was as "convinced" as McCarthy was of the vital need for protecting Wisconsin's fur-bearing mammal growers or trappers against foreign competition. Robertson and Byrd of Virginia, Johnson and Daniel of Texas, Beall and Butler of Maryland, Martin and Duff of Pennsylvania, Cotton and Bridges of New Hampshire, Morse and Neuberger of Oregon, would all have made interesting studies from this standpoint. As it happened, I did most of my interviewing with representatives simply because senators' schedules are so much more complex, and it is more difficult to see them. A first-term senator may serve on as many as fourteen subcommittees, something unimaginable in the House.

For those whose focus is on the communication between a representative and his district, and who are not necessarily confined to a particular issue, there are still better cases for study. For instance, several districts in Maryland elect seven members to its Lower House, and Massachusetts has a number of three- and two-member districts (as have other states and cities). Considering the wide factional and personality differences of incumbents at the same time, an analysis of the messages they "hear" from their districts would be of considerable value.

V

How a congressman was "influenced" by his district: A transactional relationship.

Mr. Serious-Consideration provides a very good case study of how a particular constellation of factors in the district may lead to a particular vote. The vote cannot be understood unless we recognize that both a congressman—as a personality and at a particular time— and the "district," as understood by him, are variables.

During the spring of 1954, my old friend Mr. Straightforward did considerable canvassing in the district with a view to running for Congress in the primary against Mr. Serious-Consideration. Mr. Straightforward, incidentally, has held public office in the area several times before. He told me, in effect:

> There's practically no interest in trade or tariff matters in the district; if you are thinking as we were of interviewing businessmen and labor leaders about it, don't bother. None of them know anything about it; it just doesn't bulk large in their sight.

Mr. Serious-Consideration, however, in the same year reported that in his view it was one of the most significant issues to his constituents.

Why the difference? It can be explained, I think, partly by the fact that Mr. Serious-Consideration is, consciously, or unconsciously, looking for ways in which he can appeal to local labor without offending local business. Protection against "low-wage foreign imports" is, as trade association executives have pointed out to us, an excellent issue for *uniting* labor and management in depressed or dying industries (of which there are several in the district). Mr. Straightforward, on the other hand, has a program for economic redevelopment and reform of labor legislation which deflects the attention of those whom he meets, whether they agree with him or not, from such issues as the tariff. He, therefore, rarely hears about the tariff as an issue. Then, too, in manner and bearing, Mr. Straightforward is clearly an intellectual, and one of the popular conceptions of the intellectual is his belief in free trade.[8] Mr. Serious-Consideration is not at all of this type. Finally, Mr. Straightforward's worst fault as a politician is a rather curt dismissal of anything he regards as nonsense. Mr. Serious-Consideration, on the other hand, might justly be criticized for not being able to distinguish between more or less unmotivated grumbling and serious pleas for effective action.

Mr. Serious-Consideration is a worrier. He seems genuinely to believe that we must shore-up NATO by strengthening trade relations. Therefore, he called a meeting of everyone in his district who might be interested and wanted to come to discuss the problem. After this meeting, his office, which had already received a good deal of mail on the subject, was simply overwhelmed by protectionist mail. This came about because people who had attended the meeting told their friends and business acquaintances about his indecision. Mr. Serious-Consideration had called upon persons whom he thought might be interested. Naturally most of those who turned up were from protection-minded industries. It is much easier for the businessman who is, or thinks he is, in considerable economic danger from foreign imports to take a day off to attend a meeting on trade and tariffs called by the congressman (he can charge this as a business expense) than it is for the businessman who *might* benefit economically if international trade were increased in total. It is more difficult, of course, for nonbusinessmen to take such time off and it is usually quite impossible for them to charge the cost off as business expense.

So this meeting was "stacked" in this particular district. If, on the other hand, Congressman Lankford of the Fifth Maryland had called such a meeting it might well have been stacked the other way. His district is a big tobacco-growing area which is well aware of its dependence on sales to Switzerland, and there have been Swiss threats to cut off purchases unless the U.S. withdrew its trade barriers to Swiss watches. Congressman Serious-Consideration or Congressman Lankford, however, by some planning could have gotten a more balanced attendance. A different picture would have developed if leaders of those unions in the district whose headquarters favor reciprocal trade had been consulted; and if the several college

---

[8] See Dexter, *Congressmen and the People They Listen To*, Ch. XIX; and "Where the Elephant Fears to Dance Among the Chickens: Business in Politics? The Case of DuPont," *Human Organization*, 19 (1960–61), pp. 188–194.

professors of economics in the district and representatives of the Grange and the Farm Bureau had been invited. Or several organizations could have been asked to do what the League of Women Voters has done in some areas—study the dependence of the local industries on foreign trade.

Mr. Serious-Consideration would have had to be a different kind of man to provide wider representation at his meeting. However, three or four imaginative supporters of reciprocal trade could have produced the same result. And if the agricultural commodity in which Mr. Serious-Consideration himself has had an interest were on an export basis (as it was prior to World War II), his picture of the situation might well have been altered. He would then have been hearing from his own associates in his own trade association.

Mr. Serious-Consideration finally decided to vote against the party leadership on the key votes on reciprocal trade. He justified himself by objecting to various procedural aspects of the legislation—for instance the so-called "gag rule" under which the bill was brought to the floor. But he had not objected to this gag rule, which is standard parliamentary practice, in other cases where it was invoked. He continues to regard himself as a strong advocate of reciprocal trade.

When a congressman was not much influenced by his district.

Representative Warburton (R., Del., 1953–5) provided a particularly clear example of the way in which a congressman may select the kind of communications he hears. In answer to a question from me, he said to his secretary, "Am I right? We haven't received mail from more than five people on this tariff business." I looked somewhat astounded and she replied, "Yes, except of course for the pressure groups." The congressman had instructed her to segregate all recognized pressure-group mail. And he added, quite offhandedly, that he would discount, "because of his self-interest," one out of the five people who had written him about the tariff. His attitude may, in part at least, explain why the chemical companies and other industries in the state had never given him "any particular specifications" on the tariff. It certainly clarifies his assertion that his approach to the problem of communications had "choked off" pressure-group mail.

Such an approach is relatively easy in Delaware,[9] where DuPont,

---

[9] *Ibid.*

because of its tremendous size and consciousness of its own vulnerability, has developed a practice and to some extent a doctrine of self-restraint. In a sense, Congressman Warburton's procedure[10] was made much easier because of the effect upon DuPont of the munitions investigations of twenty years ago and its subsequent earnest effort never, never, never to get into that sort of trouble again. Thus it could happen when a prominent Delaware Democrat was asked why DuPont had not put on a campaign in regard to tariff matters (if, as it was reported, DuPont was hostile to the Reciprocal Trade Extension Act) that he said in a genuinely shocked voice, "Oh, the company would never allow that, two or three letters at the most."

A congressman's reputation among those who might want to influence him, determines in large measure what actually is said to him.

Most lobbyists appear to follow the principle of going to see only those who already agree with them. "Work with your friends, but don't stir up your enemies" is a principle fairly widely believed by Capitol Hill lobbyists. There is a reason for this prudence. Most investigations of lobbying and of particular lobbyists seem to have been started by congressmen who were annoyed at being continually approached by lobbyists with whom they disagreed. There is also another possible reason—it makes the job easy for the lobbyist. Representatives of the League of Women Voters and of labor union councils, who do not follow this principle, make themselves unpopular in some quarters. In other words, survival and comfort for the lobbyist may depend upon not lobbying very much—and it is safer to stay away from somebody who may be an enemy and react negatively than to take a risk.

The tendency to abstain from trying to influence those whom you believe to be against you affects the districts back home as well as professional Capitol Hill lobbyists. The Farm Bureaus in Congressman Stubborn's district, like most Farm Bureaus, were definitely committed to the reciprocal trade program. Nevertheless, when a delegation went to see him, they made no effort to talk in favor of

---

[10] Congressman Warburton followed the same procedure on other matters. He was, it is true, rather badly beaten in his try for the Senate in 1954 by the incumbent Democrat, Frear, but there is no reason to suppose that this handling of communications had anything to do with the outcome. Far more significant political factors, such as the opposition to integration, probably explain that.

reciprocal trade. Our correspondent in Mr. Stubborn's district inquired of Farm Bureau representatives why they made no such effort and he summarized their attitude as follows:

> The farmers deliberately avoided mention of tariffs; when I asked one of them why he didn't beard old "Stubborn" in his high-tariff den, he replied, "Nothing in the world will change his thinking on tariffs, so why bother? He knows how we feel and can't help but feel a little nervous about the situation. So we can take that nervousness and get him to go along with us on things he isn't so dead-set against."

The probability is that they didn't *change* him on anything, but that they may have influenced him to take a more aggressive and effective part on an issue of importance to them—an issue on which he did not disagree, but which he considered less important than they did.

In another instance, the congressmen from a certain area are inclined to be rather blunt and not to rely on any indirection. Before the 1955 vote on reciprocal trade, the Farm Bureau sent representatives in to talk with these congressmen. One of them, Congressman Ridge, told me that the farmers said, "National asked us to pass the word along that we're in favor of reciprocal trade—but we shan't be mad if you vote against it." Then, according to Mr. Ridge, one of the congressmen asked the Farm Bureau men if any one of them really favored reciprocal trade. Anyone who knows the congressmen present can be sure that at least two of them would look ready to slay on the spot any farmer bold enough to say "Yes." Apparently no one did say "Yes," and the reason may have been similar to that advanced by the Farm Bureau member from Mr. Stubborn's district. So Mr. Ridge, who is not as strongly opposed to reciprocal trade as some of his colleagues, was pushed to this conclusion: "Everybody in my state is against reciprocal trade. . . . The only ones for it would be the ultra-internationalists." Of course, if Mr. Ridge were a devoted supporter of reciprocal trade, or if he were a really sophisticated analyst of interpersonal relations, he might well have felt that the conclusion is not that easy. But he is neither of these and so he allied himself entirely with his colleagues' opposition to the reciprocal trade program.

Several congressmen told me, in effect, that they tell their constituents: "I want a letter of such and such a kind, or I won't pay any attention to it."

One of the most dedicated opponents of reciprocal trade in the country is a man who has often pointed out that reciprocal trade is really an invention of Karl Marx himself, designed to "make us captives of the Kremlin," developed and implemented by Harry Dexter White. This congressman states that he tells his constituents that he is only interested in "factual, thoughtful" letters, nothing mass-produced or propagandistic. He also told me that in three months he had not received one single letter opposing his views on reciprocal trade; he had received over 2,000 supporting his position, 1,750 of which were definitely individual letters. The very extremity of his position apparently leads those who might disagree with him to feel, "Oh, what's the use?" Senators who make statements of this kind, however, may simply not know what mail they receive, since the mail clerks handle it. Most members of the House do have a fairly good idea of what is coming in to them. Of course, protectionist mail was mass-produced in a way that reciprocal trade mail was not, and it is far more likely that a protectionist congressman would receive nothing in opposition to his stand rather than the reverse. Oil interests on the Atlantic seaboard did mass-produce mail protesting the fuel-oil quota, but few of the congressmen to whom they wrote favored a fuel-oil quota, whatever their general tariff views.

We need more studies of what the image of a person to whom a communication is sent is in the minds of the sender.[11] By and large, I strongly suspect that the bulk of political communications in the United States today tends to be addressed to those believed most likely to be sympathetic. Exceptions may occur when an issue becomes one of great involvement (as reciprocal trade did *not,* in 1953–1955), or of interest to persons politically very unsophisticated who have no image of specific political figures. (Occasionally, too, a writer may regard his request as one for a personal service but in the recipient's view, it may involve an issue. A sympathetic response is expected, of course, to a request for a personal service.)

Some communications tend to be unclear in their meaning.

A good deal of so-called "lobbying" by constituents tends to be nothing more than a social visit and a general discussion. One senator's assistant said:

---

[11] The work of Erving Goffman, *The Presentation of Self in Everyday Life* (Garden City: Doubleday-Anchor, 1960), seems to me to be methodologically of extreme value for this purpose, as is also that of Everett C. Hughes, *Men and Their Work* (Glencoe: The Free Press, 1958).

You know, many of these guys who come in here from back home never talk about issues at all. I've seen lots of them supposedly lobbying. Now, "Roughie," [the senator] takes me to lunch with them and we go out to lunch, but they don't necessarily talk about anything. "Roughie," just knows a good guy may be going out of business because he doesn't get more trade or so. It's the spirit that influences him.

Interestingly enough, some weeks later I found that this particular assistant was completely ignorant of the quite strong feelings (verbalized in other quarters) on tariff matters of an important industry in the state. This is an industry whose representatives had visited him and the senator, and in whose behalf he personally had spent many hours performing other chores in administrative agencies.

Mr. Busy represents a district very much like those of Messrs. First, Second, and Third discussed above, and he is home every weekend. He was professedly strongly opposed to reciprocal trade, but when I questioned him, he said he really did not know whether people talk about the tariff with him or not. At first, it seemed as though this might be because of his schedule which is so heavy that most men could not stand it, and he must be, as a result, always fatigued. But the real point appears to be that Mr. Busy's focus and attention in oral conversations back home are given to requests for personal services. He is the archtype of the errandboy congressman and the only things he seems attuned to hear are requests for personal services. He shunts comments on issues to one side or regards them as preliminaries to requests for favors. When Mr. Second hears someone talk about unemployment caused by foreign imports, he regards this as a request to fight reciprocal trade. Mr. First regards it as nonsense, although possibly nonsense of which he should be cognizant. But Mr. Busy pays only vague attention to it except insofar as it leads or may lead to a request for him to perform a service. In this he may well be correct, for very few constituents talk about an issue with a congressman just to talk about the issue. I spent about twenty man-days in the winter of 1956 acting as co-manager of a candidate in a congressional primary campaign and about half of this time I was actually with the candidate. During the entire twenty days only four people raised any national or international issues whatsoever with him or me. (Others who worked for him at the same time and in the same area had similar reports to make.)

It's partly accident if anybody's listening.

There is a highly unpredictable element in the kind of response a particular communication will get. As a senatorial assistant said:

> I've seen it a dozen times. One time some letter or call will come in from "Minerville" and nobody will pay any attention to it. They might say, for instance, the miners are all worried about this foreign fuel oil. Another time a call will come in in the same words almost and everybody will get worried as hell about it; it might be that the State Chairman was in the day before and says, "We're not doing so well in 'Coal County'" so we all jump to the conclusion that it's fuel oil that is hurting us there. Or it may be just accident; one time the Senator is preoccupied, another in a relaxed mood, but the third time he listens eagerly. You know how it is.

VI

Important instances when congressmen were changed by their districts.

The two statistically notable shifts on reciprocal trade in 1955 as compared with previous years were: (1) Southern congressmen, mostly representing textile manufacturing districts, who for the first time voted against the Hull reciprocal trade program, in spite of a traditional veneration for free trade in the South; and (2) Farm Belt congressmen, from districts where "isolationist" sentiment had been fairly strong, who for the first time supported reciprocal trade on the key votes. The latter were presumably influenced by the organized efforts of national Farm Bureau leaders to get their local leaders to understand the (actual or alleged) dependence of farm prosperity upon international trade and the (actual or alleged) values of a trade not aid program. But those who were influenced were not, so far as is known, men to whom the issue mattered much one way or another.

In the case of the Southern congressmen the matter is clearer. Here "pressure education"—agitation in the district—worked. They broke with the leadership of Speaker Rayburn, generally said to be the most powerful Speaker since Speaker Cannon. They broke with the Southern tradition and the tradition of Cordell Hull, the father of reciprocal trade. They challenged and to some degree pressured that highly respected Southern Senator, Walter George, on his long-standing pro-reciprocal trade position. And they gave, in this case, a weapon to Herman Talmadge, George's potential opponent in the senatorial primary in 1956, in spite of the fact that practically none of them would have preferred Talmadge to George. This breaking with precedent was chiefly the result of the communications they received from their districts, largely from textile interests. Some Southern congressmen received more mail on the reciprocal trade question in a few weeks than they normally do in months on all issues combined. That the mail was more or less synthetic and stimulated is shown by the fact that some congressmen, whose positions are known to be unchangeable, received not a single letter! For these Southern congressmen, such a flood of mail was apparently like the first engagement in a war for inexperienced troops. They had never seen anything of the sort before. The results: most of the Georgia delegation opposed reciprocal trade on the key votes. Hugh Alexander, successor to "Muley" Doughton who as leader of Ways and Means had year after year pushed reciprocal trade through committee and the House much as Cordell Hull wanted it, voted against the program of Hull and Doughton similarly.

This does not controvert what has been said before. Most of these men, although traditionally "free-traders," care very little about the issue one way or the other. If industry and the workers in their district are convinced that reciprocal trade will hurt them, they are willing enough to go along—just as most of them would go along with their farmers if the latter wanted new soil conservation legislation. In either case, they would regard themselves simply as serving their constituents.

Mr. Lanham's shift.

The leader of the Southeastern congressmen was the late Henderson Lanham of Georgia. He played a part, perhaps a large part, in making it respectable for ten to fifteen men from his section to reject the leadership of Sam Rayburn, Jere Cooper, and Wilbur Mills, and support the textile industry's protectionist claims. How did he happen to bolt?

In January, 1955, he received a large quantity of mail from workers in the textile industry saying that they wanted protection against foreign goods. Shrewd enough to realize that they must have been "put up to it" by manufacturers, Mr. Lanham said:

> I did not appreciate it. I wrote to a friend of mine who is in business, saying, in effect, "call your fellows off." I asked

my friend, "Don't peril point and escape clause protect you?"
He replied, "No, they don't." That shocked me. I started making inquiries. I found out I'd been pretty naive. Peril point
and escape clause did not protect our people.

(Peril point and escape clause refer to provisions of earlier Reciprocal Trade Acts, professedly designed to protect U.S. industry against
"ruination" through goods introduced under the Reciprocal Trade
Act.)

It is significant that the congressman made his inquiries in his
home state almost (if not quite) entirely among people in the
textile industry. Despite the fact that at least half of the economy
of his district is agricultural, producing cotton among other commodities, he made no inquiry among his farmers. A superficial
analysis, however, would suggest that most of his farmers profit
from foreign trade, directly or indirectly, and that many of them
are affiliated with farm organizations which have endorsed reciprocal
trade. Mr. Lanham actually represented the town more than the
countryside. The town is where his roots were, where his friends
were, and he thought in its terms. Populationwise, it would be perfectly conceivable that his district and several other districts over
whose congressmen he had influence, might be represented by men
to whom the farmer is more important than the manufacturer. Although I cannot prove it to be so, and I did not realize its significance until 1959, I suspect that the Talmadge-George senatorial
rivalry was a very significant matter to Mr. Lanham and his Georgia colleagues. Walter George had won national renown as a
"world-minded" statesman; Herman Talmadge intended to challenge him for the Senate. The most vulnerable—in terms of local
interests and concerns—aspect of George's internationalist position
was his support of reciprocal trade. In whatever manner he responded to the organized pressure from back home on protection
for textiles he would be weaker. (George himself, as late as 1954,
was, as my interview with him suggested, probably quite ignorant
of the potential strength of the drive for textile protection.) Consequently, Talmadge in the nature of the case espoused the interests
of the textile industry as that industry interpreted them; and,
naturally, Congressmen from the state would have been inclined
to feel that if they continued to support reciprocal trade they might
be out on a limb which Talmadge (a younger, politically stronger,
and probably more organization-minded man than George) could
saw off.

VII

Reverse English.

When Mr. Lanham became convinced that there was merit to the contention of the textile and allied industries, he then went to the state organization representing textiles. According to his account, he politely pointed out to them that they really hadn't been on the ball—he should have heard more about the matter and so should his colleagues. Presumably, this did increase the communications on the subject, by mail and personal visits, to his colleagues.

Reverse lobbying—from congressmen to interest groups—is by no means unusual. I asked another prominent congressman how much he heard from the organizations on his side of the issue.

> Hell no, it's just the other way. It's me calling them up and trying to shaft them to get off their fat asses and get out and do something.

More common, probably, is the senator or representative who asks the lobbyists on his side to do something which they then generalize. A senatorial assistant needed some figures in preparing a speech and tried to get them from the lobbying group: "I absolutely had to beat them over the head to get those things." But not long after, the same figures were cited by the organization as "proving" their point.

VIII

Pressure is how you see it.

"Pressure" and "pressure politics" are regarded by most "sophisticated" people today as "explaining" a great deal that happens. But it was frequently impossible to find any admission of or apparently any awareness of "pressure." That was not because shrewd and worldly politicians were concealing what really goes on from this naive and innocent interviewer and his naive and innocent colleagues.[12]

---

[12] On Beacon Hill in Massachusetts, when with Governor Furcolo (D.), and to a lesser extent with Governor Volpe (R.), the writer noted pressure, possibly from Representative Cleveland Bailey on his colleagues. The journalistic, traditional notion of pressure certainly seemed to apply to highway contracts and some patronage matters in the Furcolo administration. In all probability, the pressure (not so much on congressmen but on the relevant officials in the Defense Department) on defense contracts might be much "rougher" than any-

The reason is explained by Senator Service's assistant:

There are very few people actually pressuring us, even if you count all we hear about all issues. Seriously, the sense of being pressured is a matter of reaction. Other people who get no more mail than we do in this office would say, "See how much pressure is on me." We don't feel it. . . . Sure, you get mail. It's just that so-and-so makes more 'phone calls than somebody else. The result is purely physical. It isn't a representation of what or how or when people are going to vote in elections. . . . My personal opinion is that members of most organizations make up their minds on what they read in the papers without reference to organizations.

With this theory of voting behavior, Senator Service's assistant naturally will not be too much worried by a good deal of effort to get him or his boss to change policies—he simply will not regard it as pressure.

Congressman Widesight amusingly illustrated the point made by Service's assistant. Mr. Widesight has moods when he reaches way out into left field looking for things to worry about, things which might possibly defeat him. One day, discussing reciprocal trade, he said that things were very bad indeed. His reason was that he was getting "so much" mail against it. "I, whom they never used to bother at all." When I checked with his secretary later, I found he couldn't possibly have received more than fifty letters opposing reciprocal trade. This was only a fraction of the mail Senator Service received on the same matter. It was also a fraction of what Congressman Widesight himself has several times heard on other matters such as postal pay increases. However, Widesight is accustomed to communications on that issue and he wasn't accustomed to them on the reciprocal trade issue.

As a matter of fact, on the reciprocal trade issue, most of the congressmen interviewed reported that no one had come to see them. Several of them expressed the wish that someone would make the issue clear. This does not mean, of course, that they were not approached; but simply that they had forgotten the approach or had not realized its purpose. Some of them tried to question me about the matter in what I think was a serious effort to get some guidance.

---

thing congressmen generally experience on reciprocal trade. But it will be noted that contracts and patronage are matters of direct, demonstrable interest to determinate people. Reciprocal trade is *general* legislation.

Our interviews confirmed the observation of the late Sam Jacobs, then newly appointed to the staff of Senator McNamara (D., Mich.), who said, speaking generally and not talking just about reciprocal trade:

> I was very much surprised how few representatives of organizations come around to make themselves known. The Senator is, as you know, on the subcommittee dealing with "ruanga" and "minorca" manufacturing; yet nobody came around to see us either from the Ruanga Makers, AFL, or the Minorca Setters, CIO. I raised hell with them about that because I know some of their top guys through AVC; but some, who should have been here, haven't been. . . . Of course, there might have been some reason they hesitated, although, hell, they ought to know the Senator is pro-labor if anybody is; and if they were in any doubt as to how they might be received, there are a dozen ways of throwing your hat in to see if it gets tossed back.

Later he continued:

> You know we are very much interested in educational legislation. I had some representatives of . . . organizations here to talk with us. I sent for them, they didn't try to see us. We thought about some changes in the educational bill which looked desirable in terms of their program and worked them out. We did get their O.K. They went along with us.

The question here is: How much lobbying or pressure was there?

Even where there is a considerable amount of what the outsider would consider pressure, the point made by Senator Service's assistant is entirely valid. What you call pressure, or what you feel to be pressure, depends on how thick your skin is. Mr. Second, for instance, told me that he had been subject to no "pressure—that is, no threats." To many men in politics, threats alone represent real pressure because they know very well that few votes are actually lost on any one given issue such as reciprocal trade. But, of course, what is a threat to one man is not a threat to another.

The most strongly felt kind of "pressure" on the reciprocal trade issue came, apparently, from Speaker Rayburn and the Democratic leadership against the potentially recalcitrant Democrats. Speaker Rayburn attended a breakfast for freshmen congressmen shortly before the vote and said, in effect, that he's discovered that those who go along, get along. One new member regarded this as pressure—a threat. Another new member (actually probably more vulnerable in terms of his factional position and his position within the delegation) did not. Both of them failed to "go along." Aside from this speech, most of the "pressure" on the doubtful members seems to have come through the grapevine or from their own apprehensions as to what might happen if they bolted the party leadership. One reason why fairly few members seem to have felt pressure on this matter is to be explained in terms of their background and associations in local politics. In many states, "pressure" on matters like highway contracts or patronage, or even for or against gubernatorial programs, must be relatively heavy—that is, threats are far more common at the state level than they are in Washington. Many congressmen come from such a background and a good many are still involved in local conflicts about patronage, contracts, etc. As a result, Washington to them seems mild.

It should never be forgotten that most congressmen respect—although in an inarticulate or almost subconscious way—the right of petition. They have a general feeling that everyone should have a right to talk or write to them about any public issue—that's what they're there for. But they aren't as worried about each communication as college professors might expect. They generally feel they have an equal right to disregard the petitioner's point, once it has been courteously received and acknowledged. Until a congressman definitely makes up his mind, it isn't pressure—it's communication or instruction. Much of what Mr. Fourth, for instance, believes about reciprocal trade he learned from his mail.

IX

Opportunism is also where you see it.

Outsiders, nonpoliticians, tend to attribute many political decisions to opportunism. Also, opponents in politics sometimes attribute the decisions of the other party or faction to "opportunism." However, in the interviews which I conducted, few congressmen attributed their friends' decisions or their own to opportunism. When friends differ on a particular issue it may be explained in terms of "the heat being on." Whether any significant number of politicians anywhere would have an image of themselves as opportunists, I do not know. It is certainly true that in these interviews many men were amazingly—and often embarrassingly—frank about events, relationships, and personal opinions. But insofar as the

overt picture which they have of themselves is concerned, opportunism does not play a prominent role. Even Congressman District,
who related his obligation to his district directly to his chances for
reelection, spoke of his "duty" to get reelected. No one used a
systematically opportunistic vocabulary of motives to explain himself or his action. Perhaps a different type of interview, some sort
of "depth-interviewing," would bring out a hidden set of self-images
at variance with this surface picture. However, I have no evidence
to that effect and am inclined to doubt it.

* * *

X
CONCLUSION

   Attention has been focused in the present study on the ways
congressmen view representation and on the ways in which their
pictures of the world determine what they hear, how they interpret
it, whom they represent, how they influence representation by
others, and how they view other representatives. It omits many
equally significant facets of the representative process—for example,
the formal and informal structure of the congressional system.
Elsewhere[23] I have discussed the formal structure. It is obvious
that there is an informal structure and that it is highly significant.
That it is an exceptionally complex structure to study, because
congressmen are members of several different groups simultaneously,
is also apparent. I have made only random observations concerning it.

   Obviously, it would be enlightening and helpful to have comparative studies of state legislatures to follow up the brilliant work
of Garceau and Silverman.[24] It would also be useful to have additional studies of other issues coming before Congress.

   The study here reported was defective in that it lacked the
precision of, for example, many sociological reports on industrial
plants. One reason for this is the problem of anonymity. To describe the factional conflicts in a particular congressional district,
or even more personal interrelationships within a congressional
committee, could hardly be done with fairness to the subjects of

---

[23] Dexter, *Congressmen and the People They Listen To.*
[24] Oliver Garceau and Corinne Silverman, "A Pressure Group and the
Pressured," *American Political Science Review*, 48 (1954), pp. 672–691.

the study. Such details are safe enough when the study concerns a factory. But aside from this problem, the "group memberships," reference groups, and so on, of politicians, are substantially more complex than those reported in many professional journals. Our reciprocal trade study devoted an unusual degree of attention to the districts from which some of the congressmen we interviewed came. However, we devised no technique for observing the relationship between a congressman and his constituency in detail over a period of time. Probably, considering the workload of congressmen, this can only be done by those who become helpers and thereby preclude themselves from reporting. Studies of state and city legislatures and of the representative process therein offer more hope for the development of a sociology of representation. It should be remembered that representation exists in many cultural frameworks. How for instance, does all that is said here apply to other systems? In connection, it is noted that the representative process exists in the church, in trade unions, in trade associations, and in fraternal organizations. So far, the process has been studied only occasionally in such contexts.

PART TWO

Work Groups in the House

CHAPTER TWO

II

COMMITTEE ASSIGNMENTS*

Nicholas A. Masters

ANY ATTEMPT to understand the legislative process, or to reckon how well it fulfills its purported functions, calls for a careful consideration of the relationships among congressmen. The beginning weeks of the first session of every congress are dominated by the internal politics of one phase of those relationships, the assignment of members to committees. Since congressmen devote most of their energies—constituents' errands apart—to the committees on which they serve, the political stakes in securing a suitable assignment are high. Competition for the more coveted posts is intense in both houses; compromises and adjustments are necessary. Members contest with each other over particularly desirable assignments; less frequently, one member challenges the entire body, as when Senator Wayne Morse fought for his committee assignments in 1953.[1]

The processes and patterns of committee assignments have been only generally discussed by political scientists and journalists. Perhaps the reason for this is too ready an acceptance of the supposition that these assignments are made primarily on the basis of seniority. Continuous service, it is true, insures a member of his place on a committee once he is assigned, but seniority may have very little to do with transfers to other committees, and it has virtually nothing to do with the assignment of freshman members. On what basis, then, are assignments made? Surely, not on the basis of simple random selection.

A recent student sees the committee assignment process as analogous to working out a "giant jig saw puzzle" in which the

* Reprinted from *American Political Science Review*, LV (June, 1961), 345–57. Copyright © 1961, The American Political Science Association. This study was made possible by the support of the Ford Foundation and Wayne State University. Neither of them, of course, is responsible for any errors of fact or interpretation.
    [1] Ralph K. Huitt, "The Morse Committee Assignment Controversy: A Study in Senate Norms," *American Political Science Review*, LI (June, 1957), 313–329.

committees-on-committees observe certain limitations. These committees

> . . . must, of course, be guided by the number of vacancies and by the number of applications for transfer. Care is taken to attain geographical distribution, if not balance. Attention is paid to group desires and to the experience and training of individual legislators. And balance among the various factions of the party is sought. Beyond these more or less objective factors, being in the good graces of the party leader is certainly important in getting on major committees.[2]

This statement leaves significant questions unanswered. What, for example, is meant by geographical distribution or balance? Is every section or region represented in each party on each committee? Or does the committee's subject matter jurisdiction guide the type of geographical representation the committee-on-committees considers? Is the number of assignments allotted to a state party delegation on particular committees restricted? Do state party delegations develop a "vested interest" in certain committees and attempt to maintain continuous representation on them? What groups actively seek representation for their interests on the various committees by campaigning for an individual congressman to fill a vacancy? How influential are they? The study of committee assignments should also throw light on party factionalism, the differences between the parties in performing this organizational task, and the importance attached to the professional and group backgrounds of legislators.

As a step toward answers to these questions this study looks into the formal and informal processes of committee assignments in the House of Representatives.[3]

The special hazards of this study deserve mention. No attempt was made to sample the House. The information derived from each Congressman must be used with caution, for legislators view events from a variety of perspectives. And finally, in all likelihood, some

[2] George Goodwin, Jr. "The Seniority System in Congress," *American Political Science Review*, LIII (June, 1959), 412–436.

[3] Data have been derived from unstructured interviews with members and staffs of the various committees, personal letters and similar papers, official documents of various types, and personal observations. I interviewed members of the committees-on-committees, deans of state delegations, and other members affected by the decisions. The survey covered the 80th through the 86th Congresses, with special attention to the 86th.

of the subtleties and nuances of the process have escaped observation. Despite these limitations, relatively crude techniques of analysis can yield significant results. For what sometimes frustrates our understanding of the most unique part of the American legislative process—the committee system—is the lack of organized data and the failure to analyse readily available data.

I. THE COMMITTEES-ON-COMMITTEES

In one of the more notable features of the reorganization of Congress in 1911, each party created a committee-on-committees to distribute committee assignments, on the theory, still asserted, that a party committee offers at least an opportunity for all party members to receive suitable assignments. Such a committee would go a long way toward eliminating the arbitrary judgments of the Speaker who, in the past, had used committee assignments as rewards and punishments, to help insure his control of pending legislation.

Though both parties use a committee for this purpose, their methods of selecting its members differ. Each committee therefore needs separate treatment, with comparisons from time to time.

Democrats

By custom the Democratic members of the House Ways and Means Committee, together with the Speaker and Majority Floor Leader (or the Minority Floor Leader when Democrats are in the minority), have constituted the committee-on-committees since 1911. This arrangement is evidently an outgrowth of the former practice of selecting the chairman of Ways and Means as the Majority Floor Leader. Because the Democratic members serve in this dual capacity, and although they are formally designated by the Democratic caucus, they are in fact self-perpetuating. The Speaker and Majority Floor Leader participate extensively in the Committee's deliberations and, of course, have considerable influence on the decisions.

The method of organizing the work of the Committee-on-committees in the 86th Congress was typical. Each member of the Committee was assigned a geographical zone within which his own district lies. (See Table I) All zones except two were geographically contiguous. Requests for committee assignments coming from members were handled by their respective zone committeeman.

For example, Representative Aime Forand from Rhode Island was responsible for the assignment and re-assignment requests of all Democratic representatives from districts within his zone, which includes, in addition to his own state, Connecticut, Maine, Massachusetts and Vermont. As can be seen from Table I, each zone representative served an average of approximately 18 members.

Although committee deliberations are closed, the procedure followed is well known among most House members. Each zone representative, speaking in order of seniority, nominates candidates from his zone for the various committee vacancies, usually with supporting arguments. Thereupon the Committee votes on each of the vacancies, and the nominee receiving the highest number of votes is designated to fill it.

The volume of work before the Committee varies, depending chiefly on the changes resulting from the preceding election. Almost always, however, there are more applications than vacancies; in the 86th Congress 124 applications were made for 75 places to be filled. The major committees were naturally most in demand; applications exceeded vacancies for all committees except District of Columbia, House Administration, Merchant Marine and Fisheries, Post Office and Civil Service, and Science and Astronautics—all regarded as lesser committees. Applicants usually list their order of preference, taking into account not only their personal desires but also advice from other members and their own assessments of where they stand the best chance to land at least an acceptable assignment. Without encouragement from above, an applicant, however much he might prefer to be on the Appropriations Committee, say, would hardly bother (or venture) to ask for what he realizes he has virtually no chance of getting.

Much more than committee structure and manner of procedure is involved in making assignments. Animating and guiding these formal mechanisms are the norms and customs observed when assignments are sought. The pervasive seniority rule, for example, works in a manner not commonly appreciated. Members seeking assignments, and particularly freshmen, channel their requests through the "dean" or senior member of their state party delegation. In negotiations between the Committee-on-committees and the applicants he plays a crucially important role in securing assignments. It is his special responsibility to see that his members receive adequate representation on the various committees. In performing this task, he tries to protect or maintain the delegation's place on

TABLE I

House Democratic Committee-on-Committees and Zone Assignments, 86th Congress

Committee Member	Zone	Dems. in State Del.	Fresh-men	Committee Member	Zone	Dems. in State Del.	Fresh-men
Mills (Ark.)	Ark.	6	(1)	Herlong (Fla.)	Fla.	7	(0)
	Del.	1	(1)		Ga.	10	(0)
	Kans.	3	(2)			—	—
	Okla.	5	(0)			17	(0)
		—	—				
		15	(4)	Ikard (Texas)	Texas	21	(1)
					N. Mex.	2	(1)
Forand (R.I.)	R.I.	2	(0)			—	—
	Conn.	6	(6)			23	(2)
	Me.	2	(1)				
	Mass.	8	(1)	Frazier (Tenn.)	Tenn.	7	(0)
	Vt.	1	(1)		N.C.	11	(1)
		—	—			—	—
		19	(9)			18	(1)
King (Calif.)	Calif.	16	(4)	Machrowicz	Mich.	7	(1)
	Alas.	1	(1)	(Mich.)	Ind.	8	(6)
	Ariz.	1	(0)		Ohio	9	(3)
	Nev.	1	(0)			—	—
	Utah	1	(1)			24	(10)
		—	—				
		20	(6)	Metcalf (Mont.)	Mont.	2	(0)
					Colo.	3	(1)
O'Brien (Ill.)	Ill.	14	(4)		Idaho	1	(0)
	Wis.	5	(2)		Nebr.	2	(2)
		—	—		N. Dak.	1	(1)
		19	(6)		Ore.	3	(0)
					S. Dak.	1	(0)
Boggs (La.)	La.	8	(1)		Wash.	1	(0)
	Ala.	9	(0)			—	—
	Miss.	6	(0)			14	(4)
		—	—				
		23	(1)	Green (Pa.)	Pa.	16	(4)
					N.J.	5	(2)
Keogh (N.Y.)	N.Y.	19	(2)			—	—
		—	—			21	(6)
		19	(2)				
				Watts (Ky.)	Ky.	7	(2)
Harrison (Va.)	Va.	8	(1)		Md.	7	(3)
	S.C.	6	(0)		W. Va.	5	(2)
		—	—			—	—
		14	(1)			19	(7)
Karsten (Mo.)	Mo.	10	(0)	Total		283	(63)
	Iowa	4	(3)				
	Minn.	4	(1)				
		—	—				
		18	(4)				

a major committee when a vacancy occurs and the seat has previously been held by a member of the delegation; he consults with,

and advises, the members of his delegation seeking assignments as to what their chances are, and which committee assignments he will support for them. The dean's decisions must be made in consideration of the needs of his state, the qualifications of his own members, and the necessity for adjusting the requests among his members to prevent duplication on committees. It falls to his lot also to discourage and dissuade members who have unrealistic designs on the major committees—Appropriations, Rules, and Ways and **Means.**

The importance of the deans of the state delegations may be illustrated negatively. Connecticut, for the first time since 1936, elected six freshman Democrats in 1958. Since the entire delegation was composed of freshmen, no senior member could serve as the dean and apparently there was no time or forethought to form an agreement to become part of an area delegation. So when the committee assignments were made, only one of the six, Chester Bowles, felt that he had been given as good representation as he was entitled to. Bowles got the assignment of his choice, Foreign Affairs. Frank Kowalski was assigned to Armed Services because of his extensive military experience although it was not an assignment he wanted. The remaining four were given committee places they did not prefer, namely Science and Astronautics, Education and Labor, Government Operations, and a dual appointment to the District of Columbia and Post Office and Civil Service Committees. Several dissatisfied Connecticut congressmen complained, two of them quite bitterly, that their committee positions would not help them to be reelected—that they had received the "left over" assignments. These assignments had not been made from any desire to penalize them, but apparently because they were orphans with no dean or senior member to fight for their preferences or look after their interests.

If the Democratic Committee-on-committees is judged as a system of collective responsibility among men of equal status, then it is clear that the use of members of a permanent standing committee for this purpose has had almost the opposite effect. Each member does not carry equal weight on the committee. The status and rank of each Democratic member of Ways and Means are carried over to the Committee-on-committees. The ranking Democrat serves as chairman and the status of the other ranking members is unquestionably enhanced by the fact that they also serve as Ways and Means subcommittee chairmen when the Democrats are in the majority. These are the senior members in an institution that respects seniority.

Ways and Means members have had considerable congressional experience prior to their assignment. For the period 1913 to 1958, only five of 86 assignments to this Committee were given to congressmen without any seniority; and each of these five had had previous, but interrupted, congressional service. On the average, members have served at least three consecutive terms prior to being placed on the Committee, and the average is closer to five terms if computations are based simply on prior, rather than continuous, service before selection. The stability of the Committee's membership is also increased by the fact that, although a congressman may sometimes shrink from its responsibilities, only one member has ever left the Committee by his own request. What turnover there is results from death, resignation, or loss of party control, rather than from transfers or election defeat.

For a key functioning unit of the Democratic party's legislative apparatus, so much continuity in the Committee-on-committees makes it ill-designed for flexibility and responsiveness to electoral changes and public opinion trends. Rather, it is more analogous to a firmly entrenched bureaucracy, not completely immune but well insulated, and capable of considerable resistance to any pressures placed upon it.

Republicans

The Republican Committee-on-committees is specially set up for its function and is responsible for no other. It is composed of one member from each state having Republican representation in the House; thereby, a lone Republican from any state is automatically included. Each state delegation determines its member on the Committee. This method might be thought to provide an opportunity to select a new member for each new Congress, but the normal pattern, on the contrary, is for the senior member of the delegation, usually the dean, to assume membership on the Committee and hold it as long as he desires or remains in Congress. Table II shows the membership of the Republican Committee-on-committees for the 86th Congress.

The point is sometimes argued that the Republicans make it possible for each state delegation to assume a greater share of the organizational responsibility than the Democratic committee assignment process allows, and consequently that the decentralized

TABLE II
House Republican Committee-on-Committees, 86th Congress

State	Member	Votes	State	Member	Votes
Arizona	John J. Rhodes	1	New Jersey	Frank C. Osmers	9
California	James Utt	14	New York	Mrs. K. St. George	24
Colorado	J. Edgar Chenoweth	1	North Carolina	Chas. R. Jonas	1
Florida	William C. Cramer	1	North Dakota	Don L. Short	1
Idaho	Hamer Budge	1	Ohio	Clarence J. Brown	14
Illinois	Leo E. Allen	11	Oklahoma	Page Belcher	1
Indiana	E. Ross Adair	3	Oregon	Walter Norblad	1
Iowa	Charles B. Hoeven	4	Pennsylvania	Richard Simpson	14
Kansas	Edward H. Rees	3	South Dakota	E. Y. Berry	1
Kentucky	Eugene Siler	1	Tennessee	Howard H. Baker	2
Maine	Clifford G. McIntire	1	Texas	Bruce Alger	1
Massachusetts	William H. Bates	6	Utah	Henry A. Dixon	1
Michigan	Clare E. Hoffman	11	Virginia	Joel T. Broyhill	2
Minnesota	H. Carl Anderson	5	Washington	Jack Westland	6
Missouri	Thomas B. Curtis	1	West Virginia	Arch A. Moore	1
Nebraska	Phil Weaver	2	Wisconsin	John W. Byrnes	5
New Hampshire	Perkins Bass	2	Wyoming	E. Keith Thomson	1

Total—153

Subcommittee Appointed by Minority Leader

State	Member	Votes	Seniority
California	James Utt	14	4 consecutive terms
Idaho	Hamer H. Budge	1	5 consecutive terms
Illinois	Leo E. Allen	11	14 consecutive terms
Michigan	Clare E. Hoffman	11	13 consecutive terms
New Jersey	Frank C. Osmers	9	7 non-consecutive terms
New York	Katharine St. George	24	7 consecutive terms
North Carolina	Charles Raper Jonas	1	4 consecutive terms
Ohio	Clarence J. Brown	14	11 consecutive terms
Pennsylvania	Richard M. Simpson	14	7 consecutive terms

Total—99

Republican method is much more responsible to electoral changes. Actual Republican practice tends to contradict this argument. For the Republicans allow each representative on the Committee-on-committees to cast as many votes as there are Republicans in his delegation. This concentrates the power over committee assignments in the hands of the senior members from the large state delegations. In the 86th Congress, members from seven states—California, Illinois, Michigan, New Jersey, New York, Ohio, and Pennsylvania—controlled 97 of the 153 committee votes.

Not to mask the realities of power, the Republican committee assignments are handled by a Subcommittee which, in the 86th Congress for example, was composed of the senior members from these seven states and two others, with one vote each, evidently added to give a voice to large geographical areas (intermountain and southern) that would otherwise have gone entirely unrepresented. Together the Subcommittee members controlled about two-thirds of the full committee's votes. None of them had served less than four terms in Congress. By custom the Subcommittee is appointed by the Minority Leader (or Speaker, as the case may be) on the authority granted by a resolution of the full Committee. The resolution leaves the membership of the Subcommittee apparently at the discretion of the party leader, but the example just given shows how far he is hemmed in by the practice of appointing the same members from the larger delegations each time a new Congress convenes. The change in the minority leadership in the 86th Congress had no discernible effect on this part of the organizational process.

The Subcommittee receives and considers *all* applications for assignment and transfer, and the full Committee invariably accepts all of its recommendations. Subcommittee sessions are informal and each member is free to speak for or against any assignment. Information on newly elected members is obtained from the Republican Congressional Campaign Committee and the party leaders pride themselves on having extensive knowledge not only of the professional and personal backgrounds of their colleagues, but also of the constituencies they represent. Members of the full Committee who are not on the Subcommittee are entitled to participate in the determinations if they desire, but they seldom do.

Republicans from small states sometimes object that as a result of the system of proportional voting and large-state domination of the Subcommittee they have no real voice in committee assignments and are often overlooked for assignments to the better committees. Along the same line they complain that the Republican procedure allows no mechanism whereby the small state delegations can combine their voting power in the Committee-on-committees. The critics point to the Democratic practice of letting smaller state delegations select a joint dean in order to be able to negotiate for committee assignments from a position of strength.

Actually, the principal difference between Republican and Democratic practice in formal organization is that the Republicans have built into their system a voting formula that rewards heavy Republican areas; the Democrats offer no comparable leverage to the large delegations. Nor is it likely the Democrats would even consider such a plan as long as the seniority system prevails. For it would only lessen the power of the Southern Democrats by putting more control over committee assignments into the hands of the larger northern, midwestern, and western delegations, with their very different traditions and interests.

There is little to distinguish the manner and procedure followed by an individual Republican or Democratic congressman in securing an assignment. Republican freshman members also work through the deans of the state delegations, but the deans, unlike their Democratic counterparts, are usually members of the Committee-on-committees.

Despite these differences the arrangements in both parties for handling committee assignments have one basic feature in common. Both committees-on-committees are so constituted as to be virtually immune to immediate pressures brought about by electoral changes. This is no accident. Its justification rests on a number of considerations congenial to the norms and customs of the entire body. If junior or freshman members had the responsibility for making committee assignments they would immediately be thrust into difficult and delicate positions, particularly in deciding on transfer requests from senior members. Such decisions might well be controversial enough to damage permanently a junior member's career within the legislature and possibly outside of it. In private as well as public life, organizations seldom allow the newcomer—unfamiliar with the subtleties and the institutional trappings of the process—to make important personnel decisions; and committee assignments are party personnel decisions of the most crucial importance. Senior members simply would not willingly tolerate decisions made in this way. If forced to do so, the pressures, roadblocks and penalties they could evoke might be so severe and difficult to overcome that order in the whole legislative process might be endangered. The system has evolved as it has for these reasons, as well as for more positive benefits, such as the desire to rely on the more knowledgeable judgments of those with greater experience in the legislature.

Finally, the system is intended to give the process a tone of moderation and detachment. Members with seniority are less threatened by an election two years hence, being less subject to the vicissitudes of a competitive district. After years of experience in a collective body, senior members are readier to recognise the need for compromise and adjustment if work is to be done. Although competitive ambitions among members may be intense, prolonged debate over committee assignments would delay the conduct of legislative business which is already too long delayed by the employment of exist-ing institutional and parliamentary devices.

The Role of Party Leaders

The role of the party leaders in making committee assignments is difficult to define; no simple definition fits all the realities. Gen-erally speaking, the leadership of each party in the House is formi-dable and independent to a great degree, though the leaders' power varies with their personal relations with the other members. David Truman explains the dependence of the rank-and-file upon the party leaders as follows:

> The machinery of the House and of its parties is normally available to the ordinary member only, so to speak, on its own terms, because the source of its strength is also the source of its disabilities, namely, numbers. In a House of 435 or in a body roughly half that size, as one of the parties, there is a tendency . . . for the real and formal leadership closely to coin-cide. A formal, standardized system of communication and con-trol is indispensable to the conduct of affairs in a body of that size. . . . This standardization of the communication structure implies that initiative tends to be centralized or at least that there are central controls on the flow of business. These the rank-and-file member cannot command or, as sometimes hap-pens in the Senate, supplant. Hence, excepting some aspects of his own voting decisions, the independence of the ordinary member is restricted.[4]

The Democratic and Republican leaders not only play the prin-cipal role in the selection of the members of their respective committees-on-committees, but their personal judgments also tend to become the norm for major committee assignments. In practice, the leadership of both parties is directly involved in assignments to all the major committees, though the leaders do not usually concern themselves with applicants to lesser ones.

The party leaders use their power over committee assignments vari-ously, to reward members who have been loyal and cooperative, and to reinforce the strength of their own positions by rewarding mem-bers whose loyalty may be suspected but whose strength may no longer be safely disregarded. Party leaders working with the com-

---

[4] *The Congressional Party: A Case Study* (New York, 1959), p. 195.

mittee-on-committees have in a number of instances offered important committee positions to members with demonstrated followings
who were regarded as prospective threats. Such offers are made for
the obvious purpose of securing cooperation, and so are frequently
labelled as "sell-outs" or "the buying-off process" by some discontented members. Value judgments on particular cases will vary with
individual viewpoints, but it must be recognized that Congress is
not the only place where adjustments in the power structure are
designed to accommodate or to absorb potentially strong rivals.

A specific example may be offered from the 86th Congress. Prior
to the opening of the first session a group of liberal Democrats
announced their intention to mobilize forces in the House in order
to bring about the passage of legislation they favored. While the
movement was underway—letters were being sent to the new Democratic members, as well as to incumbents sympathetic to their cause—
Speaker Rayburn intervened, promising to use his influence to prevent the Rules Committee from blocking their bills. The Speaker,
working with Chairman Wilbur Mills of the Ways and Means Committee and Majority Leader John McCormack, in order to demonstrate his willingness to cooperate with the group, offered one of
their leaders, Lee Metcalf of Montana, an appointment to the Ways
and Means Committee. Contrary to expectations, Metcalf said he did
not want the assignment; he contended that he preferred to be on
Interior and Insular Affairs—important for Montana. The leaders insisted, however, that he had a responsibility to his party to accept
the post, and he finally did. Metcalf was the logical choice in a
move to head off a possible revolt, because his previous behavior
had satisfied the party leaders that he was a "responsible" legislator—a concept that warrants further examination presently.

II. CRITERIA FOR COMMITTEE ASSIGNMENTS

The committees-on-committees have rules to govern them in
assigning members to the twenty permanent standing committees.
The Legislative Reorganization Act of 1946 limited members of
the House to service on a single committee, but this provision has
since been amended as follows: (1) Three committees are *exclusive*—namely, Appropriations, Rules, and Ways and Means. A member who serves on any of these can serve on no other committee.
An occasional exception is made, however. (2) Ten committees are

semi-exclusive; members may serve on any one of them and any one of the seven non-exclusive committees. The ten are: Agriculture, Armed Services, Banking and Currency, Education and Labor, Foreign Affairs, Interstate and Foreign Commerce, Judiciary, Post Office and Civil Service, Public Works, and Science and Astronautics. (3) Seven committees are *non-exclusive.* A member may serve on any two of these seven, or any one of them and any one of the ten semi-exclusive committees. The seven are: District of Columbia, Government Operations, House Administration, Interior and Insular Affairs, Merchant Marine and Fisheries, Un-American Activities, and Veterans Affairs.

The 1946 Act also fixes the total membership of each committee, although changes can be and are made for the duration of a Congress by means of a House resolution. Party ratios on the Rules and Ways and Means committees are fixed by agreement among the party leaders, while the ratios on other committees ordinarily reflect the House division.[5]

Beyond these ground rules, experience has developed other criteria used in determining committee assignments. In discussing them here, the exclusive committees are treated separately first, because of the special attention given to filling vacancies on them. I will then turn to the variables that affect assignments to all of the committees.

Assignments to Major Committees

The three exclusive committees, Appropriations, Rules, and Ways and Means are regarded by all in both parties as being of special importance. Other committees—among them Agriculture, Armed Services, and Public Works—deal with issues that affect vital congressional and national interests, but none can lay con-

---

[5] In the 87th Congress a serious conflict arose over the Rules Committee ratio. There was newspaper talk of "purging" the ranking Democratic member, William Colmer from Mississippi, who had supported the Dixiecrat presidential candidacy of Mississippi's Governor Barnett in the 1960 campaign, and who regularly voted with Chairman Howard Smith in the coalition of southern Democrats and conservative Republicans that controlled the Rules Committee. But Speaker Rayburn, in order to break the "stranglehold" the coalition would have over the impending legislation of the Kennedy Administration, advocated instead an increase in the Committee's size. The conflict was resolved in Rayburn's favor by a narrow margin with the entire House participating in the vote. The subsequent appointments, however, were made along the lines suggested in this article.

tinuous claim to the power and prestige of the top three. As one Congressman stated, "If you get appointed to one of the top three, you have 'arrived.'"

Although the manner of attaining positions on these committees varies, each nominee must fit a bill of particulars. In practice, as indicated earlier, these lesser leaders are selected by the party leaders in consultation with the members of the committee-on-committees, rather than the other way around. A nominee's name may be first brought up by the party leaders, a committee member, or even by someone not involved in the mechanics, but whatever the technical circumstances surrounding the introduction of his name, if the nominee is assigned, he bears the party leaders' stamp of approval. This is true in both parties.

The principal factors involved in selecting members for a major committee may be grouped under three broad headings: (1) legislative responsibility, (2) type of district represented, and (3) geographical area represented.

(1) Legislative Responsibility. The most crucial test is whether a candidate is a "responsible" legislator, as the leaders of both parties use that term. What does a member have to be or do—or avoid—in order to be regarded as a responsible legislator?

According to the party leaders and the members of the committees-on-committees, a responsible legislator is one whose ability, attitudes, and relationships with his colleagues serve to enhance the prestige and importance of the House of Representatives. He has a basic and fundamental respect for the legislative process and understands and appreciates its formal and informal rules. He has the respect of his fellow legislators, and particularly the respect of the party leaders. He does not attempt to manipulate every situation for his own personal advantage. In the consideration of issues, he is careful to protect the rights of others; he is careful to clear matters that require clearance; and he is especially careful about details. He understands the pressures on the members with whom he cannot always agree and avoids pushing an issue to the point where his opponents may suffer personal embarrassment. On specific issues, no matter how firm his convictions and no matter how great the pressures upon him, he demonstrates a willingness to compromise. He is moderate, not so much in the sense of his voting record and his personal ideology, but rather in the sense of a moderate approach; he is not to be found on the uncompromising extremes of the political spectrum. Although the notions of those interviewed were somewhat vague on this point, a responsible legislator is apparently one who does not believe that the Congress is the proper place to initiate drastic and rapid changes in the direction of public policy. On the contrary, he is more inclined to be a gradualist, and to see public policy as a sort of "synthesis of opposing viewpoints." In short, a responsible legislator is politically pliant, but not without conviction.

A legislator can demonstrate his responsibility in many ways: how he manages a major bill; what he contributes in committee work; the sort of testimony he presents before other committees; the nature of his remarks on the floor—all these are tests of his responsibility. If he behaves properly in these settings and refrains from criticizing the party leadership—and gets reelected at home—his chances of being selected for a major committee post are very good. In the interviews, both Democrats and Republicans emphasized repeatedly the attention paid to the past performance of major committee applicants. For the major committees are "closed corporations," and their membership is composed only of those who have served their "apprenticeships" on lesser committees for considerable periods of time. Even in an instance in which party leaders feel compelled to appoint a member of a dissident wing of the party in order to gain greater cooperation, they will tend to select the member who most closely conforms to the norms of responsibility.

When the question was raised how Southern Democrats, who might be regarded as uncompromising on many questions, yet were appointed to major committees, the interviewees immediately pointed out how the Southerners differ from many of their "uncompromising" northern colleagues: they never denounce the legislative process as ill suited for public policy formation, they are never frustrated by its intricacies; rather, they master its techniques and use them skillfully and artfully to support their positions. "After all," one Congressman commented,

the Southerner usually joins this body free from the pressures many of the rest of us face and is usually eager to make his mark. Membership in Congress is the highest political office he is likely to attain and he will devote full time to the legislature. Other members often entertain higher political ambitions or may have to devote the majority of their time to keeping things running smoothly in their districts.

(2) Type of District Represented. It would be rare indeed for a member to earn regard as "responsible" in only one or two terms. No freshman has been assigned to the Rules Committee since the Legislative Reorganization Act was passed and only 14 have been assigned to the larger Appropriations Committee and two to the Ways and Means Committee (Table III). So the con-

TABLE III

Committee Assignments to Freshmen, House of Representatives, 80th–86th Congresses

Committee	Number of Freshman Assignments	
	Repub.	*Dem.*
Exclusive Committees:		
Appropriations	8	6
Rules	0	0
Ways and Means	2	0
Semi-Exclusive Committees:		
Agriculture	13	11
Armed Services	1	11
Banking and Currency	15	20
Education and Labor	17	27
Foreign Affairs	4	10
Interstate and Foreign Commerce	8	10
Judiciary	15	14
Post Office and Civil Service*	22	35
Public Works	20	20
Science and Astronautics†	0	8
Non-Exclusive Committees:		
District of Columbia	13	8
Government Operations	24	26
House Administration	11	19
Interior and Insular Affairs	17	28
Merchant Marine and Fisheries	24	26
Un-American Activities	6	1
Veterans' Affairs	33	30
Totals	253	310

* Reams of Ohio, Independent, assigned to Post Office and Civil Service in 82d Congress.
† Created by 86th Congress.
Data from *Congressional Directory*, 1st Session of each Congress. Includes only Representatives with *no* previous service at any time. Some Representatives received double assignments, so totals shown are higher than the total of freshmen in each Congress.

cept of responsibility is connected with an element beyond the member's personality, an element that takes into account the nature of his district. The members of the committees-on-committees have something more in mind here than simply a particular member's ability to be reelected. Long tenure by itself is an obvious objective fact, and common sense proof that a district is "safe"; but this is not enough. It is not necessarily to the point either that the member's district may be safe for the incumbent but not for any one else. The essence of the criterion lies in the terms on which the member is returned rather than in the fact of his return alone. The committee-on-committees wants to feel that his district will not only reelect him but also allow him to operate as a free agent, enabling him to make controversial decisions on major policy questions without constant fear of reprisals at the polls. His district must not be one that forces him to take definite, uncompromising positions, for this would jeopardize his usefulness in committee work. In the terminology of Eulau, Wahlke *et al.,* the district should be one that elects its member as a "trustee" or a "politico" and not as a "delegate."[6] This requirement is of special importance in considering assignments to the Rules Committee; many members would not relish being on this committee despite its power, simply because it is inevitably involved in practically every issue before the Congress.

A related reason for the "safe" district requirement is based on the idea that important committee posts should belong to the professional, the veteran politician who has earned his way up the ladder—the "politico" in preference to the "trustee." A politician from a safe district has fought and won enough political battles to nail down a district and thus help his party maintain control of the House. In short, he is a sure vote in the battle for control and he should receive the rewards of the system.

Members of the committees-on-committees felt no compulsion to explain away or camouflage this requirement. On the contrary, they argue that a realistic appraisal of the factors operating in our political system reveals that if a member sits on a congressional committee in which compromises must continually be made on matters of major policy, he cannot come from a district that does not allow him flexibility.

(3) Geographical Area. A legislator who is responsible and who comes from a district that allows him considerable independence on issues still has no guarantee that he will be selected to fill a major committee vacancy. He simply has a better chance than others. A third factor serves to narrow the range of choice. For both party committees tend to follow the practice of selecting a

---

[6] "The Role of the Representative: Some Empirical Observations on the Theory of Edmund Burke," *American Political Science Review,* LIII (Sept. 1959), 742–756.

member from the same state party delegation as the member who vacated the seat, in order not to disturb the existing geographical balance. For example, upon the death or defeat of three members of the Ways and Means Committee, the Kentucky, Michigan, and Pennsylvania Democratic delegations asserted a prescriptive right to have members from their respective delegations chosen to fill the vacancies. Moreover, this practice sometimes extends to other committees. The Ohio Republican delegation, for example, insists that it should have one of its members on the Public Works Committee at all times.

Along this line, each party attempts to have every section of the nation represented on the Appropriations and Ways and Means committees. These are the only two committees, however, on which geographical balance is regarded as especially important. Actually the only geographical rule applied to all committee assignments provides that no state party delegation shall have more than one representative on any committee, except for the largest state delegations where strict application of the rule would be impossible.

General Criteria for All Committee Assignments

The most important single factor in distributing assignments to all other committees is whether a particular place will help to insure the reelection of the member in question. So although it might abstractly seem desirable and logical to place an urban congressman on the Agriculture Committee to protect consumer interests, there is little operative political warrant for such an assignment. Not only do congressmen from urban areas usually refrain from applying for such vacancies when they occur, but the committees-on-committees also insist that members coming from predominantly agricultural areas have first call on them in order that they may use the assignments to protect their tenure in office. Both parties take it for granted that wheat, cotton and tobacco areas should have the majority of representation on the committee. The leaders know from previous experience that assignment of an urban congressman to the Agriculture Committee would only make him "fair game" for each of the farm lobbies.

The same general reasoning applies to other committees as well. Assignments to Public Works, Interior and Insular Affairs or Merchant Marine and Fisheries are usually based on the ecological make-up of the members' districts, so as to allow them to serve their constituent interests and protect their incumbency. For example, South Dakota Democrat George McGovern's application for transfer to the Agriculture Committee from the Education and Labor Committee was approved primarily on the grounds that his former assignment handicapped his effectiveness in providing service to his constituents and was a disadvantage to him since it had become a major campaign issue in his farm district.

When two or more members stake a claim to the same assignment, on the ground that it is essential to their electoral success, both party committees usually, if not invariably, will give preference to the member with longer service. Members have often maneuvered for a position on a particular committee long before a vacancy existed, and sometimes even long before other applicants were first elected. But open importunity may be self-defeating, for no one likes a pest.

Some Special Cases

The assignment of members to the Education and Labor Committee—with jurisdiction over the explosive issues of school aid, segregation and labor-management relations—has called for the most careful attention to the constituencies of applicants. As the party committees have seen it in recent years, this assignment is no place for a neutral when there are so many belligerents around. Their assignments have produced a standoff between antagonists,[7] and a suggestion during the 86th Congress, dropped in the end, for a partition of the Committee as an alternative to the prospective accession of Adam Clayton Powell of New York to its chairmanship upon the retirement of Graham Barden of North Carolina. Apart from the Southerners and a handful of others from districts safe enough to allow them comfortable independence, Democrats have felt that only members who can afford politically to take an outright pro-labor position—*i.e.*, who get union support for election—should be assigned to this committee.

Members from farm or middle-class suburban districts are discouraged from applying. Service on this committee by a member whose district is relatively free of labor-management or segregation conflicts would only result in raising issues in his district that could prove embarrassing and even politically fatal to the member.

---

[7] *Cf.* Seymour Scher, "Congressional Committee Members as Independent Agency Overseers: A Case Study," *American Political Science Review*, LIV (Dec. 1960), 911–920.

Republicans appear to have concluded, too, that it is impossible to take a moderate position on labor-management issues. They also dissuade members from applying for this committee when it might impair their chances for reelection. Republican assignees, however, are more likely to take a pro-management or non-labor view for the obvious reason that fewer Republicans receive overt political support from organized labor; more have close ties with management groups.

For the Democratic Committee-on-committees, a special issue affects assignments to what has been commonly described as an unimportant committee, the District of Columbia Committee. Southern legislators attach a great deal of importance to their efforts to maintain representation on that committee and to control it. The objective is to block home rule for the District, with all the implications of extensive Negro participation in District political affairs.

More generally, southern congressmen have a more or less collective understanding that in order to maximize their influence on the legislative process they need to spread their strength over all the committees. This involves maneuvering for positions on the "housekeeping" committees. Although *a priori* calculations might seem to argue that dispersing members over twenty committees would weaken rather than strengthen southern control of the House, in actual practice the seniority rule vindicates their strategy. Collectively, congressmen from the South build up more seniority than any other sectional contingent and reap their rewards in committee and sub-committee chairmanships when the Democrats are in the majority.

Organized Interest Group Participation

All members of the committees-on-committees recognized that organized groups outside Congress take a hand in the assignment process from time to time. The influence of such groups is thought to be important, but little evidence is available on its nature and extent. Sometimes, though not often, organized groups formally endorse a nominee for a committee vacancy. For example, Representative Harold B. McSween (Dem., La.), when applying for assignment to the Agriculture Committee, had letters of endorsement from American Farm Bureau representatives placed in his application file. Democrats attempt to placate organized labor by placing pro-labor representatives on the Education and Labor Committee, while Republicans attempt to satisfy the National Association of Manufacturers by appointing pro-business members to the same Committee. The most widely publicized groups connected with assignments to the Ways and Means committee are spokesmen for the oil interests. Democratic members and staff personnel frequently mentioned in interviews that a nominee's acceptability for assignment to this committee often hinged on whether he demonstrated a willingness to oppose any attempts to reduce the oil depletion tax allowance.

Nevertheless, organized groups, with occasional exceptions, appear to refrain from direct intervention in committee assignments; overt intrusion is apt to be resented and so be self-defeating. Rather, they have certain "expectations" about the type of person who should be selected for the vacancies on committees which affect their interests. Each group usually counts several members "friendly" or responsive to their needs. Organized interests do not often concern themselves too much with the selection of a particular member of the "friendly" group so long as one of them is eventually chosen.

Other Considerations

The proposition is sometimes advanced that geographical balance is a deliberate objective in distributing assignments to all committees. If so, it has a low priority. There is no evidence of systematic effort to provide each section with representation on the various committees proportional to its representation in the House. The Appropriations and Ways and Means committees may be considered as exceptions, but even here a much more pressing consideration is representation for the large tax-paying states. An examination of the membership of the Interior and Insular Affairs Committee clearly shows that geographical balance is not necessarily a primary goal for all committees. Of the 19 Democratic members of this committee in the 86th Congress, 17 were from districts west of the Mississippi, and of the twelve Republican members six were from western states. Both committees-on-committees will, indeed, listen sympathetically to an applicant who argues that his section of the nation has no representation on the committee of his choice, but this argument is not a compelling reason for making the assignment. Ordinarily, applications are based on district and state delegation, not regional, considerations. Republican New Englanders, for instance, do not approach committee assignments from the viewpoint that each committee should have a New Englander on it. A notable exception to this generalization sets the Southern Democrats apart; as stated earlier, they regularly try to have Southern representation on all committees.

Party factionalism is a more serious concern than geographical balance. Republicans and Democrats alike, who were responsible for making committee assignments, vigorously denied the existence of factions within their parties; but readily admitted that their respective groups harbored members with widely divergent viewpoints. Occasional alignments emerge, they acknowledged, but these are regarded as fleeting in character. They asserted that no committee's party representation should be composed exclusively of members who view political issues from the same perspective and claimed to have made a reasonable effort to see that divergent viewpoints within each party find expression on each committee. We have already noted, however, that members on the extremes of the political spectrum are usually passed over for vacancies in the major committees; and a member's location on the spectrum is assessed by the party leadership and the committee-on-committees. It is a matter of opinion, therefore, how well founded is the frequent claim that party representation on each committee is balanced ideologically.

Unfavorable assignments, of little political value to the recipients, are sometimes deliberately given by the powers that be as a mark of disapproval, or for reasons that might be described as "for the good of the order." In one recent instance Dale Alford, Democrat from Arkansas, was said to have been assigned to the Post Office and Civil Service Committee because some members of the Committee-on-committees felt that he had violated the "rules of the game" in his campaign that displaced former Representative Brooks Hays, a widely respected member, in the wake of the Little Rock controversy. Two years later, after he had voted with the leadership to "pack" the Rules Committee, he was given a place on the Appropriations Committee. Also, there was surprising agreement among those interviewed that the original Democratic transfers to the newly created Science and Astronautics Committee—not taken seriously in the House at its founding—were made in order to provide the transferees with sinecures, and so to remove some of the less qualified members from the other committees. The transfer offers were made attractive to senior members by promises that they would receive subcommittee chairmanships, which would provide them opportunities to build their niches within the legislative bureaucracy.

The professional background of an individual legislator is seldom in and of itself the controlling factor in his assignment. However, some general rules relating to the professional backgrounds of legislators are followed by both parties. Almost without exception, lawyers only are appointed to the Judiciary Committee. Members with outstanding experience in international relations or with extensive military service are regarded as excellent choices for the Foreign Affairs and Armed Services committees respectively. Other things being equal, former bankers and financiers may be given a slight edge over competing applicants for such committees as Appropriations, Ways and Means, and Banking and Currency. The same holds true for farmers who apply for the Agriculture Committee and for members closely identified with the labor movement who apply for the Education and Labor Committee. But all agreed that holding elective office, particularly a state legislative office, outweighed any other type of professional experience as a qualification for any committee assignment. Holding elective office is regarded as a profession by members of the committees, and they feel that the rewards of the system should go to the professionals. Although the patterns of committee assignments tend to document the importance of professional background, it would be a mistake to assume that the committees-on-committees seek out applicants on this ground. Normally, the reverse is true. Applicants tend to apply for assignments where they think their professional skills can be used to best advantage.

The manner in which a congressman campaigns for a committee is an important factor in the outcome. For example, a member seeking an assignment often solicits the support of members already on the committee. Another technique is to obtain the support of influential political leaders, such as endorsements from the governor, senators, or members of the state legislature. If an individual is comparatively unknown in national politics, he may attempt to familiarize the members of the Committee-on-committees with his background and training as it relates to the type of service he can give on the committee he desires. All these tactics, properly employed, can go a long way toward helping a member get favorable consideration by his party. He must be careful, however, to avoid giving the impression of exerting undue political pressure on the members of the Committee-on-committees. For example, if the committee tells him that a vacancy has already been promised to another, he is *expected* to accept this decision. Attempts to challenge either committee's decisions are generally regarded as serious departures from the norms of conduct in the House.

Religious considerations are not ignored in judging the qualifications of applicants. Most Democratic members interviewed conceded that it was important, when possible, to have at least one Roman Catholic on the major committees, and particularly on the Ways and Means and Education and Labor Committees. Republicans, on the other hand, contended that religious factors had no bearing on their assignments.

Racial and ethnic factors also enter into the calculations occasionally. For example, the Democratic committee-on-committees thought it made sense to appoint Charles Diggs, Democrat and Negro from the 13th District in Michigan, to the House Foreign Affairs Committee because of his race and because of the emerging prominence of Africa in international affairs. In his letter of application to the Committee, Diggs argued on these grounds. Republicans denied considering racial factors as they denied the relevance of religion.

Finally, a few committee assignments are made virtually at random. Usually a handful of lesser places are left over after the committees-on-committees have argued and settled all the applications. These may be handed out more or less indiscriminately to freshman members. At least two circumstances contribute to this result. One occurs when members fail to make their preferences known or to attract any advance support for their applications. This may stem simply from a freshman member's innocence of the process, or, as in the case of the Connecticut Democratic delegation, from the absence of any senior spokesman in their behalf. A second arises when the committee-on-committees members, along with the party leadership, have too many prior commitments to give serious consideration to each applicant's stated preference. These commitments may extend to members who are obviously less qualified than those who were passed over.

III. SUMMARY AND CONCLUSION

Committee assignments in the House of Representatives involve all the complexities of an organization whose members "are not automatons but reasoning men and women acting in a setting in which they are subject to a bewildering barrage of conflicting or, at the least, inconsistent, demands—from within their constituencies. . . ."[8] Caution is consequently in order in formulating generalizations to describe the assignment process. In this study I have not tried to go beyond an assessment of the factors taken into account at the time the assignments were made, by those who made them. Whether the behavior, then or later, of those who were assigned is consistent with the reasons given for the assignments, or vindicated expectations expressed, is outside the scope of my endeavor.

From the data, several conclusions can be advanced as hypotheses for future **studies:**

(1) Despite some important differences in the formal structure, both the Democratic and Republican committee assignments are handled by small groups composed of senior members appointed and greatly influenced by the party leaders.

(2) Party leaders, working in conjunction with their committees-on-committees, use assignments to major committees to bargain with the leaders of party groups or factions, in order to preserve and fortify their leadership positions and conciliate potential rivals, as well as to reward members who have cooperated.

(3) Assignment to the major committees is restricted, with some exceptions, to members who have served two or more terms, who are "responsible" legislators, and who represent districts which do not require them to take inflexible positions on controversial issues.

(4) Although a number of factors enter into committee assignments—geography, group support, professional background, etc.—the most important single consideration—unless it can be taken for granted—is to provide each member with an assignment that will help to insure his re-election. Stated differently, the most impressive argument in any applicant's favor is that the assignment he seeks will give him an opportunity to provide the kind of service to his constituents that will sustain and attract voter interest and support. In distributing assignments the party acts as a mutual benefit and improvement society, and this for the obvious reason that control of the House depends on the re-election of party members.

(5) With minor differences, both parties apply the same criteria for making committee assignments. This does not necessarily imply

---

[8] Truman, *op. cit.*, p. 279.

that there are no differences between Republican and Democratic assignees. It does show that both parties tend to emphasize factors beyond the ideological commitments of the members, and that calculations of party advantage lead them both to substantially the same criteria.

III

THE FUNCTIONS OF INFORMAL GROUPS:
A STATE DELEGATION*

Alan Fiellin

SOCIAL SCIENTISTS have long recognized the value of the two approaches combined in the analysis reported in this paper—namely, functional analysis and the study of informal groups. Political scientists, however, have been slow to apply them *systematically* in their investigations of political institutions and behavior. Neither has as yet achieved a permanent place in the methodology of our discipline. For this latter reason, it will be worthwhile to examine briefly the meaning of these concepts before presenting the substantive analysis.

The relationship of political scientists to functional analysis is roughly that of M. Jourdain to prose; not fully conscious of his methodology, the analyst fails to use it systematically and thus fails to take full advantage of its potential. A quick review of the literature of political science would reveal many references to the functions of political behavior patterns and institutions, but self conscious systematic uses of the concept and approach would be hard to find. Moreover, owing to our traditional emphasis upon legal-constitutional and prescriptive analysis, many investigations have been limited to either the constitutionally prescribed functions[1] or functional prescriptions based upon the authors' values. Though both of these may be legitimate enterprises, they do not fully exploit functional analysis and without supplementation

---

* Reprinted from "The Functions of Informal Groups in Legislative Institutions," *Journal of Politics,* XXIV (February, 1962), 72–91. Copyright © 1962, Southern Political Science Association.
[1] For a discussion of the limitations of traditional frameworks see Gabriel Almond's introductory chapter, "A Functional Approach to Comparative Politics," in Gabriel Almond and James S. Coleman, *The Politics of the Developing Areas* (Princeton, New Jersey: Princeton University Press, 1960), especially pp. 3–4.

may lead to incomplete understanding and therefore superficial evaluation.[2]

Functional analysis is one way of viewing, understanding, or explaining behavior within a system. The observer asks what consequences a given behavior pattern has for the systems of which it is a part. For example, what are the functions and dysfunctions of boss-controlled political machines for the social, economic, and governmental systems of which they are a part,[3] or of seniority and the committee system for the legislative system, party system, and inclusive political system? The conclusions of such an analysis provide an understanding of the item as a functional unit of the institutions for which it is relevant.

Systematic functional analysis of social behavior requires more than the usual precision in the use of the term "function" and also requires that some distinctions between kinds of functions be made. The definition to be used here is that of Merton. "Functions are those observed consequences which make for the adaptation or adjustment of a given system."[4] As adapted to the present study, consequences make for the adaptation or adjustment of a given system when they (1) constitute positive and necessary contributions to the existence of the system, or (2) merely contribute to the achievement of participants' goals. Criterion 1 raises the issue and problems of the functional prerequisites of the systems considered. By supplementing this with the less demanding criterion 2, the problems involved in determining whether or not a particular function is vitally necessary are avoided. As the purpose of the analysis is to explain the existence of legislative informal groups, it seems justified to call attention to a variety of consequences without limiting attention to only those without which the various systems could not survive. Consequences which merely contribute to goal attainment are thus included not primarily for the purpose of avoid-

---

[2] A single example will clarify this point. The report of the Committee on Political Parties of the American Political Science Association, *Toward a More Responsible Two-Party System,* concentrates almost exclusively on the dysfunctions of United States parties and the functions which the authors feel they should perform (not actually do). A complete functional analysis in providing a more thorough understanding of the parties, would provide an appropriate basis for an evaluation of the net contribution of our parties to the political system and democracy.

[3] See the systematic analysis of Robert K. Merton in *Social Theory and Social Structure* (Glencoe, Illinois: The Free Press, 1957), pp. 71–82.

[4] Merton, *op. cit.,* p. 51.

ing problems but, more importantly, to permit a more complete explanation of informal groups.

The concept "dysfunction" is then used to refer to those consequences "which lessen the adaptation or adjustment of the system."[5] Merton points out that our analytical framework must also take into account the possibility of non-functional consequences—those which are irrelevant to the adaptation of adjustment of the system. It should be noted that a given behavior pattern may have all three kinds of consequences.

In addition to the above, there is the equally important distinction between manifest and latent functions. "Manifest functions are those objective consequences contributing to the adjustment or adaptation of the system which are intended and recognized by participants in the system; latent functions, correlatively, being those which are neither intended nor recognized."[6] The principal importance of this distinction is that it brings the frequently overlooked latent functions to the attention of the observer. Perceptive explorations of the latent functions of behavior patterns, because they go beyond the frequently common knowledge of manifest functions, are likely to result in new insights. A few examples will most adequately demonstrate this point—Veblen's analysis of conspicuous consumption,[7] the catharsis and legitimizing functions of congressional committee hearings, the social mobility function of political machines.

The framework to be used here thus consists of three categories —behavior patterns to which consequences are imputed, the general and specific consequences of those patterns, and units or systems for which the behavior has consequences. The behavior patterns to be analyzed are those of individuals in informal legislative groups. The general consequences will be described using the classifications developed above—manifest, latent; functional, dysfunctional, nonfunctional. Only where the distinction seems to be of theoretical importance and there are sufficient data, will functions be classified as manifest or latent. Specific consequences are the ways in which the pattern promotes adaptation and adjustment—for example, the communication channels of informal groups facilitate negotiation and coalition formation. The several systems for which the behavior

---

[5] *Ibid.*
[6] *Ibid.*
[7] *Ibid.*, p. 69.

analyzed in this case study has consequences will be specified in the following section which outlines the kinds and sources of data used for the functional analysis.[8]

NEW YORK DEMOCRATS AND INFORMAL GROUP BEHAVIOR

The analysis presented in the following pages is based upon part of a larger study of one informal group in the House of Representatives.[9] All of the members of the group are New York Democratic Representatives. The existence of an informal group within the delegation was not, however, inferred from the common membership of the Representatives in a state delegation.[10] Interview data on the interactions of the members were used to determine the existence and boundaries of a genuine interaction group. Thus the approximate correspondence of delegation and group boundaries was not assumed in the research design.[11]

Interviews in conjunction with participant-observation provided the data on the behavior patterns of the members.[12] These behavior

---

[8] For more extensive discussions of functional analysis and some inherent problems see Merton, *op. cit.*, Chap. 1; Ernest Nagel, *Logic Without Metaphysics* (Glencoe, Illinois: The Free Press, 1956), Chap. 10; Carl G. Hempel, "The Logic of Functional Analysis," in *Symposium on Sociological Theory,* ed. Llewellyn Gross (Evanston, Illinois: Row, Peterson and Co., 1959); Marion J. Levy, Jr., *The Structure of Society* (Princeton: Princeton University Press, 1952).

[9] Alan Fiellin, "The Behavior of a Legislative Group in the House of Representatives: A Case Study of New York Democrats" (Unpublished Ph.D. dissertation, Department of Government, New York University, 1960). The author wishes to express his special thanks to Professor Joseph Tanenhaus of New York University for his helpful supervision of this project.

[10] Cf. David Truman, *The Congressional Party: A Case Study* (New York: John Wiley and Sons, 1959), Chap. 7.

[11] A brief statement of the procedure followed and the results obtained will clarify this point. The members of the New York Democratic delegation in the 85th Congress were selected as the *initial* respondents for the interviews. It was thought likely that these respondents' frequent reference to Representatives outside the delegation would lead to the identification of an informal group consisting of both delegation and non-delegation members. This proved not to be the case. The seventeen members of the delegation constituted a rather uncohesive group; thirteen of these seventeen constituted the highly cohesive, relatively closed group of interactors. Each of these thirteen represented a district within New York City as did three of the others. Congressman Leo O'Brien of Albany was the only member of the delegation not from New York City.

[12] The collection of data was made possible by a Congressional Fellowship for which the author wants to thank the American Political Science Association and the donors to the program.

patterns are of two types—(1) those interactions (communication and organization for example) which are group behavior patterns, and (2) individual behavior patterns common to all members which are not, however, group behavior.

The empirical basis for both the analysis and the hypotheses which are developed (the latter are outlined in the conclusion) was supplemented with information on informal group activities found in the literature. Though not rich in systematic analyses of informal groups, books and articles by both political scientists and congressmen do contain many scattered references to their activities and functions.[13]

Despite the use of supplementary information, the limitations of a case study have not been entirely avoided. We know that the members of Congress form a variety of kinds of groups. These groups find their roots in a variety of common experiences—party membership, state and regional representation, religion, committee membership, similarity of views on the issues of the day, friendship, and so forth. Some are cohesive, some not. Some are relatively permanent, others ad hoc and temporary. In some, leadership roles are differentiated and clearly defined, while in others leadership is quite informal, perhaps shifting from one member to another. Some groups have only a few members, others are quite large. They also differ, undoubtedly, in the functions they perform. A classification scheme which could be used for distinguishing the functions different kinds of groups perform may eventually be developed. In the present exploratory study, no such attempt is made. Thus the extent to which the findings are appropriately generalized from this one group to all others is problematic.[14]

For purposes of this analysis an informal group is defined as an identifiable, self-conscious, relatively stable unit of interacting members whose relationships are not officially prescribed by statutes

---

[13] See especially the following: Stephen K. Bailey and Howard D. Samuel, *Congress at Work* (New York: Henry Holt and Co., 1952); David Truman, *The Governmental Process* (New York: Knopf, 1951) and *The Congressional Party* (New York: John Wiley and Sons, 1959); Jerry Voorhis, *Confessions of a Congressman* (Garden City, New York: Doubleday and Company, 1947).

The literature does contain at least two systematic studies of interpersonal relations in state legislatures. See Garland Routt, "Interpersonal Relationships and the Legislative Process," *Annals*, CXCV (January, 1938), pp. 129–36; Samuel Patterson, "Patterns of Interpersonal Relations in a State Legislative Group," *POQ*, XXIII (Spring, 1959), pp. 101–09.

[14] For the complete analysis of the internal structure of the New York Democratic group see Fiellin, *op, cit.*, Chap. 3.

and rules. The justification for approaching the study of Congress with this conceptual tool rests upon the assumption that such units exist and have important consequences for the nature of the legislative process. That the use of the approach will prove valuable seems likely in the light of the success researchers in other fields of social and political science have had with this approach[15] and our knowledge that Congress is a relatively unstructured legislative institution.[16] David Truman has indicated the reasons for using this approach in studying Congress.

> Such a body is not properly conceived as a collection of individual men, unorganized and without internal cohesion. Nor is it any better accounted for exclusively in terms of the formal, legal structure of the legislature. *A legislative body has its own group life, sometimes as a unit, perhaps more often as a collection of subgroups or cliques.* It has its own operating structure, which may approximate or differ sharply from the formal organization of the chamber.[17]

The following is an initial attempt to be reasonably systematic in analyzing the consequences of informal groups in the House of Representatives. Some limitations of the analysis, as previously explained, stem from primary reliance on data from a single case study. In addition, no attempt has been made to test rigorously hypotheses stating the functions of such groups. Rather the analysis is used for the purpose of generating hypotheses which may prove to be useful for future research.

In each of the following sections, one pattern of behavior is

---

[15] In the related fields of public administration and industrial management, the importance of informal groups as both facilitating and disturbing factors seems to be generally accepted. See Fritz J. Roethlisberger and William J. Dickson, *Management and the Worker* (Cambridge: Harvard University Press, 1939); Herbert A. Simon, *Administrative Behavior: A Study of Decision-Making Processes in Administrative Organization* (New York: Macmillan Co., 1947), pp. 147–49 and *passim;* Marshall E. and Gladys O. Dimock, *Public Administration* (New York: Rinehart and Co., 1953), pp. 104–06 and works cited therein. In the field of voting behavior see Bernard Berelson, Paul F. Lazarsfeld, and William N. McPhee, *Voting: A Study of Opinion Formation in a Presidential Campaign* (Chicago: University of Chicago Press, 1954), Chap. 6. For a thorough review of the literature in sociology and social-psychology as well as the report of an empirical study of opinion formation see Elihu Katz and Paul F. Lazarsfeld, *Personal Influence: The Part Played by People in the Flow of Mass Communications* (Glencoe, Illinois: The Free Press, 1955).

[16] The meaning of "unstructured" as used here is made more explicit in footnote 43, below.

[17] *The Governmental Process,* p. 343, emphasis added. Truman goes on to point out that this informal structure will have important consequences for the access of interest groups.

identified and explained and then the consequences of the pattern for relevant systems are suggested. The relevant systems for this analysis are (1) the members of the New York Democratic group, (2) the leadership of the group, (3) other members and groups in the House of Representatives, (4) the House itself as a legislative institution, (5) the electoral Democratic Party leaders of New York City and State, (6) New York City as the collective constituency represented by the group.

COMMUNICATION

From what is known about the behavior and functions of informal structures in other kinds of large scale organizations,[18] it is not surprising that the communication activities of the New York Democrats are functional for several units within the House. In fact, because of the absence of an effective hierarchical structure in the House, probably the most important functions of informal groups and relationships result from their use as communication networks.

The New York Democratic Congressmen

The communications network of the group performs three services for the individual members. It provides them with (1) "trustworthy" information on bills and legislative politics; (2) cues for making voting decisions;[19] and (3) adaptive norms, perceptions and rationalizations. All of these, since they are shared within the group, are socially supported. Providing social support for members' attitudes and behavior may thus be a latent function of informal groups.

It is a truism that legislators need information and advice. They

---

[18] Literature cited in footnote 15.

[19] For the data and statistical verification of this point see Fiellin, *op. cit.*, Chap. 5. Truman's study of state delegations and congressional committees is also relevant. *The Congressional Party*, Chap. 7. Duncan MacRae, on the basis of the results of scale analysis, also infers that face-to-face relationships affect roll call vote decisions. "Roll call votes are taken in sequence, sometimes with a considerable interval of time between them. That social controls have ample time to operate accounts, in part, for the higher degree of consistency in scaling obtainable with roll calls than with questionnaire data. One result of these Social controls may be that those individuals who change position on the continuum do so in groups on the basis of face-to-face association." "Some Underlying Variables in Legislative Roll Call Votes," *Public Opinion Quarterly*, XVIII, no. 2 (Summer, 1954), p. 194. On patterns of advice giving and taking in the U.S. Senate see Donald Matthews, *U.S. Senators and Their World* (Chapel Hill: University of North Carolina Press, 1960), pp. 251-54.

must be informed on both the technical and political aspects of legislation in order to make those decisions which may determine their political futures.[20] Members of the House of Representatives, of course, receive information from many sources—committee hearings and reports, floor debate, personal staff, the Legislative Reference Service, interest groups, mass media, and so forth. In fact this profusion of information from so many sources probably complicates the problem of decision-making rather than facilitating its solution.[21] It is for this reason that communication within informal groups may be particularly valuable to the individual member. Information, advice, and voting cues come from trusted sources— those with similar or identical interests and views. Several interview respondents attested to the value of such information and suggested the reasons for its special quality.

> I can take the advice of other members of the group on what to do and how to vote because they not only have expert opinions, their districts are essentially similar to mine. They have the same kinds of problems and the same basic viewpoint.[22]

In the particular case of the New York Democrats and other informal legislative groups based on the similar constituencies of the members, the reliability of information and advice is built-in. The constituencies of the members are essentially similar and the electoral party organizations and interest groups upon which they rely are either the same or have similar views and expectations.[23]

---

[20] See David Truman, *The Governmental Process*, pp. 334–35; Roland Young, *The American Congress* (New York: Harper and Bros., 1958), pp. 78–79.

[21] "Literally tons of information are available to Congress to keep it informed about what is happening in its own bailiwick and elsewhere in the government. The trouble is that the data are not in a form that can be used easily. Members are supposed to keep up with the executive agencies by reading their annual reports. The latter are voluminous, and those who compile them tell Congress and the people to a considerable extent, only what they want known. But with the pressure of work already imposing a physical strain on many legislators, very few have time to read the reports." Estes Kefauver and Jack Levin, *A Twentieth-Century Congress* (New York: Duell, Sloan and Pearce, 1947), p. 203.

[22] Reconstructed from interview responses.

[23] For some groups of legislators, establishing "sameness" of party organization and "similarity" of constituencies and relevant interest groups would present some difficult problems and definition and require the use of precise indices. Refined measurement seemed unnecessary for this case study since all but one of the members of the delegation in the 85th Congress were from New York City. Though New York City congressional districts do vary in socioeconomic composition, the variations are relatively minor. For occupational

Most important of all, perhaps, is that the member in taking cues from the New York group cannot get into electoral difficulties as a result of deviation. There is security in numbers. If the member honors this maxim and follows the advice of his informal group colleagues, he cannot be singled out for an "incorrect" decision.[24] A division of labor, corresponding to the committee structure of the House, develops in some groups and provides benefits for the individual. By virtue of his informal ties, the New York Democrat, for example, has ready access to committees of which he is not a member. Individual members may, and do, use group connections to check on the status and prospects of legislation in committees other than their own.[25] In the absence of personal ties with members of most House Committees, the task of quickly getting trustworthy information on the work of many committees would be most difficult.[26] The New York Democrat may save many hours of leg-work, reading, and anxious deliberation by holding a brief conversation with a likeminded colleague who knows the material and has previously sifted through it.

Members on first entering the House have much to learn. They must learn to make sense of this new world and understand their place in it—in short, become socialized in a new institution and

---

distributions within congressional districts see Duncan MacRae, Jr., *Dimensions of Congressional Voting* (Berkeley: University of California Press, 1958), Appendix B. All members of the group were, of course, within the jurisdiction of the same state party organization. The several county organizations involved, though independent and sometimes in conflict over local affairs, do frequently work together in city-wide affairs of concern to all and do seem to hold a common view of congressional politics. Certainly New York Democrats in the House tend strongly to identify themselves with the larger collective constituency, New York City.

[24] Cf. Bailey and Samuel, *op. cit.*, "In general, however, [Congressman Smith] was not inclined to compile a voting record that contrasted too sharply with the records of the other six members of the Mississippi delegation in the House." p. 131. "Often his decision followed hasty conferences with other members of the Mississippi delegation in the cloakroom outside of the Chamber." p. 132. On state delegation unity see also Bailey and Samuel, pp. 120–121; Voorhis, *op. cit.*, Chap. 7; Senator Tom Connally as told to Alfred Steinberg, *My Name is Tom Connally* (New York: Thomas Y. Crowell Co., 1954), p. 89.

[25] It is also quite possible that this access to other committees is used to secure action on members' own bills. Thus, access to committees may be used to exert influence as well as secure information.

[26] In the 86th Congress, 2d Session, there were New York Democrats on all House committees with the following exceptions: Armed Forces, Government Operations, House Administration, Un-American Activities, and Veterans Affairs. U.S. Congress, *Congressional Directory*, 85th Congress, 2nd Session, 1958, pp. 241–47.

role. By providing the new member with a social and political home away from home, by offering him viable conceptions of the national legislative process and his role in it, the group performs important functions for the individual. Since the "regular" New York Democrat is automatically a member of the group by virtue of his election, some of his difficult initial role problems are solved by his acceptance of the group and its "folkways."[27]

This function may be of greater than normal importance for the New York Democratic Representative because of his membership in what is pejoratively referred to as the "Tuesday to Thursday Club," *i.e.,* the "deviant" practice of too often restricting one's stay in Washington to these three days of the week.[28] Because of his membership in the group, however, this deviant behavior and the accompanying rationalization are socially sanctioned and supported.[29]

Though the group's provision and support of role conceptions and norms is in general an important function in a loosely structured situation,[30] that some conceptions in this case are deviant may be dysfunctional for the individual. This is true to the extent that these particular deviations reduce the members' influence.[31]

Other Informal Groups and the House as a Legislative Institution

The communication which occurs through the channels of informal groups is functional not only for the individual members, but also for the institution and its component groups as well. It would be nearly impossible for the members of Congress to perform

---

[27] Evidence of this function can also be found in the literature. "The other members [of the Ohio Republican delegation], all of whom were veterans, had been helpful in showing him [Congressman Ayers] the ropes of Congressional procedure." Bailey and Samuel, *op. cit.,* p. 121. "Through our Young Turks meetings [an informal House group], through my committee meetings, through contacts on the floor and elsewhere I was learning about Congress and about congressmen as they actually are—not as they are reported to be by the columnists or the humorists of the country." Voorhis, *op. cit.,* p. 31.

[28] See discussion below and Donald Matthews, *op. cit.,* pp. 94–95.

[29] For a complete discussion of this behavior and the reasons for it see Fiellin, *op. cit.,* pp. 24, 26 ff., 52 f., 147 ff., 163 ff.

[30] On the role problems of legislators and politicians see Edward A. Shils, "The Legislator and His Environment," *University of Chicago Law Review,* XVIII (1950–1951), pp. 571–84; William C. Mitchell, "Occupational Role Strains: The American Elective Public Official," *Administrative Science Quarterly,* III (September, 1958), pp. 210–28.

[31] See discussion below, pp. 86–87.

their legislative functions in the absence of such communication channels.[32] Committees, political parties, and floor debate solve only part of the communication problem of Congress. Informal groups supplement and fill in the remaining gaps. The following example of the operation of informal groups suggests that the functions of communication within and between such groups may lie especially in the area of forming coalitions, negotiating compromises, and developing legislative strategy.

An informal group of "Democratic Young Turks" was established during the 85th Congress.[33] The stated purpose of the group was to enhance the strength of Western and Northern Democratic "liberals" in Democratic Party and House politics. *Congressional Quarterly* expressed the view that the chief spokesman, Eugene McCarthy, was opposed to any formal organization as " . . . it might be construed as a direct challenge to Rayburn's leadership." The report goes on to state that nevertheless ". . . communication among the 80 signers of the program is effective even without a formal organization."[34] The relationship between this group and the New York Democrats, 14 of whom joined the "Young Turks," is instructive in demonstrating how a pre-existing informal group facilitated this communication.

Though much communication among the members took place in informal conversations on the floor of the Chamber and in the cloakrooms and dining rooms, the communication channels of informal groups were also used to disseminate messages quickly and effectively to all members. For example, Congressman Multer, the Democratic whip for New York State and a leader of the informal group, became an unofficial "whip" of the "Young Turks." In this way, liaison was established between the two informal House groups. The New York Democratic group "tied" its members to the outside legislative world while at the same time facilitating communication from outside groups to its members. Many messages were transmitted through these channels. At least in some of the "Young Turks' " meetings and conversations to plan program and strategy, one New York Democrat "represented" the entire group.

---

[32] In other legislatures which are highly organized by parties or other agencies, communication through informal groups may be less important.

[33] Eighty members of the House who had signed a manifesto were members. Information is from informal interviews and *Congressional Quarterly Weekly Report*, XV (February 22, 1957), 224–25.

[34] *Ibid.*, p. 225.

Though in this particular example the communication channels may have become more regularized than is customary, it does illustrate the kind of function which may be served by such groups. Until the business and politics of Congress becomes more completely structured by other kinds of organizations, one may expect informal groups to arise and facilitate a variety of essential kinds of communication.

New York Party and Public Officials

It was expected by the author that group channels would be used by both party and public officials in New York City and State to communicate their views on legislation. Available data, which may be incomplete, suggest that this is not the case. On the contrary, interview data indicate that the few messages members receive in which public officials state their views on pending legislation are sent directly to the individual members rather than being channeled through group leaders.

GROUP MEETINGS

It is not uncommon for members of informal legislative groups to meet together regularly—frequently for lunch or dinner. In the extent to which business is formally conducted and group decisions reached during these meetings, there is probably considerable variation from group to group. The following procedure is that normally followed by the New York Democratic delegation. That it is not an entirely unique case is evident from the descriptions of other group meetings found in the literature.[35]

Congressman Multer, the Assistant Whip for the New York Democrats, acts as the coordinator of these monthly meetings—setting the time and place and calling the members together. The manifest function of these meetings for the leaders is to discuss legislation and crystallize the position of the delegation. When a measure is scheduled for consideration in the House, Congressman Multer requests a summary of the bill and the pros and cons from that member of the delegation serving on the committee. At the next meeting of the group, Multer presents this information to-

---

[35] For information on the meetings of other legislative groups see Voorhis, *op. cit.*, pp. 30–31; Kefauver and Levin, *op. cit.*, pp. 89–90; Bailey and Samuel, *op. cit.*, pp. 108–09, 120–21, 125.

gether with his and the committee member's recommendations for group action. The measure is then discussed and an attempt is made to arrive at a group decision.

In arriving at group decisions, the delegation follows rules similar to those of the party caucus. When there is disagreement within the group, the members of the majority, through persuasion, attempt to bring about unanimity. "Members in the minority are told what the New York City interest is, they are informed of the party position as expressed in the platform, and the interests of their constituencies are analyzed."[36] But if individuals persist in their dissent because of contrary campaign pledges or the dictates of conscience, then, in the words of one member, "we don't try to stop them."

Bailey and Samuel, in discussing the meetings of the Ohio Republicans, present additional evidence of the informational function of regular group meetings.

> For the members themselves, the weekly luncheons usually provided some information of value; at least one of the fourteen Ohio Republicans was bound to be a member of the committee handling the current legislation. Finally, for the Republican leadership, it was helpful to get the fourteen Ohio Republicans around the same table. After the meetings, Representative J. Harry McGregor of the 17th District who served as the Ohio whip could estimate with fair accuracy how his fellow members would vote.[37]

Thus the manifest functions of these meetings for members and leaders are (1) dissemination of information, (2) exchange of views on pending legislation, and (3) at least for the New York Democrats, determination of the group's position.

An important latent function of these meetings results from the social, convivial nature of the occasion. It is well known that for many groups such affairs have the effects of developing *esprit de corps* and of reinforcing group identity. These in turn contribute to unity of action which is necessary for the realization of group goals. From very meagre information on the New York Democrats' dinner meetings, it seems probable that they also have this latent emotional function in addition to their manifest functions of information, discussion, and decision.

---

[36] Paraphrased interview response.
[37] Bailey and Samuel, *op. cit.*, p. 121.

BLOC VOTING

In contributing to the achievement of goals in the House, bloc voting is functional for the group members and leaders, the electoral party leaders, and the collective constituency, New York City. Its special contribution to goal attainment consists in providing the group with a measure of influence out of proportion to the number of its members.

Leaders especially are aware of the positive consequences of bloc behavior, whereas some of the rank-and-file seem to be totally unaware of any purpose served by the group's cohesive voting. These variations in awareness of the benefits of group cohesion can be explained in part by the greater involvement of leaders in House politics and their greater concern for the strategic problems of acquiring influence and achieving goals. As representatives of the group in negotiations concerning legislation, committee assignments, and so forth, the leaders of the delegation are made aware of the potential contribution of group unity to the achievement of desired ends.[38] Votes are one medium of exchange in political bargaining; the ability to "deliver" a large bloc of votes may contribute mightily in bringing negotiations to a successful conclusion.[39]

Two minor incidents which were brought to the attention of the author suggest specific ways bloc voting might be used to advantage in House politics. On one occasion, reportedly, it was suggested to the members of the delegation that all vote in the Democratic caucus in favor of the appointment of a *non*-New York Democrat to a committee vacancy. It was argued that unanimity on the part of the delegation on this vote would enhance its future bargaining position for favorable committee assignments for its own members.

The other example comes from the administrative assistant of a House Democrat. With great admiration, he spoke of the "smooth" operation of the New York Democrats. He had observed his "boss" rounding up votes for a bill in which the latter was interested. In doing so, the Representative contacted, among others, only one New

---

[38] Group leadership and its roles are discussed in Fiellin, *op. cit.*, pp. 58 ff.

[39] Connally in his autobiography calls attention to the function of clannishness within the Texas delegation. "Although we Texans were a smaller House group than the member's from New York, Pennsylvania, Illinois, or Ohio, as a rule the eighteen of us exerted a degree of influence far out of proportion to our numbers. For we generally voted together on a bill and this unity helped make up for the fact that we held no committee Chairmanships and that none of us was important except John Garner, then only fifth ranking man on the Ways and Means Committee." Connally, *op. cit.*, pp. 89–90.

York Democrat. He confidently relied upon this single contact as sufficient for obtaining the full support of the New York Democrats (17 votes) ; he was not disappointed by the final results.

Truman also describes an example which illustrates the advantages of bloc behavior.

> An excellent illustration of logrolling . . . occurred in connection with appropriations in 1950 for unemployment relief and farm parity payments. During that session the Farm Bureau's supporters in Congress had been in opposition to representatives from some of the Eastern cities on these two measures and on others. Neither had sufficient reliable votes on these bills to assure it a majority in the House. Under the leadership of Mayor LaGuardia of New York and President O'Neal of the Farm Bureau, an arrangement was made during the voting on parity payments in the House of Representatives. The votes of a number of urban congressmen on that measure were exchanged for those of certain representatives from farm areas on general relief appropriations.[40]

Such arrangements may of course be worked out in the absence of an appropriate informal group structure. Nevertheless, there is no doubt that such a structure facilitates the formation of coalitions, and that willingness to play the game increases the influence of stable groups. In contrast, individual members outside of the bloc structure will only in the case of very close votes have the necessary influence to enter into negotiations with sufficient leverage to expect a reasonably favorable *quid pro quo*.

These examples suggest how bloc behavior might be used by the leaders for their own success as well as the promotion of the interests of rank-and-file members, the group, the constituencies and interest groups.[41] They also provide additional evidence of the function of groups in facilitating legislative negotiations.

To appreciate fully the contribution of bloc voting to a member's legislative life and career it must be seen within the context of his

---

[40] *The Government Process*, p. 368.

[41] Truman's point regarding interest groups' relations with legislators is pertinent to the above analysis. "A group [interest group] is handicapped if its only connections are with a maverick or a newcomer. It is not enough for the legislator to be a member, in some sense, of the interest group or even to be in a position of formal power. He must 'belong' within the legislature as well." *The Governmental Process*, p. 345. Influence in legislative negotiations depends upon one's ability to "tie in" to appropriate informal networks at some point.

total situation in the legislature. New York Democrats who come to Congress rarely achieve great individual influence. For a variety of reasons, their approach to Congress typically limits the likelihood of their joining the "inner circle." Their membership in the "Tuesday to Thursday Club," short tenure as congressmen, and a tendency to limit personal contacts to other New York Democrats combine to make it less than likely that individual members will be accepted by their colleagues as "congressmen's congressmen." Since we expect our representatives to acquire influence in order to further constituency interests (ample evidence from interviews indicates that New York Democrats define this as a central role expectation), the individual New York Democrat without the group as a channel of participation and influence might have some difficulty in meeting his role expectations. From this perspective, bloc voting and the resulting collective influence can be viewed as a substitute for individual influence. The members' obligations (manifest function) to promote and defend the common interests of their constituencies (New York City) is thus fulfilled. Success in this should be functional also for the electoral party's goal of winning elections.

Collective action may also provide, probably latently, a defense and protection for the individual in his relationship with lobbyists. For much the same reason that the British backbencher is relatively free of pressures from outside groups, the rank-and-file New York Democrat may be less besieged by them than is usual for members of the House.

The psychological, cue-giving function of informal group membership as it relates to the re-election problems of members was previously mentioned in discussing the communication functions of the group. It is pertinent to refer again to this function because of its direct connection with bloc voting. Voorhis in his insightful autobiography poignantly calls attention to the psychological and electoral problems of members, which may be partially solved by informal group memberships.

> Everyone desires the inner warmth that comes from the knowledge that he has friends who can be counted upon. The members of the organized groups desire this. So do the congressmen. It is, again, a formula for re-election.
>
> *   *   *   *   *
>
> Thus I have been able to understand why members sought a kind of political "home" in the bosom of some strong group, whose interests they would always protect and who could then

be depended upon to go all out for the candidate for re-election whenever the need arose.[42]

In order fully to appreciate the importance of Voorhis' point for an understanding of the New York Democrats' group behavior in Congress, it is necessary to be aware of the ties between the congressional delegation and the electoral parties. Faithful membership in the delegation group is one way for the member to remain in good standing with party officials regarding his activities in Washington. In situations where party support is normally a *sine qua non* of re-election (and it probably is for most New York Democratic Congressmen) "belonging" is likely to be a high priority objective.

THE "TUESDAY TO THURSDAY CLUB"

A practice which has both manifest functions and latent dysfunctions for the individual is his membership in the Tuesday to Thursday Club—that is, spending only three or four days in Washington while the House is in session. It is likely that the commuting involved is not welcomed by all members. Evidence from interviews suggests that party leaders and constituents partly because of established tradition *expect* their congressmen to maintain close contact with them by making frequent trips home. Both for re-election and for "promotion" to higher political office, their time should be divided between Washington and New York. Thus the practice has manifest functions for the individual's political career.

Many members also take advantage of the economic opportunities by maintaining their previously established law practices and businesses. In this way, they supplement their incomes and maintain non-political careers to which they may return in the event of electoral defeat or political retirement.

Though functional for the member's New York political career, it seems probable that "Tuesday to Thursday Club" membership is dysfunctional for his congressional career. Frequent absence from "the Hill" earns the member a reputation as a parttime congressman. For many House colleagues, particularly those that count, this is a violation of the norm requiring that each member carry his share of the work load and spend nearly full-time in Washington while the House is in session. Some individuals (perhaps Con-

---

[42] Voorhis, *op. cit.*, p. 37.

gressman Celler, for example) may substantially overcome this handicap after long service and gain considerable influence both formally and informally. For most members, however, the deviation results in some reduction in prestige and influence with House colleagues.

CONCLUSION

The foregoing analysis of the functional meaning of some standardized behavior patterns of the members of one informal group in the House of Representatives suggests hypotheses for further research. Only those which may prove fruitful for the understanding of the functions of informal groups in general (as opposed to those whose meaning is limited to the particular characteristics of the New York Democrats) will be reformulated. Again the reader must be warned that these are suggested hypotheses, not firmly established propositions.

1. Informal groups arise in unstructured legislative situations.[43]

2. These groups perform manifest and latent functions (dysfunctions) for the members and the institutions.

3. Informal groups are the principal "socializing" agencies in such legislatures.

    a. Members learn role expectations and institutional norms within informal groups.

4. Informal groups may function to provide support for behavior adjudged to be deviant in the light of institutional norms.

5. Decisions of legislators depend, in part, on their informal group memberships.

6. Conscious bloc behavior is characteristic of informal groups under conditions of "sufficient" integration of the members and similarity of interests between them.

---

[43] This hypothesis asserts nothing about structured legislative situations. These terms, "structured" and "unstructured," will need to be more precisely defined. In the loose usage here, the distinction is being made between situations such as that of the British House of Commons, where much if not most of what transpires is determined by party and cabinet, and that of Congress, where no such all-important agencies exist. In the latter case, individuals are "forced" to be free, their behavior not having been "pre-determined" to the same extent, and they must "improvise" mechanisms to perform functions which party and cabinet perform in the British example.

a. This bloc behavior is, by defination, manifestly related to political strategy and goal attainment.

7. Latent functions for the individuals and the group leadership result from the division of labor within these groups,
e.g., access to a variety of committees in order to secure information and exercise influence.

8. Legislative functional requisites[44] are among the consequences of informal groups in legislatures.

a. One function performed by informal groups is the
exchange of political and technical information.

b. Informal groups structure otherwise hopelessly confused legislative situations.

b. 1. The politics of otherwise unstructured legislatures occur, for the most part, within and
between these groups and through their channels, e.g. negotiation, compromise, and the
formation, of coalitions.

b. 2. "Generalized support" will be characteristic
of the relationship between these groups.[45]

Applying this orientation to the House of Representatives, it is
hypothesised that House politics is not unintelligibly complex, consisting only of the individual behavior of each of 435 isolated
members. Rather, it is much more simply structured through a
network of informal groups and relationships. This network provides channels for information exchange, political negotiation, and
the formation of compromises—probably impossible tasks for 435

---

[44] Using Merton's explanation of this concept, "it is assumed that there are
certain *functions* which are indispensable in the sense that, unless they are performed, the society (or group or individual [in this application it is the legis-
lature]) will not persist." Merton, *op. cit.*, p. 33.
[45] This hypothesis has a theoretical basis in Talcott Parson's formulations on
the American political system. See his " 'Voting' and the Equilibrium of the
American Political System," in *American Voting Behavior,* eds. Eugene Burdick
and Arthur Brodbeck (Glencoe: The Free Press, 1959), pp. 89–90. Professor
Parsons suggests that generalized support of leadership on the part of the
electorate (a relationship in which *specific* policy commitments are absent)
is necessary for "the political integration of a complex social system." The
hypothesis stated above suggests that in the absence of *vertical* generalized
support in the House (probably characterized of the British House of Commons)
one would expect *horizontal* generalized support (between groups and individuals) to develop. In other words, "logrolling" in which there is a specific and
explicit quid pro quo will be relatively rare.

atomized units.[46] Just as this structure makes House politics understandable for the participants, so it is through this perspective that the observer may understand them. It is by locating and "mapping" such groups and their intra- and inter-relationships that the observer may simplify the task of understanding what seem to be hopelessly confused political institutions and processes.[47]

---

[46] Katz and Lazarsfeld point out that in a variety of areas of social behavior, a simplified model of atomized individuals is inappropriate and misleading. *Op. cit.*, Introduction; Part I, Chaps. 1–4. Many scholars are coming to realize that the same is true of Congress. In addition to the references cited throughout the paper, the works of Roland Young and Holbert Carroll contain references to the functions of informal relationships. Young writes, "In formulating policy Congress carries out its work through various types of units and alliances. Some of these units and alliances are recognized in the official rules; others are free-forming, as it were, operating within the legislative structure while not being a constituent part of the legal framework." *The American Congress* (New York: Harper and Bros., 1958), p. 47. Also see pp. 56, 157. Holbert N. Carroll, *The House of Representatives and Foreign Affairs* (Pittsburgh: The University of Pittsburgh Press, 1958), pp. 101, 237, 263.

[47] Truman's warning should be kept in mind. "It is important not to assume that these interactions produce an integrated, hierarchical structure. They may, but the life of the legislative group as of others may as easily involve a loosely allied collection of cliques." . . . "Party government is a form of legislative group life, but it is not the only or the most common form in the United States." *The Governmental Process*, p. 346.

IV

THE APPROPRIATIONS COMMITTEE
AS A POLITICAL SYSTEM*

Richard F. Fenno, Jr.

STUDIES OF Congress by political scientists have produced a time-tested consensus on the very considerable power and autonomy of Congressional committees. Because of these two related characteristics, it makes empirical and analytical sense to treat the Congressional committee as a discrete unit for analysis. This paper conceives of the committee as a political system (or, more accurately as a political subsystem) faced with a number of basic problems which it must solve in order to achieve its goals and maintain itself. Generally speaking these functional problems pertain to the environmental and the internal relations of the committee. This study is concerned almost exclusively with the internal problems of the committee and particularly with the problem of self-integration.[1] It describes how one congressional committee—The Committee on Appropriations of the House of Representatives—has dealt with this problem in the period 1947–1961. Its purpose is to add to our understanding of appropriations politics in Congress and to suggest the usefulness of this type of analysis for studying the activities of any congressional committee.

* Reprinted from "The House Appropriations Committee as a Political System: The Problem of Integration," *American Political Science Review*, LVI (June, 1962), 310–24. Copyright © 1962, the American Political Science Association. The author wishes to acknowledge his indebtedness to the Committee on Political Behavior of the Social Science Research Council for the research grant which made possible this study, and the larger study of legislative behavior in the area of appropriations of which it is a part. This is a revised version of a paper read at the Annual Meeting of the American Political Science Association at St. Louis, September, 1961.
[1] On social systems, see: George Homans, *The Human Group* (New York, 1950); Robert K. Merton, *Social Theory and Social Structure* (Glencoe, 1957); Talcott Parsons and Edward Shils, *Toward A General Theory of Action* (Cambridge, 1951), pp. 190–234. Most helpful with reference to the political system has been David Easton, "An Approach to the Analysis of Political Systems," *World Politics* (April, 1957), pp. 383–400.

The necessity for integration in any social system arises from the differentiation among its various elements. Most importantly there is a differentiation among subgroups and among individual positions, together with the roles that flow therefrom.[2] A committee faces the problem, how shall these diverse elements be made to mesh together or function in support of one another? No political system (or subsystem) is perfectly integrated; yet no political system can survive without some minimum degree of integration among its differentiated parts. Committee integration is defined as the degree to which there is a working together or a meshing together or mutual support among its roles and subgroups. Conversely, it is also defined as the degree to which a committee is able to minimize conflict among its roles and its subgroups, by heading off or resolving the conflicts that arise.[3] A concomitant of integration is the existence of a fairly consistent set of norms, widely agreed upon and widely followed by the members. Another concomitant of integration is the existence of control mechanisms (*i.e.,* socialization and sanctioning mechanisms) capable of maintaining reasonable conformity to norms. In other words, the more highly integrated a committee, the smaller will be the gap between expected and actual behavior.

This study is concerned with integration both as a structural characteristic of, and as a functional problem for, the Appropriations Committee. First, certain basic characteristics of the Committee need description, to help explain the integration of its parts. Second comes a partial description of the degree to which and the ways in which the Committee achieves integration. No attempt is made to state this in quantitative terms, but the object is to examine the meshing together or the minimization of conflict among certain subgroups and among certain key roles. Also, important control mechanisms are described. The study concludes with some comments on the consequences of Committee integration for appropriations politics and on the usefulness of further Congressional committee analysis in terms of functional problems such as this one.

---

[2] On the idea of subgroups as used here, see Harry M. Johnson, *Sociology* (New York, 1960), ch. 3. On role, see specifically Theodore M. Newcomb, *Social Psychology* (New York, 1951), p. 280; see generally N. Gross, W. Mason and A. McEachern, *Explorations in Role Analysis: Studies of the School Superintendecy Role* (New York, 1958). On differentiation and its relation to integration, see Scott Greer, *Social Organization* (New York, 1955).

[3] The usage here follows most closely that of Robert Merton, *op. cit.,* pp. 26–29.

I

Five important characteristics of the Appropriations Committee which help explain Committee integration are (1) the existence of a well-articulated and deeply rooted consensus on Committee goals or tasks; (2) the nature of the Committee's subject matter; (3) the legislative orientation of its members; (4) the attractiveness of the Committee for its members; and (5) the stability of Committee membership.

Consensus

The Appropriations Committee sees its tasks as taking form within the broad guidelines set by its parent body, the House of Representatives. For it is the primary condition of the Committee's existence that it was created by the House for the purpose of assisting the House in the performance of House legislative tasks dealing with appropriations. Committee members agree that their fundamental duty is to serve the House in the manner and with the substantive results that the House prescribes. Given, however, the imprecision of House expectations and the permissiveness of House surveillance, the Committee must elaborate for itself a definition of tasks plus a supporting set of perceptions (of itself and of others) explicit enough to furnish day-to-day guidance.

The Committee's view begins with the pre-eminence of the House—often mistakenly attributed to the Constitution ("all bills for raising revenue," Art. I, sec. 7) but nevertheless firmly sanctioned by custom—in appropriations affairs.

It moves easily to the conviction that, as the efficient part of the House in this matter, the Constitution has endowed it with special obligations and special prerogatives. It ends in the view that the Committee on Appropriations, far from being merely one among many units in a complicated legislative-executive system, is *the* most important, most responsible unit in the whole appropriations process.[4] Hand in hand with the consensus on their primacy goes a

---

[4] This and all other generalizations about member attitudes and perceptions depend heavily on extensive interviews with Committee members. Semi-structured interviews, averaging 45 minutes in length were held with 45 of the 50 Committee members during the 86th Congress. Certain key questions, all open-ended, were asked of all respondents. The schedule was kept very flexible, however, in order to permit particular topics to be explored with those individuals best equipped to discuss them. In a few cases, where respondents encouraged it, notes were taken during the interviews. In most cases notes were not taken, but were transcribed immediately after the interview. Where unattributed quotations occur in the text, therefore, they are as nearly verbatim as the author's power of immediate recall could make them. These techniques were all used so as to improve *rapport* between interviewer and respondent.

consensus that all of their House-prescribed tasks can be fulfilled by superimposing upon them one, single, paramount task—*to guard the Federal Treasury.* Committee members state their goals in the essentially negative terms of guardianship—screening requests for money, checking against ill-advised expenditures, and protecting the taxpayer's dollar. In the language of the Committee's official history, the job of each member is, "constantly and courageously to protect the Federal Treasury against thousands of appeals and imperative demands for unnecessary, unwise, and excessive expenditures."[5]

To buttress its self-image as guardian of public funds the Committee elaborates a set of perceptions about other participants in the appropriations process to which most members hold most of the time. Each executive official, for example, is seen to be interested in the expansion of his own particular program. Each one asks, therefore, for more money than he really needs, in view of the total picture, to run an adequate program. This and other Committee perceptions—of the Budget Bureau, of the Senate, and of their fellow Representatives—help to shape and support the Committee members in their belief that most budget estimates can, should and must be reduced and that, since no one else can be relied upon, the House Committee must do the job. To the consensus on the main task of protecting the Treasury is added, therefore, a consensus on the instrumental task of *cutting whatever budget estimates are submitted.*

As an immediate goal, Committee members agree that they must strike a highly critical, aggressive posture toward budget requests, and that they should, on principle, reduce them. In the words of the Committee's veterans: "There has never been a budget submitted to the Congress that couldn't be cut." "There isn't a budget that can't be cut 10 per cent immediately." "I've been on the Committee for 17 years. No subcommittee of which I have been a member has ever reported out a bill without a cut in the budget. I'm proud of that record." The aim of budget-cutting is strongly internalized for the Committee member. "It's a tradition in the Appropriations Committee to cut." "You're grounded in it. . . . It's ingrained in you from the time you get on the Committee." For the purposes of a larger study, the appropriations case histories of 37 executive bureaus have been examined for a 12-year period,

---

[5] "History of the Committee on Appropriations," House Doc. 299, 77th Cong., 1st sess., 1941–1942, p. 11.

1947–1959.[6] Of 443 separate bureau estimates, the Committee reduced 77.2 per cent (342) of them.

It is a mark of the intensity and self-consciousness of the Committee consensus on budget-cutting that it is couched in a distinctive vocabulary. The workaday lingo of the Committee member is replete with negative verbs, undesirable objects of attention, and effective instruments of action. Agency budgets are said to be filled with "fat," "padding," "grease," "pork," "oleaginous substance," "water," "oil," "cushions," "avoirdupois," "waste tissue," and "soft spots." The action verbs most commonly used are "cut," "carve," "slice," "prune," "whittle," "squeeze," "wring," "trim," "lop off," "chop," "slash," "pare," "shave," "fry," and "whack." The tools of the trade are appropriately referred to as "knife," "blade," "meat axe," "scalpel," "meat cleaver," "hatchet," "shears," "wringer," and "fine-tooth comb." Members are hailed by their fellows as being "pretty sharp with the knife." Agencies may "have the meat axe thrown at them." Executives are urged to put their agencies "on a fat boy's diet." Budgets are praised when they are "cut to the bone." And members agree that "You can always get a little more fat out of a piece of pork if you fry it a little longer and a little harder."

To the major task of protecting the Treasury and the instrumental task of cutting budget estimates, each Committee member adds, usually by way of exception, a third task—*serving the constituency to which he owes his election.* This creates no problem for him when, as is sometimes the case, he can serve his district best by cutting the budget requests of a federal agency whose program is in conflict with the demands of his constituency.[6a] Normally, however, members find that their most common role-conflict is between a Committee-oriented budget-reducing role and a constituency-oriented budget-increasing role. Committee ideology resolves the conflict by assigning top, long-run priority to the budget-cutting task and making of the constituency service a permissible, short-run exception. No member is expected to commit electoral suicide; but no member is expected to allow his district's desire for federal funds to dominate his Committee behavior.

---

[6] The bureaus being studied are all concerned with domestic policy and are situated in the Agriculture, Interior, Labor, Commerce, Treasury, Justice and Health, Education and Welfare Departments. For a similar pattern of Committee decisions in foreign affairs, see Holbert Carroll, *The House of Representatives and Foreign Affairs* (Pittsburgh, 1958), ch. 9.

[6a] See, for example, Philip A. Foss, "The Grazing Fee Dilemma," Inter-University Case Program, No. 57 (University, Alabama, 1960).

Subject Matter

Appropriations Committee integration is facilitated by the subject matter with which the group deals. The Committee makes
decisions on the same controversial issues as do the committees
handling substantive legislation. But a money decision—however
vitally it affects national policy—is, or at least seems to be, less
directly a policy decision. Since they deal immediately with dollars
and cents, it is easy for the members to hold to the idea that they
are not dealing with programmatic questions, that theirs is a "business" rather than a "policy" committee. The subject matter, furthermore, keeps Committee members relatively free agents, which
promotes intra-Committee maneuvering and, hence, conflict avoid-
ance. Members do not commit themselves to their constituents in
terms of precise money amounts, and no dollar sum is sacred—it
can always be adjusted without conceding that a principle has been
breached. By contrast, members of committees dealing directly with
controversial issues are often pressured into taking concrete stands
on these issues; consequently, they may come to their committee
work with fixed and hardened attitudes. This leads to unavoidable,
head-on intra-committee conflict and renders integrative mechanisms
relatively ineffective.

The fact of an annual appropriations process means the Committee members repeat the same operations with respect to the
same subject matters year after year—and frequently more than once
in a given year. Substantive and procedural repetition promotes
familiarity with key problems and provides ample opportunity to
test and confirm the most satisfactory methods of dealing with them.
And the absolute necessity that appropriations bills do ultimately
pass gives urgency to the search for such methods. Furthermore,
the House rule that no member of the Committee can serve on another standing committee is a deterrent against a fragmentation
of Committee member activity which could be a source of difficulty
in holding the group together. If a committee has developed (as
this one has) a number of norms designed to foster integration,
repeated and concentrated exposure to them increases the likelihood that they will be understood, accepted and followed.

Legislative Orientation

The recruitment of members for the Appropriations Committee
produces a group of individuals with an orientation especially conducive to Committee integration. Those who make the selection

pay special attention to the characteristics which Masters has described as those of the "responsible legislator"—approval of and conformity to the norms of the legislative process and of the House of Representatives.[7]

Key selectors speak of wanting, for the Appropriations Committee, "the kind of man you can deal with" or "a fellow who is well-balanced and won't go off half-cocked on things." A Northern liberal Democrat felt that he had been chosen over eight competitors because, "I had made a lot of friends and was known as a nice guy"—especially, he noted, among Southern Congressmen. Another Democrat explained, "I got the blessing of the Speaker and the leadership. It's personal friendships. I had done a lot of things for them in the past, and when I went to them and asked them, they gave it to me." A Republican chosen for the Committee in his first term recalled,

> The Chairman [Rep. Taber] I guess did some checking around in my area. After all, I was new and he didn't know me. People told me that they were called to see if I was—well, unstable or apt to go off on tangents . . . to see whether or not I had any preconceived notions about things and would not be flexible—whether I would oppose things even though it was obvious.

A key criterion in each of the cases mentioned was a demonstrable record of, or an assumed predisposition toward, legislative give-and-take.

The 106 Appropriations Committee members serving between 1947 and 1961 spent an average of 3.6 years on other House committees before coming to the Committee. Only 17 of the 106 were selected as first term Congressmen. A House apprenticeship (which Appropriations maintains more successfully than all committees save Ways and Means and Rules[8]) provides the time in which

---

[7] Nicholas A. Masters, "House Committee Assignments," *American Political Science Review*, Vol. 55 (June, 1961), pp. 345–357. [Chapter II of this volume.]

[8] In the period from 1947 through 1959, (80th to 86th Congress) 79 separate appointments were made to the Appropriations Committee, with 14 going to freshmen. The Committee filled, in other words, 17.7 per cent of its vacancies with freshmen. The Rules Committee had 26 vacancies and selected no freshmen at all. The Ways and Means Committee had 36 vacancies and selected 2 freshmen (5.6 per cent). All other Committees had a higher percentage of freshmen appointments. Armed Services ranked fourth, with 45 vacancies and 12 freshmen appointed, for a percentage of 26.7. Foreign affairs figures were 46 and 14, or 30.4 per cent; UnAmerican Activities figures were 22 and 7, or 31.8 per cent. cf. Masters, *op. cit.*

legislative reputations can be established by the member and an assessment of that reputation in terms of Appropriations Committee requirements can be made. Moreover, the mere fact that a member survives for a couple of terms is some indication of an electoral situation conducive to his "responsible" legislative behavior. The optimum bet for the Committee is a member from a sufficiently safe district to permit him freedom of maneuver inside the House without fear of reprisal at the polls.[9] The degree of responsiveness to House norms which the Committee selectors value may be the product of a safe district as well as an individual temperament.

Attractiveness

A fourth factor is the extraordinarily high degree of attractiveness which the Committee holds for its members—as measured by the low rate of departure from it. Committee members do not leave it for service on other committees. To the contrary, they are attracted to it from nearly every other committee.[10] Of the 106 members in the 1947–1961 period, only two men left the Committee voluntarily; and neither of them initiated the move.[11] Committee attractiveness is a measure of its capacity to satisfy individual member needs—for power, prestige, recognition, respect, self-esteem, friendship, etc. Such satisfaction in turn increases the likelihood that members will behave in such a way as to hold the group together.

The most frequently mentioned source of Committee attractiveness is its power—based on its control of financial resources. "Where the money is, that's where the power is," sums up the feeling of the members. They prize their ability to reward or punish so many other participants in the political process—executive officials, fellow Congressmen, constituents and other clientele groups. In the eyes of its own members, the Committee is either the most powerful in the House or it is on a par with Ways and Means or, less frequently, on a par with Ways and Means and Rules. The second

---

[9] In the 1960 elections, 41 out of the current 50 members received more than 55.1 per cent of the vote in their districts. By a common definition, that is, only 9 of the 50 came from marginal districts.

[10] The 106 members came to Appropriations from every committee except Ways and Means.

[11] One was personally requested by the Speaker to move to Ways and Means. The other was chosen by a caucus of regional Congressmen to be his party's representative on the Rules Committee. Of the 21 members who were forced off the Committee for lack of seniority during a change in party control, or who were defeated for reelection and later returned, 20 sought to regain Committee membership at the earliest opportunity.

important ingredient in member satisfaction is the government-wide scope of Committee activity. The ordinary Congressman may feel that he has too little knowledge of and too little control over his environment. Membership on this Committee compensates for this feeling of helplessness by the wider contacts, the greater amount of information, and the sense of being "in the middle of things" which are consequent, if not to subcommittee activity, at least to the full Committee's overview of the federal government.

Thirdly, Committee attractiveness is heightened by the group's recognizable and distinctive political style—one that is, moreover, highly valued in American political culture. The style is that of *hard work;* and the Committee's self-image is that of "the hardest working Committee in Congress." His willingness to work is the Committee member's badge of identification, and it is proudly worn. It colors his perceptions of others and their perceptions of him.[11a] It is a cherished axiom of all members that, "This Committee is no place for a man who doesn't work. They have to be hard working. It's a way of life. It isn't just a job; it's a way of life."

The mere existence of some identifiable and valued style or "way of life" is a cohesive force for a group. But the particular style of hard work is one which increases group morale and group identification twice over. Hard work means a long, dull, and tedious application to detail, via the technique of "dig, dig, dig, day after day behind closed doors"—in an estimated 460 subcommittee and full committee meetings a year. And virtually all of these meetings are in executive session. By adopting the style of hard work, the Committee discourages highly individualized forms of legislative behavior, which could be disruptive within the Committee. It rewards its members with power, but it is power based rather on work inside the Committee than on the political glamour of activities carried on in the limelight of the mass media. Prolonged

---

[11a] A sidelight on this attitude is displayed in a current feud between the House and Senate Appropriations Committees over the meeting place for their conference committees. The House Committee is trying to break the century-old custom that conferences to resolve differences on money bills are always held on the Senate side of the Capitol. House Committee members "complain that they often have to trudge back to the House two or three times to answer roll calls during a conference. They say they go over in a body to work, while Senators flit in and out. . . . The House Appropriations Committee feels that it does all the hard work listening to witnesses for months on each bill, only to have the Senate Committee sit as a court of appeals and, with little more than a cursory glance, restore most of the funds cut." *Washington Post,* April 24, 1962, p. 1.

daily work together encourages sentiments of mutual regard, sympathy and solidarity. This *esprit* is, in turn, functional for integration on the Committee. A Republican leader summed up,

> I think it's more closely knit than any other committee. Yet it's the biggest committee, and you'd think it would be the reverse. I know on my subcommittee, you sit together day after day. You get better acquainted. You have sympathy when other fellows go off to play golf. There's a lot of *esprit de corps* in the Committee.

The strong attraction which members have for the Committee increases the influence which the Committee and its norms exercise on all of them. It increases the susceptibility of the newcomer to Committee socialization and of the veteran to Committee sanctions applicable against deviant behavior.[12]

Membership Stability

Members of the Appropriations Committee are strongly attracted to it; they also have, which bears out their selection as "responsible legislators," a strong attraction for a career in the House of Representatives. The 50 members on the Committee in 1961 had served an average of 13.1 years in the House. These twin attractions produce a noteworthy stability of Committee membership. In the period from the 80th to the 87th Congress, 35.7 per cent of the Committee's membership remained constant. That is to say, 15 of the 42 members on the Committee in March, 1947, were still on the Committee in March, 1961.[13] The 50 members of the Committee in 1961 averaged 9.3 years of prior service on that Committee. In no single year during the last fourteen has the Committee had to absorb an influx of new members totalling more than one-quarter of its membership. At all times, in other words, at least three-fourths of the members have had previous Committee experience. This extraordinary stability of personnel extends into

---

[12] This proposition is spelled out at some length in J. Thibaut and H. Kelley, *The Social Psychology of Groups* (New York, 1959), p. 247, and in D. Cartwright and A Zander, *Group Dynamics: Research and Theory* (Evanston, 1953), p. 420.

[13] This figure is 9 per cent greater than the next most stable House Committee during this particular period. The top four, in order, were Appropriations (35.7%), Agriculture (26.7%), Armed Services (25%), Foreign Affairs (20.8%).

the staff as well. As of June 1961, its 15 professionals had served an average of 10.7 years with the Committee.[14]

The opportunity exists, therefore, for the development of a stable leadership group, a set of traditional norms for the regulation of internal Committee behavior, and informal techniques of personal accommodation. Time is provided in which new members can learn and internalize Committee norms before they attain high seniority rankings. The Committee does not suffer from the potentially disruptive consequences of rapid changeovers in its leadership group, nor of sudden impositions of new sets of norms governing internal Committee behavior.

II

If one considers the main activity of a political system to be decision-making, the acid test of its internal integration is its capacity to make collective decisions without flying apart in the process. Analysis of Committee integration should focus directly, therefore, upon its subgroups and the roles of its members. Two kinds of subgroups are of central importance—subcommittees and majority or minority party groups. The roles which are most relevant derive from: (1) positions which each member holds by virtue of his subgroup attachments, *e.g.*, as subcommittee member, majority (or minority) party member; (2) positions which relate to full Committee membership, *e.g.*, Committee member, and the seniority rankings of veteran, man of moderate experience, and newcomer;[15] (3) positions which relate to both subgroup and full Committee membership, *e.g.*, Chairman of the Committee, ranking minority member of the Committee, subcommittee chairman, ranking subcommittee member. Clusters of norms state the expectations about subgroup and role behavior. The description which follows treats the ways in which these norms and their associated behaviors mesh and clash. It treats, also, the internal control mechanisms by which behavior is brought into reasonable conformity with expectations.

---

[14] The Committee's permanent and well integrated professional staff (as distinguished from its temporary investigating staff) might be considered as part of the subsystem though it will not be treated in this paper.

[15] "Newcomers" are defined as men who have served no more than two terms on the Committee. "Men of moderate experience" are those with 3–5 terms of service. "Veterans" are those who have 6 or more terms of Committee service.

Subgroup Integration

The day-to-day work of the Committee is carried on in its sub-committees each of which is given jurisdiction over a number of related governmental units. The number of subcommittees is determined by the Committee Chairman, and has varied recently from a low of 9 in 1949 to a high of 15 in 1959. The present total of 14 reflects, as always, a set of strategic and personal judgments by the Chairman balanced against the limitations placed on him by Committee tradition and member wishes. The Chairman also determines subcommittee jurisdiction, appoints subcommittee chairmen and selects the majority party members of each group. The ranking minority member of the Committee exercises similar control over subcommittee assignments on his side of the aisle.

Each subcommittee holds hearings on the budget estimates of the agencies assigned to it, meets in executive session to decide what figures and what language to recommend to the full Committee (to "mark up" the bill), defends its recommendations before the full Committee, writes the Committee's report to the House, dominates the debate on the floor, and bargains for the House in conference committee. Within its jurisdiction, each subcommittee functions independently of the others and guards its autonomy jealously. The Chairman and ranking minority member of the full Committee have, as we shall see, certain opportunities to oversee and dip into the operations of all subcommittees. But their intervention is expected to be minimal. Moreover, they themselves operate importantly within the subcommittee framework by sitting as chairman or ranking minority member of the subcommittee in which they are most interested. Each subcommittee, under the guidance of its chairman, transacts its business in considerable isolation from every other one. One subcommittee chairman exclaimed,

> Why, you'd be branded an imposter if you went into one of those other subcommittee meetings. The only time I go is by appointment, by arrangement with the chairman at a special time. I'm as much a stranger in another subcommittee as I would be in the legislative Committee on Post Office and Civil Service. Each one does its work apart from all others.

All members of all subcommittees are expected to behave in similar fashion in the role of subcommittee member. Three main norms define this role; to the extent that they are observed, they promote harmony and reduce conflict among subcommittees.[16] Subcommittee autonomy gives to the House norm of *specialization* an intensified application on the Appropriations Committee. Each member is expected to play the role of specialist in the activities of one subcommittee. He will sit on from one to four subcommittees, but normally will specialize in the work, or a portion of the work, of only one. Except for the Chairman, ranking minority member and their confidants, a Committee member's time, energy, contacts and experience are devoted to his subcommittees. Specialization is, therefore, among the earliest and most compelling of the Committee norms to which a newcomer is exposed. Within the Committee, respect, deference and power are earned through subcommittee activity and, hence to a degree, through specialization. Specialization is valued further because it is well suited to the task of guarding the Treasury. Only by specializing, Committee members believe, can they unearth the volume of factual information necessary for the intelligent screening of budget requests. Since "the facts" are acquired only through industry an effective specialist will, perforce, adopt and promote the Committee's style of hard work.

Committee-wide acceptance of specialization is an integrative force in decision-making because it helps support a second norm—*reciprocity*. The stage at which a subcommittee makes its recommendations is a potential point of internal friction. Conflict among subcommittees (or between one subcommittee and the rest of the Committee) is minimized by the deference traditionally accorded to the recommendation of the subcommittee which has specialized in the area, has worked hard, and has "the facts." "It's a matter of 'You respect my work and I'll respect yours.'" "It's frowned upon if you offer an amendment in the full Committee if you aren't on the subcommittee. It's considered presumptuous to pose as an expert if you aren't on the subcommittee." Though records of full Committee decisions are not available, members agree that subcommittee recommendations are "very rarely changed," "almost

---

[16] A statement of expected behavior was taken to be a Committee norm when it was expressed by a substantial number of respondents (a dozen or so) who represented both parties, and varying degrees of experience. In nearly every case, moreover, no refutation of them was encountered, and ample confirmation of their existence can be found in the public record. Their articulation came most frequently from the veterans of the group.

always approved," "changed one time in fifty," "very seldom changed," etc.

No subcommittee is likely to keep the deference of the full Committee for long unless its recommendations have widespread support among its own members. To this end, a third norm—*subcommittee unity*—is expected to be observed by subcommittee members. Unity means a willingness to support (or not to oppose) the recommendations of one's own subcommittee. Reciprocity and unity are closely dependent upon one another. Reciprocity is difficult to maintain when subcommittees themselves are badly divided; and unity has little appeal unless reciprocity will subsequently be observed. The norm of reciprocity functions to minimize inter-subcommittee conflict. The norm of unity functions to minimize intra-subcommittee conflict. Both are deemed essential to subcommittee influence.

One payoff for the original selection of "responsible legislators" is their special willingness to compromise in pursuit of subcommittee unity. The impulse to this end is registered most strongly at the time when the subcommittee meets in executive session to mark up the bill. Two ranking minority members explained this aspect of markup procedure in their subcommittees:

> If there's agreement, we go right along. If there's a lot of controversy we put the item aside and go on. Then, after a day or two, we may have a list of ten controversial items. We give and take and pound them down till we get agreement.

> We have a unanimous agreement on everything. If a fellow enters an objection and we can't talk him out of it—and sometimes we can get him to go along—that's it. We put it in there.

Once the bargain is struck, the subcommittee is expected to "stick together."

It is, of course, easier to achieve unity among the five, seven, or nine members of a subcommittee than among the fifty members of the full Committee. But members are expected wherever possible to observe the norm of unity in the full Committee as well. That is, they should not only defer to the recommendations of the subcommittee involved, but they should support (or not oppose) that recommendation when it reaches the floor in the form of a Committee decision. On the floor, Committee members believe, their power and prestige depend largely on the degree to which the norms of reciprocity and unity continue to be observed. Members warn each other that if they go to the floor in disarray they will be "rolled," "jumped," or "run over" by the membership. It is a cardinal maxim among Committee members that "You can't turn an appropriations bill loose on the floor." Two senior subcommittee chairmen explain,

> We iron out our differences in Committee. We argue it out and usually have a meeting of the minds, a composite view of the Committee. . . . If we went on the floor in wide disagreement, they would say, 'If you can't agree after listening to the testimony and discussing it, how can we understand it? We'll just vote on the basis of who we like the best.'

> I tell them (the full Committee) we should have a united front. If there are any objections or changes, we ought to hear it now, and not wash our dirty linen out on the floor. If we don't have a bill that we can all agree on and support, we ought not to report it out. To do that is like throwing a piece of meat to a bunch of hungry animals.

One of the most functional Committee practices supporting the norm of unity is the tradition against minority reports in the subcommittee and in the full Committee. It is symptomatic of Committee integration that custom should proscribe the use of the most formal and irrevocable symbol of congressional committee disunity—the minority report. A few have been written—but only 9 out of a possible 141 during the 11 years, 1947–1957. That is to say, 95 per cent of all original appropriations bills in this period were reported out without dissent. The technique of "reserving" is the Committee member's equivalent for the registering of dissent. In subcommittee or Committee, when a member reserves, he goes on record informally by informing his colleagues that he reserves the right to disagree on a specified item later on in the proceedings. He may seek a change or support a change in that particular item in full Committee or on the floor. But he does not publicize his dissent. The subcommittee or the full Committee can then make an unopposed recommendation. The individual retains some freedom of maneuver without firm commitment. Often a member reserves on an appropriations item but takes no further action. A member explained how the procedure operates in subcommittee,

> If there's something I feel too strongly about, and just can't go along, I'll say, 'Mr. Chairman, we can have a unanimous

report, but I reserve the right to bring this up in full Committee. I feel duty bound to make a play for it and see if I can't sell it to the other members.' But if I don't say anything, or don't reserve this right, and then I bring it up in full Committee, they'll say, 'Who are you trying to embarrass? You're a member of the team, aren't you? That's not the way to get along.'

Disagreement cannot, of course, be eliminated from the Committee. But the Committee has accepted a method for ventilating it which produces a minimum of internal disruption. And members believe that the greater their internal unity, the greater the likelihood that their recommendations will pass the House.

The degree to which the role of the subcommittee member can be so played and subcommittee conflict thereby minimized depends upon the minimization of conflict between the majority and minority party subgroups. Nothing would be more disruptive to the Committee's work than bitter and extended partisan controversy. It is, therefore, important to Appropriations Committee integration that a fourth norm—*minimal partisanship*—should be observed by members of both party contingents. Nearly every respondent emphasized, with approval, that "very little" or "not much" partisanship prevailed on the Committee. One subcommittee chairman stated flatly, "My job is to keep down partisanship." A ranking minority member said, "You might think that we Republicans would defend the Administration and the budget, but we don't." Majority and minority party ratios are constant and do not change *i.e.*, in 1958) to reflect changes in the strength of the controlling party. The Committee operates with a completely non-partisan professional staff, which does not change in tune with shifts in party control. Requests for studies by the Committee's investigating staff must be made by the Chairman and ranking minority member of the full Committee and by the Chairman and ranking minority member of the subcommittee involved. Subcommittees can produce recommendations without dissent and the full Committee can adopt reports without dissent precisely because party conflict is (during the period 1947–1961) the exception rather than the rule.

The Committee is in no sense immune from the temperature of party conflict, but it does have a relatively high specific heat. Intense party strife or a strongly taken presidential position will get reflected in subcommittee and in Committee recommendations. Sharp divisions in party policy were carried, with disruptive impact, into some areas of Committee activity during the 80th Congress and subsequently, by way of reaction, into the 81st Congress.[17] During the Eisenhower years, extraordinary presidential pleas, especially concerning foreign aid, were given special heed by the Republican members of the Committee.[18] Partisanship is normally generated from the environment and not from within the Committee's party groups. Partisanship is, therefore, likely to be least evident in sub-committee activity, stronger in the full Committee, and most potent at the floor stage. Studies which have focussed on roll-call analysis have stressed the influence of party in legislative decision-making.[19] In the appropriations process, at any rate, the floor stage probably represents party influence at its maximum. Our examination, by interview, of decision-making at the subcommittee and full Committee level would stress the influence of Committee-oriented norms—the strength of which tends to vary inversely with that of party bonds. In the secrecy and intimacy of the subcommittee and full Committee hearing rooms, the member finds it easy to compromise on questions of more or less, to take money from one program and give it to another and, in general, to avoid yes-or-no type party stands. These decisions, taken in response to the integrative norms of the Committee are the most important ones in the entire appropriations process.

Role Integration

The roles of subcommittee member and party member are common to all.

Other more specific decision-making positions are allocated among the members. Different positions produce different roles, and in an integrated system, these too must fit together. Integration, in other words, must be achieved through the complementarity or reciprocity of roles as well as through a similarity of roles. This may mean a pattern in which expectations are so different that

---

[17] See, for example, the internal conflict on the subcommittee dealing with the Labor Department. 93 *Cong. Record,* pp. 2465–2562 passim; 94 *Cong. Record,* pp. 7605–7607.

[18] See, for example, the unusual minority report of Committee Republicans on the foreign aid appropriations bill in 1960. Their protest against Committee cuts in the budget estimates was the result of strenuous urging by the Eisenhower Administration. House Report No. 1798, *Mutual Security and Related Agency Appropriation Bill,* 1961, 86 Cong. 2d sess. 1960.

[19] David Truman, *The Congressional Party* (New York, 1959); Julius Turner, *Party and Constituency: Pressures on Congress* (Baltimore, 1951).

there is very little contact between individuals; or it may mean a pattern in which contacts require the working out of an involved system of exchange of obligations and rewards.[20] In either case, the desired result is the minimization of conflict among prominent Committee roles. Two crucial instances of role reciprocity on the Committee involve the seniority positions of old-timer and newcomer and the leadership positions of Chairman and ranking minority member, on both the full Committee and on each subcommittee.

The differentiation between senior and junior members is the broadest definition of who shall and who shall not actively participate in Committee decisions. Of a junior member, it will be said, "Oh, he doesn't count—what I mean is, he hasn't been on the Committee long enough." He is not expected to and ordinarily does not have much influence. His role is that of apprentice. He is expected to learn the business and the norms of the Committee by applying himself to its work. He is expected to acquiesce in an arrangement which gives most influence (except in affairs involving him locally) to the veterans of the group. Newcomers will be advised to "follow the chairman until you get your bearings. For the first two years, follow the chairman. He knows." "Work hard, keep quiet and attend the Committee sessions. We don't want to listen to some new person coming in here." And newcomers perceive their role in identical terms: "You have to sit in the back seat and edge up little by little." "You just go to subcommittee meetings and assimilate the routine. The new members are made to feel welcome, but you have a lot of rope-learning to do before you carry much weight."

At every stage of Committee work, this differentiation prevails. There is remarkable agreement on the radically different sets of expectations involved. During the hearings, the view of the elders is that, "Newcomers . . . don't know what the score is and they don't have enough information to ask intelligent questions." A newcomer described his behavior in typically similar terms: "I attended all the hearings and studied and collected information that I can use next year. I'm just marking time now." During

---

[20] The ideas of "reciprocity" and "complementarity," which are used interchangeably here, are discussed in Alvin Gouldner, "The Norm of Reciprocity," *American Sociological Review* (April, 1960). Most helpful in explaining the idea of a role system has been the work of J. Wahlke, H. Eulau, W. Buchanan, L. Ferguson. See their study, *The Legislative System* (New York, 1962), esp. Intro.

the crucial subcommittee markup, the newcomer will have little opportunity to speak—save in locally important matters. A subcommittee chairman stated the norm from his viewpoint this way: "When we get a compromise, nobody's going to break that up. If someone tries, we sit on him fast. We don't want young people who throw bricks or slow things down." And a newcomer reciprocated, describing his markup conduct: "I'm not provocative. I'm in there for information. They're the experts in the field. I go along." In full Committee, on the floor, and in conference committee, the Committee's senior members take the lead and the junior members are expected to follow. The apprentice role is common to all new members of the House. But it is wrong to assume that each Committee will give it the same emphasis. Some pay it scant heed.[21] The Appropriations Committee makes it a cornerstone of its internal structure.

Among the Committee's veterans, the key roles are those of Committee Chairman and ranking minority member, and their counterparts in every subcommittee. It is a measure of Committee integration and the low degree of partisanship that considerable reciprocity obtains between these roles. Their partisan status nevertheless sets limits to the degree of possible integration. The Chairman is given certain authority which he and only he can exercise. But save in times of extreme party controversy, the expectation is that consultation and cooperation between the chairman-ranking minority member shall lubricate the Committee's entire work. For example, by Committee tradition, its Chairman and ranking minority member are both *ex officio* voting members of each subcommittee and of every conference committee. The two of them thus have joint access at every stage of the internal process. A subcommittee chairman, too, is expected to discuss matters of scheduling and agenda with his opposite minority number. He is expected to work with him during the markup session and to give him (and, normally, only him) an opportunity to read and comment on the subcommittee report.[22] A ranking minority member described his subcommittee markup procedure approvingly:

> Frequently the chairman has a figure which he states. Sometimes he will have no figure, and he'll turn to me and say, '——, what do you think?' Maybe I'll have a figure. It's very

[21] For example, the Committee on Education and Labor, see footnote 26.
[22] See the exchange in 101 *Cong. Rec.*, pp. 3832, 3844, 3874.

flexible. Everyone has a chance to say what he thinks, and we'll
move it around. Sometimes it takes a long time. . . . He's a
rabid partisan on the floor, but he is a very fair man in the
subcommittee.

Where influence is shared, an important exchange of rewards
occurs. The chairman gains support for his leadership and the ranking minority member gains intra-Committee power. The Committee
as a whole insures against the possibility of drastic change in its
internal structure by giving to its key minority members a stake in
its operation. Chairmen and ranking minority members will, in the
course of time, exchange positions; and it is expected that such a
switch will produce no form of retribution nor any drastic change
in the functioning of the Committee. Reciprocity of roles, in this
case, promotes continued integration. A ranking minority member
testified to one successful arrangement when he took the floor in the
83rd Congress to say:

> The gentleman and I have been see sawing back and forth
> on this committee for some time. He was chairman in the 80th
> Congress. I had the privilege of serving as chairman in the 81st
> and 82nd Congresses. Now he is back in the saddle. I can say
> that he has never failed to give me his utmost cooperation, and
> I have tried to give him the same cooperation during his ser-
> vice as chairman of this Committee. We seldom disagree, but
> we have found out that we can disagree without being disagree-
> able. Consequently, we have unusual harmony on this com-
> mittee.[23]

Reciprocity between chairmen and ranking minority members on
the Appropriations Committee is to some incalculable degree a
function of the stability of membership which allows a pair of particular individuals to work out the kind of personal accommodation
described above. The close working relationship of Clarence Cannon
and John Taber, whose service on the Committee totals 68 years
and who have been changing places as Chairman and ranking minority member for 19 years, highlights and sustains a pattern of
majority-minority reciprocity throughout the group.

Internal Control Mechanisms

The expectations which apply to subcommittee, to party, to veterans and to newcomers, to chairmen and to ranking minority mem-

---

[23] 99 *Cong. Rec.*, p. 4933.

bers prescribe highly integrative behaviors. We have concentrated on these expectations and have both illustrated and assumed the close correlation between expected and actual behavior. This does not mean that all the norms of the Committee have been canvassed. Nor does it mean that deviation from the integrative norms does not occur. It does. From what can be gathered, however, from piecing together a study of the public record on appropriations from 1947 to 1961 with interview materials, the Committee has been markedly successful in maintaining a stable internal structure over time. As might be expected, therefore, changes and threats of change have been generated more from the environment—when outsiders consider the Committee as unresponsive—than from inside the subsystem itself. One source of internal stability, and an added reason for assuming a correlation between expected and actual behavior, is the existence of what appear to be reasonably effective internal control mechanisms. Two of these are the socialization processes applied to newcomers and the sanctioning mechanisms applicable to all Committee members.

Socialization is in part a training in perception. Before members of a group can be expected to behave in accordance with its norms, they must learn to see and interpret the world around them with reasonable similarity. The socialization of the Committee newcomer during his term or two of apprenticeship serves to bring his perceptions and his attitudes sufficiently into line with those of the other members to serve as a basis for Committee integration. The Committee, as we have seen, is chosen from Congressmen whose political flexibility connotes an aptitude for learning new lessons of power. Furthermore, the high degree of satisfaction of its members with the group increases their susceptibility to its processes of learning and training.

For example, one half of the Committee's Democrats are Northerners and Westerners from urban constituencies, whose voting records are just as "liberal" on behalf of domestic social welfare programs as non-Committee Democrats from like constituencies. They come to the Committee favorably disposed toward the high level of federal spending necessary to support such programs, and with no sense of urgency about the Committee's tasks of guarding the Treasury or reducing budget estimates. Given the criteria governing their selection, however, they come without rigid preconceptions and with a built-in responsiveness to the socialization processes of any legislative group of which they are members. It is crucial to Committee integration that they learn to temper their potentially disruptive welfare-state ideology with a conservative's concern for saving money. They must change their perceptions and attitudes sufficiently to view the Committee's tasks in nearly the same terms as their more conservative Southern Democratic and Republican colleagues. What their elders perceive as reality (*i.e.*, the disposition of executives to ask for more money than is necessary) they, too, must see as reality. A subcommittee chairman explained:

> When you have sat on the Committee, you see that these bureaus are always asking for more money—always up, never down. They want to build up their organization. You reach the point—I have—where it sickens you, where you rebel against it. Year after year, they want more money. They say, 'Only $50,000 this year'; but you know the pattern. Next year they'll be back for $100,000, then $200,000. The younger members haven't been on the Committee long enough, haven't had the experience to know this.

The younger men, in this case the younger liberals, do learn from their Committee experience. Within one or two terms, they are differentiating between themselves and the "wild-eyed spenders" or the "free spenders" in the House. "Some of these guys would spend you through the roof," exclaimed one liberal of moderate seniority. Repeated exposure to Committee work and to fellow members has altered their perceptions and their attitudes in money matters. Half a dozen Northern Democrats of low or moderate seniority agreed with one of their number who said: "Yes, it's true. I can see it myself. I suppose I came here a flaming liberal; but as the years go by I get more conservative. You just hate like hell to spend all this money. . . . You come to the point where you say, 'By God, this is enough jobs.' " These men will remain more inclined toward spending than their Committee colleagues, but their perceptions and hence their attitudes have been brought close enough to the others to support a consensus on tasks. They are responsive to appeals on budget-cutting grounds that would not have registered earlier and which remain meaningless to liberals outside the Committee. In cases, therefore, where Committee selection does not and cannot initially produce individuals with a predisposition toward protecting the Treasury, the same result is achieved by socialization.

Socialization is a training in behavior as well as in perception. For the newcomer, conformity to norms in specific situations is insured through the appropriate application, by the Committee veterans, of rewards and punishments. For the Committee member who serves his apprenticeship creditably, the passage of time holds the promise that he will inherit a position of influence. He may, as an incentive, be given some small reward early in his Committee career. One man, in his second year, had been assigned the task of specializing in one particular program. However narrow the scope of his specialization, it had placed him on the road to influence within the Committee. He explained with evident pleasure:

> The first year, you let things go by. You can't participate. But you learn by watching the others operate. The next year, you know what you're interested in and when to step in. . . . For instance, I've become an expert on the——program. The chairman said to me, 'This is something you ought to get interested in.' I did; and now I'm the expert on the Committee. Whatever I say on that, the other members listen to me and do what I want.

At some later date, provided he continues to observe Committee norms, he will be granted additional influence, perhaps through a prominent floor role. A model Committee man of moderate seniority who had just attained to this stage of accomplishment, and who had suffered through several political campaigns back home fending off charges that he was a do-nothing Congressman, spoke about the rewards he was beginning to reap.

> When you perform well on the floor when you bring out a bill, and Members know that you know the bill, you develop prestige with other Members of Congress. They come over and ask you what you think, because they know you've studied it. You begin to get a reputation beyond your subcommittee. And you get inner satisfaction, too. You don't feel that you're down here doing nothing.

The first taste of influence which comes to men on this Committee is compensation for the frustrations of apprenticeship. Committee integration in general, and the meshing of roles between elders and newcomers in particular, rests on the fact that conformity to role expectations over time does guarantee to the young positive rewards—the very kind of rewards of power, prestige, and personal satisfaction which led most of them to seek Committee membership in the first place.

The important function of apprenticeship is that it provides the necessary time during which socialization can go forward. And teaching proceeds with the aid of punishments as well as rewards. Should a new member inadvertently or deliberately run afoul of Committee norms during his apprenticeship, he will find himself confronted with negative sanctions ranging in subtlety from "jaundiced eyes" to a changed subcommittee assignment. Several members, for example, recalled their earliest encounter with the norm of unity and the tradition against minority reports. One remembered his attempt to file a minority report. "The Chairman was pretty upset about it. It's just a tradition, I guess, not to have minority reports. I didn't know it was a tradition. When I said I was going to write a minority report, some eyebrows were raised. The Chairman said it just wasn't the thing to do. Nothing more was said about it. But it wasn't a very popular thing to do, I guess." He added that he had not filed one since.

Some younger members have congenital difficulty in observing the norms of the apprentice's role. In the 86th Congress, these types tended to come from the Republican minority. The minority newcomers (described by one of the men who selected them as "eight young, energetic, fighting conservatives") were a group of economy-minded individuals some of whom chafed against any barrier which kept them form immediate influence on Committee policy. Their reaction was quite different from that of the young Democrats, whose difficulty was in learning to become economy-minded, but who did not actively resent their lack of influence. One freshman, who felt that "The appropriations system is lousy, inadequate and old fashioned," recalled that he had spoken out in full Committee against the recommendations of a subcommittee of which he was not a member. Having failed, he continued to oppose the recommendation during floor debate. By speaking up, speaking in relation to the work of another subcommittee and by opposing a Committee recommendation, he had violated the particular norms of his apprentice role as well of the generally applicable norms of reciprocity and unity. He explained what he had learned, but remained only partially socialized:

> They want to wash their dirty linen in the Committee and they want no opposition afterward. They let me say my piece in Committee. . . . But I just couldn't keep quiet. I said some things on the floor, and I found out that's about all they would take. . . . If you don't get along with your Committee and have their support, you don't get anything accomplished around

here. . . . I'm trying to be a loyal, cooperative member of the Committee. You hate to be a stinker; but I'm still picking at the little things because I can't work on the big things. There's nothing for the new men to do, so they have to find places to needle in order to take some part in it.

Another freshman, who had deliberately violated apprenticeship norms by trying to ask "as many questions as the chairman" during subcommittee hearings, reported a story of unremitting counteraction against his deviation:

> In the hearings, I have to wait sometimes nine or ten hours for a chance; and he hopes I'll get tired and stay home. I've had to wait till some pretty unreasonable hours. Once I've gotten the floor, though, I've been able to make a good case. Sometimes I've been the only person there. . . . He's all powerful. He's got all the power. He wouldn't think of taking me on a trip with him when he goes to hold hearings. Last year, he went to——. He wouldn't give me a nudge there. And in the hearings, when I'm questioning a witness, he'll keep butting in so that my case won't appear to be too rosy.

Carried on over a period of two years, this behavior resulted in considerable personal friction between a Committee elder and the newcomer. Other members of his subcommittee pointedly gave him a great lack of support for his non-conformity. "They tried to slow him down and tone him down a little," not because he and his subcommittee chairman disagreed, but on the grounds that the Committee has developed accepted ways of disagreeing which minimize, rather than exacerbate, interpersonal friction.

One internal threat to Committee integration comes from new members who from untutored perceptions, from ignorance of norms, or from dissatisfaction with the apprentice role may not act in accordance with Committee expectations. The seriousness of this threat is minimized, however, by the fact that the deviant newcomer does not possess sufficient resources to affect adversely the operation of the system. Even if he does not respond immediately to the application of sanctions, he can be held in check and subjected to an extended and (given the frequency of interaction among members) intensive period of socialization. The success of Committee socialization is indicated by the fact that whereas wholesale criticism of Committee operations was frequently voiced among junior members, it had disappeared among the men of moderate experience. And what these middle seniority members now accept as the facts of Committee life, the veterans vigorously assert and defend as the essentials of a smoothly functioning system. Satisfaction with the Committee's internal structure increases with length of Committee service.

An important reason for changing member attitudes is that those who have attained leadership positions have learned, as newcomers characteristically have not, that their conformity to Committee norms is the ultimate source of their influence inside the group. Freshman members do not as readily perceive the degree to which interpersonal influence is rooted in obedience to group norms. They seem to convert their own sense of powerlessness into the view that the Committee's leaders possess, by virtue of their positions, arbitrary, absolute, and awesome power. Typically, they say: "If you're a subcommittee chairman, it's your Committee." "The Chairman runs the show. He gets what he wants. He decides what he wants and gets it through." Older members of the Committee, however, view the power of the leaders as a highly contingent and revocable grant, tendered by the Committee for so long and only so long as their leaders abide by Committee expectations. In commenting on internal influence, their typical reaction is: "Of course, the Committee wouldn't follow him if it didn't want to. He has a great deal of respect. He's an able man, a hard-working man." "He knows the bill backwards and forwards. He works hard, awfully hard and the members know it." Committee leaders have an imposing set of formal prerogatives. But they can capitalize on them only if they command the respect, confidence and deference of their colleagues.

It is basic to Committee integration that members who have the greatest power to change the system evidence the least disposition to do so. Despite their institutional conservatism, however, Committee elders do occasionally violate the norms applicable to them and hence represent a potential threat to successful integration. Excessive deviation from Committee expectations by some leaders will bring counter-measures by other leaders. Thus, for example, the Chairman and his subcommittee chairmen exercise reciprocal controls over one another's behavior. The Chairman has the authority to appoint the chairman and members of each subcommittee and fix its jurisdiction. "He runs the Committee. He has a lot of power," agrees one subcommittee chairman. "But it's all done on the basis of personal friendship. If he tries to get too big, the members can whack him down by majority vote."

In the 84th Congress, Chairman Cannon attempted an unusually broad reorganization of subcommittee jurisdictions. The subcommittee chairman most adversely affected rallied his senior colleagues against the Chairman's action—on the ground that it was an excessive violation of role expectations and threatening to subcommittee autonomy. Faced with the prospect of a negative Committee vote, the Chairman was forced to act in closer conformity to the expectations of the other leaders. As one participant described the episode,

> Mr. Cannon, for reasons of his own, tried to bust up one of the subcommittees. We didn't like that. . . . He was breaking up the whole Committee. A couple of weeks later, a few of the senior members got together and worked out a compromise. By that time, he had seen a few things, so we went to him and talked to him and worked it out.

On the subcommittees, too, it is the veterans of both parties who will levy sanctions against an offending chairman. It is they who speak of "cutting down to size" and "trimming the whiskers" of leaders who become "too cocky," "too stubborn" or who "do things wrong too often." Committee integration is underwritten by the fact that no member high or low is permanently immune from the operation of its sanctioning mechanisms.

III

Data concerning internal committee activity can be organized and presented in various ways. One way is to use key functional problems like integration as the focal points for descriptive analysis. On the basis of our analysis (and without, for the time being, having devised any precise measure of integration), we are led to the summary observation that the House Appropriations Committee appears to be a well integrated, if not an extremely well integrated, committee. The question arises as to whether anything can be gained from this study other than a description of one property of one political subsystem. If it is reasonable to assume that the internal life of a congressional committee affects all legislative activity involving that committee, and if it is reasonable to assume that the analysis of a committee's internal relationships will produce useful knowledge about legislative behavior, some broader implications for this study are indicated.

In the first place, the success of the House Appropriations Committee in solving the problem of integration probably does have important consequences for the appropriations process. Some of the possible relationships can be stated as hypotheses and tested; others can be suggested as possible guides to understanding. All of them require further research. Of primary interest is the relationship between integration and the power of the Committee. There is little doubt about the fact of Committee power. Of the 443 separate case histories of bureau appropriations examined, the House accepted Committee recommendations in 387, or 87.4 per cent of them; and in 159, or 33.6 per cent of the cases, the House Committee's original recommendations on money amounts were the exact ones enacted into law. The hypothesis that the greater the degree of Committee unity the greater the probability that its recommendations will be accepted is being tested as part of a larger study.[24] House Committee integration may be a key factor in producing House victories in conference committee. This relationship, too, might be tested. Integration appears to help provide the House conferees with a feeling of confidence and superiority which is one of their important advantages in the mix of psychological factors affecting conference deliberations.

Another suggested consequence of high integration is that party groups have a relatively small influence upon appropriations decisions. It suggests, too, that Committee-oriented behavior should be duly emphasized in any analysis of Congressional oversight of administrative activity by this Committee. Successful integration promotes the achievement of the Committee's goals, and doubtless helps account for the fairly consistent production of budget-cutting decisions. Another consequence will be found in the strategies adopted by people seeking favorable Committee decisions. For example, the characteristic lines of contact from executive officials to the Committee will run to the chairman and the ranking minority member (and to the professional staff man) of the single subcommittee handling their agency's appropriations. The ways in which the Committee achieves integration may even affect the success or failure of a bureau in getting its appropriations. Committee members, for instance, will react more favorably toward an administrator who conforms to their self-image of the hard-working master-of-detail than to one who does not—and Committee response to individual administrators bulks large in their determinations.

Finally, the internal integration of this Committee helps to

---

[24] *Cf.* Dwaine Marvick, "Congressional Appropriations Politics," unpublished manuscript (Columbia, 1952).

explain the extraordinary stability, since 1920, of appropriations procedures—in the face of repeated proposals to change them through omnibus appropriations, legislative budgets, new budgetary forms, item veto, Treasury borrowing, etc. Integration is a stabilizing force, and the stability of the House Appropriations Committee has been a force for stabilization throughout the entire process. It was, for example, the disagreement between Cannon and Taber which led to the indecisiveness reflected in the short-lived experiment with a single appropriations bill.[25] One need only examine the conditions most likely to decrease Committee integration to ascertain some of the critical factors for producing changes in the appropriations process. A description of integration is also an excellent base-line from which to analyze changes in internal structure.

All of these are speculative propositions which call for further research. But they suggest, as a second implication, that committee integration does have important consequences for legislative activity and, hence, that it is a key variable in the study of legislative politics. It would seem, therefore, to be a fruitful focal point for the study of other congressional committees.[26] Comparative committee analysis could usefully be devoted to (1) the factors which tend to increase or decrease integration; (2) the degree to which

[25] See Dalmas Nelson, "The Omnibus Appropriations Act of 1950," *Journal of Politics* (May, 1953).

[26] This view has been confirmed by the results of interviews conducted by the author with members of the House Committee on Education and Labor, together with an examination of that Committee's activity in one policy area. They indicate very significant contrasts between the internal structure of that Committee and the Appropriations Committee—contrasts which center around their comparative success in meeting the problem of integration. The House Committee on Education and Labor appears to be a poorly integrated committee. Its internal structure is characterized by a great deal of subgroup conflict, relatively little role reciprocity, and minimally effective internal control mechanisms. External concerns, like those of party, constituency and clientele groups, are probably more effective in determining its decisions than is likely to be the case in a well-integrated committee. An analysis of the internal life of the Committee on Education and Labor, drawn partly from interviews with 19 members of that group, will appear in a forthcoming study, *Federal Aid to Education and National Politics*, by Professor Frank Munger and the author, to be published by Syracuse University Press. [See Chapter VIII of the present volume.] See also Nicholas R. Masters, *op. cit.*, note 7 above, pp. 354–355 [Reprinted as Chapter II of the present volume.] and Seymour Scher, "Congressional Committee Members as Independent Agency Overseers: A Case Study," *American Political Science Review*, Vol. 54 (December, 1960), pp. 911–920.

integration is achieved; and (3) the consequences of varying degrees of integration for committee behavior and influence. If analyses of committee integration are of any value, they should encourage the analysis and the classification of congressional committees along functional lines. And they should lead to the discussion of interrelated problems of committee survival. Functional classifications of committees (*i.e.*, well or poorly integrated) derived from a large number of descriptive analyses of several functional problems, may prove helpful in constructing more general propositions about the legislative process.

V

THE AGRICULTURE COMMITTEE AND THE
PROBLEM OF REPRESENTATION*

Charles O. Jones

STUDENTS OF American politics are told that our political system is fundamentally a *representative* democracy. Concepts of representation, since Burke, have commonly employed his distinction between action taken in response to instructions from constituents and action based on an independent appraisal of the national interest.[1] A very recent analysis has offered a refinement of this, by distinguishing three types: "delegate," "trustee" and "politico."[2] Theory and history alike tell us, however, that a representative does not invariably act in only one of these roles. There have been a number of empirical studies of representatives, few of which con-

* Reprinted from "Representation in Congress: The Case of the House Agriculture Committee," *American Political Science Review*, LV (June, 1961), 358–67. Copyright © 1961, The American Political Science Association. The author wishes to acknowledge the generosity of Congressman E. Y. Berry (R–South Dakota) in providing office space and other aids, as well as the helpful suggestions and comments of Leon D. Epstein and Ralph K. Huitt, University of Wisconsin; Samuel C. Patterson, State University of Iowa; and Wayne G. Rollins, Wellesley College.
[1] Some of the most useful studies of representation are: Charles Beard and J. D. Lewis, "Representative Government in Evolution," *American Political Science Review*, Vol. 26 (April, 1932), pp. 223–40; Francis M. Carney, "Concepts of Political Representation in the United States Today," unpublished Ph.D. dissertation, University of California, Los Angeles, 1956; Alfred de Grazia, *Public and Republic* (New York, 1951); John A. Fairlie, "The Nature of Political Representation," *American Political Science Review*, Vol. 34 (April and June, 1940), pp. 236–48 and 456–66; H. F. Gosnell, *Democracy, The Threshold of Freedom* (New York, 1948); James Hogan, *Election and Representation* (Oxford, 1945). For an extended bibliography see Charles O. Jones, "The Relationship of Congressional Committee Action to a Theory of Representation," unpublished Ph.D. dissertation, University of Wisconsin, 1960, pp. 413–28, from which materials for this article were drawn.
[2] Heinz Eulau et al., "The Role of the Representative: Some Empirical Observations on the Theory of Edmund Burke," *American Political Science Review*, Vol. 53 (Sept., 1959), pp. 742–756.

centrate on specific policy fields;[3] and studies also of the play of interests in the enactment of specific legislation, but without a systematic account of the legislative committee members involved, acting in their representative capacities as they saw them. How then can we tell when to expect a representative to view his role in one way rather than another? The aim of this article is to shed a little light on some aspects of this broad question by means of a case study.

The subjects of the study were the members of the House Agriculture Committee and their action on the omnibus farm legislation (H. R. 12954 and S. 4071) in 1958 (85th Congress, second session).[4] Most of the data were obtained from interviews[5] with thirty of the thirty-four Committee members, but, in addition, the specific stands of members in subcommittees, the full committee, and on the House floor were traced, through the printed hearings and the *Congressional Record* of floor debates. Finally, other interested and knowledgeable people were interviewed, newspaper accounts were studied, and the characteristics of constituencies were examined.

For analytical purposes the most useful concept I developed, to account for the behavior of a representative, was one I shall call his "policy constituency." This may be defined as those interests within his geographical or legal constituency which he perceives to be affected by the policy under consideration. When he regards these interests as actively and homogeneously concerned, they are ordinarily sufficient to determine his public stand. When he sees them as weak, indifferent or divided, other factors come into play.

---

[3] Two studies which do concentrate on specific policies are: Lewis Dexter, "The Representative and His District," *Human Organization*, Vol. 16 (Spring, 1957), 2–13 [Reprinted as Chapter I of the present volume]; and L. E. Gleeck, "96 Congressmen Make up Their Minds," *Public Opinion Quarterly*, Vol. 4 (March, 1940), 3–24.

[4] I selected a committee which is more likely than most to be constituency-oriented. Commonly, representatives from farm areas are anxious to get on this committee to represent their constituency interests, though interviews with Republican members indicate that this generalization would now need modification since recent farm policies have not been notably successful. See the accompanying article by Nicholas A. Masters, "House Committee Assignments," *American Political Science Review*, Vol. 53 (June, 1961), pp. 345–357 [Reprinted as Chapter II of the present volume].

[5] Focused interviews were conducted in March, 1959. An interview guide was followed but it was kept flexible. I wrote as the respondents discussed the questions and typed the responses immediately after the interview. All respondents were guaranteed anonymity.

But he is affected too by the nature of the committee institution within which the policy is being formed.

I. THE HOUSE AGRICULTURE COMMITTEE AND ITS WORK

Organization

In 1958 a Republican President was again faced with a Democratic Congress in a congressional campaign year. The margin of control for Democrats in the House Agriculture Committee was a less-than-comfortable four votes; the split was 19 to 15. The margin in subcommittees was one vote in most cases.

Harold D. Cooley (D–North Carolina) was chairman in 1958, as he had been in every Democratic Congress since 1949. Members did not class him among the strong House committee chairmen, but respected him as fair and honest. W. R. Poage (D–Texas) was vice-chairman. The Agriculture Committee was the only House committee in 1958 to have a vice-chairman and one member suggested that this was due to the chairman's complete and admitted willingness to share the responsibility of leadership with the very forceful, knowledgeable, and capable "Bob" Poage.

The ranking minority member in 1958 was William S. Hill (R–Colorado). Like Cooley, he was not considered a strong leader and it became apparent that Charles Hoeven (R–Iowa) was recognized as the spokesman of the minority viewpoint. Hoeven has since become the ranking minority member.

The principal work units in the House Agriculture Committee are the subcommittees. In 1958 there were 18 subcommittees of two kinds—ten commodity subcommittees and eight special-action subcommittees. The former are more important since they consider legislation designed to solve the many crises for specific commodities. Usually a member is assigned to at least one commodity subcommittee of his choice. The chairman consults the ranking minority leader but has the last word on appointments. Actually few decisions have to be made, since most commodity subcommittees are permanent and their membership is continuing; only the new members need assignments. The size of subcommittees varies considerably (from 12 for tobacco to five for rice), giving the chairman some flexibility in case several members are interested in one commodity.

Finally, the House Agriculture Committee has been able to rely on a small expert staff consisting of a counsel, research director, majority and minority clerks, and five staff assistants.

Representing Agriculture

As might be expected, congressmen from constituencies with significant interests in farm policy make up the membership of the House Agriculture Committee. In 1958 there was but one exception to this rule—Victor Anfuso, Democrat from Brooklyn. Thirteen of the 19 Democrats came from areas where tobacco, cotton, peanuts, and rice are the principal commodities. Republican Committee members came from areas producing corn, hogs, small grain, wheat, and areas where the farming is diversified. Table I shows the geographical distribution of members.

Committee members may be classified by commodities of greatest interest to their constituencies, as in Table II. Commodities receiving price supports are grown in the constituencies of members of all six groups there listed. The *basic* commodities, so labeled by the Agricultural Adjustment Act of 1938, are corn, cotton, tobacco, rice, wheat, and peanuts; price supports have been mandatory for them. An increasing number of *non-basics* have also received price supports, e.g., milk and wool. The "diversified" (mainly non-basics) group often find their interests conflicting with those of representatives in the other groups. They complain that their farmers are at a disadvantage since their non-basics either do not receive price supports or receive less support than the basics; the price supports for the few basics grown do not make up for the deprivation of profits attributable to acreage and marketing controls (the complaint of California cotton farmers); and they must pay higher prices for the basics as well as pay higher taxes.

TABLE I

*Geographical Representation on the House Agriculture Committee**

Land-Use Area	Democrats	Republicans	Totals
Northeast	1	3	4
Appalachian	5	—	5
Southeast	3	—	3
Mississippi Delta	2	—	2
Southern Plains	3	1	4
Corn Belt	2	3	5
Lake States	2	2	4
Northern Plains	—	3	3
Mountain	—	2	2
Pacific	1	1	2
Totals	19	15	34

* Based on the areas presented in Bureau of Census and Department of Agriculture, Bureau of Agricultural Economics, *Land Utilization, A Graphic Summary, 1950* (December, 1952), p. 5.

TABLE II

*Committee Members and Their Constituencies' Commodities**

1. *Corn and Livestock*
   Harrison (R-Nebraska)
   Harvey (R-Indiana)
   Hill (R-Colorado)†
   Hoeven (R-Iowa)
   Polk (D-Ohio)
   Simpson (R-Illinois)†
2. *Cotton and Rice*
   Abernethy (D-Mississippi)
   Albert (D-Oklahoma)
   Gathings (D-Arkansas)
   Grant (D-Alabama)
   Jones (D-Missouri)
   Poage (D-Texas)
   Thompson (D-Texas)
3. *Dairy, Livestock, Small Grains*
   Johnson (D-Wisconsin)
   Knutson (D-Minnesota)
   Quie (R-Minnesota)
   Tewes (R-Wisconsin)
   Williams (R-New York)†

4. *Diversified* (non-basics)
   Anfuso (D-New York)
   Dague (R-Pennsylvania)
   Dixon (R-Utah)
   Hagen (D-California)
   McIntire (R-Maine)
   Teague (R-California)
5. *Tobacco*
   Abbitt (D-Virginia)
   Bass (D-Tennessee)
   Cooley (D-North Carolina)
   Jennings (D-Virginia)
   McMillan (D-South Carolina)
   Matthews (D-Florida)
   Watts (D-Kentucky)
6. *Wheat*
   Belcher (R-Oklahoma)
   Krueger (R-North Dakota)†
   Smith (R-Kansas)

* Members were classified on the basis of their constituencies' principal commodities, as listed in the *Census of Agriculture*, Vol. I, 1956, and interviews with the members.
† These members were not interviewed. Simpson, Williams and Krueger clearly belong to the groups to which they have been assigned. Hill might also have been included in the wheat group.

Almost without exception the six groups show an alignment between commodity interests and party allegiance. The corn and livestock group has five Republicans and one Democrat; the cotton and rice group, seven Democrats; the dairy, livestock, small grains group, two Democrats and three Republicans; the diversified group, four Republicans and two Democrats; the tobacco group, seven Democrats; and the wheat group, three or four Republicans.[6] Consequently, different commodities will ordinarily be favored when different parties are in control. For example, cotton, rice, and tobacco usually receive more attention when the Democrats are a majority in the Committee.[7]

Committee organization has been strongly influenced by the commodity problems in agriculture. First, subcommittees are established to deal with currently critical commodity problems. Sec-

---

[6] Four, if Hill were also assigned to it. Anfuso is assigned to the diversified (non-basics) group because he does not fit elsewhere. The overlap between the corn and livestock, and the dairy, livestock, small grains group is explained by the fact that livestock production is important to both but corn is more important in one and dairy products in the other.

[7] Recent Democratic victories in the middle west have changed the pattern somewhat. There are more Democrats from corn, livestock, and dairy constituencies than previously.

ond, members are assigned to commodity subcommittees on the basis of their constituency interests. Table III shows the high correlation prevailing. Only one Democrat (Anfuso) was assigned to no commodity subcommittee representing producers in his constituency and he has no agricultural production at all in his Brooklyn district, though the poultry trade is important there.[8] Two Republicans (Harrison and Dixon) found themselves on subcommittees of little or no concern to their constituencies. Significantly both of these members were identified by other members as being supporters of Secretary Benson's recommendations.

Party considerations dictate that some members must be on subcommittees of no concern to their constituencies: there must be Republicans on the cotton subcommittee and Democrats on the wheat subcommittee. For the most part, members who have little interest in the proceedings are expected either to remain silent during hearings or not to attend.

The Work of the Committee—1958

In 1958 serious problems existed for cotton, rice, wheat, dairy products, and corn. These crises involved four of the six commodity groups shown in Table II, leaving the tobacco and diversified groups with little direct and positive interest in the legislation. The Committee decided to employ the "omnibus" procedure so as to get as much backing for the bill as possible. Apparently the leadership on both sides agreed to this, though some Republicans complained about such obvious "logrolling."

The work of the Committee proceeded according to plan with the cotton, dairy products, livestock and feed grains, and wheat subcommittees holding extensive hearings. The result was a 62-page bill (H. R. 12954) which included eight titles. In addition to titles designed to solve immediate crises, titles to extend certain popular programs were added so as to increase the bill's dubious chances of passage.[9]

The Committee voted on June 13 to report H. R. 12954 favorably, but on June 25, the Rules Committee's motion to debate

[8] Anfuso almost monopolized the Committee hearings on the extension of the Agricultural Trade Development and Assistance Act, since many New York City firms were testifying. His activity in these hearings provided unexpected evidence of constituency-representative relationships.

[9] The titles were: I—Foreign Trade; II—Rice; III—Cotton; IV—Wool; V—Wheat; VI—Milk; VII—Feed Grains; and VIII—Miscellaneous. Titles I and IV in particular were included because they were popular programs.

TABLE III

*Constituency Interests and Commodity Subcommittee Assignments**

Member†	Major Agricultural Interests In Constituency	Commodity Subcommittees
Democrats		
Poage	Cotton, Livestock, Peanuts	Cotton; Livestock & Feed Grains (C)
Grant	Cotton, Peanuts, Wood Products	Forests (C); Peanuts
Gathings	Cotton, Rice, Soybeans	Cotton (C); Rice; Soybeans-Oilseeds
McMillan	Cotton, Tobacco, Peanuts	Forests; Peanuts (C); Tobacco
Abernethy	Cotton	Cotton; Dairy Products (C); Soybeans-Oilseeds
Albert	Cotton, Livestock	Livestock and Feed Grains; Peanuts; Wheat (C)
Abbitt	Tobacco, Peanuts	Tobacco (C); Peanuts
Polk	Feed Grains, Livestock, Dairy	Dairy Products; Tobacco
Thompson	Rice, Cotton, Peanuts	Rice (C); Poultry-Eggs
Jones	Cotton, Livestock, Soybeans	Rice; Soybeans-Oilseeds (C); Wheat
Watts	Tobacco, Feed Grains, Seeds	Tobacco; Wheat
Hagen	Cotton, Alfalfa Seed, Potatoes, Fruit	Cotton; Soybeans-Oilseeds
Johnson	Dairy, Forests, Livestock	Dairy Products; Forests; Poultry-Eggs
Anfuso	None	Poultry-Eggs
Bass	Tobacco, Cotton	Tobacco; Wheat
Knutson	Wheat, Dairy, Feed Grains	Dairy Products
Jennings	Tobacco, Livestock	Livestock and Feed Grains; Tobacco; Wheat
Matthews	Tobacco, Peanuts, Vegetables	Livestock and Feed Grains; Tobacco
Republicans		
Hoeven	Feed Grains, Livestock	Livestock and Feed Grains; Soybeans-Oilseeds
Simpson	Feed Grains, Livestock	Cotton; Livestock and Feed Grains; Soybeans-Oilseeds; Tobacco
Dague	Tobacco, Truck Farming, Poultry, Dairy	Tobacco; Wheat
Harvey	Feed Grains, Livestock	Livestock & Feed Grains; Soybeans-Oilseeds
Belcher	Wheat	Cotton; Peanuts; Wheat
McIntire	Forests, Poultry, Potatoes	Forests; Poultry-Eggs; Tobacco
Williams	Dairy, Truck Farming	Dairy Products; Rice
Harrison	Feed Grains, Livestock	Peanuts; Poultry-Eggs
Dixon	Wheat, Potatoes, Small Grain, Sugar Beets	Forests; Poultry-Eggs
Smith	Wheat	Peanuts; Wheat
Krueger	Wheat, Small Grains	Rice; Wheat
Teague	Vegetables, Fruit, Small Grains, Cotton	Cotton; Forests
Tewes	Dairy, Tobacco, Livestock	Dairy Products; Tobacco
Quie	Dairy, Feed Grains, Livestock	Dairy Products; Tobacco

* The major interests were deduced from the *Census of Agriculture, 1954*, Vol. 1, 1956, and from interviews with members.
† Members listed according to committee rank. Chairman Cooley, whose principal interests were tobacco, cotton and poultry, and William Hill, whose principal interests were wheat, feed grains, and sugar beets, were *ex officio* members of all subcommittees by virtue of their positions as chairman and ranking minority member, respectively.

the bill (H. Res. 609) was lost in the House, thereby defeating the bill.[10] Shortly afterword, on June 27, the Senate passed its farm bill (S. 4071) and sent it to the House. The House Agriculture Committee amended S. 4071 to bring it into line with their previously defeated bill and reported it on August 4. On August 6, Chairman Cooley moved that the House suspend the rules and pass S. 4071 as amended. The motion received a simple majority, but not the two-thirds vote required for such a motion, and so S. 4071 was also defeated. The House Agriculture Committee made a final attempt to modify their amendments to S. 4071, and on August 14 Chairman Cooley once again moved that the House suspend the rules and pass the bill as amended. This time S. 4071 was accepted after a short debate by a voice vote, and on August 28 it was signed into law by the President. (P.L. 85-835).

In general, H. R. 12954 solved the cotton, rice, and feed grain problems to the satisfaction of Committee representatives from those areas and they were apparently willing to trade their support. Their modifications of S. 4071 were attempts to bring that bill closer to the provisions of H. R. 12954 for these commodities. The wheat and dairy titles in H. R. 12954 had little support outside the groups representing those interests. Though the Secretary of Agriculture and the American Farm Bureau Federation had objections to all titles in H. R. 12954, their most serious protests were directed against the dairy and wheat titles. Cotton and rice representatives were willing to drop these objectionable titles when the bill reached the House floor in order to save the sections of the bill they wanted most. Neither wheat nor dairy was included in S. 4071.[11]

S. 4071 was more in line with the Secretary of Agriculture's recommendations for fewer controls and lower supports.[12] Its ultimate passage, even with the modifications to bring it closer to H. R. 12954, was generally conceded to have been a victory for the Eisenhower Administration.

---

[10] The reported vote in Committee was 21–10. The House vote on H. Res. 609 was 171–214.

[11] The dairy situation illustrates the in-fighting. Evidently the cotton and rice Democrats were opposed to any dairy legislation. Hearings were held but only after long delays. The Secretary of Agriculture's objections to the "self-help" bill proposed by dairy representatives were given the spotlight of a full committee hearing rather than a less sensational subcommittee hearing. The title which resulted was developed at the last minute and had little support, even among the national dairy groups.

[12] See *The Congressional Digest*, Vol. 37 (March, 1958), pp. 75–7, for details of the Administration's recommendations.

II. MEMBER DISCUSSION AND EVALUATION

The vote on the rule to debate H. R. 12954 was split along party lines (Democrats for, Republicans against) with the major exception of urban Democrats. Of the 59 Democrats who indicated opposition (either by voting against, pairing against, or answering the *Congressional Quarterly* poll), 47 were from metropolitan or mid-urban districts. Several Committee members charged that the opponents of H. R. 12954 had tried to identify it as a "consumers' tax" bill in order to win the support of the urban representatives. The Committee vote, also split along party lines, is indicated in Table IV.

TABLE IV

House Agriculture Committee Vote on House Resolution 609

Democrats		Republicans	
Yea	*Nay*	*Yea*	*Nay*
Cooley	Hagen	Harvey	Hill
Poage		Smith	Hoeven
Grant		Quie	Simpson
Gathings			Dague
Abernethy			Belcher
Albert			Harrison
Abbitt			Dixon
Polk			Krueger
Thompson			Teague
Jones			Tewes
Watts			
Johnson	Not Voting		Not Voting
Anfuso	or Paired		or Paired
Bass	———		
Knutson	McMillan		McIntire
Jennings	(paired for)		(paired against)
Matthews			Williams

	Totals		
	Yea	*Nay*	*Not Voting or Paired*
Democrats	18	1	1
Republicans	3	11	2
Committee	21	12	3

* Compiled from data in the *Congressional Quarterly Almanac*, 85th Cong., 2d sess., 1958, pp. 392–3. Members are listed according to committee rank.

Opinion of the Legislation

Members were asked in interviews for their opinions of the legislation, both H. R. 12954 and S. 4071. Two conclusions emerged. First, there was little unqualified opinion in support of either bill.

Of the 30 members interviewed in regard to H. R. 12954, three considered it good, five said that most of it was good, fifteen were equivocal (some sections good, some sections bad); and seven considered it poor. Of the 28 who were interviewed in regard to S. 4071, four labeled it good, eight thought it "mostly good", fourteen were equivocal, and only two considered it bad. Table V distributes the opinions by commodity group.

Several comments are appropriate. The commodity groups can be classified into the principal beneficiaries of H. R. 12954 (corn and livestock, cotton and rice) who enjoyed broad support; the champions of controversial titles who were also directly and positively affected (dairy, wheat); and the onlookers who were not involved or only indirectly affected (diversified, tobacco). Examined in this way the most favorable opinions were offered by those most affected: six of the eight "good" or "mostly good" responses came from representatives of the main beneficiaries. The middle category, concerned with controversial titles, tended to be suspicious of the

TABLE V

*Member Opinion of the Legislation, by Commodity Group**

Commodity Interest	H. R. 12954				S. 4071			
	Good	Mostly Good	Equiv-ocal	Bad	Good	Mostly Good	Equiv-ocal	Bad
Corn and Livestock								
Democrats†			1					
Republicans		1	1	1	1	2		
Cotton and Rice								
Democrats	3	2	2		1		6	
Dairy, Livestock, Small Grains								
Democrats			2					2
Republicans				2		2		
Diversified								
Democrats#			1	1		1		
Republicans		1	2	1	2	1	1	
Tobacco								
Democrats		1	6			1	6	
Wheat								
Republicans			2			1	1	
Totals	3	5	15	7	4	8	14	2

* In answer to the question, "Did you consider H. R. 12954 (S. 4071) a good bill, a bad bill, something in between, or just what?"
† Polk not interviewed on S. 4071.
# Anfuso not interviewed on S. 4071.

bill. Both dairy and wheat members suggested that their titles would be sacrificed once the bill got to the floor.

Though it might be expected that Democratic tobacco representatives would actively support a bill from a Democratic committee, they were equivocal about H. R. 12954. On the basis of such comments as, "Frankly, I didn't think it would help very much," indications were that the tobacco representatives did little more than vote for the rule to debate. Nothing in either bill was of primary concern to their constituencies.

The diversified group offered very little favorable comment on H. R. 12954 and only one of them, a Democrat, voted for the bill on the floor. Once again, the bill gave very little direct, positive benefit to the group's constituencies though, as will appear, it soon became evident that they did have a constituency interest in the bill.

Opinion on the second bill shows a party split. Though the Republicans had less direct constituency interest in the bill (except for the corn and livestock group which considered it "good" or "mostly good"), nine of eleven committee Republicans considered the bill "good" or "mostly good." The Democrats were more qualified, with many of the cotton and rice group stating, "It was the best we could get." The tobacco group was no more enthusiastic about S. 4071 than they had been about H. R. 12954. Republicans obviously considered this a better bill because it was not a clear-cut victory for Democratic commodities. Though Republican commodities had not fared too well, the Democrats were not able to write the legislation with a free hand. Republicans from diversified farming areas were much more satisfied with S. 4071 since it reduced controls and price supports.

Second, the members' opinions, not only of the bill as a whole but also of specific titles, were influenced by their constituencies' interests. When asked what they liked most and least about the bills, members whose constituencies were directly affected replied that they liked best those sections which were designed to solve commodity problems in their own constituencies. On H. R. 12954, four from the cotton and rice group mentioned those titles, one from corn and livestock, both members from wheat, and two from dairy. The same held true for S. 4071.

Members were reluctant to say what sections they liked least. Some spoke in general terms, mentioning the over-all cost, the politics involved, the issues not faced, etc. Only the dairy title drew much critical comment. Ten members (six Democrats and four

Republicans) suggested that the dairy title was not good legislation and was harmful to the bill. The most numerous response for S. 4071 was that no sections were "least liked."

As a follow-up question, members were asked which sections had beneficial or adverse effects on their constituencies. Once again, the replies supported the conclusion. In discussing H. R. 12954 all groups directly affected by the bill mentioned most often, as being beneficial, those titles of greatest interest to their respective constituencies. The most frequent response from the two least affected groups (diversified, tobacco) was that no section was beneficial. For S. 4071, those most affected were the cotton and rice and corn and livestock members. They all mentioned the titles of interest to their constituencies as most beneficial. Other groups either chose some section which was of tangential importance or stated that none was beneficial. Hardly any member admitted that any sections adversely affected his constituency.

Concepts of Representation

Members were also asked to discuss what they relied on in their action on the first bill (H. R. 12954)—independent judgment, constituency wishes, a combination of factors, or something else. The results are summarized in the following conclusions.

First, a majority of members stated that in making up their minds they relied on independent judgment or a combination of factors (22 of 27 interviewed on this question). There was no important difference between Republicans and Democrats on this question. (See Table VI.)

Second, analysis by commodity groups reveals that those groups least positively affected by the legislation most often responded that they relied on "independent judgment." But the record shows that the diversified group did act to benefit constituency interests.

The members' replies must be weighed after taking into consideration both the importance of the legislation to their constituencies and the effect of their action for their constituencies. Of the ten who said that they followed independent judgment, four were from the tobacco group and three from the diversified. One other member from the diversified group said he supported his party in this instance but usually relied on independent judgment.

Despite these replies, two observations are pertinent: (a) all tobacco representatives who relied on independent judgment nevertheless voted in support of their party[13] and (b) the voting action (against the bill) of the diversified group tended to favor the best interests of their farmers—as they themselves described these in-

TABLE VI

Bases Asserted for Action on H. R. 12954*

Commodity Groups	Independent Judgment	Constituency Wishes	Combi- nation	Other (Party)
Corn and Livestock† Republicans	1		2	
Cotton and Rice Democrats	1	2	3	1
Dairy, Livestock, Small Grains Democrats Republicans	1		2 1	
Diversified # Democrats Republicans	1 2		1	1°
Tobacco** Democrats	4		2	
Wheat Republicans		1	1	
Totals	10	3	12	2

* In answer to the question, "What did you rely on in your action on H. R. 12954: (1) independent judgment, (2) the wishes of your constituency, (3) perhaps a combination of these, or (4) something else?"
† Polk not included.
# Anfuso not included.
° Usually relied on independent judgment.
** Cooley not included.

terests. As one member put it: "Benson is an asset to me. I agree with him and there is nothing political involved because his philosophy is good for my farmers." All of the diversified group who responded "independent judgment" indicated that a continued program of high supports and controls for *basic* commodities was bad for their farmers, who grow principally non-basics.

The other three members who mentioned independent judgment were from the corn and livestock group (an admitted Administration and American Farm Bureau Federation supporter—he thought

---

[13] Some tobacco representatives noted the importance of the wheat and feed grain titles for their constituencies. They thought these might eventually affect their livestock farmers (using the slogan, "cheap feed means cheap livestock"). Many of their farmers relied on wheat as an alternative crop.

their programs would be best for his constituency in the long run);
the cotton and rice group (a generally inactive member who "didn't
have too much information from my constituency") ; and a dairy
Republican who said, "I only had this chance to vote against the
cotton deal."

Third, those groups most directly and positively affected by the
legislation relied on a "combination" or on "constituency wishes."
Replies of these members indicated they were well aware of the
problems involved in representing *all* interests in their legal constituency on such a piece of legislation.

Nine of the twelve responses indicating a reliance on a combination of factors came from members whose constituency interests
were directly affected by the legislation. Some of the most detailed
analyses of the process of representation were offered by senior
members who replied that representation on policy was not a simple choice between independent judgment on the one hand and
constituency wishes on the other. Typical of the extended remarks
are the following:

> I understand the problems of that area [his district]. I know
> what is best for the farm section. And I think that the majority
> in my area reflect my views.

> I am in close contact with them at all times. I meet with
> them, ask their opinions on all matters. I don't use polls. I
> know the people. I vote my convictions and hope that they
> [constituents] will follow these. They expect this—unless a real
> organized group is excited about something. They generally
> expect that you have more information than they do.

> I am sent here as a representative of 600,000 people. They
> are supposed to be voting on all the legislation. I try to follow
> my constituents—to ignore them would be a breach of trust—
> but I use my judgment often because they are misinformed. I
> know that they would vote as I do if they had the facts that
> I have. A lot of people expect you to use your judgment.

> Under our form of government you have to rely on a com-
> bination. If I know the views of the constituents I will vote
> these views—as a representative, I must—but when I don't know
> I substitute my best judgment. There is not one case in a
> hundred where I do know their views fully. I figure if they
> knew what I know . . . they would understand my vote. Most
> of us vote what we believe is sound, based on the information
> and our judgment. This can be changed if the people express

themselves clearly enough. This, however, is improbable and doesn't happen very often.

Even the junior members in these groups had definite ideas about how their constituencies were affected:

> I thought that it was a good bill and then I thought that I could go ahead in view of the referendum and support the bill. If there weren't a referendum [included in the bill], I would have checked [with the constituency] but I felt I could go ahead. On some legislation I hear from the people and rely on their judgment . . . [after probing for specifics]. On labor legislation I rely on groups in my area since I don't know too much about it.

> I depend on a combination. I should educate them; they don't really care how you vote. I make up my mind and then temper it with what the people want. After all, I think as they do.

One member who relied on constituency wishes was frank in explaining his position:

> I vote for what I think will be the best economic interests of my people. Throughout the years I have gained an idea of what those best interests are. This is the way representative government should work.

Fourth, an analysis of members' extended discussions coupled with an examination of their interest and activity on the legislation reveals the importance of a concept of "constituency" in the action of members.

Those who purported to rely on independent judgment were of three types: members who had no commodities to represent on the legislation but opposed the bill—an action evidently in the best interests of their constituencies; members in the tobacco group who supported their party but had no direct interest in the legislation (though some expressed indirect interest); and members who had a constituency interest in the bill but said they relied on independent judgment in their actions, though this did not seem the case in fact.

Those relying on a combination of factors argued that defining constituency interests was no simple, straightforward interpretation. In their subcommittee work on the bill, however, these members—

the most active of all who worked on the bill—evinced a shrewd conception of their constituencies' commodity interests.

Clearly, more evidence than the self-explained motivation for voting is relevant in appraising a representative's action and in interpreting his conception of representation: his work in subcommittee on acceptable compromises, e.g., or his interrogation of witnesses in hearings, or his part in the Committee's executive sessions. The data gathered here from such successive stages of action as these tend to confirm Eulau's typology of "delegates," "trustees" and "politicos," and his suggestion that a representative might act in more than one of these roles.[14]

Knowing the Constituency

In order to discover some of the relationships and means of communication between the representative and his constituency, members were asked how they knew their constituency wishes on H. R. 12954. Table VII summarizes the responses. The most im-

TABLE VII

Methods for Determining Constituency Wishes*

Method	Democrats† Mentioning	Republicans Mentioning	Totals
Just know it (live there, sense it)	8	5	13
Meetings	6	3	9
Correspondence	4	3	7
Questionnaire	1	2	3
Newspaper	—	2	2
Testimony	1	1	2
Advisory Committee (to advise on agricultural policy)	—	1	1
Telephone calls	—	1	1
Visitors	1	—	1

* In answer to the questions, "How did you find out what your constituency wishes were on this bill?" and "Are there other ways you use to tap opinion and get information about your constituency's agricultural interests? What are these?"
† Does not include Cooley, Polk, or Anfuso.

portant method, members said, was a type of individual "sounding-board" procedure. Some of those mentioning "intuition" or "sixth sense" observed that their own identity with the culture or mood of the district made it natural that they would know their neighbors' wishes. Responses which typified the members' analyses were:

You are in a position to know, of course, on a lot of things. I live there—there are many things I just know. I don't have

---
[14] Above, note 2.

to ask anybody. There are very few bills where I have to guess.
If I did, I wouldn't be here as the representative.
I am a native of ——. I get letters—though I don't get
very much mail. I have sent out questionnaires but I don't
now. It is just the fact that I know and I can judge their needs.

Some of the members pointed out that they were farmers and
reasoned that this gave them a special ability to know the needs
of fellow farmers. Others indicated that their familiarity with the
district through campaigns or frequent visits made it possible for
them to know. Either way, they were identifying a "policy constituency."

Though such responses suggest that the representative has a
concept of his constituency interests on legislation, there is still
no reliable evidence as to how he develops it. But whether he
gets it by divination, intuition or instruction, it appears to dominate
his behavior as a representative where its outline is sharp.

III. CONCLUSIONS

The conclusions suggested by this case study can be set forth
somewhat more systematically as follows:

1. If a policy measure is seen to affect substantial interests in a
representative's legal constituency, then he will rely on his perception of the interests affected (his "policy constituency") when he
acts at the working level (usually the subcommittee) in regard to
this measure.

   A. Institutional arrangements affect his ability to represent his
   policy constituency. The House Agriculture Committee is organized to allow a maximum of constituency-oriented representation.

   B. The representative has a "sense" of constituency interests drawn
   from first-hand experience in the "legal" constituency and this
   "sense" influences his perception of a policy constituency.

   C. Party allegiance is an important modifying factor.

      (1) The legislative majority party may demand a vote in sup-
      port of its policies. The legislative minority party may
      demand a vote in opposition to the majority's policies.
      The Administration may press for support for its stands.

      (2) Representatives, whether or not affected by the legislation,
      tend to support their party's position more as the action

moves beyond the basic working level, and most at the final vote.

2. If a measure is seen to have little or no direct effect on interests in a representative's legal constituency, then he will tend more readily to look to his political party for a cue when he acts in regard to this measure.

A. The representative will tend the more to suggest that he relies on "independent judgment," the less his constituency's interests are seen to be directly or positively affected by a policy.

B. He will vote in support of his political party but will not actively support the policy in other ways if his constituency interests are not perceived to be affected.

A final comment suggests a further and more tentative generalization. In this case study it became necessary to reconcile actions of certain members who seemed motivated by different forces at different action points. Table IV shows that 11 Republicans voted or paired against the rule to debate H. R. 12954. Of these, seven were from constituencies which had a direct, positive interest in the legislation. Four of the seven were particularly active in effecting compromises in titles of major concern to their constituencies. They were apparently satisfied with the respective titles, yet had no difficulty in rationalizing opposition to the entire bill on the House floor. Further, while members of the diversified group apparently did little to obstruct the work on H. R. 12954 at the subcommittee level (thereby following an apparent norm for Agriculture Committee members), it nevertheless became obvious that some of them worked actively to defeat the bill on the House floor.[15]

An adequate concept of representation should account for a total action pattern, not merely a final vote. The representative on the House Agriculture Committee can view his composite role retrospectively as one in which he has taken several separate actions to make up a total pattern in regard to the omnibus farm legislation. He also can recognize that on different occasions he felt differing demands upon him in his several capacities, as a member of a party, a representative of a constituency, a member of a committee, of a Congress, of interest groups, etc. He was able to reconcile,

---

[15] Minority party members are more likely to feel conflicting demands since the majority party's commodities will probably be favored. Some majority party members will find, however, that they are not as directly concerned with the legislation and so will be less actively involved at all stages of action.

compromise or avoid some of the inherent conflicts in these demands, at least in part, because of the multiple action points. Examples of such reconciliations in this case study justify a final hypothesis which merits separate study:

3. If a representative has a multiplicity of conflicting demands upon him in any series of actions on policy, he can satisfy many of them, over a period of time, because of the multiplicity of action points at successive stages in the legislative process.

THE ENLARGED RULES COMMITTEE*

Robert L. Peabody

WHAT SHOULD be the relationship between the formal leadership of the House of Representatives, the over four-hundred House members, and the Committee on Rules, the principal scheduling and policy committee of the House? Both the Eighty-seventh and Eighty-eighth Congresses began with floor fights attempting to re-solve, in George Galloway's terms, a fundamental question: Should the Committee on Rules serve as the agent of the majority party or should it operate as the instrument of a bipartisan coalition which may control a majority of the votes in the House?[1] Early in the Eighty-seventh Congress, in an attempt to make the committee more responsive to the Speaker and the newly formed Kennedy Adminis-tration, the House voted 217 to 212 in favor of increasing the committee size. Almost two years later, when the House adopted its rules for the Eighty eighth Congress, it voted 235 to 196 to permanently enlarge the Committee on Rules from twelve to fif-teen members.[2] By adding two pro-Administration Democrats and only one Republican to a committee previously dominated by two

---

* This study was made possible by a grant from the Committee on Public Affairs, the Johns Hopkins University. In addition to a number of readers who made helpful comments on earlier versions of this paper, I am particularly in-debted to Chairman Howard W. Smith and the members of the Committee on Rules, without whose cooperation this study could not have been accomplished.
[1] George B. Galloway, *History of the United States House of Representatives,* 87th Cong., 1st sess., H. Doc. 246 (Washington, D.C.: U.S. Government Print-ing Office, 1962), p. 137. This question oversimplifies the issues. The majority party leadership is not always united. The Republican–Southern Democratic conservative coalition is effective on only a limited number of votes in a given session of Congress. As will be elaborated upon in the concluding section of this paper, this question needs reformulation in terms of the degree of inde-pendence exercised by the Committee on Rules in its relationships with the leadership and the members of the House of Representatives.
[2] H. Res. 5 read as follows: *"Resolved,* That the Rules of the House of Representatives of the Eighty-seventh Congress, together with all applicable provisions of the Legislative Reorganization Act of 1946, as amended, be, and they are hereby, adopted as the Rules of the House of Representatives of the

conservative southern Democrats and the four Republican minority members, a six-to-six stalemate was converted to an eight-to-seven majority generally sympathetic to the needs of the Democratic leadership. From a longer time perspective, these enlargement controversies of 1961 and 1963 can be seen as but two of many episodes in the often uneasy and sometimes changing relationships among the formal majority leadership, the Committee on Rules, and the membership of the House as a whole.

The House Committee on Rules has been vested with powers affecting the flow of legislation which are both indispensable and potentially a source of conflict.[3] These powers are indispensable to the majority leadership of the House because some form of coordination is needed in a legislative body of such a large size. Furthermore, the leadership is too preoccupied with other functions to provide detailed scrutiny and oversight of the over one hundred complex and potentially controversial bills coming before the House each session.[4] The Committee on Rules also performs valuable

---

Eighty-eighth Congress, with the following amendment therein as a part thereof, to wit:

Strike out subsection (p) of rule X and insert in lieu thereof the following:

'(p) Committee on Rules, to consist of fifteen Members.' " *Congressional Record,* 88th Cong., 1st sess. (January 9, 1963), p. 13. Without the above amendment introduced by majority leader Carl Albert of Oklahoma, the Committee on Rules would have automatically reverted to a twelve-member committee as prescribed in the House Rules and the Legislative Reorganization Act of 1946. Traditionally, the Chairman of the Committee on Rules has introduced resolutions similar to the above, without the amending language; but in this instance, the majority leadership wished to maintain control of the floor. See, for example, the opening day adoption of the rules in the Eighty-seventh Congress, *Congressional Record,* January 3, 1961, p. 24.

[3] The formal powers and duties of the Committee on Rules are specified by Rule XI, cl. 16, in Lewis Deschler, *Constitution, Jefferson's Manual and Rules of the House of Representatives of the United States,* 87th Cong., 2d Sess., H. Doc. 459, pp. 352–53. For a comprehensive description of the use of these powers from 1937 to 1962, see James A. Robinson, *The House Committee on Rules* (Indianapolis: Bobbs-Merrill, forthcoming). A brief but useful summary of committee powers is contained in *Congressional Quarterly Almanac* (Washington, D.C.: Congressional Quarterly, Inc., 1961), XVII, 402–3.

[4] Of the over 20,000 measures introduced in the Eighty-seventh Congress, only 885 public bills and 684 private bills were enacted into law, "Resumé of Congressional Activity of Eighty-seventh Congress," *Congressional Record,* 87th Cong., 2d sess. (November 2, 1962), p. D 973. About 90 per cent of these measures are generally killed in the legislative committees. As James A. Robinson has observed with regard to the balance: "Approximately nine-tenths of the business of the House is relatively noncontroversial and this portion of the work is considered by expeditious procedures, such as the Consent or Private calendars,

services for rank-and-file members; these include the provision of
information and voting cues and protection against pressures exerted by the executive branch and external interest groups. Yet the
Committee on Rules is potentially irksome to some members, particularly the newly elected and more liberal members, because the
powers of the committee operate so as to enhance the policy predilections of the particular congressmen who are its members. The
appointment of most committee members from safe districts, the
operation of the seniority system, and the heightened influence of
the Democratic South and the Republican Midwest in the Congress
all tend to produce a majority on the Rules Committee that is
relatively insulated from the broad shifts of sentiment that affect
the Presidency and, on occasion, a majority of the members of the
House and Senate.

As a result, the relations among the House membership, the
House leadership, and the Committee on Rules may shift from
relative consensus to conflict. On the one hand, there can be general consensus, marred only by an occasional arbitrary action by a
Rules Committee Chairman, as there was in the 1920's and early
1930's when the House leadership, most members, and the House
Rules Committee generally agreed on the substance and flow of
legislation. On the other hand, underlying differences may erupt,
leading to revolt, purges, or attempts to bypass the powers of the
committee such as occurred in 1910, 1938, and 1949.[5] Controversy
over the activities of the committee continued through the 1950's,
with the exception of the period of the Republican-controlled

---

or on special legislative days, including District of Columbia Day. The other
one-tenth of the House's program—numbering approximately one hundred bills
and resolutions each session—is controversial enough to be debated for three or
more pages each in the *Congressional Record* (approximately 30 minutes) . . . .
More than half of these controversial items will be handled under special resolutions from the Committee on Rules." "The Role of the Rules Committee in Arranging the Program of the U.S. House of Representatives," *Western Political
Quarterly,* XII (September, 1959), 653, 653–69.

[5] For a balanced overview of the events leading up to the overthrow of
Speaker Joseph Cannon in 1910, President Roosevelt's successful "purge" of
Chairman of the Committee on Rules James O'Connor of New York in 1938,
and the adoption and abandonment of the twenty-one-day rule in 1949 and
1951, see Galloway, *op. cit.,* pp. 50–52, 133–40. For more comprehensive
treatments of these events, see Joseph Cooper, "Progressive Attitudes toward the
Proper Role of Committees in the House of Representatives, 1908–1929" (Cambridge, Mass.: Multilithed, 1962), pp. 32–58; and Lewis J. Lapham, "Party
Leadership and the House Committee on Rules" (Unpublished Ph.D. dissertation, Department of Government, Harvard University, 1953).

Eighty-third Congress. The issue became most sharply drawn during the Eighty-sixth Congress, when the largest Democratic majority since 1937 attempted to enact a legislative record on which to campaign in 1960. It was the Rules Committee's refusal to grant a special order permitting House conferees to meet with Senate conferees on a school construction bill that had passed both Houses, which, as much as any factor, brought on the 1961 rules enlargement.[6] Conservative control of a twelve-member committee could not be tolerated by the newly-formed Kennedy Administration. After considering several alternatives, the Democratic House leadership settled for a moderate but important change—an increase in committee size for the duration of the Eighty-seventh Congress.[7]

The principal purpose of this chapter will be to sketch four main policy alternatives to a question posed at the end of Chapter VII: What should be the composition of the House Committee on Rules and in whose interests should committee control be exercised?

> Should the committee be an instrument of the House majority leadership? If so, should it be composed solely of members of the majority party, and should the Speaker himself be a member? Alternatively, should the committee be as nearly representative as possible of the total membership of the House—a microcosm of the whole? Or should the committee overrepresent groups who are in a minority in the House, thus making the agreement of concurrent majorities a necessary prerequisite for action in the American governmental system?[8]

Before discussing these and other policy alternatives, three subsidiary purposes must be fulfilled. The first will be to review the range of functions performed by the Committee on Rules as seen from the perspectives of its members. A second purpose will be to outline briefly some of the consequences of increasing the committee size from twelve to fifteen members. Finally, the floor fights of 1961 and 1963 will be contrasted and compared for the insights they may

---

[6] See, for example, criticisms of the Committee on Rules during the post-convention session of the Eighty-sixth Congress, *Congressional Record,* August 26, 1960, pp. 16698–706. During the floor debate preceding the 1961 enlargement vote, Chairman Smith accused several members of the Democratic Study Group of opening the assault on the Committee on Rules. *Congressional Record,* 87th Cong., 1st sess. (January 31, 1961), p. 1505.

[7] Milton C. Cummings, Jr. and Robert L. Peabody, "The Decision to Enlarge the Committee on Rules," Chapter VII of this volume.

[8] *Ibid.,* pp. 192–93.

bring to underlying political strategies, party alignments, and incremental change in the House of Representatives.

I. PERCEPTIONS OF COMMITTEE FUNCTIONS

How do Rules Committee members perceive the functions they perform for the House membership and leadership?[9] James A. Robinson has carefully examined the role of the Committee on Rules in arranging the program and regulating debate in the House of Representatives.[10] Building on his detailed descriptions, the focus here is on the internal operations of that Committee, and, in particular, how the views of the fifteen members affect policy outcomes. The interpretations which follow are primarily based on semistructured interviews with the fifteen members and observation of over twenty-five hearings during the Eighty-seventh Congress.[11]

Following several questions about the strategy and consequences of the 1961 rules enlargement controversy, each member was asked, "What would you say are the two or three most important functions performed by the Committee on Rules"? In order of the frequency with which they were mentioned by the members, the functions cited were: (1) substantive control over legislation, (2) regulation of debate, (3) technical review and oversight, (4) timing, or holding up the release of a bill, (5) communication of information and voting cues, and (6) protection of members from external pressures. Table I reports these frequencies for the total committee and for

---

[9] An explicit distinction is made here between functions performed and the members' *perceptions* of these functions. For elaboration on functional analysis, see Robert K. Merton, *Social Theory and Social Structure* (rev. ed.; Glencoe, Ill.: The Free Press, 1957), pp. 19–84; Gabriel Almond and James S. Coleman, *The Politics of the Developing Areas* (Princeton, New Jersey: Princeton University Press, 1960), esp. chap. i; and Alan Fiellin, "The Functions of Informal Groups in Legislative Institutions," *Journal of Politics*, XXIV (February, 1962), 72–91. Reprinted as Chapter III of this volume.

[10] James A. Robinson, *The House Committee on Rules, op. cit.*

[11] More generally, this chapter is based on three sets of interviews: (1) some twenty informal interviews held during the summer of 1961 with the majority and minority leadership, six of the fifteen members of the Committee on Rules, and a number of representatives and staff members who had been active in the 1961 rules fight; (2) thirteen focused interviews in 1962 with members of the Rules Committee, using a fifteen-question semi-structured interview schedule; and (3) ten more informal interviews with congressmen and key staff members immediately following the 1963 rules controversy, including three follow-up interviews with Rules Committee members. Notes were taken during the interviews, reworked immediately afterwards, and later transcribed for subsequent analysis.

the two primary voting alignments on the committee, which, for want of a better term, have been labeled pro-administration and anti-administration.[12]

On most (perhaps three-fourths) of the bills and resolutions which come before the Committee on Rules, the members act with unanimity or near unanimity.[13] It is only on the most controversial measures that the dominant cleavage comes into play. This division is not strictly on party lines—the Committee is composed of ten members of the majority party (in the Eighty-seventh Congress, the Democratic party) and five members of the minority party. Rather, the division is along ideological lines, conservative and liberal.[14] The pro-administration group is composed of the eight least-senior and more moderate and liberal members of the ten-member Democratic majority. The anti-administration group is made up of the two ranking Democrats—Chairman Howard W. Smith of Virginia and Representative William M. Colmer of Mississippi—and the five minority Republicans.

Two generalizations are immediately apparent from the summary of interview data reported in Table I. Although the members differ greatly as to what legislation they consider "good" or "bad" for the country, they appear to be in near-unanimous agreement, from their own point-of-view, that the Committee on Rules should and does exercise substantive control over legislation. Thirteen of the fifteen

---

[12] Members of the majority eight had an average Kennedy-support score of 90 per cent in 1961 and 83 per cent in 1962. The average scores for the seven minority members (five Republicans and two ranking Democrats) were 28 per cent in 1961 and 34 per cent in 1962. The scores for all Democratic members in the House were 73 per cent in 1961 and 72 per cent in 1962; for Republicans they were 37 per cent in 1961 and 42 per cent in 1962.

[13] As Walter Kravitz has observed in an apt metaphor: "It must be kept in mind . . . that the unique circumstances of the Committee's duties . . . tend to emphasize the negative rather than the normal aspects of its work. We usually watch the legislative scene much as we view a lake bottom through clear water, largely unaware of the transparent separation until the water roils and makes the view transluscent. In the same way, the work of the Rules Committee is seldom noticed until it becomes involved in conflict." See "The House Committee on Rules' Influence on Legislation in the 87th Congress" (Library of Congress, Legislative Reference Service, Washington, D.C., Multilithed, 1963), p. 1.

[14] The terms "conservative" and "liberal" are much abused. However, if one uses as an index the *Congressional Quarterly* "larger federal role" support scores on eighteen test roll call votes in the Eighty-seventh Congress, again, the pattern is clear-cut. The eight majority Democrats have scores ranging from 89 to 100 per cent, with an average of 95 per cent. The two "conservative" southern Democrats and the five Republicans range from 0 to 22 per cent with an average "larger federal role" support score of 9 per cent. *Congressional Quarterly Weekly Report*, XX (December 28, 1962), 2290–95.

members, or 87 per cent, elaborated and justified this function of substantive control.

A second point to be stressed is that one or more functions were endorsed by at least two members each from the pro- and anti-administration groupings. There is considerable agreement, cutting across party and ideological cleavages, on the merits of all of these functions.[15] While any classification, such as Table I, oversimplifies

TABLE I

Functions of the Committee on Rules as Perceived by Pro-Administration and Anti-Administration Members, Eighty-seventh Congress

| | Number Mentioning* | | |
Function	Total Committee on Rules N = 15	Pro-Admin- istration† Group N = 8	Anti-Admin- istration‡ Group N = 7
Substantive control of legislation, independent judgment as to merits ..	13	7	6
Regulation of debate, type of rule, and kind of amendment	8	4	4
Holding and timing release of bill, "waiting for grass-roots reaction"	7	3	4
Technical review and oversight of bills .	6	4	2
Communication of information, vote cueing during debate	5	3	2
Protection of members, "heat shield" or buffer function	5	2	3

* The number of responses total more than fifteen since members were asked to give two or three important functions performed by the committee.
† Eight Democrats, in order of their ranking on the committee from third to tenth, Representatives Ray J. Madden of Indiana, James J. Delaney of New York, James W. Trimble of Arkansas, Homer Thornberry of Texas, Richard Bolling of Missouri, Thomas P. O'Neill, Jr. of Massachusetts, Carl Elliott of Alabama, and B. F. Sisk of California.
‡ Two Democrats, Chairman Howard W. Smith of Virginia and second-ranking majority member William M. Colmer of Mississippi; and five Republicans, in order of their committee seniority, Clarence J. Brown of Ohio, Katherine St. George of New York, H. Allen Smith of California, Elmer J. Hoffman of Illinois, and William H. Avery of Kansas.

---

[15] Given the pronounced ideological cleavage, which, with the major exceptions of Smith and Colmer, closely parallels party divisions, greater disagreement among these two blocs in their identification of important committee functions were initially expected. As the following section will reveal, the major difference between the majority and minority blocs is not *which functions* are to be exercised, but in *whose interests*. Since the Committee on Rules plays a unique policy role and has no permanent subcommittees, it does not lend itself to ready comparisons with other House committees, but see the discussion of minimum partisanship and high committee integration in Richard Fenno, "The House Appropriations Committee as a Political System: The Problem of Integration," reprinted as Chapter IV of this volume; and Charles O. Jones, "The Role of the Congressional Subcommittee," *Midwest Journal of Political Science*, VI (November, 1962), 327–44.

the richness and divergency of beliefs about committee functions, some of this diversity will become more apparent as each of these functions is examined and illustrated in some detail.

Substantive Control Over Legislation

While rank-and-file members of Congress might take quite a different view as to what the principal function of the Committee on Rules should be, there is widespread consensus among committee members that they do exercise independent judgment about the merits of legislation and on occasion vote their policy predilections in deciding whether or not a particular bill should go to the floor for debate. Seven out of eight of the least-senior Democratic members, and six out of seven of the conservative minority emphasized the committee's exercise of substantive control over legislation. One member of the pro-leadership bloc expressed this point of view:

> It [the Committee on Rules] screens the legislation. It saves for the consideration of the House the bills that are important for the national defense and for our economy—that *we* think are important for national defense and our economy, and our foreign relations. . . .
> When a legislative committee comes down, knowing it has to go through the Rules Committee—it controls legislation in that sense, a kind of indirect control of legislation. On things that we don't think are in the best interests of the country, we don't allow a rule.

And a member of the conservative bloc concurred in this point of view, although professing quite different policy predilections:

> Quite frankly, to stop a lot of crackpot legislation from going through. A lot of legislation which is introduced should not be—people put it in with tongue in cheek. They just do it to humor some constituent; they don't expect it to get out, and they want the Rules Committee to stop it. There are too many laws already without opening the floodgates. If you didn't have the Rules Committee, you couldn't get through one year's output; we'd be here more like ten. It's absolutely necessary.

A number of the members tempered their remarks by indicating that they sometimes vote in favor of a rule, reserving the right to vote against the bill when it reaches the floor. Perhaps the remarks of another Democratic majority member were more typical:

I don't go along with those who argue that the Rules Committee should superimpose its judgments over the members of the House, but I do feel that on occasion we should exercise judgment on the committee that an issue is of such importance to the country that it ought to be debated.

I don't go so far as some people either—that the Rules Committee should be a traffic cop only. I have once or twice voted against granting a rule to a bill when I felt it wouldn't pass and we shouldn't take up the time of the House with it. Yet people are entitled to have it debated, even if sometimes we know it won't pass. . . . I'm not going to deny it's a question of judgment.

While there was near-unanimous agreement that the members exercise independent judgment, there was great divergency in opinion as to whose interests should be served by the substantive control. This question of the orientation of control will be re-examined after the remaining functions put forward by Rules Committee members in the Eighty-seventh Congress have been elaborated upon.

Regulation of Debate—The "Traffic Cop" Function [16]

As the response of the last Rules Committee member illustrates, substantive control over legislation—the imposition of the Rules Committee's views over and above those of the legislative committee's views—is often contrasted with an alternative function of regulating debate—a policy-neutral activity in which the committee merely expedites the orderly flow of legislation. As one member of the majority put it:

We're traffic cops; that's what we are. We grant rules on the timing of debate, the kinds of amendments that can be offered. The rules are flexible. You can waive certain things, such as points of order; do this, do that. You try to go along with the majority of the legislative committee. If they're on the Veterans Committee, Agriculture, Public Works, then they should know a bit more about the bill than we do.

Eight members of the Rules Committee developed this function at some length by commenting upon the importance of granting a

---

[16] It should be noted that as early as 1955 and on a number of occasions since, Chairman Smith in defense of the committee's discretionary powers has stated, "My people did not elect me to Congress to be a traffic cop." *Congressional Record,* 84th Cong., 1st sess. (July 19, 1955), p. 10944.

rule, determining the amount of debate, and limiting the kinds of amendments which may be offered from the floor. There was little difference in emphasis among the majority and minority voting alignments on the committee. Only one or two members saw this function as even partially irreconcilable with the exercise of independent judgment as to the merits of legislation.

It seems clear from a number of preliminary interviews with the House majority and minority leadership, interviews with a number of the more articulate and aggressive participants in the Rules fights who were not members of the Committee on Rules, and a reading of the *Congressional Record,* that an important core of the House would prefer to see a more neutral Rules Committee.[17] Under this conception of its principal functions, the Committee on Rules would emphasize *procedural* rather than *substantive* control, generally bringing bills to the floor under open rules, so that "the House could work its will." These views, however, must be interpreted with caution. Most of the critics as well as the supporters of the Committee on Rules in Congress are highly sophisticated "politicians" in the finest sense of the word. All of them would make optimum use of the Rules Committee to further what they believe to be in the best interests of their country, their constituents, their party, and themselves—and in about that order.[18] That is to say, all sides are in favor of the House's "working its will"; again, they differ in their perceptions of just what that will is and should be.

One final point about the function of regulating debate should be made explicit. The type of rule and the number and kind of

---

[17] Further research is needed, including follow-up interviews with the leadership and a cross-section of the House, in order to confirm or qualify these impressions. But see, for example, Speaker Rayburn's remarks at the close of the 1961 debate, *Congressional Record,* 87th Cong., 1st sess. (January 31, 1961), p. 1508, and the emphasis placed on the *procedural* aspects of the Committee on Rules by Speaker McCormack and Majority Leader Albert during the 1963 rules debate, *Congressional Record,* 88th Cong., 1st sess. (January 9, 1963), pp. 17, 20. There is, of course, an equally adamant group of members, mainly conservatives, who defend the committee's substantive control over legislation which they oppose. As one member of the minority leadership expressed this view, "I'm a conservative. If you're against a bill, you try to beat it in the legislative committee or then hold it up in the Rules Committee. If that doesn't work, then you try to defeat it on the floor."

[18] As Republican Representative Charles Goodell of New York commented upon the 1961 Rules Committee enlargement three months later, "Those who talked about reform earlier were not interested in real reform. They were interested in power. They did not want to eliminate the bottleneck, they just wanted to choose the corks themselves." *Congressional Record,* 87th Cong., 1st sess. (April 20, 1961), p. 6143.

amendments which may be offered from the floor are often crucial to the passage or defeat of a particular bill. Thus, a closed rule on reciprocal trade in the Eighty-seventh Congress was almost mandatory; an open rule on the labor reform bill in the Eighty-sixth Congress opened the bill to amendments resulting in one of Speaker Rayburn's most severe defeats, the adoption of the Landrum-Griffin substitute bill. Whichever faction controls the Rules Committee can often dominate legislative strategy. A key member of the majority eight summed up this point:

> Part of the first function is the parliamentary advantage. That was one of the most difficult things to get across in 1961. It's the timing and manner of debate. In a tight fight with two or three votes making the difference, that can be all important. It gives us a tremendous advantage—the ability to pop through in a hurry or to slow up a bill and wait until support can be mobilized.

This strategic advantage needs further elaboration.

Timing—Waiting for "Grass-Roots" Reaction

A third function of the Committee on Rules as perceived by its membership is one of timing—holding up or delaying the release of a bill from the committee in order to allow members and constituents to become familiarized with and take a stand on controversial measures. By allowing some time to elapse between a legislative committee chairman's request for a rule and the hearing, or, after public hearings, before voting out a special order, "grass-roots" sentiments, either for or against the bill, can make their presence felt. As Table I suggests, minority members were somewhat more inclined to emphasize this function than majority members. One senior Republican made this point:

> We have these hearings so that everyone can find out what the bill is all about. Information, you might say. Now you might not believe it, but I can show you bills—some of these bills might take eighteen months in the legislative committees—and they want to come to us and have us report the bill out in three days. It just can't be done. And that's the other thing the Rules Committee has to do—somebody has to do it—slow down or sit on some of these bills.

And a less senior Democratic member enlarged upon this theme:

Then, timeliness. There are many people who may disagree
with me on this, but I believe it is also important. Members
will take rather precipitous action, move too quickly, sometimes without adequate hearings. . . . If the bill has been
brought out in great haste, if there have been pressures on
the members, if it is felt that certain elements have not been
adequately explored, then that is where the Rules Committee
enters in. . . .

We must sometimes be deliberately slow in granting a rule.
By that time, there is an opportunity for reaction from the
country, from the newspapers. More knowledge is available.
We hear about it, and other congressmen get mail, too. That
is the obligation of timeliness; that is what I mean.

As the above quotations suggest, substantive control over legislation is at least implicit in the function of timing or holding up
the release of controversial legislation in the committee. The
fourth function—technical review—also contains policy implications.

Technical Review and Oversight

A further difference between the two major voting alignments
on the Rules Committee concerned technical review and oversight
of complex legislation. Four of the eight majority Democrats
stressed this function as against only two of the minority seven.
Committee members with law backgrounds, who might be expected
to pay more attention to bill drafting and technicalities, were only
slightly more predisposed than non-lawyers to elaborate upon this
function.[19] In part, these differences might reflect a somewhat
greater dependence by minority members on the skills displayed
in this area by Chairman Howard Smith of Virginia and ranking
Republican Clarence Brown of Ohio.

A Rules Committee hearing on the College Academic Facilities
Act, held January 24, 1962, and subsequent action on the floor of
the House on January 30, 1962, provide examples of how technical
review of seemingly unimportant details may suddenly loom large
in its policy implications. During the committee hearing, Chairman
Smith questioned Representative Edith Green of Oregon, the bill's
chief sponsor, about the language of the short title of the bill and
certain provisions in the section on loans for construction of aca-

---

[19] Nine of the fifteen members (60 per cent) on the Committee on Rules
have legal backgrounds as compared with 244 of 437 representatives (56 per
cent) in the Eighty-seventh Congress.

demic facilities.[20] Chairman Adam Clayton Powell and Representative Green assured the Committee on Rules that the short title would be amended and that the amount of loans for college facilities would be controlled through annual appropriations. Chairman Smith concluded his admonishments of members of the Education and Labor Committee with a polite suggestion: "Why invite controversy? I've known committees to reconsider bills. . . ."

During the floor debate on the rule one week later, ranking Republican Brown urged the Education and Labor Committee to amend the title so as to strike any references to student scholarships. Mrs. Green subsequently complied. Chairman Smith urged the Committee to eliminate any reference to Treasury loans. Chairman Powell acquiesced. At the end of two hours of debate, both Smith and Brown joined the great majority of their colleagues in supporting passage of H. R. 8900 by a vote of 319 to 79.[21] Late in the session, however, a House-Senate compromise bill, held up on the question of scholarship loans, was recommitted.[22]

More typically, the committee members' concern with technical review would not have such immediate policy implications. One member of the majority Democrats summed up this function:

We have an obligation to see that a bill is well written, that it is not bad legislative language, that the language is constitutional. By that I don't mean that we're the Supreme Court, although we may act that way sometimes. I question whether

---

[20] The title of H. R. 8900 contained a clause authorizing financial assistance for undergraduate study (scholarship loans), even though the language of the bill itself was limited to grants and loans for the construction of academic facilities. This clause was subsequently deleted on the floor of the House at the request of Smith and Brown. The section on loans could have been misconstrued as "back door spending," or the expenditure of public debt receipts by governmental agencies borrowing from the Treasury with congressional authorization but without annual appropriations.

[21] *Congressional Record*, 87th Cong., 2d sess. (January 30, 1962), pp. 1000–41, esp. pp. 1002, 1005, 1038, 1040–41.

[22] The 214–186 vote to recommit the College Facilities Act on September 20, 1962, is a good illustration of the southern Democratic–Republican coalition in action. Eighty-four Democrats, many of them southerners objecting to grants to private parochial colleges, and 130 Republicans, many of them objecting to student loan provisions, combined to recommit the bill. Previously, the bill had been prevented from going to conference until the House conferees assured Chairman Smith and the Committee on Rules that a separate vote would be taken on student scholarships. *Congressional Quarterly Weekly Report*, XX (September 21, 1962), pp. 1574, 1596–97.

we should be the Supreme Court—we are not. . . . On some
bills we waive points of order. All of that is important.

In addition to technical review and oversight, the Rules Committee
performs a fifth function—communicating information and voting
cues.

Information and Vote Cueing

Rules Committee members, more than any other group in the
House with the possible exception of the leadership, are uniquely
situated to observe and understand the workings of the House and
the strategy of legislative outcomes. Practically all important bills
must filter through the committee at least once, and generally twice,
if the bill goes to conference. In any given session, almost all of the
committee chairmen and ranking minority members will appear
a number of times before the committee. Other congressmen, particularly those who develop a subject-matter expertness, will also
appear before the committee to testify on particular provisions of
legislation. Through these public hearings and the seeking out of
the congressmen on each of the substantive committees who are
most aware of the strengths and weak points of legislation, an industrious Rules Committee member soon becomes one of the best-
informed members of the House. Furthermore, key members of the
committee will be in weekly, and frequently daily, contact with their
respective leadership. Hence, it is not surprising that Rules Committee members become storehouses of knowledge and that they
are sought out by other members, not only for information but also
for advice on voting. While only one-third of the members specifically discussed this aspect of their work, this influence is probably
oftentimes as important as other voting cues, such as state delegation and whip pressures.[23] There did not seem to be any appreciable

---

[23] As the work of Julius Turner, V. O. Key, Jr., Duncan MacRae, Jr., and
David Truman demonstrate, party affiliation remains the most powerful explanatory factor in the analysis of roll call voting. Turner, *Party and Constituency: Pressures on Congress* (Baltimore: The Johns Hopkins Press, 1951); Key,
Parties, Politics and Pressure Groups (4th ed.; New York: Crowell, 1958),
pp. 727–41; MacRae, *Dimensions of Congressional Voting* (Berkeley: University of California Press, 1958); and Truman, *The Congressional Party* (New
York: Wiley, 1959). Members of the Rules Committee, as spokesmen for the
leadership, often help to eliminate uncertainty or lack of information about
bills on which the leadership's stance is unclear. Furthermore, Judge Smith's
pronouncements on legislation have a considerable influence on a substantial
bloc of southern conservatives. Much more research needs to be undertaken

difference among majority or minority members in the degree to which they emphasized this function. One extended response from one of the newly added Republican members may illustrate this function of communication of information and vote cueing:

> A second thing, having a statement on the rule for the convenience of members who haven't read the bill. I just came from a meeting where they were asking me about the trade bill. I've read it. I study them all. When you give the rule on the floor, you take time to explain what is in the bill. Lots of members listen to the Rules presentation and decide how to react. We try to tell the fellows what is in the bill, a cursory review of the bill. . . .
>
> Members come to us and ask, "What's in the bill?" We don't know all the answers, but we do know the chairmen and the ranking members, what the leadership is going to do this week, and the next. I'll be going to a meeting at five o'clock, and there will be . . . fellows there. The first thing they will ask me will be, "What's going to happen next week?" . . .
>
> Now you take the trade bill, a lot of members will ask me about that.

As this quotation intimates, the debate on the rule is seldom concerned with the merits of the rule per se, but is almost immediately concerned with the substantive merits of the bill itself. One final function remains to be developed.

Protection of Members—The "Heat Shield" or Buffer Function

A final function elaborated upon by one-third of the members was protecting other members from external pressures—from constituents, from organized interest groups, and, in the case of Democratic members, from the White House and the executive branch. Again, as Table I suggests, minority members were somewhat more inclined to stress this function than were members of the majority eight. One Republican member illustrated this theme with an example of the way in which congressmen sometimes use the Rules Committee as a "whipping boy":

> There are some bills that just shouldn't get to the floor, and the members know it. I had this congressman come to me

focusing on alternative cue mechanisms to party, such as state delegations, committee influence, and personal influence; but see, for example, Truman, *The Congressional Party*, esp. chap. vii; Alan Fiellin, "The Functions of Informal Groups, in Legislative Institutions," *Journal of Politics*, XXIV (February, 1962), 72–91. Reprinted as Chapter III of the present volume.

and say, "You've got to keep that bill from coming on to the floor. I've got a primary coming up, and its going to be close, and which ever way I vote on that bill, I'm dead." So I told him that I would do him a favor, and I sat on the bill, and what happened? A week later, I get this letter from one of his constituents, a lady, and she has written to all of the members of the Rules Committee. She says, "Why haven't you let such and such a bill out of your committee? I know that you're holding it up because I have the proof right here," and she encloses a letter from her congressman, this fellow that I'm taking the pressure off, saying that he favors her bill and is most sympathetic to it, but he can't get the Rules Committee to let the bill out on the floor so he can vote on it.

So there you are. A lot of congressmen want us to keep bills from coming to the floor. We take the pressure off them. That's why a member should come from a district where he doesn't have to worry about being re-elected or which way the wind is blowing on every bill that comes up.

A veteran Democratic member made the same point and at the same time illustrated the substantive control exercised by committee members:

Of course, there are some bills which shouldn't go to the floor. There are some bills which are just too controversial. The education bill was one of them. After you have been around here as long as I have, you get a feel or sense about a bill and whether or not it should go to the floor. But you have to use judgment, and you have to be independent. There may be some bills that should go to the floor even if you don't believe in them yourself. You have to be fair. But there are some bills which shouldn't go to the floor.

Now, you might say that a congressman ought to be allowed to stand up and be counted, that he ought to be able to stand the gaff. If we all had to stand the gaff, there wouldn't be too many of us who would be around after one term.

But which bills are "just too controversial" and which bills should go to the floor following clearance from legislative committees and at the request of the leadership? Here, the members differ. The following section elaborates on some of these differences by outlining a number of important consequences of enlargement. But first, the theme of this section will be briefly recapitulated.

Six functions perceived as important by the fifteen members of the Committee on Rules have been sketched. They range from a theoretically-neutral regulation of debate to a highly policy-charged substantive control over legislation. Between these extremes, members may be more or less involved in policy formation through functions such as technical review and oversight, the communication of information and voting cues, the protection of congressmen from outside pressures by preventing bills from reaching the floor, and the timing or holding up of bills while "grass-roots" support is activated. In the final analysis, all of these functions have important policy implications. Whoever controls the Committee on Rules—and it is inevitably a shifting and subtle control as long as the committee is composed of both Democrats and Republicans—will dominate policy formation in the House of Representatives.

II. CONSEQUENCES OF ENLARGEMENT

What were the consequences of increasing the size of the House Committee on Rules from twelve to fifteen members? By adding two pro-administration Democrats—Representatives Carl Elliott of Alabama and B. F. Sisk of California—and only one Republican, Speaker Rayburn hoped to convert what had at times been an unresponsive six-to-six stalemate to an eight-to-seven majority which would vote out or hold up bills at the leadership's request. Four kinds of evidence can be assembled to support the conclusion that, on balance, the Speaker's and the administration's objectives were achieved.

First, the perceptions of the fifteen members will be examined as to whose interests the committee's substantive control should serve. Second, a brief overview of the Kennedy Administration's successes and failures during the Eighty-seventh Congress will be attempted. Third, the Rules Committee members' own evaluations of the shift in control will be marshalled. Finally, the fourth piece of evidence—that the President and the majority leadership believed it necessary to convert the temporary enlargement to a permanent one—will be evaluated in the third section of this paper.

The importance of this shift in committee control should not obscure four by-products of the enlargement, consequences which for the most part were unanticipated. Since these by-products were developed at some length in a previous paper, they will only be quickly reviewed and slightly modified here.[24] By increasing the

---

[24] Robert L. Peabody, "The Committee on Rules and the House Leadership: Some Consequences of Enlargement," in James A. Robinson, ed., *Political Parties* (New York: Atherton Press, 1963).

size of the committee from twelve to fifteen members, the interest base of the committee became that much more diversified. Where the broader base had its most readily apparent consequence was with regard to a middle level of legislation, bills which were primarily regional in scope and impact. A second result, closely related to the first, was the broadening of geographical representation on the committee. The Committee on Rules was made more representative of the country in general, and of the Far West in particular, with the addition in 1961 of two California representatives, Democrat B. F. Sisk and Republican H. Allen Smith. A third consequence was that while Republicans continue to occupy one-third of the committee seats, the conversion reduced the Republican minority's effectiveness within the committee.[25] Under the present alignment, a Republican vote becomes decisive only if one of the eight moderate-to-liberal Democratic members decides to vote contrary to the majority leadership's wishes. Finally, the appointment of Elliott and Sisk, coupled with a change in the speakership, brought about not so much a "widely shared" as a diffused leadership among the majority eight.[26]

As has already been suggested, debate over whether a twelve- or a fifteen-member committee, most generally, "allows the House to work its will" is largely rhetorical. The important question is not *how many* bills or resolutions are released, blocked, or delayed in committee. Any size Committee on Rules would, of necessity, exercise substantive control. The more important question is *which* bills and resolutions are controlled. In other words, the question

---

[25] Representative Clarence Brown of Ohio made this point in his defense of a twelve-member committee during the 1963 debate: "As the ranking minority member of the Rules Committee I am just a bit provoked, discouraged and disheartened by statements to the effect that legislation will be emasculated in our committee unless the committee is packed by the addition of three new members which, of course, in turn would reduce the effectiveness of the minority Members of the House, and of the committee itself." *Congressional Record*, 88th Cong., 1st sess. (January 9, 1963), p. 17.

[26] In the "consequences" paper mentioned above, the extent of "shared leadership" among the majority eight was probably overstated. It is perhaps more accurate to say that several of the more junior members assumed portions of a leadership role previously exercised almost exclusively by Representative Bolling of Missouri. Except for a temporary hiatus in January, 1962, when McCormack first assumed the speakership, Bolling continued to act as the Speaker's principal strategist on the Committee on Rules, but without the close personal ties that characterized his relationship with the late Speaker Rayburn. See Nelson W. Polsby, "Choosing a Majority Leader, 1962," Chapter IX of the present volume, for an elaboration of this relationship.

pertains to whose interests are being served by the exercise of the admittedly broad powers of the Committee on Rules.

The Orientation of Substantive Control

It seems clear from the views of the fifteen members of the Committee on Rules that there are not just two major alternatives to this question. As Table II suggests, the dominant difference of opinion dividing the committee pertains to whether the committee should operate as an instrument of the party leadership or as a spokesman for the majority of the House. At least two additional interests might be, and frequently are, in conflict with these major alternatives. The committee may also operate so as to further the interests of the constituents of specific districts or regions, or it may operate independently of *both* the leadership and the members of the House in "the best interests of the country." Indeed, while nine of the fifteen members, including seven of the eight majority Democrats, emphasize their allegiance to their party leadership, almost as many members, including some of these same majority members, *also* stress the need for independent judgment. In contrast, none of the majority eight, but four of the minority seven, places primary emphasis on representing the will of the House. And of course, with regard to all of these interests—majority leadership, majority of the House, particular constituents or mem-

TABLE II

Perceptions of Rules Committee Members as to Whose Interests Should Be Served by Substantive Control of the Committee, Eighty-seventh Congress

Interest	Number of Members Perceiving*		
	Total Committee on Rules N = 15	Pro-Admin-istration† Majority N = 8	Anti-Admin-istration‡ Minority N = 7
The party leadership (majority of the majority)	9	7	2
Consensus of the House (bipartisan majority)	4	0	4
Constituents of particular districts, or the benefits of particular members	4	2	2
Independent judgment as to the best interests of the country	8	4	4

* The number of responses total more than fifteen since some members of the Committee on Rules elaborated on more than one interest.
† For the composition of the pro-administration majority, see footnote †, Table I.
‡ For the composition of the anti-administration minority, see footnote ‡, Table I.

bers, and/or the needs of the country—it is the individual member who interprets and defines the interests.

Selected excerpts from the interviews, some of which suggest more than one allegiance in a single response, may serve to illustrate these four main alternatives.

A number of members stressed the importance of party or their loyalty to the party leadership:

> It's a policy committee for the majority. Formerly it was eight to four, and now it's ten to five. If the Republicans win, the next committee would be ten Republicans and five Democrats. The committee interprets policy and the program of the party in power. But nothing in a straitjacket—you can't always tell what will happen. . . .
>
> * * *
>
> The whole function is as an arm of the leadership, an arm of the majority of the majority, which is the elected leadership of the House.
>
> * * *
>
> I'm a party man. I like to work through a party. Not all of the members of Congress have that orientation. But I believe that is the strength of our political system. The day we lose the Democratic party or the Republican party, either of them, we're in real trouble. My predilection is to go along as much as I can.

If these interviews were being conducted during a Republican-controlled Congress, such as the Eightieth or the Eighty-third, probably similar responses would be forthcoming from Republican *majority* members. As it were, most of the Republicans adopted an opposing stance—that the Rules Committee should reflect the consensus of the House:

> The committee speaks for the House regardless of size.
>
> * * *
>
> The House can always work its will. They tried Calender Wednesday on the education bills, and the House voted that down. They don't want to vote on controversial issues, and that's where we come in. "Let it simmer and you get a better soup."

And Chairman Smith emphasized the norm of House majority rule in a television appearance before the 1961 fight:

> Now, remember this, and everybody ought to be willing to recognize it—that if there's one rule in the House of Repre-

sentatives that is inviolate, and that is majority rule; and if the majority of the House wants to debate a rule, there are ways provided in the rules by which they can do it; and neither the Rules Committee nor the leadership or anybody else can stop them, the majority of the House, from working their will on legislation.[27]

The Committee on Rules also serves the interests of particular members, their constituents, or even, on occasion, a regional point of view. Attention has already been directed to the "heat shield" or buffer function performed by the committee. In addition, all representatives, on occasion, feel a conflict between constituency pressures and party demands, or between what they perceive to be their constituencies' interests and the best interests of the country.[28] Two responses from majority members illustrate these conflicts:

> I'm a party man. . . . My predilection is to go along as much as I can. I draw the line where the interests of those I serve, the local interests, are deeply involved. I have a strong feeling about that. It's seldom that I would vote different from a known variance of a great majority of the wishes of my constituents. Of course, that's allowing for an exchange of views, imagination—some leadership. I know more on some issues than the people, and then it's my responsibility to educate. But the dominant reason a man comes to Congress is to represent the views of his people.

* * *

> You can't be too parochial or too provincial. That's a charge that every member may have to face—that he's becoming too much of a statesman. You can't get too unparochial

---

[27] Transcript of "The Keeper of the Rules: Congressman Smith and the New Frontier," *CBS Reports*, January 19, 1961 (Multilithed, 1961), p. 17. Chairman Smith was referring to alternate methods of bringing bills to the floor such as suspension of the rules, Calendar Wednesday proceedings, and the use of the discharge petition. For divergent views as to the merits of these alternative methods, see the exchange between Representatives Bolling and Brown in the transcript of this same program, pp. 29–30. See also, Majority Leader Albert's rebuttal during the 1963 debate in *Congressional Record*, January 9, 1963, p. 13.

[28] For elaboration on these dilemmas of representation in the House, see Lewis A. Dexter, "The Representative and His District," *Human Organization*, XVI (1947), 2–13. Reprinted as Chapter I of this volume; Charles O. Jones, "The Agriculture Committee and the Problem of Representation," *American Political Science Review*, LV (June, 1961), 358–67. Reprinted as Chapter V of this volume; and Polsby, "Choosing a Majority Leader, 1962," Chapter IX of this volume. For a discussion of similar problems of representation in state legislatures, see John C. Wahlke *et al., The Legislative System* (New York: Wiley, 1962), chaps. xi–xv.

here. But, practically all legislation we face here affects the whole nation.

And Chairman Smith, in his attempt to retain the support of his southern colleagues during the debate on the 1963 enlargement, restated a theme which extends back to Calhoun's doctrine of the concurrent majority:

> Mr. Speaker, I would like to say a few plain words to some folks who come from my part of the country. . . .
> I am a conservative Democrat, I am a southern Democrat, and I believe my country's welfare is more important than any political party and I further believe that this matter of packing the Rules Committee affects more closely our area of the country than anywhere else. . . .
> I hope none of my southern friends are going to be complaining around here when certain measures come up that are going to come up, and come up quite promptly, if the Committee on Rules is packed again. And, I hope that when they go to vote on this resolution that they will remember that there are some things involved in this that will greatly and adversely affect their States; not just how many people should be on the Committee on Rules or who shall govern the Committee on Rules.[29]

Finally, at least eight of the members interviewed firmly believe in the need to exercise independent judgment on legislation, as most of them would put it, for the good of the country. When asked, "What characteristics make for an effective member of the House Rules Committee?", these members were apt to reply as follows:

> Calling your shots as you see them, rather than just going along.
>
> * * *
>
> Some say you should do what ever the leadership wants. That's not what I believe. Rayburn put me on because he thought my judgment was good. . . . Exercise your judgment and your own vote, and be there.
>
> * * *
>
> It all depends on your point of view. From the leadership point of view, a man who asks no questions, but votes and clears bills like they want.
> The other one is the opposite point of view, that a member feels he has a responsibility similar to that of a legislative

---

[29] *Congressional Record,* 88th Cong., 1st sess. (January 9, 1963), p. 17.

committee—what's in the best interests of the country, not the party.

Given these diverse and shifting orientations held by the fifteen members of the Committee on Rules, the mixed record of the committee in the Eighty-seventh Congress is hardly surprising.

The Record of the Committee on Rules in the Eighty-seventh Congress

The major consequence of increasing the size of the House Committee on Rules from twelve to fifteen members in 1961 has already been suggested. Until the last few weeks of the second session, when Chairman Smith once again assumed control, both the late Speaker, Sam Rayburn, and the new Speaker, John W. McCormack, had been able to depend on a slender, if uneasy, working majority of eight, with but one exception each.[30] Fourth-ranking Democrat, James Delaney of New York, representing a strong Catholic district, broke with the administration over the issue of federal aid to parochial schools in July, 1961.[31] Two southern Democratic Congressmen, Carl Elliott of Alabama and James Trimble of Arkansas, temporarily joined with the minority seven to table Kennedy's Department of Urban Affairs bill in January, 1962.[32] At the end of the Eighty-seventh Congress, confronted with the traditional logjam of bills, the majority leadership was again forced to reckon with the enhanced powers and strong bargaining position of Chairman Smith.[33] While the majority leadership got some bills out, the final result was that the Committee on Rules took no action on at least twenty significant bills, including the youth employment bill,

---

[30] Rayburn, his health failing, left Washington for Bonham, Texas, in August, 1961, and Majority Leader McCormack became Speaker *pro tempore*. Following Rayburn's death on November 16, 1961, McCormack was elected Speaker at the opening of the second session of the Eighty-seventh Congress, January 10, 1962.

[31] Hugh Douglas Price, "Race, Religion, and the Rules Committee: The Kennedy Aid-to-Education Bills," in Alan F. Westin, ed., *The Uses of Power* (New York: Harcourt, Brace & World, 1962), pp. 1–71, esp. p. 64.

[32] *Congressional Quarterly Weekly Review*, XX (January 26, 1962), 99.

[33] As Chairman, Smith determines the committee agenda, when the committee shall meet, who will testify, and in what order. Toward the end of a session, these powers for expedition or delay of bills can become crucial. The leadership must either assign priorities and negotiate with Smith or use its votes to take the committee away from its chairman, an alternative which a new leadership could use only as a last resort.

the mass transit program, and a number of education and labor bills.[34]

From the subsequent legislative history of four of these measures—federal aid to schools, creation of a Department of Urban Affairs, the youth employment bill, and federal aid for mass transit—a persuasive case can be made that, in these instances, the Committee on Rules was indeed reflecting the will of the majority. The House refused to consider a hastily assembled compromise school aid bill under Calendar Wednesday proceedings on August 30, 1961, by a vote of 170 to 242. The President's urban affairs reorganization plan, submitted after his bill was tabled in the Rules Committee, was decisively defeated on February 21, 1962, by a vote of 264 to 150. Attempts to bypass the Committee on Rules on the youth employment and mass transit bills under Calendar Wednesday proceedings on September 19, 1962, proved abortive.[35]

Yet these and other administration defeats should not obscure the basic consequence of enlargement: when the eight votes were needed, they could almost always be counted upon. As has already been suggested, control of the committee allowed the majority leadership to take bills to the floor under more favorable strategic conditions. Perhaps the most important single piece of evidence was the eight-to-seven vote for a closed rule on the President's major legislative accomplishment in the Eighty-seventh Congress—the Trade Expansion Act of 1962.[36] Furthermore, control of the committee was particularly vital during the first session of Congress when such economic measures as the distressed areas bill and minimum wage legislation were passed. A Democratic member of the minority seven late in the summer of 1961 summed up the decisiveness of this shift:

> It was strictly a matter of control—whether it should be twelve men or the Speaker—that's it. He packed the Committee, and that's working for him. As far as the Rayburn eight votes—they go along.

---

[34] In his comprehensive survey, Walter Kravitz estimates that the Committee on Rules failed to grant rules to thirty-four significant measures in the Eighty-seventh Congress, including twenty-eight bills that were technically still pending at adjournment. "The House Committee on Rules' Influence on Legislation in the 87th Congress" *op. cit.*, p. 3.

[35] *Congressional Quarterly Almanac*, XVII (1961), 214, 230–34; *Congressional Quarterly Weekly Report*, XX (February 23, 1962), 275–77, 310–11; XX (September 21, 1962), 1562.

[36] *Congressional Quarterly Weekly Report*, XX (June 29, 1962), 1083–84, 1118–19.

And even as late as early summer of 1962, a member of the majority could still assess the consequences of enlargement as follows:

> The answer is to be found in the votes of the Rules Committee, the record of this Congress. Important bills, such as the trade bill and the farm bill have been voted out of the Rules Committee by an eight-to-seven vote. The spirit of the situation has been such that the new frontier would have absolutely fallen on its face were it not for the enlargement of the Committee on Rules. Conservative groups had gained control of this key committee. This committee was able to block legislation. If it had continued as it had before, there would have been no legislative accomplishments for the past year and one-half. Oh, there would have been a few titles passed, but they would have been empty of content. A few rewrites of old bills, but that would have been all the bills that would have been passed.
>
> I would say that enlargement of the Committee on Rules was the most significant happening in my time in Congress, and that has been . . . years.

From interviews conducted during the summers of 1961 and 1962, it seems clear that an overwhelming majority of the fifteen members believed that enlargement had had a considerable impact. As would be expected, members of the majority eight tended to emphasize the importance; members of the minority, in contrast, generally played down the consequences. But even the minority members, including the southern conservatives, would admit that "they have a working majority" or "they successfully packed the committee" or "Rayburn has his way." By the middle of the summer of 1962, the majority members who were interviewed were less sanguine, and some downgrading of consequences appears to have taken place. Toward the close of the Eighty-seventh Congress, at least four members felt that enlargement probably had not made much difference. As one Republican summed up these views when asked what, if any, had been the result:

> Virtually none. All along it has reflected what the House wants, and it's not so different now. Oh, there is a little more positive trend to favor the Democratic leadership. But on most issues, the committee works the will of the House, regardless of the leadership . . . and it continues to work that will.

The major consequence—a shift in control—and four by-products of the enlargement of the Committee on Rules during the Eighty-seventh Congress have been outlined. Until the final weeks of the second session, on all but two of its major bills coming out of legislative committees, the Kennedy administration and Speakers Rayburn and McCormack were in control. They were able to count on eight of the ten Democratic members to grant the kinds of rules which would give bills a strategic advantage on the floor. For most of the Eighty-seventh Congress, at least, the fundamental question which had governed the relationship between the Committee on Rules and the formal elective leadership since 1910 had been resolved. While the committee continued to exercise considerable independence, in the main it operated as the instrument of the majority leadership rather than as an agent of a bipartisan majority.

One final piece of evidence as to the importance of committee enlargement remains to be assessed—President Kennedy's request for and Speaker McCormack's strong support of a continuing fifteen-member Committee on Rules. These events culminated in permanent enlargement on the opening day of the Eighty-eighth Congress in 1963.

III. THE 1961 AND 1963 ENLARGEMENT VOTES

In 1961, Speaker Sam Rayburn won what he called "the worst fight of my life"—a narrow 217 to 212 roll-call vote on the resolution temporarily increasing the size of the Committee on Rules from twelve to fifteen members.[37] Two years later, at the opening of the Eighty-eighth Congress, his successor, Speaker John McCormack of Massachusetts had a comparatively easy time winning a floor fight which permanently enlarged the committee. In 1961, Speaker Rayburn of Texas had only been able to attract a little over one-third of his southern colleagues to support enlargement. On the surface, McCormack's odds appeared hardly better.[38] He

---

[37] D. B. Hardeman, "Rayburn and the Committee on Rules" (Unpublished manuscript, Washington, D.C., 1962), p. 1. Close observers—such as Hardeman, John Holton of Speaker Rayburn's staff, and Lewis Deschler, parliamentarian—seem to concur in the judgment that Rayburn adopted the standard format for increasing the size of a committee for a single Congress, both as a line of least resistance and to give the enlarged committee a pragmatic test. For a somewhat different interpretation from Chairman Smith, see Laurence Stern, "Rayburn Curb on Rules Unit Increase Cited," *Washington Post,* December 24, 1962, p. A 2.

[38] According to a *Congressional Quarterly* analysis published three days after the November 6, 1962, election: "The President has lost 33 members of the 87th Congress who backed him on enlarging the Rules Committee for the

began with five fewer Democratic party members, 258 as compared to 263 in 1961. After only one year in the speakership, McCormack had built up neither the backlog of personal obligations nor the public prestige that Rayburn had amassed as Speaker during sixteen of the previous twenty years, even though McCormack had spent an equally impressive number of years as Majority Leader. Yet, Speaker McCormack—ably assisted by Majority Leader Carl Albert of Oklahoma, Majority Whip Hale Boggs of Louisiana, and the White House liaison group—won handily in 1963 by a vote of 235 to 196.[39]

What made the difference? What can these two votes—the first a narrow five-vote victory, the second, a comfortable thirty-nine-vote margin—tell us about political strategy, party alignments, and incremental change in the House of Representatives? Only tentative and preliminary answers to these questions will be attempted here.

Several generalizations emerge from party and regional comparisons summarized in Table III. The vote in 1963 was primarily a party-line vote, just as in 1961. Eighty-one per cent of the Democrats opposed 84 per cent of the Republicans in 1963; in 1961, 75 per cent of the Democrats opposed 87 per cent of the Republicans. As in 1961, the representatives who broke ranks in 1963 were primarily conservative southern Democrats and liberal northeastern Republicans.[40] While Rayburn received only thirty-six supporting votes from his southern colleagues in 1961, the majority leadership was able to attract fifty votes, or 54 per cent of southern Democrats, to its cause in 1963. Furthermore, the support for enlargement increased from twenty-two to twenty-eight votes among Republicans.

A preliminary analysis of the two groups which broke party

---

duration of Congress. He gains 27 known supporters for his program in the new Congress. This is a net loss of six. . . . Obviously this will be touch and go if the attempt is again made in 1963." XX (November 9, 1962), 2133.

[39] For a comparison of the 1961 and 1963 votes enlarging the House Committee on Rules, see *Congressional Quarterly Weekly Report,* XXI (January 11, 1963), 2–4, 42–43.

[40] More precisely, forty-four of the forty-eight Democrats who opposed enlargement in 1963 represented districts in states of the old Confederacy. Of the twenty-eight Republicans who voted for Rules Committee enlargement in 1963, twenty-two came from New England or Atlantic seaboard states. Four freshmen Republicans voted for enlargement. Three-fourths of the remaining twenty-four Republicans had Kennedy support scores of 57 per cent or higher in 1962, including all ten of the Republicans with the highest Kennedy support scores on sixty Kennedy-issue roll-call votes in that year. *Congressional Quarterly Weekly Report,* XX (October 26, 1962), 2035–39, esp. 2037.

ranks in both 1961 and 1963—the conservative southern Democrats and the (primarily) northeastern liberal Republicans—reveals some interesting comparisons and contrasts. The Democratic leadership held its own or improved its position in every one of the eleven states of the old Confederacy.[41] The leaders picked up the bulk of their new support in three state delegations, North Carolina, Florida, and, above all, Georgia. In 1961, only two Georgians, Representatives Vinson and Pilcher, supported enlargement; in 1963, all ten Georgian members voted with the leadership for reasons elaborated below. The twenty-eight Republicans who voted for enlargement in 1963 included sixteen members who also voted affirmatively in 1961, two Republicans who did not vote in 1961, six members who reversed their position, and four freshmen representatives (three from New York and one from Pennsylvania). Only two Republicans who supported the rules change in 1961—Curtis of Missouri and Fulton of Pennsylvania—reversed their votes in 1963.

Further analysis of the 1963 vote (unlike the 1961 vote), using data concerning the characteristics of the congressmen and the constituencies they represent, would have diminishing returns. The generalizations developed by Milton C. Cummings and this author in an earlier paper (see Chapter VII), still seem to hold, and what discrepancies are revealed can largely be explained by other causes. Seven interrelated factors that seem to have made the difference between these two roll-call votes may be singled out for brief elaboration.[42]

---

[41] The percentage of southern Democratic House delegations voting in favor of enlargement were (with the 1961 percentage in parentheses): Georgia, 100 per cent (20 per cent); Arkansas, 75 per cent (67 per cent); Texas, 67 per cent (70 per cent); Louisiana, 63 per cent (63 per cent); Tennessee, 60 per cent (57 per cent); Florida, 50 per cent (14 per cent); Alabama, 50 per cent (44 per cent); North Carolina, 44 per cent (9 per cent); South Carolina, 17 per cent (0 per cent); Virginia, 12 per cent (12 per cent); and Mississippi, 0 per cent (0 per cent). All eleven southern Republican congressmen voted against enlargement in 1963, an increase of four votes over 1961.

[42] Other observers, and certainly the participants themselves, might stress different or additional factors than those developed here. My conclusions are based on observation of the two floor debates, examination of newspaper accounts and the *Congressional Record,* and informal interviews with ten congressmen and key staff members during and immediately following the January, 1963, enlargement controversy. I am also indebted to Donald Tacheron and the 1962–63 American Political Science Association congressional fellows for an invaluable evening session early in February, 1963, during which time many of these impressions were formed, modified, or confirmed.

TABLE III

The 1961 and 1963 Votes to Enlarge the House Committee on Rules, by Party and Region

	1961 Democrats			1963 Democrats		
REGION	Number of Votes Against	Number of Votes For	Per Cent for En-largement	Number of Votes Against	Number of Votes For	Per Cent for En-largement
Northern and western..	0	129	100	1	132	99
Border states*	2	30	94	3	25	89
Southern states†	62	36	37	44	50	54
Total Democrat	64	195	75	48	207	81
	Republicans			Republicans		
Northern and western..	137	20	13	130	27	17
Border states*	4	2	33	7	1	13
Southern states†	7	0	0	11	0	0
Total Republican	148	22	13	148	28	16
Total vote‡	212	217		196	235	

* The border states are Kentucky, Maryland, Missouri, Oklahoma, and West Virginia.
† States classified as southern are the eleven states of the former Confederacy: Alabama, Arkansas, Florida, Georgia, Louisiana, Mississippi, North Carolina, South Carolina, Tennessee, Texas, and Virginia.
‡ These totals do not include paired votes.

The House Adapts to Incremental Change

In the first two sections of this paper, two central if somewhat contradictory themes were developed: (1) that regardless of committee size, the House Committee on Rules continued to perform certain basic functions; and (2) that there was a major shift in control from a bipartisan coalition to an eight-member majority generally responsive to the Democratic leadership. Yet the committee also continued to demonstrate its independence on notable occasions, such as the urban affairs and federal aid-to-education bills. In general, the Committee on Rules continued to carry out its indispensable functions, such as the regulation of debate and the communication of information. As one member of the majority leadership put it: "If the Committee on Rules did not exist, we'd have to create something like it." Finally, Howard W. Smith was able to utilize his still very sizable discretion as chairman and his almost universally admired skills as a parliamentary strategist to protect and further many of the interests held by himself and a substantial bloc of southern conservatives. At times this Smith-led bloc wielded the balance of power in the House. And as the congressional session, particularly the second session, came to a close,

Smith's formal authority and informal influence were considerably enhanced. In sum, it seems plausible that, on one ground or another, a substantial majority of the House could adapt to a fifteen-member Committee on Rules. Even Minority Leader Halleck could observe during the 1963 debate, ". . . [I]t did not make much difference that the membership of the Rules Committee was increased from 12 to 15."[43]

A second, and in my opinion, the decisive factor, was that the Eighty-eighth Congress was not very different in its composition from the Eighty-seventh Congress. In contrast to the traditional pattern of midterm losses, the 1962 congressional elections resulted in a standoff. While sixty-seven new members were elected, only twenty seats shifted from the control of one party to the other.[44] Observers were in general agreement that while the Democratic party lost four seats, the Kennedy administration may have gained slightly in liberal support for its programs.[45] A twenty-seat Republican gain would probably have brought about a return to a twelve-member committee, just as a twenty-eight-seat Republican gain in 1950 resulted in the abandonment of the twenty-one-day rule.[46]

President Kennedy's endorsement of a fifteen-member committee on a three-network, nation-wide television "Conversation with the President" in mid-December was a third important factor.

> I hope the Rules Committee is kept to its present number, because we can't function if it isn't. We might as well—we're through if we lose—if they try to change the rules. Nothing controversial, in that case, would come to the floor of Congress. . . .
> The whole program, in my opinion, would be emasculated.[47]

The President's strong rhetoric, his transfer of the onus of change to the opposition, or even an admiration for the skillful use of

---

[43] *Congressional Record,* January 9, 1963, p. 13.

[44] Republicans picked up eleven seats previously held by Democrats, and the Democrats picked up nine seats previously held by the GOP.

[45] See, for example, John D. Morris, "President May Gain Four Votes in House Despite Party Loss," *New York Times,* November 12, 1962, p. 1; " 'Frontier' May Have Gained in House But Key Issues in Doubt," *Congressional Quarterly Weekly Report,* XX (November 9, 1962), 2133–37.

[46] *Congressional Record,* XCV, 10–11; XCVII, 9–19.

[47] Transcript of "A Conversation with the President," December 17, 1962 (Washington, D.C.: CBS Television, 1962), p. 3.

his "powers to persuade," should not lead us astray.[48] The President was committing the prestige of his office and his high personal popularity which followed the Cuban crisis to a cause that had been substantially won in the November elections.

A fourth factor enhancing the majority leadership's chances in 1963 was the performance and personal popularity of the two Democratic additions to the committee—Carl Elliott of Alabama and B. F. Sisk of California. Both had forfeited substantial seniority on other committees in assuming positions on the Rules Committee at Rayburn's personal request. Both had performed creditably in committee and on the floor. Elliott, the Alabamian, and Sisk, a transplanted Texan, were both personally popular in the House and among southerners. Finally, as the largest Democratic delegation in the House, the twenty-four-member California Democratic delegation could make a strong case for representation on the powerful Rules Committee.

A fifth factor was a lack of enthusiasm, if not outright opposition, among a substantial number of Republican congressmen as to the wisdom of opposing enlargement of the Rules Committee in what appeared to be another losing cause. Unlike 1961, Charles Halleck, the Minority Leader, stayed out of Washington and remained uncommitted until two days before the vote. While a number of older Republicans opposed "packing" the Rules Committee as a matter of principle, others expressed the view that the whole issue was a "phony," or fears that the G.O.P. would be labeled "obstructionist."[49] Whatever plans the Republican leadership may have had to unite with conservative southern Democrats were cast into disarray by a "revolt" within Republican ranks the day before the Eighty-eighth Congress opened. A group of middle-level "Young Turks," led by Charles Goodell of New York and Robert Griffin

---

[48] Richard E. Neustadt, *Presidential Power* (New York: Wiley, 1960), esp. chap. iii. The Democratic leadership could make the persuasive argument that it was maintaining the *status quo* in 1963, although technically the Committee on Rules would revert to twelve members (see note 2, *supra*).

[49] Representative Thomas B. Curtis of Missouri, a leader among the group of twenty-two Republicans who broke party ranks in 1961, voted against enlargement in 1963, terming the whole issue a "phony." Curtis believed the Republicans should vote "present" on the issue. For development of this strategy, see Roscoe Drummond's column in the *Washington Post*, December 31, 1962, p. A 9. Fears that the Republican party would again be labeled an "obstructionist party" if Republicans voted with southern Democrats were frequently voiced among liberal Republicans in 1963 as in 1961.

of Michigan, successfully challenged their more senior party leaders. The afternoon before the Rules' vote the Republican Conference voted eighty-six to seventy-eight to replace its chairman, Charles Hoeven of Iowa, with aggressive forty-nine-year-old Gerald Ford of Michigan.[50] Conference debate over just what strategy the Republicans should adopt as far as the Rules Committee was concerned was settled by adoption of three "fair-play" amendments sponsored by Representative Melvin Laird of Wisconsin. The first of these amendments called for a fifteen-member committee, but a different ratio of nine Democrats to six Republicans, instead of ten and five.

The Republican "revolt" took the Republican leadership by surprise. It also made the Democratic leadership uneasy, perhaps unnecessarily so, since the "fair-play" amendments antagonized most of the southern Democrats who firmly believed in the principle of a twelve-member committee. As a consequence, the vote on the previous question cutting off debate after one hour became the key vote. Halleck made one last effort to form a combination which would defeat this vote, thus opening up Majority Leader Albert's motion to amendment.[51] Only 7 southern Democrats, 5 of them from Mississippi, voted "no" along with 176 Republicans. Fearing even less palatable changes should the majority leader's motion be open to amendment, the vast majority of southern conservatives joined Chairman Smith in support of the Democratic leadership on this question. The subsequent vote adopting the rules of the previous Congress, including an amendment enlarging the Committee on Rules, was anticlimactic.

A sixth factor—a tacit understanding between the Dean of the House, Carl Vinson of Georgia, and Speaker McCormack, that if the Georgia delegation supported Rules Committee enlargement, Speaker McCormack would back Phillip Landrum of Georgia for one of two vacancies on Ways and Means—was widely publicized if never completely documented.[52] Despite disavowals of any "deals,"

---

[50] Congressman Charles Goodell's newsletter dated January 23, 1963, contains a summary of strategy followed by the younger Republicans in their "revolt" against the more senior members. See also, *Congressional Quarterly Weekly Report*, XXI (February 8, 1963), 149–56.

[51] *Congressional Record*, 88th Cong., 1st sess. (January 9, 1963), p. 20.

[52] While rumors circulated about an alleged "agreement" between Vinson and McCormack even before Christmas, the tip-off on the swing in the Georgia delegation came in a letter from Phillip Landrum to Howard W. Smith announcing that he could not endorse a return to a twelve-member committee. Frank Eleazer, "Kennedy Rules Victory Seen by Vinson, Landrum," *Washington Post*, December 30, 1962, p. 1; Peter J. Kumpa, "Kennedy May Win

all ten members of the Georgia delegation supported the Speaker in 1963. Undoubtedly, other factors also entered in, including at least one member's dissatisfaction with Chairman Smith, and a changing political climate in Georgia state politics.[53] Voting by secret ballot on January 14, 1963, the Democratic caucus rejected the leadership's endorsement of Landrum and selected Representatives Ross Bass of Tennessee and Pat Jennings of Virginia to fill the two vacancies on Ways and Means. These two moderate southerners were more likely to support the Kennedy administration on such measures as tax reduction and medicare. Perhaps as important in its long-run implications, Bass and Jennings also became members of the Democratic Committee on Committees. Subsequent committee appointments generally reflected the leadership's tendency to reward the faithful for support on the enlargement votes.[54]

A seventh and final factor should not be overlooked. The 1963 rules fight took place on opening day in contrast to the 1961 fight in which a roll-call vote was put off until four weeks into the session. Having withstood the challenge of mid-term election losses, the Democratic leadership was able to capitalize on a momentum built up in electing a Speaker by a party division. Unlike 1961, there was little time for the opposition to mobilize its forces or to suggest viable compromises. Since the Democratic Study Group professed to want further rules change, the leadership could adopt the stance of mediating between opposing extremes.[55] By making

Battle on Rules," *Baltimore Sun,* January 3, 1962, p. 1. While the Democratic caucus met the day before the vote, the two vacancies on Ways and Means were not filled until the following Monday.

[53] Smith's obstinacy in preventing the creation of a peanut laboratory in one Georgia member's district allegedly cost him one vote. The primary defeat of conservative Representative James C. Davis following the outlawing of the Georgia county unit rule as well as the victory of the "moderate" candidate in the gubernatorial primary, also made it easier for the Georgia delegation to shift its votes.

[54] Committee assignments were perhaps the principal leverage used by McCormack in the 1963 rules fight. As the third-ranking member on Ways and Means, Hale Boggs of Louisiana, the Democratic whip, is strategically placed to reinforce the leadership's wishes. These impressions, of course, need more systematic confirmation. For policy considerations in general, see Nicholas A. Masters, "Committee Assignments," *American Political Science Review,* LV (June, 1961), 345–57. Reprinted as Chapter II of this volume.

[55] While not as intimately involved in the 1963 strategy as in the 1961 plans, the Democratic Study Group made more "extreme" requests for rules reforms which made more persuasive the "middle ground" assumed by the Democratic leadership. It was largely the threat posed by this group which kept southern Democrats in line on the previous-question vote.

permanent a temporary increase in the size of the Committee on Rules, a change that all parties could live with, the House of Representatives had adapted to incremental change.

IV. CONCLUSIONS: SOME POLICY ALTERNATIVES

This study of the House Committee on Rules in the Eighty-seventh Congress has had four objectives. First, it has suggested six important functions performed by the Committee on Rules for the leadership and membership, as the fifteen members of the committee perceive these functions. Second, this paper has developed the major consequence—a shift in control—and four by-products of increasing the size of the committee from twelve members to fifteen members, at first "temporarily," and then, "permanently." Third, the events leading up to and including two roll-call votes on enlargement have been briefly contrasted and compared. Fourth and finally, some tentative answers to the question posed at the beginning of this paper can now be attempted. What should be the composition of the House Committee on Rules and in whose interests should its control be exercised?

Political scientists cannot decide what values are to be preferred; they can, however, suggest what ends seem to follow from the adoption of one or another means. Several extreme policy alternatives can be eliminated either as unrealistic or politically unfeasible reforms. It seems highly improbable that the committee could ever be reduced to a mere "traffic cop" regulating debate with no concern as to the policy implications of the functions it performs. Given present methods of committee selection, the Committee on Rules will never be a microcosm of the whole House, since its members will inevitably be more senior, and hence, generally more conservative, than the House as a whole. At the other extreme, hardly any member of the House would advocate a return to the pre-1910 situation in which the Speaker dominated the Committee on Rules and the House of Representatives. It is also unlikely that a policy committee composed solely of members of the majority party would be acceptable to the minority or that it could continue to perform the same functions as the present Rules Committee.

Short of these extremes, there are four main policy alternatives. The size of the committee, the party ratio, and the particular ideological orientations of individual members must all be taken into account, depending on what type of "majority rule" is preferable:

1. If control by a *concurrent majority* is preferred, then an even-numbered committee divided not so much by party as by ideology, would be the appropriate means. (Example: the six-to-six liberal-conservative cleavage which controlled the Committee on Rules throughout most of the Eighty-sixth Congress).[56]

2. If control by a *bipartisan majority* is preferred, then an odd- or even-numbered committee with a shifting party and ideological ratio more characteristic of the House as a whole would be the appropriate means. (Examples: a nine-to-six division such as the Laird "fair-play" amendment proposed during the 1963 debate; or the composition of the committee prior to 1958, when a Republican liberal could sometimes be persuaded to vote bills out).[57]

3. If *moderate control by the majority party leadership* is preferred, while at the same time some committee independence is retained, then an odd-number committee divided along party or ideological lines so as to give one-vote control to the leadership, would be the appropriate means. (Example: the Committee on Rules in the Eighty-seventh Congress).[58]

4. If *strong control by the majority party leadership* is preferred, then reduction of the committee size and an increase in party ratio would seem to be the appropriate means. (Examples: a twelve-member Democratic committee with a party ratio of nine-to-three; or the twelve-member committee in the Republican-controlled Eightieth and Eighty-third Congresses, which gave conservative Republicans and southern Democrats eight or more votes).[59]

Of course, these alternatives highly oversimplify the possible com-

---

[56] John C. Calhoun, *A Disquisition on Government and Selections from the Discourse*, ed. C. Gordon Post (Indianapolis: Bobbs-Merrill Co., 1953), pp. 37–38; James Burnham, *Congress and the American Tradition* (Chicago: Regnery, 1959), pp. 315–16.

[57] See Willmoore Kendall's development of the thesis that a tension exists between two "majorities" in the American political system: one, liberally oriented and focused on the Executive, and the other, more conservatively oriented, expressed through Congress. "The Two Majorities," *Midwest Journal of Political Science*, IV (November, 1960), 317–45.

[58] Robert A. Dahl, *A Preface to Democratic Theory* (Chicago: University of Chicago Press, 1956), esp. chap. v.

[59] James MacGregor Burns, *The Deadlock of Democracy* (Englewood Cliffs, N.J.: Prentice-Hall, 1963), esp. chaps. xiii–xiv; Walter Lippmann, "The Third House," *Washington Post*, January 8, 1963, p. A 11.

binations that could be achieved by alternately controlling committee size and varying party ratio. But the House of Representatives is not sympathetic to radical change. There would be as much opposition to changing traditional party ratios on the three main committees of the House—Rules, Ways and Means, and Appropriations—as was generated by increasing the size of the Rules Committee. Some of these same purposes could be obtained by carefully controlling subsequent appointments to the Committee on Rules. Yet Speakers of the House are as aware as are Presidents with their Supreme Court appointments, that while general policy predilections may be calculated, subsequent decisions on specific issues can neither be predicted nor controlled. Thus, the Committee on Rules will continue to shift from representing the interests of one type of majority to another from Congress to Congress, occasionally alternating even within the same Congress. The tenuous control by the eight pro-administration members may dissolve on specific issues. Prolonged illness or death could shift committee domination to its conservative members or strengthen the narrow majority responsive to the Democratic party leadership. The majority eight may yet find it necessary to take control of the committee agenda from its chairman. The increase in size is not necessarily permanent. The relationships between the majority leadership, the Committee on Rules, and the members of the House of Representatives will continue to shift and change—and that is their continuing fascination.

PART THREE

Leadership and the Legislative Process

VII

THE DECISION TO ENLARGE THE COMMITTEE ON RULES: AN ANALYSIS OF THE 1961 VOTE*

Milton C. Cummings, Jr.
Robert L. Peabody

ON JANUARY 31, 1961, after an intense two-hour session, the United States House of Representatives, by a vote of 217 to 212, adopted House Resolution 127:

> *Resolved,* That during the Eighty-seventh Congress the Committee on Rules shall be composed of fifteen members.[1]

Simply phrased and innocuous in wording, this resolution was no routine exercise of congressional powers under the constitutional provision that "Each House may determine the Rules of its Proceedings . . . ." At stake in this action to increase the size of the Committee on Rules from twelve to fifteen members were the power and prestige of the newly elected President, John F. Kennedy, the Speaker of the House, Sam Rayburn of Texas, and the Chairman of the Committee on Rules, Howard W. Smith of Virginia. At stake, also, was the crucial issue of who was to control the powers lodged in the Committee on Rules: Rayburn and through him the President as head of the majority party, or the Chairman of the Rules Committee, acting independently and representing the views of the conservative southern Democratic-Republican voting alignment.

---

* This study was made possible by the support of The Brookings Institution. We are also indebted to numerous readers for helpful comments on early drafts of the manuscript. For any errors of interpretation or fact that remain, we alone are responsible.

[1] *Congressional Record,* January 31, 1961, p. 1502. This resolution temporarily amended Rule X, Clause 1 (p), of the House of Representatives, which sets the size of the Committee on Rules at twelve members. Lewis Deschler, *Constitution, Jefferson's Manual,* and *Rules of the House of Representatives of the United States,* House Document 479, 86th Cong., 2nd sess., 1961, p. 325. All references to the *Congressional Record* are to the unbound daily edition unless otherwise noted.

The outcome of this contest for control of the Committee on Rules had important implications for the way in which the House would conduct its business during the remainder of the Eighty-seventh Congress. As the key coordinating committee of a 435-member legislative body, the committee possesses extraordinary powers. It not only acts as the traffic controller for legislation, it also determines time limits on debate and the kind and number of amendments that may be offered from the floor.

> It may kill a bill by refusal to recommend a rule; it may expedite legislation by recommending appropriate rules; it may limit debate drastically; it may limit the amendments to be offered to bills; it may, in effect, determine the form of the question to be voted on by the House. The committee may even control the substance of the measures submitted to the House by declining to grant a rule until the legislative committee modifies the bill to meet its wishes.[2]

Furthermore, unless unanimous consent is obtained, a special rule must be granted by the Committee on Rules before House conferees can meet with Senate conferees to discuss disagreements between the two houses on legislation. The committee also may recommend to the House the creation of select committees and direct them to make investigations.

The purpose of this study of the 1961 House Rules controversy is threefold: first, to outline the events leading up to the crucial vote on the floor of the House; second, to analyze the vote itself, particularly the behavior of the sixty-four Democrats and twenty-two Republicans who bolted party lines; and, finally, to speculate briefly on some of the broader questions that were raised by the decision which the House made.[3]

---

[2] V. O. Key, Jr., *Politics, Parties and Pressure Groups* (4th ed.; New York: Thomas Y. Crowell, 1958), p. 719. See James A. Robinson, "The Role of the Rules Committee in Arranging the Program of the U.S. House of Representatives," *Western Political Quarterly,* XXII (September 1959), 653–69; and James A. Robinson, "The Role of the Rules Committee in Regulating Debate in the U.S. House of Representatives," *Midwest Journal of Political Science,* V (February, 1961), 59–69, for an extensive analysis of the actions of the Committee on Rules in the 76th–84th Congresses.

[3] At this point, a word of disclaimer is in order. In the subsequent analysis, we are less concerned with explaining why *individual* representatives voted the way they did than in establishing generalizations about the way groups of congressmen behaved in the *aggregate*—as, for example, the southern Democrats who broke with their party leadership. We gained our initial impressions about the 1961 House Rules controversy from observation of the floor fight and the

I. THE GROWTH OF DISSATISFACTION

During the early years of the American Republic, the House Committee on Rules operated as a select committee set up at the beginning of each Congress with authorization to report a system of rules and no other important function.[4] As the House increased in size, the powers and privileges of the Rules Committee grew. In 1858, the Speaker became a member of the committee; and in 1880, the committee was made a standing body of five members with the power to issue special orders. In subsequent years, the Speaker, as chairman of the committee, increasingly made it a device by which his party could control legislation. By 1910, opposition to the power which Republican Speaker Joseph Cannon of Illinois had acquired was sufficiently strong that insurgent Republicans combined with minority-party Democrats to remove the Speaker from his *ex officio* status as a member of the committee.[5]

---

open meetings of the Committee on Rules and from the coverage by the mass media. The core of the analysis, however, rests upon a detailed examination of the vote using data concerning the characteristics of the congressmen and the constituencies they represent. These findings then served as a basis for informal discussion with more than twenty congressmen and congressional staff members. For their assistance and insights, we extend our thanks.

[4] For a brief history of the Committee on Rules, see George B. Galloway (revised by Walter Kravitz), "A Short History of the Development of the House Committee on Rules" (Washington, D.C.: Library of Congress, Legislative Reference Service, Mimeographed, 1961). See also, Floyd M. Riddick, *Congressional Procedure* (Boston: Chapman & Grimes, 1941), pp. 79–83.

[5] The 1961 House Rules controversy presents an intriguing contrast to the overthrow of Speaker Cannon. On March 19, 1910, a "coalition" of insurgent Republicans led by George Norris of Nebraska and minority-party Democrats headed by Champ Clark of Missouri adopted a resolution which removed the Speaker from the Rules Committee, enlarged the committee's membership from five to ten (six from the majority party and four from the minority party), and assigned to the House as a whole the selection of its members. *Congressional Record*, 61st Cong., 2nd sess., 1910, XLV, Part 4, 3425–36; and Charles R. Atkinson, *The Committee on Rules and the Overthrow of Speaker Cannon* (New York: Columbia University, 1911). Three years later, a future Speaker of the House, Sam Rayburn, became a member of the Sixty-third Congress. Almost fifty-one years after the 1910 revolt, the power which had been used by Speaker Cannon to prevent bills opposed by the Taft Administration from reaching the floor was partially restored to Speaker Rayburn in order that the Kennedy legislative program might reach the floor of the House. See Arthur Krock, "A Curious Interplay of Reform and Reaction," *New York Times,* January 26, 1961, p. 28. Of course, few of Cannon's formal powers were restored to Speaker Rayburn, despite the fact that at least one congressman proposed putting the Speaker back on the Committee on Rules. *Congressional Record*, August 26, 1960, p. 16699. In both cases, however, the Committee on Rules was enlarged to prevent certain bills from being blocked in the committee. See also George B. Galloway, "Leadership in the House of Representatives," *Western Political Quarterly*, XII (June, 1959), 438–41.

While the size of the committee has fluctuated between ten and fourteen members since 1910, the majority party has maintained an approximately two-to-one advantage in membership. Thus, when the Democratic party controlled the House, as in the Eighty-fourth, Eighty-fifth, and Eighty-sixth Congresses, the Committee on Rules was composed of eight Democrats and four Republicans. In periods when the majority party was united, it was able to dominate the committee and thereby to control the order and rules governing legislation brought to the floor. From 1910 until 1937, except for occasional independent action by its chairman, the Committee on Rules functioned as a responsible instrument of the majority party leadership. But by 1937, a bipartisan coalition of dissident Democrats and conservative Republicans who were united in their opposition to President Roosevelt's legislative program had come to dominate the committee, and the House Democratic leadership was forced to use the discharge petition to get the bill that became the Wages and Hours Act of 1938 to the floor.[6]

Although Chairman John J. O'Connor was defeated in 1938, other members of the Rules Committee, including Smith of Virginia, survived Roosevelt's attempted "purge." Between 1939 and 1961, except for the Republican Eightieth and Eighty-third Congresses, the Committee on Rules tended to be dominated by a bipartisan conservative bloc, despite Rayburn's occasional successful use of personal influence with its members to work his will. One major attempt to restrict the formal powers of the Committee on Rules, the twenty-one-day rule, proved successful in getting bills to the floor of the House, but this rule was short-lived.[7]

During each succeeding Congress, controversy over the activity of the committee continued. The issue became most sharply drawn in the Eighty-sixth Congress, when the largest Democratic majority in the House since 1937 attempted to enact a legislative record on which to campaign in the 1960 elections. On January 3, 1959, Ray-

---

[6] Robinson, "The Role of the Rules Committee in Arranging the Program . . . ," *op. cit.*, p. 659.

[7] On January 3, 1949, the Eighty-first Congress adopted the "twenty-one-day rule," a procedure by which the chairman of a legislative committee which had reported a bill favorably and requested a rule from the Committee on Rules could bring the bill directly to the House floor if the Rules Committee failed to grant the rule within twenty-one calendar days of the request. Following Republican gains in the 1950 mid-term elections, Congress repealed the "twenty-one-day rule" on the opening day of the Eighty-second Congress. *Congressional Record*, 81st Cong., 1st sess., 1949, XCV, Part 1, 10–11; 82d Cong., 1st sess., 1951, XCVII, Part 1, 9–19. See also Galloway, "Leadership in the House . . . ," *op. cit.*, p. 440–41.

burn promised the leaders of the Democratic Study Group, a loose organization of some 100 to 120 liberally oriented Democratic representatives, that "legislation which has been duly considered and reported by legislative committees will be brought before the House for consideration within a reasonable time."[8] Three days later, however, House Republicans chose Charles Halleck of Indiana to replace Joseph Martin of Massachusetts as Minority Floor Leader. Martin had alternated as Minority Floor Leader and Speaker with Rayburn since 1940; and, by working through Martin, Rayburn had occasionally been able to pick up one or two votes from Republican moderates on the Rules Committee in order to get legislation to the floor.[9]

During the Eighty-sixth Congress, the two ranking majority members of the Committee on Rules, Chairman Smith of Virginia and William M. Colmer of Mississippi, consistently aligned themselves with the four Republican members of the committee, Leo E. Allen of Illinois, Clarence J. Brown of Ohio, B. Carroll Reece of Tennessee, and Hamer H. Budge of Idaho. Table I illustrates the ideological split that existed between the pro-Rayburn "moderates" and "liberals" and the anti-Rayburn "conservatives" on the Rules Committee, both before and after the decision to enlarge its membership. Whether one uses a "liberal" rating scale such as that compiled by Americans for Democratic Action, or a "conservative" index compiled by the business-orientated Civic Affairs Associates, the same basic voting pattern on the Committee on Rules is revealed.[10] The table indicates that, except on civil rights legislation, the voting record of Smith and Colmer on major issues was almost identical

---

[8] *Congressional Quarterly Weekly Report,* XVII (January 9, 1959), 45.

[9] To fill two vacancies formerly held by moderate Republicans on the Committee on Rules, Halleck appointed two conservative Republicans—B. Carroll Reece of Tennessee, who had had previous service on the committee, and Hamer H. Budge of Idaho.

[10] Interest group rating scales, as congressmen are among the first to point out, have a number of limitations. Not only are they usually restricted to a few selected issues in one or two sessions of Congress, but the issues and particular votes are sometimes chosen so as to demonstrate a pattern of voting sympathetic or opposed to the interest group's ends. Other rating scales, such as the AFL-CIO Committee on Political Education scale or the "conservative" Americans for Constitutional Action voting records, could have been used to demonstrate approximately the same gross distinctions. The Americans for Democratic Action scale, which is used in Table I and elsewhere in this study, was selected because it was based on nine issues in the most recent session of Congress (1960), several of which would again confront House members in the first session of the Eighty-seventh Congress. The derivation of the ADA and CAA (Civic Affairs Associates) indices are discussed in more detail in Table I, notes * and †.

with that of the committee's four Republican members during the Eighty-sixth Congress. It also suggests the combination of five "liberal" and three southern Democratic "swing" votes that made up the Rayburn majority following enlargement of the committee on January 31, 1961. Finally, Table I indicates clearly that the four new Republicans appointed to the committee in 1961 were apt to vote just as "conservatively" as the Republicans they replaced.

TABLE I

Members of the Rules Committee and Their Records on ADA and CAA Approved Measures During the Eighty-sixth Congress

	RULES	COMMITTEE	MEMBERS		
Members, 86th Congress	*Votes Approved by:* ADA* (Per	CAA† cent)	*New Members,* 87th Congress	*Votes Approved by:* ADA (Per	CAA cent)
Democrats					
Pro-Rayburn					
Madden (Ind., 1)	100	0			
Delaney (N.Y., 7)	100	0			
Bolling (Mo., 5)	100	0			
O'Neill (Mass., 11)	100	14			
			Sisk (Calif., 12)	100	0
			Elliott (Ala., 7)	75	15
Trimble (Ark., 3)	67	21			
Thornberry (Tex., 10)	67	36			
Anti-Rayburn					
Smith (Va., 8) Chairman	0	93			
Colmer (Miss., 6)	0	69			
Republicans‡					
Allen (Ill., 16)	11	100	St. George (N.Y., 28)	13	100
Brown (Ohio, 7)	11	93			
Reece (Tenn., 1)	11	93	Avery (Kansas, 1)	22	100
Budge (Ida., 2)	0	100	Smith (Calif., 20)	0	93
			Hoffman (Ill., 14)	0	93

* For a detailed description of the roll calls on which the ADA (Americans for Democratic Action) "liberalism-conservatism" index is based, see *Congressional Quarterly Weekly Report*, XVIII (October 7, 1960), 1655–66. The percentages indicate the degree to which each member voted in accordance with the ADA's position on nine selected issues during the second session of the Eighty-sixth Congress (1960), including an increase in the minimum wage, federal aid for school construction, a depressed areas bill, appropriations for the mutual security program, and the Civil Rights Act of 1960. See note 10 for the limitations of such rating scales.
† The CAA (Civic Affairs Associates) index is based on fourteen selected issues during the Eighty-sixth Congress (1959–60), including federal employee salary increases, a minimum wage, school construction, distressed areas, and the 1959 labor reform bill (Landrum-Griffin Act). The percentages indicate the degree to which each member supported the Civic Affairs Associates' orientation in favor of the private enterprise system as against "bureaucratic planning under a government enterprise system." *Ibid.*, pp. 1655–66, esp. p. 1656.
‡ Representative Allen retired, and Representative Budge was defeated for re-election in 1960. On March 28, 1961, Representative Avery was named to the Committee on Rules to replace Congressman B. Carroll Reece, who died March 19, 1961.

By a six-to-six tie vote, the conservative members of the committee were able to block, delay, or force revision of a number of social welfare measures in the Eighty-sixth Congress.[11] Under the leadership of Speaker Rayburn and Majority Floor Leader John McCormack, however, liberal Democratic members were able to use Calendar Wednesday proceedings to pass the aid to distressed areas bill, and, through threatened use of the discharge petition, to force release of what was to become the Civil Rights Act of 1960.[12] When Congress recessed for the 1960 nominating conventions, both political parties adopted platform planks critical of existing congressional procedures.[13] Shortly thereafter, criticism of the control exercised by the House Committee on Rules reached a high point during the post-convention August session, when the committee refused to grant a special rule allowing House conferees to meet with Senate conferees on the education bill.[14]

---

[11] For a detailed analysis of the events of the second session of the Eighty-sixth Congress, see Ivan Hinderaker, "From the 86th to the 87th Congress: Controversy over 'Majority Rule,'" *American Government Annual, 1961–62* (New York: Holt, Rinehart & Winston, 1961), pp. 76–98, esp. pp. 90–94. The activity of the Democratic Study Group in the House Rules controversy is given extended coverage in National Committee for an Effective Congress, *Congressional Report*, X, No. 1 (March 4, 1961), 1–5.

[12] Members of the House of Representatives who wish to circumvent or override the decisions of the Committee on Rules have recourse to a number of procedures: principally, unanimous consent, suspension of the rules, Calendar Wednesday proceedings, and the discharge petition. For a brief summary of each of these procedures, see *Congressional Quarterly Weekly Report*, XVIII (December 30, 1960), 1994. Some of the dilatory motions which can be used against Calendar Wednesday proceedings are demonstrated in the debate on the distressed areas bill, *Congressional Record*, May 4, 1960, pp. 8737–44. But see the remarks of Congressman Thomas B. Curtis, *Congressional Record*, July 25, 1961, p. 12466.

[13] The Democratic party platform urged that "the rules of the House of Representatives . . . be so amended as to make sure that bills reported by legislative committee reach the floor for consideration without undue delay." *The Rights of Man*, Democratic Platform, Report of the Committee on Resolutions and Platforms as adopted by the Democratic National Convention, Los Angeles, California, July 12, 1960, p. 47. Congressmen Chester Bowles and Chet Holifield, both leaders in the Democratic Study Group, were key members of the Democratic Platform Committee. The Republican platform specially criticized the Senate's Rule XXII. *Building a Better America*, Republican Platform, Adopted by the Republican National Convention, Chicago, Illinois, July 27, 1960, p. 29.

[14] On August 26, 1960, eleven Democratic representatives made or inserted statements critical of the House Committee on Rules. *Congressional Record*, August 26, 1960, pp. 16698–706. During the floor debate preceding the roll-call vote on the Rayburn resolution, Chairman Smith accused these representatives of opening the assault on the Committee on Rules. *Congressional Record*, January 31, 1961, p. 1505.

Maneuvering Before the Floor Fight[15]

In the November, 1960, elections, the Democratic party captured the White House and maintained control of both houses of Congress; but the Republicans made a net gain of twenty-one House seats, thus apparently diminishing the possibilities of a change in the House rules. In November, Democratic Chairman Smith announced his opposition to any change. Subsequently, he met with Republican Floor Leader Halleck to discuss plans for maintaining the status quo.[16]

When Speaker Rayburn returned to Washington three days before the Eighty-seventh Congress convened, he was convinced that some change had to be made, but he had not yet decided on which alternative to pursue.[17] After presenting Smith with an opportunity to introduce a resolution enlarging the Committee on Rules from twelve to fifteen members, which Smith refused, Rayburn met with the leaders of the Democratic Study Group. Representatives Chet Holifield of California, Frank Thompson, Jr. of New Jersey, and John Blatnik of Minnesota, reported back to other Democratic Study Group members on January 2, 1961, that while Rayburn was committed to some change, they were not free to say what that change would be. The next day press reports confirmed the rumor that Rayburn's plan would be to ask the Democratic Committee on Committees (Democratic members of the Ways and Means Committee) to remove Representative Colmer of Mississippi from the Rules Committee and to replace him with another, less recalcitrant, Democrat.[18] Colmer was one of the five southern Democratic Repre-

[15] For a concise résumé of the events of this period, with pertinent newspaper citations, see Walter Kravitz, "The Rules Committee Controversy in the 87th Congress: A Brief Résumé" (Washington, D.C.: Library of Congress, Legislative Reference Service, Mimeographed, 1961).

[16] *Washington Post,* November 12, 1960, p. A 9; *New York Times,* November 15, 1960, p. 35; Tom Wicker, "Coalition Chiefs Confer in House," *New York Times,* November 29, 1960, p. 30.

[17] The events of this period can be only partially reconstructed. What follows is a composite view based for the most part on newspaper accounts and unstructured interviews conducted in July and August of 1961 with over twenty key participants. Interviews, from fifteen minutes to over two hours in length, were confined for the most part to Rules Committee members and the majority and minority party leadership. In order to maintain the confidential nature of the information received, specific sources have not been cited for some statements of interpretation in the brief résumé which follows.

[18] Richard L. Lyons, "Rayburn Plans Purge of Colmer," *Washington Post,* January 3, 1961, p. A 2; John D. Morris, "Congress to Open Today; Rayburn Moving to Curb Conservative Rules Bloc," *New York Times,* January 3, 1961, p. 1.

sentatives who had publicly opposed the Kennedy-Johnson ticket during the 1960 presidential campaign.[19] Meanwhile, seven Republicans, headed by Thomas B. Curtis of Missouri and John V. Lindsay of New York, issued a manifesto deploring any coalition between Republicans and southern Democrats as contrary to the best interests of the country and the Republican party.[20]

On January 3, the 262-member Democratic majority elected Sam Rayburn to his ninth term as Speaker. Moments later, the House routinely adopted Chairman Smith's resolution that the rules of the Eighty-seventh Congress be the same as those governing the House of Representatives in the previous Congress.[21] A week later, however, Rayburn returned to his plan to enlarge the Committee on Rules, presumably on the urging of Representatives Carl Vinson of Georgia, Paul Kilday of Texas, and other southern moderates. While to some observers, Rayburn's plan to remove Colmer had been a tactical maneuver from the beginning, others felt that Rayburn backed down because such a plan would have alienated too many southerners.

On January 18, Rayburn's proposal to enlarge the committee was formally endorsed by the House Democratic caucus by a voice vote.[22] At this meeting, Chairman Smith agreed to bring the resolution to the floor when his committee was reconstituted the following week. The next day, urged on by Rules Committee member Clarence

---

[19] Other southern Democrats who openly opposed their party's presidential ticket were Jamie L. Whitten, John Bell Williams, and Arthur Winstead of Mississippi, and Otto E. Passman of Louisiana. In addition to posing problems of what to do with these representatives as far as committee assignments were concerned, the suggested ouster of Colmer raised the question of New York Representative Adam C. Powell's failure to support the Democratic ticket in 1956 without retribution. However, Colmer's removal from the Rules Committee had the advantage of being regarded as an internal party matter, thus probably preventing an open floor fight.

[20] This resolution was presented to the House Republican Policy Committee on January 2, 1961, and signed by Representatives Curtis of Missouri, Lindsay and Seymour Halpern of New York, Florence P. Dwyer and William T. Cahill of New Jersey, Perkins Bass of New Hampshire, and Silvio O. Conte of Massachusetts. All seven subsequently voted for the Rayburn resolution enlarging the Rules Committee.

[21] *Congressional Record*, January 3, 1961, pp. 21–22, 24.

[22] For the most part, Speaker Rayburn, "working things out in his own way," ignored those Democratic Study Group supporters who urged him to take advantage of certain parliamentary or party rules which might have facilitated the change. For example, the Speaker did not request a two-thirds binding caucus vote, although judging from the final roll-call vote, he probably could have obtained the approximately 175 votes necessary.

Brown, the Republican House Policy Committee unanimously rejected the enlargement plan, and on January 23, the Republican
conference supported that decision with few dissents. Two days
before the floor vote scheduled for Thursday, January 26, the Committee on Rules voted six to two to report the enlargement resolution. Only Smith and Colmer opposed House Resolution 127; the
incumbent Republican members did not attend.

Postponement of the Vote

The day before the scheduled vote, Democratic leaders decided
to postpone the vote until Tuesday, January 31. While the publicly
voiced reason for postponing the vote was that "some members are
unable to be here,"[23] this decision was at least tacit admission that
Rayburn and McCormack lacked the necessary votes to get the enlargement resolution passed on the twenty-sixth. Minority Leader
Halleck offered his own interpretation of the decision: "The New
Frontier is having trouble with its first roundup."[24] That same
evening, at his first press conference, President Kennedy announced
his position on nationwide television. While declaring that any
rules change was an internal House matter, he also said that he
hoped a "small group of men" would "not attempt to prevent the
members from finally letting their judgments be known."[25] Concurrently, members of the President's cabinet, notably Attorney
General Robert Kennedy, Secretary of the Interior Stewart Udall,
and the President's legislative liaison staff headed by Lawrence
O'Brien, contacted individual congressmen by telephone and in
person to solicit support for the resolution.[26]

---

[23] *Congressional Record,* January 25, 1961, p. 1169.
[24] *New York Times,* January 26, 1961, p. 18.
[25] Question 11, Transcript of the President's press conference, *New York
Times,* January 26, 1961, p. 10.
[26] The impact of these Administration pressures, which were widely reported
in the press, cannot be evaluated with certainty. Some observers claim that
White House intervention turned what was a toss-up vote on Thursday into a
five-vote victory on Tuesday. Not all of this Administration activity accomplished the desired objective, however, for some congressmen reacted unfavorably
to what they felt were unfair pressure tactics. See the statement inserted in
the *Congressional Record* by North Carolina's Representative Scott, January
31, 1961, pp. 1515–16, and the criticism of Secretary Udall's activities by
Representative Lennon, also of North Carolina, reprinted in the *Congressional
Record,* February 28, 1961, pp. 2615–18. One member of the majority-party
whip system placed a different interpretation on the subsequent discussions
of who was responsible for the resolution's success, remarking somewhat dourly,
"They (the Administration) get the credit if we win, and we get the blame
if we can't round up the votes!"

Over the weekend, party and interest group pressure increased. The vote-aligning techniques of the regular party whip system headed by Carl Albert of Oklahoma, abetted by an informal whip system led by Richard Bolling of Missouri and Frank Thompson of New Jersey, continued to counteract earlier activity by Chairman Smith. On Saturday, at least one attempt was made to effect a compromise. Rayburn might have been willing to call off the vote if he could have obtained Smith's written guarantee that the Rules Committee would not block any Kennedy legislative proposal during the coming session. But Smith would not go this far. Instead, he promised only to "interpose no obstacles in the Committee on Rules to the five major bills that the President has publicly announced as his program for this session."[27]

As the roll call vote neared, coverage of the issue by the mass media was intensified. On the eve of Kennedy's inauguration, *CBS Reports* devoted an hour television program to "The Keeper of the Rules: Congressman Smith and the New Frontier."[28] According to John D. Morris, of *The New York Times,* the power and prestige of "two tough and skillful septuagenarians" rode on the outcome.[29] Chalmers M. Roberts of the *Washington Post* reported that the President feared a possible "disastrous blow" to his Administration's prestige on his twelfth day in office.[30]

On Tuesday, January 31, the day of the vote, one of the largest crowds ever to attend a congressional debate competed for seats in the gallery. Shortly after twelve o'clock, Rayburn mounted the Speaker's rostrum to preside over the most critical fight of his career. One hour of debate, thirty minutes allocated to each party, preceded the vote.[31] The Republican leadership and Democratic Chairman Smith condemned the resolution as an attempt "to pack

[27] Letter from Howard W. Smith addressed to Representatives Carl Vinson and Francis E. Walter and sent to all members of the House of Representatives, dated January 28, 1961, *Congressional Record,* January 31, 1961, p. 1505. Vinson and Walter had called on Smith to suggest possible compromises after first meeting with Speaker Rayburn. The five legislative proposals at the top of President Kennedy's priority list of domestic legislation dealt with redevelopment of depressed areas, an increased minimum wage with broader coverage, expansion of housing programs, aid to education, and health insurance for the aged through social security payments.
[28] The transcript of this program, featuring interviews with Representatives Smith of Virginia, Bolling of Missouri, and Brown of Ohio, is reprinted in the *Congressional Record,* January 31, 1961, pp. 1422–27.
[29] *New York Times,* January 30, 1961, p. 12.
[30] *Washington Post,* January 30, 1961, p. 1.
[31] *Congressional Record,* January 31, 1961, pp. 1502–19.

or purge" the Committee on Rules. "I will cooperate with the Democratic leadership of the House of Representatives," Smith stated, "just as long and just as far as my conscience will permit me to go. . . ." But, he continued, "when I am asked to pledge aid to the passage of any resolution or bill in this House that I am conscientiously opposed to, I would not yield my conscience and my right to vote in this House to any person or any Member or under any conditions."[32]

Speaker Rayburn, climaxing the debate in one of his rare statements from the floor, urged adoption of the enlargement proposal in order to facilitate passage of President Kennedy's legislative program:

> I think this House should be allowed on great measures to work its will, and it cannot work its will if the Committee on Rules is so constituted as not to allow the House to pass on those things. . . .
> Let us move this program. Let us be sure we can move it and the only way we can be sure that this program will move when great committees report bills, the only way it can move, in my opinion, my beloved colleagues, is to adopt this resolution today.[33]

On the roll-call vote, the House adopted the enlargement resolution, 217 to 212. Twenty-two Republicans joined 195 Democrats voting for the resolution; against it were 64 Democrats and 148 Republicans. The next day, the new Democratic committee assignments, made by Speaker Rayburn and approved by the Democratic Committee on Committees, included the appointments of Representatives Carl Elliott of Alabama and B. F. Sisk of California to the Committee on Rules.[34]

---

[32] *Ibid.*, pp. 1504–5.

[33] *Ibid.*, pp. 1508–10. Speaking or submitting statements in favor of the resolution were Democratic Representatives Trimble, Kilday, Walter, McCormack, Yates, Blatnik, Ryan, Pucinski, Thompson of New Jersey, Moorhead, and Addonzio; and Republican representatives Curtis of Missouri, Lindsay, Conte, and Halpern.

[34] Richard L. Lyons, "Committee Seats Filled with Eye to Rules Vote," *Washington Post*, February 2, 1961, p. 1 A. The following Monday, the House formally approved these majority committee assignments. *Congressional Record*, February 6, 1961, pp. 1704–5. The balance of Republican minority committee assignments were formally agreed to on February 13, 1961, including the appointments of Katherine St. George of New York, H. Allen Smith of California, and Elmer J. Hoffman of Illinois, to the Committee on Rules. *Congressional Record*, February 13, 1961, p. 2007.

II. ANALYSIS OF THE VOTE

Party Lines Predominate Outside the South

The dramatic outcome of the vote prompted a flood of explanations in the public press. Some observers attributed Rayburn's victory to the White House or to key cabinet members, such as Attorney General Robert F. Kennedy or Secretary of the Interior Stewart Udall. For others, it was the "pragmatic liberals" of the House, both inside and outside the Democratic Study Group, who deserved the major credit or blame. Still others stressed the importance of personal and political loyalty owed to Rayburn. Yet another characteristic of the vote, and one that encompasses all of these interpretations, deserves further emphasis. The decision to enlarge the House Committee on Rules was primarily a party-line vote. As Table II illustrates, three-fourths of the House Democrats supported the Rayburn resolution, and nearly seven-eighths of the Republicans opposed it. Among congressmen from districts above the Mason-Dixon Line, every Democrat who voted supported the Speaker, and these northern Democrats were joined by all but two of their border-state colleagues. Republicans from the North were slightly less cohesive, but in all only twenty-two GOP congressmen supported the Democratic leadership. In thirty-one of the thirty-nine non-southern states, the House delegation divided along party lines —with all Democrats supporting the Rayburn resolution and all Republicans opposing it.

In the South, of course, it was different. Here the Democratic lines splintered sharply, and Rayburn was opposed by nearly two-thirds

TABLE II

The Vote to Enlarge the Rules Committee by Democratic and Republican Congressmen from the North, Border States, and South

Region	Democrats			Republicans		
	Votes Against (Number)	Votes For (Number)	Proportion For (Per Cent)	Votes Against (Number)	Votes For (Number)	Proportion For (Per Cent)
North and West	0	129	100	137	20	13
Border States*	2	30	94	4	2	33
South†	62	36	37	7	0	0
TOTAL‡	64	195	75	148	22	13

* The border states are Kentucky, Maryland, Missouri, Oklahoma, and West Virginia.
† "South" here includes the eleven states of the former Confederacy: Alabama, Arkansas, Florida, Georgia, Louisiana, Mississippi, North Carolina, South Carolina, Tennessee, Texas, and Virginia.
‡ These totals do not include paired votes.

of his southern Democratic colleagues. However, the Speaker did get a vital thirty-six votes from the South without which the enlargement proposal would have surely failed. In a contest so close, virtually every vote was critical; but in the subsequent analysis, attention will be focused on the twenty-two Republicans and thirty-six southern Democrats whose votes, when added to those of the Democrats from the North and West, enabled the Rayburn resolution to prevail.

The Vote of the Southern Democrats

Political observers are sometimes tempted to speak of southern Democrats as a unit, both in reports of legislative conflict in the House and election returns in general. Yet, as V. O. Key observed more than a decade ago: "The politics of the South is incredibly complex. Its variety, its nuances, its subtleties range across the political spectrum."[35] Few House roll calls reveal the nuances and subtleties of southern congressional politics better than the decision to enlarge the Committee on Rules. In that one vote were etched most of the basic lines of political cleavage that exist within the South today—state delegation versus state delegation, rural congressmen versus urban congressmen, black belt representatives versus House members from districts where the Negro population is relatively small, economic liberals versus economic conservatives, and committee chairmen versus those southerners with less formal authority and seniority in the House.

The amount of support which southern congressmen gave to the Rules Committee enlargement varied widely from state to state. All but a handful of the southern votes for the Rayburn resolution came from five states—Alabama, Tennessee, Louisiana, Arkansas, and, above all, the Speaker's own state of Texas. At the other extreme, Mississippi and South Carolina cast a solid bloc of twelve votes against the resolution. In every southern congressional delegation save these two, there were votes both for and against the proposal.[36]

---

[35] V. O. Key, Jr., *Southern Politics in State and Nation* (New York: Knopf, 1949), p. ix.

[36] Interviews with several congressmen and their staffs, while not reflecting a systematic sampling, suggested that state delegation solidarity was used as a rallying point in support of Rayburn in Texas and as a means of defensive protection in southern state delegations opposing the enlargement resolution, the most notable example being North Carolina. The percentage

A clearer picture of the resolution's sources of strength and weakness in the South emerges if one probes beneath the differences
among state delegations to examine the relationship between key
characteristics of an individual district and the way its representative voted on this crucial issue. As one would suspect, urban representatives in the South, confronted with the attendant problems
of industrialization and urban growth, were more likely to support
enlargement of the Rules Committee than rural congressmen.[37]
An even more clear-cut index, however, was the Negro percentage
of the population in the congressman's district. In general, the
hypothesis that southern representatives from districts with large
Negro populations would be less likely to support the Rules Committee change than those who came from districts with relatively
small Negro populations was sustained. As Table III suggests, the
bulk of the support for Rayburn came from districts where preoccupation with the race issue was likely to be less intense—those districts where less than one-fifth of the population were Negroes.
Approximately two-thirds of the thirty-two representatives from
these districts voted for enlargement. In contrast, of sixty-six congressmen from districts where the Negro population exceeded one
in five, only fifteen voted for House Resolution 127. Nonetheless,
the irregularities in the data presented in Table III indicate that
there was no simple linear relationship between the percentage of
Negroes in a district and the vote against the Rayburn resolution.

of southern Democratic House delegations voting in favor of the Rayburn
proposal were: Texas, 70 per cent; Arkansas, 67 per cent; Louisiana, 63 per
cent; Tennessee, 57 per cent; Alabama, 44 per cent; Georgia, 20 per cent;
Florida, 14 per cent; Virginia, 12 per cent; North Carolina, 9 per cent;
Mississippi, 0 per cent; and South Carolina, 0 per cent. Speaker Rayburn
did not vote on the resolution. All seven southern Republican congressmen,
two from Tennessee, two from Virginia, and one each from Florida, North
Carolina, and Texas, voted against the Rules Committee enlargement resolution. For an extended analysis of roll-call votes in which state delegation
solidarity operated as a significant alternative cue-mechanism to party membership, see David B. Truman, "The State Delegations and the Structure of
Party Voting in the United States House of Representatives," *American Political Science Review*, L (December, 1956), 1023–45.

[37] Fifty-five per cent of the twenty-nine representatives from the most urban
districts of the South (Types III and IV according to the *Congressional
Quarterly*'s method of classification) voted for the Rayburn resolution; whereas only eighteen of sixty-four southern congressmen from more rural districts
(Types I and II), or approximately 28 per cent, supported the proposal.
This analysis is based on data presented in the *Congressional Quarterly Almanac*, XII (1956), 790–91.

They also suggest that other factors than the race issue had an important bearing on the outcome of the vote.[38]

TABLE III

Southern Democratic Representatives: Votes to Enlarge the Rules Committee and Percentage of Negroes in their Districts

	Southern Democratic Representatives			
Negroes in District* (Per Cent)	*Districts (Number)*	*Members Against Enlargement (Number)*	*Members For Enlargement (Number)*	*Members For Enlargement (Per Cent)*
0–9.9	17	8	9	53
10–19.9	15	3	12	80
20–29.9	28	22	6	21
30–39.9	19	14	5	26
40–49.9	16	12	4	25
50.0 and over	3	3	0	0
TOTAL	98	62	36	37

* Figures for the percentage of Negroes in each district's total population are based on the 1950 census. The figures appear in the *Congressional Quarterly Almanac*, XII (1956), 796–97.

In the eyes of many northerners, southern Democrats are often equated with conservative Democrats—anti-labor, staunch defenders of fiscal responsibility, and resolute opponents of costly social welfare programs. Yet the fact is that the South's representatives are by no means so monolithic in their orientation. In the legislative session immediately preceding the 1960 elections, as in previous sessions of Congress, the support given to increased federal expenditures and expanded social welfare programs, or, to use the vernacular of American politics, the "liberalism" of southern House members, varied extensively.

The data presented in Table IV also make it clear that the voting records of southern Democrats were distinctly weighted in the conservative direction. Using a simple "liberalism-conservatism" rating such as that compiled by Americans for Democratic Action on nine roll-call votes in 1960, the median score for ninety-three

---

[38] Despite some radio and newspaper coverage in the South which gave the contrary impression, many southern congressmen were well aware of the limitations of the Committee on Rules as an effective roadblock to civil rights legislation even if the new Administration were to move more aggressively in this field. If northern Republicans join with northern and borderstate liberals on the Rules Committee, they were and are able to outvote the South on civil rights measures. Furthermore, both Thornberry of Texas and Trimble of Arkansas have occasionally voted to report a civil rights bill, reserving the right to vote against it on the floor.

southern Democrats re-elected to the Eighty-seventh Congress was only 29 per cent.[39] However, these congressmen ranged along the political spectrum from sixteen representatives who almost never supported ADA-approved legislation to the one Democratic congressman from Florida voting for enlargement, Dante B. Fascell of Miami, who was in agreement with the ADA position (and, incidentally, the position of most northern Democrats) on eight issues out of nine.

TABLE IV

Southern Democrats: Percentage of ADA-Approved Votes and Votes on the Resolution to Enlarge the Committee on Rules

Percentage ADA-Approved Votes*	*Southern House Members† (Number)*	*Southern Members Against Enlargement (Number)*	*Southern Members For Enlargement (Number)*	*Southern Members For Enlargement (Per Cent)*
0–9.9	16	16	0	0
10–19.9	16	15	1	6
20–29.9	16	11	5	31
30–39.9	8	4	4	50
40–49.9	9	3	6	67
50–59.9	13	7	6	46
60–69.9	7	1	6	86
70–79.9	7	0	7	100
80 and over	1	0	1	100
TOTAL	93	57	36	39

* The ADA liberalism index in this table is identical to that in Table I.
† These totals exclude freshmen representatives elected in 1960.

Furthermore, the data in Table IV indicate that liberal southern Democrats like Fascell were generally more likely than their conservative colleagues to support the Rayburn resolution. Yet it also appears that this relationship between the congressmen's support for liberal legislation and support for enlargement of the Rules Committee was curvilinear, rather than linear. The southern Democrats with ADA liberalism scores between 20 and 59.9 per cent varied considerably in how they voted on the Rayburn resolution. In fact, those with ADA liberalism scores of 50–59.9 per cent were slightly less likely to support the Speaker than those with ADA scores between 30 and 49.9 per cent. This lack of progression in the data suggests that for congressmen with moderately liberal voting records, factors other than their "liberalism" or "conservatism" probably weighed heavily. Conversely, among the southern congressmen whose voting records were either strongly "liberal" or

---

[39] See note *, Table I, *supra,* for the derivation of this index.

strongly "conservative," there was little doubt as to how they would vote—the "liberals" for the enlargement plan, and the "conservatives" against it. Only one[40] of thirty-two southern Democrats with a rating below 20 per cent supported Rayburn; and all but one[41] of the fifteen southern Democrats whose liberalism score exceeded 60 per cent backed the change.

Consider, for example, the case of Representative Pat Jennings, the one Virginian who opposed Judge Smith. Congressman Jennings' district was the "Fighting Ninth," long a center of insurgency against the Old Dominion's dominant Byrd machine. He also had the highest liberalism rating among his Virginia colleagues, 44 per cent. Rayburn picked up a few votes from southern conservatives, principally colleagues from Texas or committee chairmen, but the bulk of his support came from the more liberal representatives of the South.

Not all southern "liberals" supported Rayburn and the Kennedy administration, however. Among those southern House members who voted frequently for liberal domestic legislation, those from districts in which the Negro population was unusually high were less likely to vote for the enlargement proposal. Table V demonstrates findings derived from aggregate analysis of the data presented in Tables III and IV. Ten of the twelve southern Democrats with ADA liberalism scores of 40 to 59.9 per cent who also come from districts with relatively small Negro populations—the median for southern House districts in 1950 was 27 per cent—supported the change in the Rules Committee's composition. Not one of their six colleagues with similar records of support for liberal domestic programs who came from districts with Negro populations larger than 30 per cent supported Rayburn. Among the most liberal southern Democrats in the House—those with ADA scores of 60 per cent or higher—only one representative from a district with a large Negro population opposed the Speaker. The congressman in question, George Huddleston, Jr., of Birmingham, Alabama, at first declared himself for the Speaker, but later decided to vote against enlargement after extensive constituency pressures.

From the foregoing analyses it is clear that there was a demonstrable relationship between the nature of the southern representa-

---

[40] The late Overton Brooks (La.-4), then Chairman of the House Science and Astronautics Committee.

[41] Representative George Huddleston, Jr. (Ala.-9).

TABLE V

Southern Democrats: Percentage of Negroes in Home Districts, Voting Records, and Votes to Enlarge the Committee on Rules

Southern Democratic Vote on Enlargement*

Percentage ADA-Approved Votes	District Population under 20 Per Cent Negro			District Population 20–29.9 Per Cent Negro			District Population over 30 Per Cent Negro		
	Against	For	Per Cent For	Against	For	Per Cent For	Against	For	Per Cent For
0–19.9	4	0	0	13	0	0	14	1	7
20–39.9	3	4	57	6	2	25	6	3	33
40–59.9	2	10	83	2	2	50	6	0	0
Over 60	0	7	100	0	2	100	1	5	83

* These totals exclude freshmen representatives elected in 1960.

tives' constituencies and past voting records and their reaction to the Rayburn proposal to enlarge the Committee on Rules. The lower the Negro percentage of the total population in his district, the more likely a southern Democrat was to support the Speaker. And the more liberal his past voting record, the more likely he was to support the move to enlarge the Committee on Rules. But there also were some important exceptions to this general pattern—exceptions that point to the operation of other, special factors during the final maneuvering before the roll-call vote.

The vote of the South's committee chairmen in the House underscore this remark. Conservative southern Democrats who were the chairmen of important House committees were much more likely to back the Speaker than southern conservatives who were not committee chairmen. Four, or half, of the southern House committee chairmen with ADA liberalism scores of under 30 per cent in 1960 went along with Rayburn; whereas only one in every twenty of the southern Democrats with equally conservative voting records who were not committee chairmen supported Rayburn. Among the more liberal southern Democrats, by contrast, committee chairmen supported Rayburn by the same two-to-one ratio as the other representatives.

It was, moreover, among the chairmen of the House's most important committees that the Speaker's support was greatest. All but two of the heads of the major committees supported Rayburn. One exception was Smith himself. The other, Chairman of the Committee on Agriculture Harold D. Cooley of North Carolina, received a personal telephone call from the President requesting his support shortly before the showdown. It failed. But even so, in the supreme test of his legislative career, Rayburn had the support of a substantial number of the most authoritative leaders of the South—among them Carl Vinson of Georgia, and Oren Harris and Wilbur D. Mills of Arkansas—as well as unanimous backing from northern and border state committee chairmen, including the conservative head of the House Appropriations Committee, Clarence Cannon of Missouri.

Undoubtedly, some southern Democrats, particularly those who had served with Rayburn on the Hill for many years, surmounted constituency pressures because of a sense of personal loyalty to the Speaker. As Representative John L. Pilcher, one of two Georgians who voted for the Rayburn proposal, explained his vote in a letter to his friends:

> To have voted against Sam Rayburn, who will go down in history as one of the greatest Americans, and our own "Old War Horse" Carl Vinson, who has been here since Woodrow Wilson and knows more about the defense of our country than any man in Congress, I would have had to align myself with 150 Republicans who will take pleasure in seeing President Kennedy's program fail. I would also have been forced to vote against my conscience, and I am 62 years of age, and have held public office for 41 years, I cannot do that now. I may be wrong; only time will tell.[42]

But Rayburn needed more than party and personal loyalty to gain enough votes to offset the two-thirds of the southern Democrats who went along with the outlook and voting inclinations of another respected veteran of the House, Judge Smith of Virginia. In order to pass the Rules Committee proposal, some additional votes were required.

The Twenty-Two Republican Dissenters

The Rayburn resolution was supported by nearly all of the northern and border state Democrats and by more than a third of the Democrats from the South. But it also received twenty-two votes from the Republican side of the aisle. Although these twenty-two Republicans were but a small fraction of the total Republican House strength (seven of every eight GOP congressmen opposed the Rayburn resolution), they had a decisive effect on the roll call's outcome. Barring additional support for Rayburn from southern Demo-

---

[42] Letter to his constituents from Representative John L. Pilcher (Ga.-2), quoted in the *Washington Post,* February 2, 1961, p. A 2.

crats,[43] three more Republican "nay" votes were all that would have been required to kill the Administration-backed resolution. Yet Minority Leader Charles Halleck was unable to get them from these Republicans, mainly, it appears, because most of these twenty-two congressmen were a special type of Republican. With several notable exceptions, these Republican dissenters differed markedly from most of their party cohorts—in the areas they represented, in their support for domestic social welfare legislation, and in the enthusiasm which President Kennedy's candidacy had evoked in their home districts.

The regional concentration of the Republicans who backed the Rayburn proposal underscores this point. Eighteen of the twenty-two came from urban and industrial districts in states along the Atlantic seaboard, including three from New York City, two from Pittsburgh, and one from Washington's Maryland suburbs. Republican support for the Rules Committee change was particularly strong in New Jersey and New England. Seven of ten GOP representatives from Massachusetts, New Hampshire, and Connecticut, and four of the eight New Jersey Republicans crossed party lines to support Speaker Rayburn.[44]

Three other dissenters—Ayres of Ohio, Curtis of Missouri, and Baldwin of California—also represented urban or suburban industrial constituencies. Yet in the region where the GOP had traditionally been strongest, there was little indication of dissatisfaction with the *status quo*. Throughout the farm belt, once the heartland of Republican insurgency and the region that spawned George Norris, leader in the revolt of 1910, only one Republican—O'Konski of Wisconsin—supported the change. Republican insurgency in the Rules Committee fight of 1961 came primarily from the eastern urban wing of the party.

It also stemmed primarily from the party's liberal wing. A simple index of liberalism similar to that used in the analysis of the southern Democrats will demonstrate this point. As the data presented in Table VI indicate, the higher a Republican congressman's liber-

---

[43] It was frequently asserted on Capitol Hill that Rayburn had two or more votes among southern Democrats that he could have tapped had he needed them. While observers differed as to who these representatives were, there was some agreement that he probably could have commanded at least one more vote from Texas and one from Mississippi.

[44] In addition, former Republican Speaker Joseph Martin of Massachusetts was paired in favor of enlargement of the Committee on Rules, thus canceling one Republican opposition vote.

alism score had been on nine selected issues in the 1960 legislative session, the more likely he was to support enlargement of the Committee on Rules in 1961. Of the GOP representatives with liberalism scores of 60 per cent or higher, seven out of eight supported the Rayburn resolution. At the other extreme, among conservative Republicans who opposed the ADA position more than 80 per cent of the time, not one voted for enlargement.

For the most part, it was the liberal Republicans who backed the Rules Committee change. But, as the data in Table VI indicate, there were some notable exceptions. The more conservative voting records of four of the Republicans who supported Rayburn—Ayres of Ohio, Bass of New Hampshire, Bates of Massachusetts, and Curtis of Missouri—suggested that these congressmen would probably vote against much of the President's domestic program. One of the four, Congressman Curtis, made his position explicit in the debate immediately before the vote:

> . . . [W]hichever party obtains the responsibility to organize the Congress should have the necessary power to meet that responsibility. . . . I intend to oppose most of the legislation I have heard Mr. Kennedy is going to send up to the House for consideration. I intend to be on the floor to do the best I can to defeat the measures on the merits.[45]

TABLE VI

House Republicans: Percentage of ADA-Approved Votes and Votes on the Resolution to Enlarge the Committee on Rules

Percentage ADA-Approved Votes*	Republican House Members			
	Total† (Number)	Vote Against Enlargement (Number)	Vote For Enlargement (Number)	Proportion For Enlargement (Per Cent)
0–9.9	15	15	0	0
10–19.9	30	30	0	0
20–29.9	34	32	2	6
30–39.9	18	16	2	11
40–49.9	8	6	2	25
50–59.9	11	7	4	36
60–69.9	4	1	3	75
70–79.9	2	0	2	100
80 and over	2	0	2	100
TOTAL	124	107	17	14

* The ADA liberalism index in this table is identical to that in Table I.
† These totals exclude freshmen representatives elected in 1960 and paired votes.

---

[45] *Congressional Record*, January 31, 1961, p. 1504. Curtis was the only dissenting Republican who was allowed floor time during the debate.

Still different considerations may have affected the vote of some of the other GOP dissenters. One possibility is that urban Republicans from economically distressed areas would be less satisfied with the existing House rules. Republicans who supported the Rayburn resolution were in fact more likely to have areas with substantial unemployment in their districts than those who did not, but the data on which this finding is based, while suggestive, cannot be considered conclusive.[46]

An equally plausible hypothesis is that Republican House members who were elected by a narrow margin in the 1960 elections might be especially likely to trim their sails in a liberal direction in order to broaden their base of support. Yet, in fact, this was not the case. Republicans who supported the Rayburn resolution were only slightly more likely to hold marginal House seats than those who did not.[47] Furthermore, of the twenty-nine Republican repre-

---

[46] Some fourteen of fifty-seven Republican representatives (approximately 25 per cent) from districts bordering on or within "areas of substantial labor surplus" voted for enlargement of the Rules Committee. These findings must be interpreted with considerable caution, however, because the boundary lines of congressional districts seldom coincide with the geographical areas set forth by the Bureau of Employment Security, United States Department of Labor, in its bimonthly survey, *Area Labor Market Trends*. Furthermore, it may be that these urban representatives were predisposed to vote for a change in the rules, with the extent of unemployment in their respective districts only one of a number of factors. In Democratic districts bordering on or in areas in which surplus labor was 6 per cent or greater, eighty out of ninety-two representatives voted for enlargement. As of January, 1961, 76 of the nation's 150 major areas were classified as areas of substantial labor surplus, the largest number since the low point of the 1957–58 recession. *Area Labor Market Trends* (January, 1961), p. 2.

[47] Sixteen per cent (four in twenty-five) of the Republican congressmen elected with between 50.1 and 52.4 of the two-party congressional vote supported the Rayburn resolution. The comparable figures for the Republican congressmen who were elected with larger margins of victory were: 10 per cent of those elected with 52.5–54.9 per cent of the vote (twenty cases); 14 per cent of those elected with 55–59.9 per cent of the vote (sixty-six cases); 11 per cent of those elected with 60–69.9 per cent of the vote (fifty-two cases); and 14 per cent of those elected with 70 per cent or more of the vote (seven cases). In contrast, support for the Administration-supported resolution was strongest among Democratic congressmen from marginal seats, again a reflection of the sectional cleavage within the Democratic party and the fact that most uncontested seats were in the South. With the exception of five North Carolina dissenters, support for the resolution was unanimous among the seventy-six Democratic representatives receiving less than 60 per cent of the two-party vote in their districts in 1960 (93 per cent). The comparable figures for the Democratic congressmen who were elected with larger margins of victory were: 89 per cent of those elected with 60–69.9 per cent of the vote (fifty-three cases); 78 per cent of those elected with 70–94.9 per cent of the vote (sixty cases); and but 43 per cent of those elected with 95 per cent or more of the vote (seventy cases).

sentatives who won seats previously held by Democrats, only four voted for enlargement.[48] What is noteworthy about the districts these congressmen represented, however, is that they were all keenly fought at the presidential level. In more than half of them, Kennedy polled more votes than Nixon. The data which underpin this point appear in Table VII, in which the vote of Republican congressmen on the Rules Committee issue is related to President Kennedy's popular vote in their district in 1960. The import of the data is clear: the larger the Kennedy vote in a Republican congressman's district, the more likely the Republican was to support the Administration-backed measure to enlarge the Committee on Rules. Republican congressmen who supported the Rayburn resolution, in short, represented districts

TABLE VII

Republican Congressmen: Kennedy's Percentage of the Presidential Vote in Their Districts in 1960 and Congressmen's Vote on the Motion to Enlarge the Committee on Rules*

| Kennedy Percentage in Congressional District, 1960 | Total (Number) | Republican House Members | | |
		Vote Against Enlargement (Number)	Vote For Enlargement (Number)	Vote For Enlargement (Per Cent)
0–44.9	99	98	1	1
45–47.4	29	25	4	14
47.5–49.9	17	13	4	24
50–52.4	12	6	6	50
52.5 and over	13	6	7	54
TOTAL	170	148	22	13

* Data compiled from "Complete Returns of the 1960 Elections by Congressional District," Part II of the *Congressional Quarterly Weekly Report*, XIX, No. 10 (March 10, 1961), 3–45. Paired votes are excluded from this analysis.

where the Democratic presidential ticket had had considerable appeal.[49]

---

[48] The eight Democratic representatives who won seats formerly held by Republicans, three from New York, one in New Jersey, and four from western states, all voted in favor of the resolution.

[49] Comparable data for Democratic congressmen are less clear-cut. Outside the South, of course, the Rayburn resolution received all but two votes. Among the southern congressmen, the Kennedy-backed resolution received its greatest support in districts where the Kennedy-Johnson ticket received between 50 and 59.9 per cent of the two-party vote. Among these representatives, 54 per cent supported the enlargement resolution (thirty-eight cases). Only 17 per cent of the southern congressmen voted for the resolution in districts in which the Kennedy-Johnson ticket had less than 50 per cent of the vote (twenty-nine cases). In districts where the Democratic ticket received 60 per cent or more of the two-party vote, 36 per cent of the southern Democratic

These Republican mavericks—more conservative than the northern Democrats, yet more liberal than their Republican colleagues—occupied a crucial position in the American political system. Thirteen of the twenty-two represented districts Nixon lost to Kennedy, districts which a Republican presidential nominee would probably have to carry in order for their party to regain control of the White House. Although they themselves had fared well at the hands of the electorate, the Kennedy vote in their districts made it clear that they came from closely contested political territory. In their public statements during the rules fight, one major theme predominated. If the Republicans supported Chairman Smith as a bloc, the public image of the GOP as an "obstructionist party" in alliance with the conservative southern Democrats would be reinforced. As Representative Lindsay of New York expressed it, the action of the House Republican leadership placed "the Republican minority in the position of seeming to coalesce with southern Democrats, a posture which in the long run is contrary to the principles and best interests of the Republican party."[50] By opposing their leadership, these twenty-two representatives provided the indispensable minimum of Republican support that enabled the Rayburn resolution to pass.

III. SUMMARY AND CONCLUSIONS

The decision to enlarge the House Committee on Rules was supported by nearly all of the Democratic congressmen outside the South, and by a third of the southern Democrats and an eighth of the Republicans. Among southern Democrats, the move drew its greatest support from committee chairmen and from congressmen with moderate to liberal voting records. It drew least support from southerners representing rural districts and districts with large Negro populations. The House delegations of Alabama, Tennessee, Louisiana, Arkansas, and, above all, Speaker Rayburn's own state of Texas provided the bulk of the southern votes for the change.

Among Republicans, what support there was for the Rayburn resolution came primarily from the more liberal Republicans of the

---

congressmen supported the Rules Committee enlargement (thirty-four cases). Analysis is further complicated by the presence of third-party slates in Mississippi, Alabama, and Louisiana.

[50] Lindsay made his statement after the Republican Party Policy Committee took the unprecedented action of releasing its decision to the press, prior to the meeting of the Republican Conference. *New York Times*, January 20, 1961, p. 16.

eastern seaboard, although a handful of GOP congressmen who did not belong to the party's eastern or liberal wings also voted for the measure. Nearly all of these Republican dissenters, however, represented districts where Kennedy polled a sizable vote for President. More than half came from districts which President Kennedy carried in 1960. With this support, the Rayburn resolution was carried by the slender margin of five votes.

This victory, however, should not obscure the fact that other courses of action designed to achieve the Speaker's aim of expediting the President's legislative program were also open to Rayburn. Several of these alternatives, in fact, received serious consideration before they were rejected by the House Democratic leadership at the beginning of the session. Although compelling practical arguments could be advanced against each of them, the range of legislative tactics that might have been employed was broad. The Speaker could, of course, have done nothing about the Rules Committee, planning to rely instead on bargaining with its members and the use of existing devices for bypassing the committee—such as the Calendar Wednesday procedure. He could have again resorted to a "twenty-one-day rule," modification of the discharge petition, or some other technique designed to provide a majority of the members of the House with a means of getting bills to the floor. He could have sought a compromise with Smith, based on Smith's agreement to grant a rule for certain specified key measures of the President's legislative program. He could have pushed his proposal to remove Representative Colmer from the committee through the Democratic party caucus. Or he could have attempted to persuade the House to make a basic change in the committee's powers.

Looming behind these various tactical choices open to the Speaker were larger questions of principle, for the enlargement struggle refocused attention on the basic issue of what the function of the Committee on Rules should be. Here again, a number of lines of speculation are possible—speculation that concerns both the committee's composition and its powers. Should the committee be an instrument of the House majority leadership? If so, should it be composed solely of members of the majority party, and should the Speaker himself be a member? Alternatively, should the committee be as nearly representative as possible of the total membership of the House—a microcosm of the whole? Or should the committee overrepresent groups who are in a minority in the House, thus making the agreement of concurrent majorities a necessary prerequisite for action in the American governmental system?

Given these basic considerations, Rayburn's choice of tactics is instructive as to the workings of the House of Representatives. For Rayburn's decision for the floor fight that led to enlargement of the committee in effect enabled the Speaker to avoid a final resolution of these underlying issues. By making this choice, Rayburn opted for the positive course of action that created the minimum disturbance possible in the *status quo*. No attack was made on the committee's jurisdiction or powers. No member was unseated, nor was party discipline applied. Even the resolution to enlarge the committee was worded so as to apply to the Eighty-seventh Congress only. The enlargement resolution, as the Speaker himself said after abandoning his proposal to purge Colmer, was "the way to embarrass nobody if they didn't want to be embarrassed."[51]

The House Rules fight of 1961 thus resembled every previous battle over the powers of the Rules Committee in which some action was taken—each of which had been resolved by a change in the committee's membership or by providing a mechanism whereby a majority of the members of the House could bypass the committee. Like those previous battles, the House Rules fight of 1961 left the Committee on Rules with extensive powers to block the progress of some bills and to expedite the passage of others. The committee thus retained powers which even those committee members normally sympathetic to the House leadership might feel prompted to exercise independently on certain issues. It also held powers over which the conservatives might regain control if but one of the moderates and liberals was unable to attend meetings of the committee. Particularly toward the end of the session, the discretionary powers of the chairman would once again loom large.

Moreover, even before Rayburn's fatal illness made it necessary to select a new Speaker, it was clear that the enlargement decision itself was tentative, not permanent. When the Eighty-eighth Congress convened in January, 1963, the issue of the committee's size would be up for decision again. Whether the composition of the Committee on Rules would remain responsive to the wishes of the Democratic majority leadership in the House for long was thus an open question. It was also a question that, to a considerable extent, depended

---

[51] *New York Times*, January 1, 1961, p. 1.

upon the outcome of the mid-term elections of 1962. For only the election returns would determine the number and relative strength of congressmen who opposed or favored the policy predilections that frequently prevailed in the House Committee on Rules between 1937 and 1960.[52]

---

[52] In the 1962 midterm elections, the Democrats made the best showing by a party in control of the White House since 1934—a net loss of only four seats. In January, 1963, the House voted 235 to 196 for a rules change "permanently" increasing the size of the Committee on Rules to fifteen members (see Chapter VI of the present volume).

VIII

THE HOUSE OF REPRESENTATIVES AND FEDERAL AID TO EDUCATION*

Richard F. Fenno, Jr.

THE RESOLUTION of conflict and the building of consensus are among the major functions which Congress performs for American society. The process by which House and Senate majorities are created and authoritative congressional decisions are made helps to resolve society-wide conflicts and increase society-wide agreement on public policy. One area, however, in which Congress has tried and failed to perform these normal functions is that of federal aid to elementary and secondary schools. For ninety-two years, this issue of "general" federal aid to education has commanded congressional attention; since 1945 alone, its committees have recorded 6.5 million words of testimony on seventy-seven different legislative proposals.[1] Yet no general aid bill has ever been enacted into law. By failing to take positive action, Congress repeatedly reconfirms an existing policy consensus in opposition to general federal aid. But, at the same time, the persistence of sharp, closely fought controversy in and out of Congress testifies to the root instability of that consensus. Conflict remains widespread, deep, and unresolved.

To speak of Congress' inability to promote a new consensus on federal aid policy is to focus attention on the House of Representatives. Since 1945, federal aid bills have never lacked a Senate majority, either in the Committee on Labor and Public Welfare or on the

---

* This article has been drawn largely from Chapters 5 and 6 by the author in Frank J. Munger and Richard F. Fenno, Jr., *National Politics in Federal Aid to Education*. Copyright © 1962 by Syracuse University Press (No. 3, "Economics and Politics & Public Education Series"). The material is used here by special permission of the publisher. A special debt of gratitude is owed to Frank Munger for his assistance and stimulation at all phases of the larger project.

[1] For purposes of this study, the meaning of federal aid to education is restricted to general aid to elementary and secondary schools. A much more extensive analysis of the issues and interest groups involved and of decision-making units (for instance, the executive branch and the Senate) will be found in *ibid*.

floor. The Senate has passed each bill debated in the postwar years—in 1948, 1949, 1960, and 1961. When the body has not acted, it has been for external reasons, not because federal aid stood in any danger of defeat. By contrast, however, majorities have been extremely hard to achieve at those points in the House where they must be produced—in the Committee on Education and Labor, the Committee on Rules, and on the floor. In the late 1940's and early 1950's the Education and Labor Committee held hearings but failed to report out a bill. In the more recent past the committee has reported out a bill six times. In three of those instances the Rules Committee refused to send the bill to the House floor. Two other bills which received Rules Committee approval were subsequently defeated on the floor. On the single occasion when a federal aid bill did pass in the House, it was stopped by the Rules Committee on its way to conference. See Figure 1.

On the record, the House of Representatives has not performed conflict-resolving and consensus-building functions in the area of federal aid to education. This study presents a summary analysis of the House record from 1945 to 1962. Legislative case histories typically focus upon a single bill and relate in depth the story of how that bill became a law. This analysis, in contrast, treats many bills over a considerable span of time and attempts to explain why none of them has ever become law. Doubtless, one explanation lies in the incredible complexity and sensitivity of the problems which comprise "the" issue of federal aid—problems involving control of the educational system, aid to non-public (especially parochial) schools, and the survival of segregated schools. Some readers may conclude that it is simply impossible for any legislative body to resolve such a tangle of criss-crossing conflicts. However, the Senate has performed quite normally in dealing with the same issues. The vastly different outcome of House action can best be understood by examining the issues of federal aid as they are processed by the particular individuals and institutions of the House.

THE COMMITTEE ON EDUCATION AND LABOR

The most powerful institutions of the House are its committees, where all demands for House decisions begin their journeys—and where most of these projected journeys end. In doing its work, each House committee participates in the conflict-resolution and consensus-building functions of the parent chamber. The conflicts which are resolved in committee are the ones most likely to be

Figure I
House Action on General Federal Aid to Education Bills
1945–1962

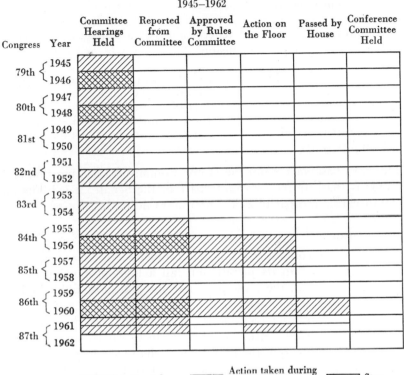

Congress	Year	Committee Hearings Held	Reported from Committee	Approved by Rules Committee	Action on the Floor	Passed by House	Conference Committee Held
79th	1945	▨					
	1946	▨					
80th	1947	▨					
	1948	▨					
81st	1949	▨					
	1950	▨					
82nd	1951						
	1952	▨					
83rd	1953						
	1954	▨					
84th	1955	▨	▨				
	1956	▨	▨	▨	▨		
85th	1957	▨		▨	▨		
	1958	▨					
86th	1959	▨					
	1960	▨	▨	▨	▨	▨	
87th	1961	▨	▨		▨		
	1962						

▨ Action taken during session   ▨ Action taken during prior session of same Congress   ☐ Step bypassed

Source: Frank Munger and Richard Fenno, *National Politics and Federal Aid to Education* (Syracuse, N.Y.: Syracuse University Press, 1962), p. 9.

resolved on the floor. If the committee majority supporting a policy agreement is cohesive and stable, the House as a whole is more likely to produce a stable legislative consensus. In the area of federal aid policy, the pattern of House activity has been fixed, to a considerable degree, by the pattern of activity in its Committee on Education and Labor.

Nearly all congressmen agree that this committee is probably the one in which it is most difficult to achieve a consensus and the one most susceptible to prolonged conflict. In the words of a leading Democratic proponent of federal aid:

It's a very discouraging committee. You can't get a resolu-tion praising God through that committee without having a three-day battle over it. . . . It's about the most difficult committee around. Our executive sessions are the most exciting things you ever saw.[2]

A Republican opponent of federal aid uses a different perspective but arrives at a similar conclusion:

We work by trying to split the Democrats on the committee. And actually we don't have to work very hard. They'll split off by themselves. . . [n]ot on the big issues on the final votes, but on amendments and in the committee. They'll shout at each other, stand up and bang their fists on the table and stomp out.

The most basic fact about the House Committee on Education and Labor is that, unlike its counterpart in the Senate, it exhibits an almost classic incapacity as a consensus-building institution.

Jurisdiction

Most of the committee's internal problems are consequences of the fact that within its jurisdiction fall a high proportion of the most controversial, the most partisan, and the most publicized issues of American domestic politics. The committee, activated in 1947, cut its legislative teeth on the Taft-Hartley Bill and has been a domestic political battleground ever since. All committee members agreed with two of their colleagues—the first a Republican, the second a Democrat—whose explanations follow:

This is where the basic philosophies of the two parties really come out strongly. It's a clash of philosophies. You don't get that on Merchant Marine and Fisheries. Oh, what battles! You should see the battles we have in executive session.

This is probably the most partisan committee in the House because this is where the fundamental philosophical battles are fought. . . . The things that identify the administration's domestic program come out of our committee. You take mini-

---

[2] All unattributed quotations in this article are taken from interviews held with twenty-one members of the House Committee on Education and Labor, one member of the Senate Committee on Labor and Public Welfare, and with staff members of both committees. The interviews were held in Washington in June, 1961. They were semi-structured interviews, and questions were open-ended. Notes were not taken during the interview but were transcribed immediately afterward. The quotations are as nearly verbatim as the author's power of immediate recall could make them. In all cases, the respondents were told that their comments would not be attributed to them.

mum wage. That's a black and white proposition there. And all of our issues are fundamental, philosophical questions. You don't get that on Space or Foreign Affairs.

If a committee is to function as a consensus-building institution, there must be considerable opportunity for compromise and mutual accommodation of views. Conditions must be maintained in which the legislative techniques of give and take, bargaining, are possible. It is the chief consequence of nationwide partisan and philosophical controversies that they seriously limit the development of such internal conditions. A former Republican member reflected on his experience in the 1950's:

> Some of us were unalterably opposed to federal aid, and some on the other side were just as unalterably in favor of it. . . . There weren't many minds changed by discussion. Everybody had a fixed position when he came there, and nobody changed that opinion that I know of.

A Democrat, speaking of the situation in 1961, agreed, "The lines are drawn pretty tight on this committee, and there isn't much flexibility."

Issues involving the degree and direction of federal participation in such fields as labor-management relations, minimum wage, and education are among those which few legislators can avoid in their election campaigns. Several Republicans recalled debating their opponents on the federal aid issue in 1960; and they recalled, too, having taken a firm stand against all federal aid or a stand, following Vice President Nixon, in support of school construction aid only. Most committee Democrats, on the other hand, campaigned along with their standard-bearer, Senator Kennedy, in favor of both a construction and a teachers' salary aid program. Since they have assumed more or less unequivocal positions on federal aid before their constituents, members come to their committee work committed in advance and are denied the freedom to maneuver so basic to the production of legislative agreement. They have come from their election campaigns trained, positioned, and girded for head-on, showdown committee conflict.

In another way, too, the jurisdiction of the committee has hampered consensus-building in the field of federal aid. When the committee was established in 1946, its main focus was considered to be the field of labor. The great majority of committee members were oriented toward labor problems and professed only minor interest in education. Though there has been a tendency for some members to specialize in educational matters, such members still remain in the minority on the committee. Since the 1946 decision that the field of education did not warrant a separate committee, many large educational programs of the national government have been placed under the jurisdiction of other House committees.[3] Thus, the decision to combine education and labor has weakened and fragmented the efforts on behalf of federal aid by members of Congress and by supporting interest groups.

Educational controversy has also been infected with the by-products of labor controversy. Internal conflict would doubtless be harsh in a single education committee, but the tradition of charge and countercharge accompanying labor-management legislation has certainly made it more difficult to build a consensus among the same people in the area of education. There is, of course, an affinity of philosophy between the supporters of organized labor and the supporters of federal aid to education; the record of the AFL-CIO on behalf of federal aid is substantial. However, the Democratic membership of the committee has been chosen so as to maximize unity on labor matters, and concern for unity on federal aid to education has been secondary. The result is that while a Catholic Democrat and a non-Catholic Democrat or a Democrat with many Negro constituents and a Democrat with few Negro constituents can reach agreement on labor matters, they may be pulled in many directions when confronted with the divisive religious and racial issues involved in federal aid.

The passage of time has increased the heat of the federal aid controversy and has done very little to reduce committee conflict. There was a period in the 1940's when information was scarce, when a variety of new approaches was being explored, when there was no legacy of controversy, and when, therefore, some attitudes had not crystallized. Now, however, each successive layer of legislative struggle compresses the participants into positions of increasing inflexibility. Committee hearings, for example, function to add current data to support old positions and to add current reaffirmations of support or opposition to the store of old political intelligence. They may serve to promote communication between the interest group spokesmen and their own membership, but they have ceased

---

[3] See Robert M. Rosenzweig, "The Congress—How It Deals With Educational Issues," *Higher Education*, XVII (April, 1961), 8–11.

to promote, if they ever did, the communication between proponents and opponents. One member described the federal aid hearings
in this way:

> They don't do any good, and nobody listens to them any-
> way. The same people say the same things every year; only the
> statistics change. But the lines are hard and fast on this issue,
> and nobody changes his mind on or off the committee. It's a
> formality. . . . The teachers' groups and these other organiza-
> tions can prove to their members that they are getting their
> money's worth for their dues. That's all. They don't change
> anything.

Hearings may serve to inform newcomers, but they do not convert
anyone. One freshman said, "I tried to keep an open mind. I went
in there and listened with the attitude, 'let's see if you can convince
me I'm wrong.' And the more I heard, the more convinced I was
that I was right." In the hearing rooms and out, committee members
tend, they say, to maintain communications with only one set of
interest groups and one set of lobbyists—those with whom they
already agree. The only people who may have something new to
present, who may represent a potential for change, and who are,
therefore, listened to by both sides, are the spokesmen for the
President and his administration.

Membership

Conflict within the Committee on Education and Labor is, ultimately, not a conflict among issues but among individual members.
The selection of committee members is, therefore, critical in
determining the degree, if not the main lines, of internal conflict.
The net result has been that the members of the House committee
come from among those in their respective parties who already are
in the widest disagreement on the issues of federal aid. The people
who control assignments to the committee exercise considerable
care. On the Republican side, new House members are ordinarily
discouraged from applying for this committee unless their convictions are firm, their talents for combat considerable, and their districts reasonably safe.[4] Those who cannot be dissuaded and those
who must be solicited tend to lean toward the more conservative

---

[4] See Nicholas A. Masters, "House Committee Assignments," *American Political Science Review*, LV (June, 1961), 354–55. Reprinted as Chapter II of the
present volume.

wing of their party. A rather senior Republican said that he advises anyone who desires a political career to stay off the Committee— unless he is deeply committed. Of himself, he said:

> My people didn't vote for me. They voted for what I stood for, my principles. I was elected as a conservative, and that's a wonderful thing. . . . It's an awfully unpopular committee. I take a terrible pounding. But my future is behind me, and I don't give a good God damn.

"I'm the kind of person," echoed an equally conservative freshman member, "who jumps right into these hot spots. So I figured if this was the most controversial committee in the House, I'd like to get on it." When the leadership has to fill a slot with a member who has not applied, it may try to ascertain his views beforehand. One member explained:

> Halleck called a friend of mine in —— and said, "What kind of a guy is this ——? We're thinking of putting him on Education and Labor, but we need someone who'll stand up, someone we can count on who won't waver in his views." My friend replied, "You don't have to worry about ——."

On the Democratic side, too, members are strongly issue-oriented, personally contentious, and vigorously committed. They tend to represent the more liberal elements of their party. Party leaders produce this result both by encouraging the appointment of labor-oriented congressmen and by discouraging the appointment of southerners. To an individual representing a manufacturing or mining constituency, a place on the committee dealing with labor matters will have positive electoral advantages. Many Democratic members (fifteen of nineteen in 1961) received financial assistance from the trade unions, and all of these are dependent upon labor support at the polls.[5] Union lobbyists sometimes actively intercede with the Democratic committee selectors on behalf of congressmen known to be sympathetic to them. On the other hand, no more than four (and usually fewer) southern Democrats have ever been placed on the committee at one time—despite the pleas of the southern committee members. No pretense is made at representativeness on this score; in 1961, 38 per cent of all Democratic congressmen (99

[5] *Congressional Quarterly*, XVII (April 10, 1959), 509–15; *Congressional Quarterly*, XVIII (November 11, 1960), 1857.

of 263) came from the eleven southern states, but only 11 per cent (two of nineteen) of the committee members did.

Despite the most careful attention to their appointment, the Democratic members of the committee constitute an extraordinarily heterogeneous group. They are personally much more predisposed to intraparty conflicts than are the Republicans. Moreover, if there is a unifying bond among most of them, it is a bond on the issues of labor, not education. The Republicans on the committee in 1961, however, were all male, non-southern, non-border-state, and Protestant—whatever their differences. They were all white, and not one of them represented a constituency with a non-white population of 10 per cent or over. Though 17 per cent of the Roman Catholic House members were Republicans, of these, none was on the committee. The 1961 Democratic members, by contrast, included two women, two southerners, two border-state members, seven Roman Catholics, and two Jews. The chairman was a Negro, and four Democrats represented constituencies with non-white populations of over 10 per cent.[6] These demographic differences are overlaid with vast differences in personality and political style. Together they make consensus-building on the Democratic side especially hazardous, particularly on the issues of school integration and private school assistance.

The combined result of Republican and Democratic appointment practices, which is most significant for this study, is not only that they guarantee sharp ideological and partisan division on the committee, but that they intensify internal committee division. The *Congressional Quarterly* selected ten roll-call votes in 1961 to distinguish those House members who supported a larger federal role in the nation's economic and social life (*i.e.,* liberals) and those House members who opposed a larger federal role (*i.e.,* conservatives).[7] A majority of committee Democrats (twelve of nineteen) voted on every occasion to expand government activity, and a majority of committee Republicans (seven of twelve) voted on every occasion in opposition to this expansion. Moreover, if the voting percentages are scaled, every Democratic committee member voted

---

[6] Data on the non-white population by congressional districts are taken from United States Bureau of the Census, *Congressional District Data Book* (Washington, D.C.: Government Printing Office, 1961).

[7] The roll-call votes used and the records of each Representative are listed in *Congressional Quarterly,* XIX (October 20, 1961), 1751–63.

more often for an expanded federal role than did any of the Republicans.

These ideological and partisan differences inside the committee
are significantly greater than differences on the same issues in the
House as a whole. Whereas average percentages among House
Democrats were 78 per cent in favor of a larger federal role and 21
per cent against, committee Democrats averaged 91 per cent in
favor and 8 per cent against. House Republicans averaged 12 per
cent in favor and 87 per cent opposed, whereas committee Republicans averaged 7 per cent in favor and 93 per cent opposed. See
Table I.

TABLE I

*Ideological Representativeness of Committee on Education and
Labor, 1961*

	Votes For Expanded Federal Role (10 Roll Calls)	Votes Against Expanded Federal Role (10 Roll Calls)	Index of Ideological Representa- tiveness*
	(Mean Percentage)		
All House Democrats	78	21	+57
House Education and Labor Committee Democrats	91	8	+83
All House Republicans	12	87	−75
House Education and Labor Committee Republicans	7	93	−86

Source: *Congressional Quarterly*, XIX (October 20, 1961), 1751–63.
* The Index of Ideological Representativeness constitutes the difference between the
mean percentage of votes in favor of an expanded federal role and the mean
percentage of those opposed.

Given the considerable degree of inflexibility within party groups,
the ratio of Democrats to Republicans has assumed considerable
importance. During the years of Republican control, it was certain
that no bill would emerge from the committee. During the years
of Democratic majorities, a coalition of Republicans plus southern
Democrats could prevent committee action. Until the Eighty-sixth
Congress in January, 1959, the Republicans plus the southern Democrats constituted a majority—hence a controlling influence whenever
they could agree. In 1959, following the sweeping Democratic congressional victory of the previous November, the liberal Democrats
and their interest-group allies succeeded in breaking the long-standing coalition majority. They persuaded Speaker Rayburn to recom-

mend a new party ratio of twenty Democrats to ten Republicans instead of the previous seventeen Democrats to thirteen Republicans. Under the previous arrangements, thirteen Republicans plus Chairman Barden and Phil Landrum (Ga.) could create a tie vote. A third, a more liberal southerner, Carl Elliott of Alabama, one of the committee's few education specialists, was placed in a strategic position at the ideological center of the committee and in the eye of most internal storms. Six new Democrats, all supported by organized labor, were given committee membership in 1959; those southerners who applied were turned down. This membership change constitutes one of the landmarks of the federal aid controversy in Congress.

Procedures

The resolution of internal strife and the formation of legislative consensus are affected greatly by the way in which a committee organizes itself for decision-making. The style of decision-making best suited to the ends of this committee would be one which would emphasize mutual accommodation within the group and develop procedures for cooperation and compromise. Frequently, informal and traditional techniques of accommodation will develop on committees—between majority and minority party leaders, between legislatively experienced members and those who are legislatively inexperienced, between the experts in a particular subject matter and non-experts. The Committee on Education and Labor has not adopted this style of decision-making to any important degree. Its style tends to be fiercely competitive; the techniques are those of naked power, and the decision goes to whoever can command a simple majority in a showdown vote. The rules of the game are the formal rules of the House, untempered by private committee traditions or informal understandings. Committee members have no sense of the committee as an entity worth worrying about. Sentiments of mutual regard and group solidarity are few. Group morale is not high. The committee's decision-making procedures do nothing to lower tension or to increase cohesion inside the group.

Democrats and Republicans find it difficult to overcome their mutual suspicions sufficiently to establish even minimally harmonious working relationships. Throughout 1961, the committee chairman and the ranking minority member, whose cooperation should provide the major lubricant of decision-making, conducted a ridiculous public feud over the amount of room space allotted to their respective staffs.[8] A marked lack of communication seems to exist at all other levels of the committee as well.

Though it is doubtless true that, in the words of one Republican, "Some of our guys hate Democrats more than anything," it often appears that some Democrats hate some other Democrats with a similar passion. Democrats freely admit their natural propensity to fight one another, and a Republican remarked, "There's never that kind of fighting between Democrats and Republicans. They don't expect to convert us. It's like the old situation where they hate the heretic more than they do the infidel." In federal aid decisions, the injection of the segregation issue—splitting northerner from southerner and moderate from liberal—and the parochial school issue—splitting urban Catholic and rural non-Catholic—exacerbates the normal problems of consensus-building on the Democratic side. Republicans, less beset by racial and religious differences and in the minority during all but four years since World War II, have tended to cohere much more frequently—though President Eisenhower's support for federal aid split the group in the late 1950's.

One of the most common House traditions that functions to check conflicts on many committees is the informal norm of apprenticeship, which prescribes that committee newcomers should defer to those senior men more experienced in the work of the committee. Accordingly, the freshman is to attend meetings, do his homework, say very little, and participate minimally in the making of the group's decisions. The Education and Labor Committee gives virtually no service to this tradition. The committee's young men, who happen to be extraordinarily bright, able, and disputatious, are expected to carry a major share of the decision-making burdens. A freshman Republican put this in the strongest language possible:

> There isn't any bigger myth than the idea that new people can't do anything. After all this talk about seniority, I was surprised. You know you aren't going to be the committee chairman, and you know you aren't going to get to sponsor a major piece of legislation, but other than that you can participate as much as you want. You can even get to take leadership on a bill in committee. . . . Every time a bill comes out, the young members are asked to take five minutes or ten minutes

---

[8] Their battle was reported in the Capitol Hill newspaper, *Roll Call* during March, April, September, and December, 1961. There is, predictably, almost no contact between majority and minority staff members on the committee.

to speak on the floor. They ask us; we don't have to ask. So it's just the opposite from what the myth and fiction of seniority would have you believe.

A first-year Democrat spoke for his colleagues when he said:

> I was amazed. I was hesitant to do all the things they asked me to do—being a newcomer. I'm the only lawyer on that subcommittee . . . and in drafting the law they relied on me a great deal. A new man has no restrictions at all.

The weakness of seniority traditions is also evident in the fact that very senior members are sometimes denied the sponsorship of a bill or the chairmanship of a subcommittee to which their rank would otherwise entitle them. Chairman Barden refused to give top Democrat Adam Clayton Powell the chairmanship he wanted, and Powell, when he became chairman, rendered this kind of treatment to high-ranking Phil Landrum of Georgia.[9] Operation without the stabilizing influence of these traditions encourages decision-making by free-for-all.

Another force which often countervails against an every-man-for-himself technique of legislative decision-making in many committees is the presence of subject-matter experts. Committee members will acknowledge the expertise of one or two of their colleagues and will defer to them—not on matters of critical importance to themselves but on technical or factual matters. The expert may not be able ultimately to swing votes, but as the legislation works its way through subcommittee and committee, his views will carry substantial weight. It is important to realize, therefore, that there are no acknowledged experts on federal aid to education in the House of Representatives. If there were, they would be found on the Committee on Education and Labor. Yet every one of the factors thus far discussed militates against the unifying presence of expertise.

Inside the committee no deference is accorded even to the work of subcommittees. Though a subcommittee may have sat many days in hearings and worked long hours over its recommendations, these

---

[9] Powell set up a battery of three subcommittees to deal with educational matters but declined to assign them permanent areas of jurisdiction. He offered the chairmanship of the Special Subcommittee on Education to Landrum. Since, however, Powell had no intention of assigning any legislation to the subcommittee if Landrum became its chairman, Landrum declined to serve.

are almost always changed by the full committee. Long-time participants are hard put to remember occasions when substantial alterations have not been made; one senior member remarked:

> You can't take a bill before that group unless you know exactly what every section, every paragraph, every line, every word means. There are so many sharpies in there. . . . Someone will try to put another interpretation on it, and if you can't refute it, it will stick. . . . Oh! it's a real circus.

The committee has, furthermore, never recruited a staff of experts on education whose independent judgment has carried any weight at all with the members.

Since the committee does not acknowledge within its own body of supposed specialists any experts on federal aid, it is hardly likely that the committee will be viewed as conveying expert opinion to the floor. This committee's views as such ordinarily carry little persuasion with the House membership. The normal impression which committee members manage to create in the floor is that of being wholly unable to agree among themselves—both between and within parties. Individual committee members often come to the floor prepared to introduce crippling amendments or, indeed, substitute bills. Members are not usually daunted should a pet amendment, e.g., the Powell Amendment, be defeated in committee. Said one Democrat in reference to an education amendment:

> I tried it in the committee . . . and I'll try it again on the floor. I haven't told them [his committee colleagues] I'm going to, but they know that I tried it in committee, and I suppose they know I'll try again. . . . I just believe in it—that's all.

Other amendments come to the floor because the committee is incapable of dealing with them: "Lots of times . . . if a person has an amendment, he'll hold it back just so we can get the damn bill on the floor. Then he'll propose it on the floor."

The House membership views the committee as "stacked" via the appointment process; the additional picture of the committee in wide disarray on the floor is not conducive to confidence. According to one experienced committee member:

> Frankly, it's not one of the authoritative committees of the Congress—not one of those whose word you take automatically. . . . It lacks stature. In fact, most of the bills we report out get completely changed on the floor. . . . It's a power strug-

gle that counts on the floor and not respect for the committee
or the influence of any one individual.

The committee's modest rank in the prestige hierarchy of House
committees operates as both cause and effect of its internal conflicts.
Because it is not regarded as having great prestige, House members
are only moderately attracted to it. Of the twenty-one committee
members interviewed, eight had designated it as their first choice
for a committee assignment; six had listed it second or third; and
seven members had been requested to go on or were simply put
on the committee. Moderate attractiveness means a relatively high
rate of turnover among committee personnel. Of the thirty members
of the group in 1961, only three had been members since 1947;
seven had been members since 1953; and less than half (fourteen)
had been on the committee for as many as four years (since 1957).
Instability of membership is, perhaps, a contributing factor to the
committee's lack of tradition and lack of group-mindedness. These
failures, in their turn, allow internal conflict to flourish, further
decreasing the prestige of the group among House members.

Leadership

To write a politically viable federal aid to education bill and to
maneuver it successfully through the House committee requires far
more cohesion than the group normally displays. Only exceptional
leadership within the committee or extraordinary pressure without—or both—can produce the requisite internal unity. The committee has had but one strong chairman since the war, Graham Barden
(D.-N.C.). Among the members of his committee, Barden's legislative abilities are already legend. He is invariably described as "a
shrewd, smart chairman," "a very effective chairman," "absolutely
brilliant," "magnificent," and "one of the ablest congressmen in
American history." For all of his eight years as chairman, Barden
led the committee so as to create rather than resolve internal conflicts. Most of the time, he worked tirelessly to defeat federal aid
legislation, and on the single occasion, in 1949, when he accepted a
federal aid bill, he did so on such restrictive and uncomprising
grounds that he triggered the most acrimonious of all committee
conflicts.

His main tactics were to delay, divide, and conquer. And his
successes were largely due to the fact that these tactics followed
the natural grain of a conflict-ridden committee. "Barden was try-

ing to keep things from being done," said a Democratic member. "He just wanted to filibuster and sow confusion. If it lagged, he would introduce some more." Another Democrat recalled, "He never shut any one up. He'd let you talk yourself around the clock and in circles if you would. One year, he brought in ninety-two witnesses from the Chamber of Commerce on the school bill and was going to let them all talk. That was his way of doing things." In support of these tactics, he relied heavily on the backstopping votes of the Republicans. A key Republican said, "He ran that committee 100 per cent. I must say that some of us on our side were in substantial sympathy with what he was doing. There was a good deal of support from the Republicans." From his perspective, a Democratic member concurred:

> You never had any leadership under Barden—not majority leadership. Under Barden, you had a club. He was a Republican; there's no doubt about that. He was a Democrat in name only. Under him, you had a coalition, and it was very skillful. The coalition ran things until 1959 when Ways and Means decided to enlarge the committee.

Barden used a skillful combination of formal prerogative, informal maneuver, and personal talent. During most of his tenure, for instance, he refused to institute formal committee rules. Among other things, the committee had no regular meeting day. "In my first year here," said one member, "we held our first committee meeting in April and the next one in June." There was, in addition, no time limit placed on the questioning of witnesses during hearings. "I remember once," said a Republican member, "when the very suggestion of a five minute limitation [for each member in questioning each witness] was made, and he hit the roof. He wouldn't hear of any such thing. And he carried the day by sheer bravado or strength of character, call it what you will."

Another prerogative which Barden employed dexterously was his authority to terminate committee meetings by declaring the absence of a quorum. "Even after 1959 Barden retained a lot of power," protested one Democrat, "we tried holding rump sessions without him but with a quorum. Barden would come in, look around and say, 'I see there's no quorum present,' bang his gavel, and it would be all over." A colleague recalled an occasion when the committee had recessed during a crucial executive session to enable the members to go to the floor to answer a roll call. Barden, however, stayed in the committee room and sent his clerk to the floor with instructions to call back as soon as the roll call was over and debate had resumed on the floor.

> I was one of the first ones back, and Barden was sitting there. He got a phone call, put down the phone, looked around and said, "No quorum" and banged the gavel. I jumped up and protested. He said, "No quorum," and left. . . . Technically, he was right. We were supposed to be sitting during debate and should have begun when the floor debate began again. . . . The timetable was such that if we didn't complete our work that day we couldn't meet for some time.

In 1956 Barden, who was opposed to the federal aid bill, refused to relinquish his right to control and manage the floor debate on the bill. His allocation of disproportionate time to the opponents plus his dramatic resignation as floor manager near the end of the proceedings added important increments to the unbelievable confusion which accompanied the floor defeat of that year. In the absence of particular committee rules and compensating informal tradition, the rules of the group had to be the same as the rules of the parent House. And in his knowledge of these, Barden far outdistanced the young and aggressive but legislatively naive liberals on his committee. "He was a master of parliamentary strategy," said one inexperienced opponent. "He'll lull you to sleep and then hit you with an uppercut. You wouldn't know what the hell had hit you." Another agreed, "We're a young committee . . . and it takes a lot of time to learn how the legislative process works. . . . We learned a lot from Barden."

As chairman, Barden could manipulate the subcommittees and staff. For considerable period of time, he refused to institute standing subcommittees with specific jurisdiction. The *ad hoc* nature of the committee structure enabled him to exert close control over the tasks of each subcommittee and over its Democratic membership. In 1957, for example, Barden used his power over subcommittees to head off an incipient liberal revolt in the committee. He won the support of one senior Democrat to his view on other procedural matters by agreeing to give him a permanent subcommittee of his own. As for the committee staff, Barden kept it small and inactive as befitted his tactical goals. Democratic committee members received so little research help they were ignorant of the names of the staff members. One staff assistant, a veteran Democrat, complained with great feeling:

> This committee has the most incompetent, inept staff of any of the Hill. Barden wanted it that way. He could manipulate a dumb staff easier than a smart one. . . . We haven't had a chief clerk or counsel on this committee for years that knew enough to come in out of the rain.

Whether accurate or not, this is the common perception of the staff shared by pro-federal aid members.

FEDERAL AID IN THE HOUSE COMMITTEE, 1945–1955

Between 1945 and 1955 the committee held federal aid hearings on seven separate occasions, but not until 1955 did a bill win the approval of a majority of the group. The peak years of controversy were 1949 and 1950—Barden was primarily responsible for the decisions adverse to federal aid in those years. In 1949 Chairman John Lesinski (D.-Mich.), whose interest was in labor matters, gave Barden the chairmanship of a thirteen-man Special Subcommittee on Federal Aid to Education. Barden selected an unrepresentative group of Democratic members—all four of the committee's southern Democrats, two of its four border-state members, and only two of its seven northern Democrats. The year 1949 was critical because for the first time, in both 1948 and 1949, the Senate had passed a federal aid bill. This bill contained both equalization (money distributed to states in accordance with criteria of need) and flat-grant (money distributed to states on some per capita basis) provisions. The money could be used for teachers' salaries and other current operating expenditures (no construction). The bill provided money for transportation and textbook aid to non-public schools in states where such "auxiliary services" were permitted by state law. The 1949 bill, S. 246, passed the Senate by a fifty-eight-to-fifteen margin on May 5. Twelve days later, when the House heard the first of its fifty-eight witnesses and took the first of its 953 pages of testimony, the prospects for federal aid legislation seemed brighter than ever.

Expressing his devotion to federal aid at every opportunity, Barden staged a counter-offensive by proposing a substitute bill and by refusing to entertain serious testimony on S. 246. At the outset, he set the ground rules. "There are some features in the Senate bill so objectionable to me that I could not find myself going over to it.

I am not going to accept it; that's all."[10] The distasteful provisions included those requiring reports to the Commissioner of Education (*i.e.,* federal control) and those providing for the possibility of aid to non-public schools. Barden dominated the hearings to a degree unequalled by any representative or senator in any federal aid hearing before or since. His colloquies with various witnesses consumed one-third of all the space devoted to questions and answers. Each witness was asked to testify and then subjected to questions on the Barden bill. Those groups, especially organized labor, who would not agree to support it were branded as uncooperative and given unsympathetic treatment. "I am frank to state to you that your idea will not pass" (to AF of L). "I wanted some help, my friend, and you have had a tendency to add chaos to confusion. . . . I don't believe you yourself have the slightest idea in the world there would be a Chinaman's chance of getting that bill through Congress, do you?" (to AF of L). "One ear is deaf and the other is partly closed when you talk to me" (to CIO).[11]

The issue which eventually rent the committee—that of aid to non-public schools—was systematically avoided. On one of the few occasions when the question faced him point blank, Barden stated, "My reason [for a public school aid bill] was that it is just so much easier and more comfortable to go around a mud hole than it is to go through it. . . . So in this bill and in this legislation, I pray that we will be spared any controversy over that point because it should not be in here."[12] To the countervailing arguments of National Catholic Welfare Conference representative he replied, "I am just as far in one direction as you can possibly be in the other. So we could not get together."[13] The fact that Barden's bill was a public school bill precipitated a national controversy as soon as it was reported (by a ten-to-three vote) from the subcommittee to the full committee. Chairman Lesinski attacked the bill as "anti-Catholic" and filled with "bigotry." "It will never be reported out of the Labor Committee . . . ," he said. "It is my opinion that he [Barden] drew it up that way purposely because he didn't want any aid to education and wanted to kill it."[14] The parallel dispute between

[10] House Committee on Education and Labor, *Public School Assistance Act of 1949*, 81st Cong., 1st sess. (1949), p. 102.

[11] *Ibid.,* pp. 628, 678, 768.

[12] *Ibid.,* p. 165.

[13] *Ibid.,* p. 744.

[14] *Congressional Quarterly Almanac*, V (1949), 266–69.

Cardinal Spellman and Eleanor Roosevelt flared and raged in the public press. The controversy over federal aid to non-public schools was not to dominate the educational policy struggle again until 1961. But in 1949 and 1950 it stirred a fatal division within the House committee.

Two key votes were taken by the committee in August of 1949. A motion to report out S. 246 was defeated eleven-to-fourteen, a vote for which there is no record. Following the heavy defeat of two substitute Republican measures, Representative John F. Kennedy (D.-Mass.) moved to postpone action until the next session. The motion, which would have killed federal aid legislation for that year, was lost thirteen-to-twelve. See Table II. Thus the

TABLE II

Federal Aid Votes—House Committee on Education and Labor, 1949 and 1950

	1949 Motion to Kill Federal Aid for 1949		1950 Motion to Report out S. 246	
	Yes	*No*	*Yes*	*No*
Democrats				
Lesinski (Mich.)	X			X
Barden (N.C.)		X		X
Kelley (Penna.)	X		X	
Powell (N.Y.)		X	X	
Wood (Ga.)		X	X	
Kennedy (Mass.)	X			X
Lucas (Texas)	X			X
Bailey (W.Va.)		X	X	
Irving (Mo.)		X	X	
Perkins (Ky.)		X	X	
Howell (N.J.)		X	X	
Sims (S.C.)		X	X	
Jacobs (Ind.)		X	X	
Burke (Ohio)	X			X
Steed (Okla.)		X		X
Wier (Minn.)		X	X	
Republicans				
McConnell (Penna.)	X			X
Gwinn (N.Y.)	X			X
Brehm (Ohio)	X		X	
Smith (Kans.)	X			X
Kearns (Penna.)		X		X
Nixon (Calif.)	X			X
Morton (Ky.)		X	X	
Werdel (Calif.)	X			X
Velde (Ill.)	X			X
TOTAL	12	13	12	13

Source: *Congressional Quarterly Almanac*, Vols. V, VI.

possibility of favorable action remained, but nothing more was, in fact, done. The vote on the Kennedy motion revealed the toll which the private school controversy had taken of the proponents of federal aid. Four Catholic members of the committee—Lesinski (Mich.), Kelley (Penna.), Kennedy (Mass.), and Burke (Ohio), all liberal Democrats, voted to kill federal aid legislation for that session. They were joined by the great bulk of the committee's conservative members. The majority group, on the other hand, could agree only to keep the issue alive. They could not, especially against the opposition of Chairman Lesinski that late in the session, agree on a bill to support. For Barden it was all or nothing, and not all of the thirteen were willing to pay his price.

Early in February of the next year, the committee met in executive session at the urging of President Truman to reconsider its negative action on S. 246. A motion to report out S. 246 again lost— this time by thirteen to twelve. The voting alignment (Table II) was similar to that of the previous August. Those who had voted to postpone the issue in 1949, voted against S. 246; those who had voted to keep the issue alive in 1949 voted in favor of S. 246. Among the five exceptions were Representative Augustine Kelley, who left his three colleagues to vote in favor of S. 246, and Representative Barden, who voted against S. 246 thus joining irrevocably with the committee group opposed to federal aid.

In view of the fact that S. 246 permitted state option on the question of auxiliary services for non-public schools, the continued opposition of Lesinski, Kennedy, and Thomas Burke requires further explanation. Since Kennedy proposed an amendment to S. 246 specifically allowing aid for transportation to non-public schools (rather than leaving it permissive), it seems likely that the three were still dissatisfied with the treatment of the question in S. 246. But it is also true that the three had spoken out against the equalization provisions of S. 246 and in favor of the flat-grant principle. All came from states which were scheduled to give far more than they would receive, and all came from districts which needed assistance. The reluctance of representatives from needy districts in wealthy states to support equalization provisions has always caused more acute problems in the House than in the Senate. Republican Carroll Kearns, a strong advocate of federal aid, reversed his decision and voted against S. 246 on precisely these grounds. From that vote until 1962, Kearns was adamant and rigid in his opposition to any equalization provision whatsoever. Since Kearns was the ranking minority member of the committee in the Eighty-sixth and Eighty-seventh Congresses, his inflexibility provided a significant example of the absence of maneuvering room within the group.

As chairman of the committee in 1951 and 1952, Barden did not allow the full committee to meet at all on federal aid questions. In 1953 and 1954, with the Republicans in control, a similar record was maintained by Chairman Samuel McConnell. In 1955, when the Republican administration sent its first program to Congress, Chairman Barden was again successful in bottling up federal aid legislation in his committee. In order to delay action, he designated the full committee as the unit to hold hearings and refused to limit questioning. He prolonged the hearings from March 2 to May 24 during which time the committee considered eleven separate bills, listened to fifty-two witnesses, and took 1,158 pages of oral and written testimony. Barden's foot-dragging ended only after he had been presented with an ultimatum by the fifteen non-southern Democrats.[15] On July 28, these Democrats plus seven Republicans formed the first federal aid majority on the committee, and they reported out a bill by a vote of twenty-two to eight. As Barden had planned, it was too late in the session for action by the Rules Committee and the House. Indeed, it was not until June of 1956, when faced with threats to bypass them and urgent proddings by the administration, that the Rules Committee consented to send the bill to the House floor. See Table III. The year-long delay furnished the first concrete evidence that majorities on the Education and Labor Committee could by no means guarantee majorities on the equally critical Rules Committee.

COMMITTEE AND CHAMBER ACTIVITY, 1956–1957

The conditions of partisanship gave basic shape to the federal aid struggles of 1956 and 1957. A Republican President faced a Democratic majority in Congress; and the Democratic majority was a slim one. In 1956, House membership stood at 232 Democrats and 203 Republicans; in 1957, it remained virtually the same, at 234 to 201. These conditions necessitated bipartisan majorities in and out of the committee if any federal aid bill were to be passed and signed into law. The bills which reached the floor in 1956 and 1957 did

---

[15] House Committee on Education and Labor, *Federal Aid to States for School Construction,* 84th Cong., 1st sess. (1955), pp. 1105–12.

command bipartisan majorities in the Committee on Education and Labor and in the Rules Committee, but supporting bipartisan majorities on the floor of the House never materialized.

An important factor in producing the committee majorities of those years was the successful effort to avoid the 1949–50 type of entanglement with parochial school issues. The technique was simply to write a different kind of bill—one embodying a type of aid for which parochial schools, by common agreement, were not eligible. The 1956 and 1957 bills, therefore, provided aid for school construction only. The 1956 "Kelley Bill" was sponsored by Representative Augustine Kelley (D.-Penna.), a devout and unmistakably Irish Catholic committee member. There was virtually no mention of private schools in the committee hearings of 1950, 1955, or 1957. Within the committee, informal taboos operated against raising "the religious issue." A former Republican member recalled:

> I guess I was the first to breach a rule on that. I made a speech on the floor about it. When I came back, Sam McConnell said to me, "That's one thing I wouldn't have said if I were you." I said, "Well, I believe it." And he said, "I know, but that's one subject we shy away from."

On the floor, majority leader John McCormack called attention to the forbearance of parochial school supporters. Said McCormack:

> No complaints, no opposition, no obstructionist proposals have come from private or parochial school sources. . . . [They have] refrained from any action that might impede passage of this bill even though it will bring no direct benefit to their schools. These people have an unselfish, statesmanlike attitude. . . . I do not know whether we shall again need to consider federal aid for current expenditures. If we do, I hope we will be spared a repetition of the ordeal of a few years ago. I hope public school authorities will have a tolerant cooperative attitude if an effort is made to try in a small way to help private and parochial school children. . . .[16]

Few, if any, committee decisions held up as well on the floor as the one which eliminated the issue of parochial school aid. In their other essentials, the 1956 and 1957 proposals represented the most fragile of compromises between the preferences of President Eisenhower and the preferences of a majority of committee Democrats.

---

[16] *Congressional Record*, 84th Cong., 2d sess. (1956), p. 11844.

The President was never more than a lukewarm advocate of federal aid. And committee Republicans, in the words of one of them, "went along holding their noses because it was the President's program." The majority of committee Democrats desired a far more ambitious program than could conceivably win presidential support. These differences were papered over by a mutual willingness to send a bill to the floor. But the coalition was not durable. Given an opportunity on the floor to act on its basic preferences, either faction might revert to a less flexible, more disruptive position.

President Eisenhower preferred a debt service approach to school construction. If he had to compromise on some sort of grant program, he preferred equalization grants, to be matched by the states. The 1956–57 bills combined a grant program with a debt service program to assist local districts in financing construction. The 1956 bill called for flat and equalization grants, also on a matching basis.

In 1956, the committee's Eisenhower Republicans accepted the compromise, but as soon as the bill reached the floor, they sought to exact a heavier price for their allegiance by changing the grant distribution formula to conform to the President's preference. Their proposal, sponsored by ranking minority member Representative Samuel McConnell (R.-Penna.), stirred confusion if not bitterness within the bipartisan coalition. Federal aid stalwart Cleveland Bailey (D.-W.Va.) protested:

> I feel compelled to question the good faith of the gentleman from Pennsylvania in offering this substitute plan. He was a member of the subcommittee that drafted the legislation and it was agreed that the Kelley Bill would be a nonpartisan-bipartisan approach to the solution of the problem. That is why the proponents of Title I, the federal grants-in-aid, agreed to accept Titles II and III of the President's program as a compromise measure to insure the approval of this legislation. The gentleman is not satisfied with two Titles of the President's plan, he wants to substitute Title III of the President's plan for Title I of the Kelley Bill.
>
> I can assure you the distinguished gentleman from Pennsylvania [Mr. Kearns] was a party to this agreement that this would be fought out on a nonpartisan-bipartisan basis and that the Kelley Bill was to be defended against all crippling amendments right down the line.[17]

Other Democrats complained that McConnell's formula was too complicated to be dealt with on the floor and added that they them-

---

[17] *Ibid.*, p. 11751.

selves could not understand it. Chairman Graham Barden further revealed the committee's disarray with his comment that "It is a little bit of an awkward position for the chairman to be caught in when the ranking minority member springs five pages of law on the committee of the whole without my ever having seen it."[18] The next day Barden formally withdrew as "floor manager" of the bill.

The public exhibition of committee disunity did no service to the bill's supporters and gave encouragement and a rationalization to its opponents. Representative Charles Halleck (R.-Ind.), a key Republican leader and a key opponent of federal aid, seized upon the division to argue that:

> The Kelley Bill never was the administration program; it is not the administration program now. . . . I hope a motion to recommit is offered, with instructions to incorporate the McConnell amendments thereby incorporating the President's recommendations.[19]

Representative McConnell did offer the recommittal motion. It was supported by eleven of the committee's thirteen Republicans (84.6 per cent) and by 76 per cent of the Republicans in the House as a whole. President Eisenhower was unwilling to state his own position positively enough to provide for Republican leadership one way or the other.

In 1957, on a bill that was said to contain "85 per cent of the specifications laid down by the President," Eisenhower's silence was even more disastrous for aid proponents. In this instance the bill was killed by a vote of 208 to 203. On the floor, committee Republicans vied with each other in attempts to fathom the presidential will. Representative Peter Frelinghuysen (R.-N.J.), the strongest Republican aid supporter on the committee, admitted, "Perhaps he has not given it his unequivocal wholehearted support, . . . [but] this bill in my opinion incorporates all the principles which the President declared are vital to sound legislation in the field."[20] Representative McConnell, senior committee Republican, attempted clarification:

> The President is in favor of a bill for school construction. This is not the most preferred bill he wishes. He has made that very clear. He also realizes that legislation is a matter of

---

[18] *Ibid.*, p. 11752.
[19] *Ibid.*, p. 11869.
[20] *Congressional Record*, 85th Cong., 1st sess. (1957), p. 12608.

compromise, and he understands an effort to compromise. He does say, however, that this is not his first preference; that he prefers a bill where financial need is more emphasized than in the compromise bill.[21]

Representative William Ayres (R.-Ohio), who had voted against reporting the bill out of committee, offered a substitute bill, saying, "This is the bill that the President is really for. This is the bill he supported in the last session. This is the bill, in my judgment, after having talked with him at a breakfast at the White House, his heart is really in."[22]

Members announced at several points that a presidential statement was imminent, but such a statement was not forthcoming. Its absence allowed each legislator to interpret the Eisenhower position to suit his own preconceptions. As Representative Halleck declared:

> I am going to follow the dictates of my own conscience. I am going to be mindful of the views of the people I represent. . . . Certainly I shall not be unmindful of the loyalties that are mine to my party and the stand of the administration insofar as I am able to determine how those various things will come up as a matter of application.[23]

Unemcumbered by presidential pressure, Halleck's conscience and that of 110 other Republicans dictated a vote to kill federal aid for 1957. A veteran federal aid supporter in the Senate summed up the sentiments of his cohorts when he stated later:

> It was what the administration did—or didn't do—that killed the legislation. The truth of the matter was that Eisenhower never wanted federal aid. I think some of his friends on the golf course must have told him that it was creeping socialism. I really do. In 1957, the bill lost in the House by five votes. He could have had a bill. A few phone calls to members of Congress, "This is the President of the United States calling congressman so and so"—and he'd have gotten the votes. If he had called up Charlie Halleck and Joe Martin and said "I want the votes," he could have gotten them. The struggle would never have been as close as it was. He just didn't want a bill. He did nothing. And in that situation, inaction meant, "No."

Amid great confusion on the floor, the Democratic supporters of

---

[21] *Ibid.*, p. 12723.
[22] *Ibid.*, p. 12750.
[23] *Ibid.*, p. 12721.

federal aid struggled to repair the damaged bipartisan coalition. When Ayres offered his substitute bill (the Eisenhower preference of 1956 and the one embodied in McConnell's amendment of that year), the committee's liberal Democrats agreed to support it. Representative Stewart Udall (D.-Ariz.) said, typically, "If in order to get the bipartisanship we need, we must have precisely the bill the President said he wanted last year, I . . . will support the amendment of the gentleman from Ohio, as I want a school bill."[24] Republicans and Democrats rose to pledge allegiance to this new coalition and, briefly, it looked as if a timely if not hardy majority might coalesce. But before any new alignment could take shape Chairman Howard Smith (D.-Va.) of the Rules Committee offered a preferential motion to strike the enacting clause of the bill, *i.e.* to kill it, and "be through with this rather futile debate." Representative Udall made a last impassioned plea:

> Finally, after two years of thrashing around in this thing, we have finally reached an agreement. We on this side have decided to go all the way with the President, cross every "t" and dot every "i" and go right down the line with precisely what the President wants. We can join hands with you. We have obviously worked out a working agreement. It is feasible in this body. We can pass a school bill today. Therefore the purpose of this motion is to derail this new coalition that we have.[25]

The motion was carried 208 to 203. The time was ripe, as Judge Smith doubtless sensed, for disrupting a coalition, not creating one. That which Republican and Democratic supporters could not accomplish over a period of years in committee or at the White House they could hardly hope to improvise in a period of minutes on the House floor.

Ineffective leadership contributed heavily to the federal aid failures of 1956–57. But even with the best of leadership, the bipartisan coalition might not have survived the effects of another deeply divisive social issue—segregation in the public schools. The crystallization of the issue by the Supreme Court's decision of 1954 had placed it before the committee with an intensity which had not existed in 1949 and 1950. Its potential for disrupting the bipartisan coalition was fully as great as the parochial school question. Where-

---

[24] *Ibid.*, p. 12751.
[25] *Ibid.*, p. 12753.

as a dearth of leadership had cost the coalition vital Republican support, the superimposition of racial issues upon federal aid issues deprived the coalitions of 1956–57 of equally vital Democratic support.

As might be expected, the segregated school issue nearly paralyzed the House committee. It was agitated by Adam Clayton Powell (D.-N.Y.) who, of all the members of that disharmonious group, was the least committee-oriented, the least legislatively oriented, and the least amenable to appeals based on the necessity for compromise and cohesion.[26] Powell was supported by some members of the bipartisan majority out of conviction; he was opposed by most of them; and, to confound the problem further, he was supported by some committee members who were strongly opposed to federal aid legislation under any circumstances. Debate of the issue inside the committee in 1955 was sufficiently heated to provoke at least one shoving incident between Powell and a Democratic opponent. The "Powell Amendment" prohibiting aid to segregated schools was ultimately rejected seventeen to ten in the committee. Six of the ten wrote additional views supporting Powell. Four of these were Democratic supporters of federal aid; two were Republicans opposed to it.[27] The lack of any committee tradition of unity in support of its votes served the cause of federal aid ill in this instance. The committee's inability to agree plus Powell's insistence on taking the issue to the floor forecast an even wider, more disastrous split within the bipartisan majority when the bill was debated and lost in 1956.

In 1956 the Powell Amendment was attached to the bill by a coalition of 77 northern Democrats and 148 Republicans. The amendment was opposed by 115 southern and border-state Democrats, 31 northern Democrats, and 46 Republicans. The voting

---

[26] Inside the committee, Powell was urged to adopt one of the following alternatives: attach his amendment to the appropriation bill for the Department of Health, Education, and Welfare; obtain a ruling from the executive branch that no funds would be distributed to segregated school districts; attach his amendment, as a first step, to the impacted areas program; or make a commitment in favor of federal aid regardless of the fate of his amendment. Powell declined to take any of these steps. Another Negro leader, Rep. William Dawson (D.- Ill.), took a more compromising stand, as did Powell himself when he became chairman of the committee. Rep. Powell's behavior can be explained in part by his great disaffection from the committee under Barden and by the political style he adopted in the light of his constituency. On the contrasting styles of Powell and Dawson, see James Wilson, "Two Negro Politicians: An Interpretation," *Midwest Journal of Political Science,* IV (November, 1960), 346–69.

[27] House Committee on Education and Labor, *House Report* 1504, 84th Cong., 1st sess., 1955.

alignment cut across and divided the ranks of proponents and opponents of federal aid. As such, it bore little resemblance to the final
alignment on passage of the bill. Ninety-six of the 148 Republicans
who had voted for the Powell Amendment voted against the bill.
Twenty-nine of the thirty-one northern Democrats who had voted
against the Powell Amendment voted for the bill, but they could
not offset the large Republican swing in the other direction. The
seventy-seven northern Democrats who voted for the Powell Amendment supported the bill, but they were unwilling to vote against
their civil rights convictions in order to improve the chances of
federal aid. The very passage of the amendment, however, irrevocably detached from the coalition some southern and border-state
congressmen who might otherwise have voted in favor of the legislation. Whatever their motivation may have been, the consequences
of 76.3 per cent Republican support for the Powell Amendment and
61.3 per cent Republican opposition to final passage were first to
divide and then to defeat the federal aid coalition.

It is difficult to know precisely how many Democratic supporters
were lost to the bill through the passage of the Powell Amendment.
Some measure of that loss, however, can be gleaned from comparing
the vote on passage in 1956 with the vote to strike the enacting
clause in 1957. At the time the 1957 bill was killed, the pending
business was a vote on the substitute bill supported by the coalition
leaders. The effect of this amendment would have been to strike
out the Powell Amendment which had been proposed by Representative Stuyvesant Wainwright (R.-N.Y.), an opponent of federal
aid, and passed by a teller vote in the committee of the whole. A
southerner who supported federal aid without the Powell Amendment could logically, therefore, have voted to keep the 1957 bill
alive. Of the ninety-four southerners who voted against passage of
the bill in 1956, only nine voted to keep the bill alive in 1957. Of
the nine border-state members who voted against passage in 1956,
four voted against killing the 1957 bill. Thirteen members, in other
words, indicated by their 1957 votes that they might have been willing, in 1956, to support federal aid legislation free from desegrega-
tion provisions.[28]

The number of votes is not sufficient to have changed the result
in 1956. How many other southern and border-state votes might

---

[28] The nine southerners were Representatives Andrews, Elliott, Grant, Hud-
dleston, Jones, Rains, Roberts, and Selden, all of Alabama, plus Representatives
Trimble and Hays of Arkansas. The four border-state representatives were Albert
(Okla.), Steed (Okla.), Jones (Mo.), and Natcher (Ky.).

have been forthcoming in 1956 if the racial issue had not been raised at all is problematical. Enough, perhaps, to have produced the sixteen votes necessary to change the result. Certainly this was the contention of the northern liberals (including Negro Congressman William Dawson [D.-Ill.]) who voted against the Powell Amendment and pleaded with their fellow liberals to do likewise. By 1957, a greater number of northern liberals had been persuaded by this argument. They announced their change of mind and their intention to vote against all antisegregation amendments in the hope of passing a federal aid bill.

But the issue of school segregation had been crystallized by the Court, and no southerner needed a Powell Amendment to be reminded of it. The pre-1954 political climate simply could not be recreated. On the racial issue most southerners agreed with veteran Representative William Colmer (D.-Miss.) when he said of the Powell Amendment in 1957:

> This is a case of tweedledee and tweedledum. It is immaterial whether this amendment is adopted or not. . . . This will be offered as an amendment on an appropriations bill. If that is not done, it will be done administratively. If that is not done, is there anybody so naive as to believe that the Supreme Court . . . is going to permit you to receive money and have segregated schools. So you lose any way it goes.[29]

The absence of a Powell Amendment would doubtless have increased the chances of federal aid passage in the House. But its absence would not have guaranteed passage. The indisputable result of the 1956 and 1957 House battles was legislative stalemate. Comparing the final result of 1957 with that of 1956, the proponents of a new federal aid consensus increased their support by a very unimpressive nine votes. In 1958, the President withdrew his support for federal aid altogether, and, once again, Representatives Barden and Landrum plus thirteen Republicans kept the question bottled up in committee.

COMMITTEE AND CHAMBER ACTIVITY, 1959–1961

The congressional elections of 1958 decisively altered the balance of party power in the House. Democratic membership jumped from

---

[29] *Congressional Record,* 85th Cong., 1st sess. (1957), p. 12738.

234 to 283, increasing thereby potential chamber support for federal aid. The change in party ratios on the Committee on Education and Labor created a new all-Democratic majority which, beginning in 1959, "picked up the committee and ran away with it." As Democratic federal aid strength increased, however, President Eisenhower's enthusiasm for a massive program correspondingly waned— to the point where, from 1958 to 1960, any such bill faced the likelihood of a presidential veto. Bipartisanship in the committee gave way to a steadily growing partisanship as both the need and the disposition to compromise weakened. The new Democratic majority found the key to its own cohesiveness in a type of permanent, flat grant for construction and for teachers' salaries, a bill quite unacceptable to the President and to committee Republicans. In 1959 and 1961, therefore, the Democratic bill was opposed unanimously by the committee's Republicans. In 1960, two Republicans joined the Democrats, but this did not affect the outcome.

These conditions of increased partisanship did not prevent aid bills from clearing the committee, but they did cost the federal aid proponents critical increments of Republican and southern Democratic support at later legislative junctures. One such juncture was the Committee on Rules. To the degree that the new Democratic majority refused to compromise with the President and Republicans inside the Committee on Education and Labor, they increased Republican intransigence on the Rules Committee. In addition, a change of two Republican members of the Rules Committee increased the opposition of that side of that group. In 1959, an alliance between the four Republicans and two consistently anti-federal-aid southern Democrats forestalled even a committee vote on the subject. One of the architects of that bill recalled:

> We got that bill out of committee, and we knew it didn't stand a chance of getting through the Rules Committee. But we just let it sit there. It put a few feet to the fire. We got enough pressure built up so that the next year when we came back with a construction bill, we got one extra vote and got it through the Rules Committee.

In 1960, one Republican vote did come from Representative B. Carroll Reece (Tenn.), who reportedly was under heavy pressure from his needy constituency to support federal aid. The bill cleared the Rules Committee by a seven-to-five vote (see Table III) and subsequently passed the House. A fatal loss of Republican and southern Democratic support in the Rules Committee did occur, however, at an even later point in the process. Every problem of consensus-building in the House is compounded by the necessity of securing cohesive majorities in two separate and distinct committees.

TABLE III

Votes in the Rules Committee to Expedite Federal Aid Legislation, 1956–1961

CONGRESSMEN	1956 Yes	1956 No	1960 1st Yes	1960 1st No	1960 2nd Yes	1960 2nd No	1961 1st Yes	1961 1st No	1961 2nd Yes	1961 2nd No
Democrats										
Smith (Va.)		X		X		X		X		X
Colmer (Miss.)		X		X		X		X		X
Madden (Ind.)	X		X		X		X		X	
Delaney (N.Y.)	X		X		X			X	X	
Trimble (Ark.)	X		X			X	X		X	
Thornberry (Tex.)	*	*	X		X		X		X	
Bolling (Mo.)	X		X		X		X		X	
O'Neill (Mass.)	X		X		X		X		X	
Elliott (Ala.)								X		X
Sisk (Calif.)								X		X
Republicans										
Allen (Ill.)		X		X		X				
Brown (Ohio)	X		X			X	X		X	
Ellsworth (Ore.)	X									
Latham (N.Y.)	X									
Reece (Tenn.)				X		X				
Budge (Ida.)				X		X				
St. George (N.Y.)								X		X
Smith (Calif.)								X		X
Hoffman (Ill.)								X		X
Avery (Kan.)								X		X
TOTAL	8	3	7	5	5	7	6	9	7	8

Source: *Congressional Quarterly Almanac,* Vols. XII, XIII, XVI, XVII. No record of 1957 and 1959 votes.
* Not present.

The 1960 House bill was, like its predecessors, a school construction measure. For lack of teachers' salaries provisions, it was far less than the legislative proponents of the 1959 bill and their allies from the National Education Association desired. It did, however, retain the flat-grant basis from the earlier bill, but in so doing, it eliminated the equalization provisions so basic to President Eisenhower's position. As a compromise with the Republicans, who were also devoted to the idea of matching grants, the bill provided direct grants for the first year and matching grants for the following two years.

Representative Bailey, the chairman of the subcommittee which had drafted it, said, "It is particularly written and tailored to receive House approval. The job that faces me and other proponents of the legislation is to see that it is not muddied up from the introduction of a lot of side issues."[30]

The design of the bill did lead to the passage of the first twentieth-century federal aid-to-education legislation in the House. When the 206 to 189 vote for passage is compared with the 1956 vote—194 to 224 against passage—two facts emerge. First, the number of Democrats in favor of the bill increased by forty-three; whereas the number opposed dropped by only eight. That is to say, the pro-aid Democratic vote, the heaviest ever cast by that party in the House, was made possible by the augmented Democratic majority arising out of the 1958 elections. Of the forty-nine Democrats who took seats away from Republicans in that election, forty-three voted in favor of federal aid, two were paired in favor, three voted against it, and one had died. Second, one-third of the House's Republicans voted for the bill. This represented a sizeable drop in number (thirty-one), but only a slight drop in percentage (6.3 per cent). On the final vote, 162 Democrats (62.5 per cent) and 44 Republicans (32.4 per cent) combined to pass the bill. It was, however, the post-1958 Democrats who most directly altered the balance of power.

At the same time, floor action constituted failure for the federal aid advocates. Representative Bailey was unable to prevent the side issues of which he warned from "muddying up the bill." Bailey's difficulty was underlined by the fact that during the floor action, one of the key committee sponsors of the bill, Representative Frank Thompson (D.-N.J.), offered a compromise amendment (affecting the grant provisions and the duration of the program) which was subsequently passed over Bailey's own vigorous opposition. When finally other items were tacked on to the Thompson amendment, Thompson and Bailey voted against it.

The key item that was added to Thompson's amendment was the Powell Amendment denying aid to segregated schools—first approved by a teller vote in the committee of the whole and later confirmed by roll call. The northern Democratic floor generals and some others voted against the Powell Amendment. But one hundred northern and western Democrats, faced with a civil rights proposition and a fall election, voted for the amendment. Said Powell, "A

---

[30] *Congressional Record*, 86th Cong., 2nd sess. (May 25, 1960), p. 10270.

vote against this amendment is a vote against the Supreme Court. A vote against this amendment is a vote against civil rights."[31] The strategic situation, as recognized by the pro-aid floor leaders, was that a bill with a Powell Amendment might be endangered at several later points—even if it could be passed. Yet House Democrats joined the anti-aid Republicans, just as they had done in 1956, in voting it into the bill. The Republicans achieved their greatest cohesion on this roll call out of the six taken in 1960. In line with their classic whipsaw pattern, however, seventy-seven Republicans who voted for the Powell Amendment subsequently voted against the bill.

Since the Senate had already passed an aid bill, only the conference committee remained. House rules provide that unless there is unanimous consent to such a conference, the Rules Committee must grant a special rule sending the bill on its way. Following an objection by Representative August Johansen (R.-Mich.), the Rules Committee procedure was invoked. There, at the hands of the four Republicans and three southern Democrats, the bill perished. Representatives Reece of Tennessee and James Trimble, a moderate Democrat from Arkansas, changed their positions from the earlier vote. For Trimble, and probably for Reece, the primary reason was the addition of the Powell Amendment to the original bill. The Rules Committee took action on June 22; Congress did not adjourn until September 1. During that summer, some aid supporters worked for compromise, but positions became ever more inflexible. Republicans feared that if a bill were passed, it might draw a presidential veto, which would be a liability in the fall election campaign. Liberal Democrats were unenthusiastic because of the elimination of teachers' salaries from the bill; they preferred a campaign issue to a watered-down bill. This paralysis revealed, once again, the essential evanescence of federal aid majorities.

Flexibility and compromise would seem to be two of the prerequisites for federal aid passage in the House. Two reasons that these attributes may be difficult to achieve are the nature of House members' constituencies and the frequency of House elections. Large numbers of representatives find that they must respond to a single dominant constituency interest—be it that of private school aid, school integration, school construction, teachers' salaries, or federal control. To the degree that his district's interests are homo-

---

[31] *Ibid.*, May 6, 1960, p. 10486.

geneous, a congressman may be bound tightly to one position on certain aspects of the federal aid controversy. And his legislative maneuverability may be further restricted by the necessity of standing for election every two years. As one committee member said, "You're tied down a lot tighter to your constituency here than in the Senate. . . . Over there at least one-third of the senators can afford to be statesmen. Here, you've got to be a politician all the time because you have to run every two years." House members pride themselves on the fact that their short tenure keeps them "close to the people." But their constant accountability to their constituents may reduce their autonomy in committee and on the floor.

Among the decisive inflexibilities of the 1960–61 period one of the most interesting was that of the National Education Association. At a point of legislative impasse, where a skillful lobbying group could be especially effective, the NEA became deliberately inactive and uncompromising. It was enthusiastically behind a teachers' salary bill. Failing to get such a provision in the House bill, its zeal disappeared. Federal aid leaders were unable to state precisely what the NEA position was.[32] In the summer of 1960, the NEA preferred to "wait till next year" rather than work to promote a compromise construction bill in conference. The group did nothing, therefore, to move the House bill off dead center in the Rules Committee. *New York Times* education columnist Fred Hechinger placed a large share of the blame for the 1960 failure on ". . . the lack of enthusiasm for any realistically attainable compromise on the part of [the] . . . powerful association of public school educators representing more than 700,000 teachers."[33]

Since the NEA is the most important interest-group ally of the legislators favoring federal aid, its insistence on teachers' salary provisions as the price of its wholehearted support has severely restricted the legislative maneuverability of its congressional cohorts. At the beginning of the 1960 session, the NEA memorialized each member of Congress and stated its terms in flat, uncompromising language:

If no satisfactory school support bill embodying the principles of the Murray-Metcalf bill [of 1959] is enacted in the

<hr>

[32] *Ibid.*, p. 10476.
[33] *New York Times,* September 4, 1960, p. 17.

next session of Congress, the association will endeavor to make this matter a major issue in the political campaigns of 1960 so that the American people may again express their mandate for the enactment of such legislation in 1961.[34]

The parliamentary inflexibility of the NEA is the cause of constant consternation and bitterness among its legislative friends. Two sympathetic members of the Education and Labor Committee commented in 1961:

They are very disappointing. They want the moon. Their attitude is that they might as well try a big bite and go down fighting rather than to establish a new area of federal responsibility in a small-scale, reasonable way. I think they've done great damage to their own cause.

They're the worst, most ineffective lobby around. . . . They don't get their people to do the one thing that gets bills passed around here—write letters. My desk should be piled that high with letters, but it isn't. They just don't do it.

A member of the committee staff summed up:

Their pavement pounders, the boys who are up here all the time, came to me when the construction bill was up and said they wanted a teachers' salaries bill. They asked me what position they should take before their convention. I said they should certainly take a position in favor of school construction and teachers' salaries both, but I said that didn't mean they couldn't support the school construction bill if that was up. There was that wondering whether they should hold out for all of their program. The AFL-CIO is much more realistic. They never backed down one inch on their position for construction and teachers' salaries, but when the chips were down on the construction bill, they were in there pounding away in favor of the construction bill long before the NEA. . . . The AFL-CIO was willing to take half a loaf. But the NEA has a tendency to want the whole loaf. They don't realize that if you get half a loaf, you have taken the first step. That's the hardest step, and you may be able to get more. They're a little idealistic—and shortsighted. If you argue for a whole loaf and won't take half a loaf, you'll argue yourself right out of a job.

The task of majority-building was renewed in 1961 under conditions which seemed to eliminate a number of earlier obstacles. A

[34] Quoted in *Congressional Record*, 86th Cong., 2nd sess., (May 26, 1960), p. 10476.

sympathetic Democratic President occupied the White House. The retirement of Representative Barden and the accession of Representative Powell to the chairmanship placed the Education and Labor Committee completely in the hands of pro-aid liberals. And, in his new role, Powell agreed to exert all of his influence to oppose any amendment concerning aid to segregated schools. Finally, the prospects for success were increased when federal aid supporters secured, with the help of Speaker Rayburn and President Kennedy, an enlarged and more liberal Rules Committee. Progress would appear to have been made, but the pattern of majority-building in the House has been more characteristically cyclical. In 1961, the familiar problems of 1949–50 recurred, and the prospective federal aid majority foundered once again on the dilemmas of aid to parochial schools.

On the impetus of a strong statement in favor of parochial school aid by the Catholic bishops, a group of Education and Labor Committee members attempted to add a private school program to the public school bill. In the committee, one group of Democrats had to manipulate the committee machinery very sharply and skillfully to prevent another group of Democrats (with Republican assistance) from altering the basic nature of the administration's construction and/or salaries bill. They succeeded, and then drafted the bill carefully so that a point of order could be raised (under the rule of germaneness) against any private school amendments offered on the floor. Defeated on their first attempt, parochial school aid supporters on the committee then wrote a provision for long-term construction loans to private schools into the National Defense Education Act, which was being amended in the committee. The public school bill, the NDEA amendments, and a bill providing for aid to colleges were in the hands of separate subcommittees. The paternal interest of each subcommittee in its particular education bill certainly did not help matters when the bills became interlocked on the way to the House floor.

Relations between party contingents inside the committee had become badly frayed, leaving all problems to be resolved within the all-Democratic majority. A description by two leading spokesmen of the committee atmosphere of 1961 reflects the extent to which the bipartisanship of the earlier period had declined:

[Republican:] The Democrats haven't made a single concession to us on anything. . . . We've dug our heels in. We don't like their tactics, and they don't like ours. But what we're doing against the bill isn't any worse than what they are doing to pass the bill. If they aren't going to do some of the things we think are reasonable, we're going to have to oppose the whole thing right down the line.

[Democrat:] Boy were they mad. We were slick. But they were trying to be slick, too. They haven't got any interest in aiding parochial schools. They were trying to raise the issue, giggle, sit back and watch the bill die. They play the game right to the hilt.

Republican opposition to the committee's public school bill was unanimous.

The question which proved insoluble was whether the public school bill or the NDEA amendments with aid for parochial schools should be sent to the House floor first. The factional struggle inside the committee was resolved in favor of the public school bill, which was reported to the Rules Committee. But that committee voted nine to six (see Table III) to take no action on it until the other two bills had reached their committee. On this vote, the majority was comprised, as expected, of five Republicans and the two anti-federal-aid southerners. But they were joined, unexpectedly, by two liberal Democrats, both Catholics representing heavily Catholic constituencies—Thomas O'Neill from Cambridge, Mass. and James Delaney of New York City.

Once again, the separate problems of majority-building on the two House committees are apparent. The factional conflict which was eventually broken inside the Education and Labor Committee helped to precipitate a conflict which could not be resolved on the Rules Committee. Three weeks later when faced with all three education bills, the Rules Committee Democrats were still unable to agree on how to break the log jam. By an eight-to-seven majority, they voted to table all three education bills for the remainder of the year. On this vote, one of the two defecting Democrats, Representative O'Neill, changed his position; but the other, Representative Delaney, was still dissatisfied with the provisions for parochial school aid and again voted against sending the public school aid bill to the floor. A month later, an improvised federal aid bill was rushed to the floor on Calendar Wednesday—thus bypassing the Rules Committee—but it stood no chance of passage. The defeat in the Rules Committee and in the course of regular legislative processes was decisive.

The Rules Committee is, by the very nature of its jurisdiction over the House's program and procedure, subject to the directive influence of the majority party leadership. In 1961, the Democratic leadership group was itself badly split on the issue of priority and strategy. Speaker Rayburn, convinced that the only possibility for a public school program lay in its being considered first, insisted that the public school bill be taken up forthwith. Majority Leader John McCormack (D.-Mass.), fearful that the bill containing aid to parochial schools would fail unless it reached the floor first, argued against Rayburn. Each was allied with a faction in the Rules Committee. Because the Rayburn faction took the initiative inside the Rules Committee, it was the two members allied with McCormack, *i.e.*, O'Neill and Delaney, who delivered the *coup de grace* to federal aid. But, had McCormack's strategy been proposed in the committee, federal aid would just as surely have perished at the hands of the Rayburn faction—men such as James Trimble of Arkansas, Carl Elliott of Alabama, Homer Thornberry of Texas, and B. F. Sisk of California. The Rules Committee Democrats had been presented with the issue in a form which made it virtually insoluble.

The watered-down bill which administration and legislative leaders hastily drew up and sent to the floor via Calendar Wednesday requires comment only because it suffered the most lop-sided defeat in the history of federal aid. It died when an undebatable motion to consider it was lost by 170 to 242. The revealing feature of the vote was the complete disintegration on the floor as in committee of the moderate bipartisanship which had characterized the consensus-building attempts of the mid-fifties. See Table IV. Only six Republicans voted to consider the bill—a drop from a high of 41 per cent in 1957 to 3.6 per cent in 1961. During the same period, Democratic support for federal aid had steadily increased—from a low of 53.1 per cent in 1956 to 66.7 per cent in 1961.

TABLE IV
Increasing Partisanship on Federal Aid Final Votes 1956–1961

Congressmen	Per Cent Supporting Federal Aid			
	1956	1957	1960	1961
Democratic Representatives	53.1	56.5	62.5	66.7
Republican Representatives	38.7	41.0	32.4	3.6
House Index of Partisanship*	14.4	15.5	30.1	63.1

* The index of partisanship constitutes the difference between the percentages of Democrats and Republicans supporting federal aid. A value of 100 would indicate unanimous support by one party, unanimous opposition by the other; a zero value would demonstrate identical divisions within both parties.

Party tensions had been further exacerbated by the manner in which the new proposal had been concocted and rushed to the floor. A normally sympathetic Republican, Representative John Lindsay (N.Y.) explained his vote:

> It is insulting to those in the minority for the majority to slap a last-minute, strung-together, and totally inadequate compromise before us in this take-it-or-leave-it procedure. . . . My vote is a protest against the procedure used and the complete inability of the majority to put its legislative house in order.[35]

As in the case of the parochial school problem, a conflict which had been laboriously resolved at one point in time, *i.e.* partisanship, had returned to plague later efforts to build consensus.

Near the end of the 1961 session, Chairman Powell could only be guardedly pessimistic:

> It is my personal opinion, and I may be totally wrong, that the temper of this House is of such nature that Federal aid to school construction, per se, is dead at least for the next year. I think it is deplorable, but we must face the stark, brutal, and disheartening fact and not dissipate the energies of this Committee nor this House on that which will bring no results whatsoever.[36]

As prophecy, Powell's assessment remained accurate through the Eighty-seventh Congress and up to the congressional elections of 1962.

CONCLUSION

An epitaph for 1961 was pronounced by Secretary of Health, Education and Welfare Abraham Ribicoff when he said, "They expected a miracle and I couldn't produce a miracle. It was impossible to bring together a majority for a bill when most members didn't want one."[37] Ribicoff's lament summarizes many years of conflict over federal aid in the House. It also helps to restate the problem of majority-building in that chamber. The problem is not that a majority of representatives have not wanted a federal aid measure or could not be persuaded to want one. The problem is that an

---

[35] *Ibid.*, 87th Cong., 1st sess. (August 30, 1961), p. 16509.
[36] *Ibid.* (September 6, 1961), p. 17096.
[37] Quoted in *Wall Street Journal*, September 6, 1961, p. 14.

over-all majority—or a federal aid consensus—cannot be obtained at any one point in time for any one legislative proposal. To put it another way, any federal aid majority must be compounded of many submajorities. Different submajorities will be needed to resolve essentially different conflicts—that is to say, conflicts on different issues, in different decision-making units, at different points in time, and in different sets of society-wide circumstances. Furthermore, each submajority must be both flexible and cohesive—flexible enough to permit agreement with other submajorities and cohesive enough to make that agreement an asset in legislative maneuver.

At one time or another, submajorities have been obtained to resolve every identifiable conflict over federal aid. And, from time to time, each of these submajorities has combined considerable flexibility and cohesiveness. But, given the issues involved and given the institutional characteristics of the House of Representatives, an over-all House majority in support of general federal aid legislation is extraordinarily difficult to create. A new, stable House consensus remains as far from—yet as close to—realization as ever.

IX

TWO STRATEGIES OF INFLUENCE: CHOOSING A MAJORITY LEADER, 1962*

Nelson W. Polsby

POLITICAL SCIENTISTS seem to be fond of debating whether traditional political theory in America is dead or only sleeping.[1] Either way, there is no argument that the speculations which occupied thinkers of other days have been little used to illuminate current political behavior. The argument, when there is one, concerns whether it is even possible to use traditional political theory in this way. Regrettably, optimists on this point have not always demonstrated that they were right in supposing that traditional political theory could contribute to the understanding of present-day politics. But this does not mean that they are wrong.

A major obstacle to the use of traditional political theory in modern political science has been theory's long standing concern with prescriptive statements. Prescriptions are not necessarily the best instruments for organizing information about the empirical world, since the preferences which they assert may not correspond

---

* This paper was originally presented at the annual meetings of The American Political Science Association, Washington, D.C., 1962. Several members of Congress, who I am sure would prefer to remain anonymous, read an early draft of this chapter and made many useful comments. I should also like to thank Lewis A. Dexter, H. Douglas Price, and Robert L. Peabody. Others who have been helpful include Aaron B. Wildavsky, Lewis A. Froman, Jr., Norman O. Brown, Luigi Einaudi, Joseph Cooper, Alan L. Otten, and Neil MacNeil. Research assistance was provided by a Ford Foundation grant to Wesleyan University.
[1] The phrase "traditional political theory" refers in this context to the history of political thinking rather than to any specific political doctrines. See, for example, David Easton, *The Political System* (New York: Knopf, 1953); Harry V. Jaffa, "The Case Against Political Theory," *Journal of Politics*, XXII (May, 1960), 259–75; Robert A. Dahl, "The Science of Politics, New and Old," *World Politics*, VII (April, 1955), 479–89; Dahl, "Political Theory, Truth and Consequences," *World Politics*, XI (October, 1958), 89–102; Norman Jacobson, "The Unity of Political Theory," in R. Young (ed.), *Approaches to the Study of Politics* (Evanston: Northwestern University Press, 1958), pp. 115–24.

to any observed (or even observable) events. However, prescriptions may in fact point to quite interesting and genuine dilemmas in the real world. In these circumstances, we have the option of converting the language of prescription to that of description if we desire to put traditional political theory to more modern uses.

The possibilities of this device have lately been explored by a group of students of the legislative process, using as their text the celebrated speech to the Electors of Bristol by Edmund Burke.[2] In this speech, on the occasion of his election as Member of Parliament from Bristol, it will be recalled that Burke undertook to state and resolve a recurring dilemma of the representative:

> Certainly, gentlemen, it ought to be the happiness and glory of a representative to live in the strictest union, the closest correspondence, and the most unreserved communication with his constituents. Their wishes ought to have great weight with him; their opinion high respect; their business unremitted attention. . . . But his unbiased opinion, his native judgment, his enlightened conscience he ought not to sacrifice to you. . . . Your representative owes you, not his industry only, but his judgment. . . . Government and legislation are matters of reason and judgment, and not of inclination; and what sort of reason is that, in which the determination precedes the discussion; in which one set of men deliberate and another decide . . . Parliament is not a *congress* of ambassadors from different and hostile interests . . . but . . . a *deliberative* assembly of *one* nation. . . . We are now members for a rich commercial city; this city, however, is but part of a rich commercial nation, the interests of which are various, multiform, and intricate. . . . All these widespread interests must be considered; must be compared; must be reconciled if possible.[3]

Six years after Burke spoke these words, he stood for election once again, and on the same topic said:

> I could wish undoubtedly . . . to make every part of my conduct agreeable to every one of my constituents. . . . But . . . do you think, gentlemen, that every public act in six years since I stood in this place before you—that all the arduous things which have been done in this eventful period, which has

---

[2] Heinz Eulau, John C. Wahlke, Leroy C. Ferguson, and William Buchanan, "The Role of the Representative: Some Empirical Observations on the Theory of Edmund Burke," *American Political Science Review*, LIII (September, 1959), 742–56.

[3] "Speech to the Electors of Bristol," November 3, 1774, *Works* (London, etc.: Oxford University Press, 1906), II, 164–66.

crowded into a few years' space the revolutions of an age—can be opened to you on their fair grounds in half an hour's conversation? . . . Let me say with plainness . . . that if by a fair, by an indulgent, by a gentlemanly behavior to our representatives, we do not give confidence to their minds, and a liberal scope to their understandings; if we do not permit our members to act upon a *very* enlarged view of things, we shall at length infallibly degrade our national representation into a confused and scuffling bustle of local agency.[4]

A brief historical detour will suggest certain empirical problems related to Burke's position. Shortly after the second speech quoted here, Burke withdrew his candidacy, feeling he could not win. He and his constituents had disagreed over several matters, in particular his vote to free Irish trade from restrictions operating in favor of Bristol. Burke remained in Parliament, however, representing a pocket borough thereafter.[5] Although acting on his principle of independence from constituent pressures was costly to him, Burke was clearly in a position to take a more luxurious stand on such a question than another member could who did not have the protection of a pocket borough and the party list.

This raises still a more general empirical point: Under what conditions will the representative be more likely to respond to the demands of "local agency"? When is he more likely to respond to a political situation as it appears to him in the light of his experience at the seat of government? Under what conditions will attempts to influence the representative through his constituency bring better results than attempts to influence him through the network of loyalties and affiliations he has built up through service in his deliberative body—and vice versa?

The United States House of Representatives is one laboratory for the exploration of questions such as these. Indeed, where the stakes are as high as they often are in House decision-making, it is not surprising that full-scale campaigns are mounted in order to sway sometimes no more than a handful of marginal votes. But are these votes swayed from the inside or the outside? Do constituencies matter more or less than colleagues?[6]

---

[4] "Speech at Bristol," September 6, 1780 in *ibid.*, III, 2, 3, 4.

[5] *Ibid.*, and F. W. Raffety, "Preface" in *Works*, II, xiv–xv.

[6] One approach to some of these questions was made by Julius Turner, who used the analysis of roll calls as his major source of data in *Party and Constituency: Pressures on Congress* (Baltimore: Johns Hopkins, 1951). See also David B. Truman, *The Congressional Party* (New York: Wiley, 1959).

Sometimes the answer is reasonably clear and unequivocal. Here
are examples of *inside* influences at work:

> Representative Cleveland Bailey is a genuinely dedicated
> opponent of reciprocal trade. . . . [He] is unusual among mem-
> bers—probably unique—in that protection is *the* most impor-
> tant issue to him and that he creates the sense of having a
> deep felt conviction on the subject. In 1953–54 he went around
> and pled individually with a number of members to vote
> against reciprocal trade and for the West Virginia miners. One
> member put it, "He was rough, real rough . . . I had to be
> rough with him." Another said, "In the 1954 vote, Cleve Bailey
> was worth 15 votes to his side easily."[7]

> The morning of one of the key votes on reciprocal trade
> [1955], Speaker Sam Rayburn attended a breakfast of the fresh-
> man Democrats in the House. I asked one of the Congressmen
> who was there about it. He chuckled: "Oh, you heard about
> that? . . . We'd just invited Mr. Sam to this breakfast. He
> turned it into a sort of speech and said he'd observed that
> *generally the new members got along better who went along,*
> but he didn't make any particular application—of course you
> could guess what he had in mind. . . ."[8]

On the other hand, it is sometimes possible to detect *outside* influences. The following example comes from the January, 1961, battle
over the size of the House Rules Committee:

> It was learned that Representative Howard Smith, Southern
> leader and Rules Committee Chairman, has held several meet-
> ings in his office in recent weeks with representatives of the
> most powerful conservative lobbies in the country, trying to
> shape a campaign to beat Rayburn by applying pressure on
> members from home. The groups included the National As-
> sociation of Manufacturers, the United States Chamber of
> Commerce, the American Medical Association and the Ameri-
> can Farm Bureau. . . . Some members have reported heavy
> mail from business interests in their home districts. . . . On the
> other side, Northern Democrats have sent out an appeal to
> organized labor for help. Yesterday, Andrew J. Biemiller,
> chief AFL-CIO lobbyist, was at the Capitol trying to line up
> votes. . . .[9]

[7] Lewis Anthony Dexter, "Congressmen and the People They Listen To"
(Cambridge: Center for International Studies, Massachusetts Institute of
Technology, Ditto, 1955), chap. ii, p. 14, chap. viii, p. 7.
[8] *Ibid.,* chap. v, pp. 4–5.
[9] Richard L. Lyons, "Pressure Rises as House Moves to Vote on Rules,"
Washington Post, January 31, 1961.

During the aid to education debate [a Roman Catholic congressman] threatened to kill the public school measure by tagging on to it a parochial school amendment. [Presidential Assistant Lawrence] O'Brien appealed to [the congressman's home district party leader] who immediately telephoned [the congressman]. "Who sent you there, me or the Bishop?" he growled. "And who's going to keep you there, me or the Bishop?"[10]

At other times strong inside and outside influences are blurred together quite inextricably:

A newspaper correspondent told me: "Oh yes, you know those two boys [congressmen] . . . well you know why Jack voted against the leadership? Just to oblige Joe to whom he's very close; Joe was afraid he'd be the only fellow from the state to vote against the leadership and he'd get into trouble with the leadership and the party organization so Jack went along with him to prevent his sticking his neck out all alone. . . ."[11]

The whip from the area told me . . . "Tom rather wanted to go along with the leadership, but he found Dave and Don and four other guys from surrounding districts were against the leadership, and he decided he'd better go along with them, because after all he's hearing a lot from his district against it, and how could he explain his being for it and Dave and Don and the rest being against it?"[12]

The recent contest for the majority leadership of the House provides, as it happens, a rather good contrast between the two strategies of influence. In turn, the close examination of this case may begin to suggest answers to some of the questions posed above.

I

On January 10, 1962, the Democratic members of the House met in caucus in the House chamber and nominated John McCormack

---

[10] *Time* (September 1, 1961), p. 14. The congressman is not identified here, as he was in the *Time* article, first, because he denies the conversation took place (*Congressional Record*, 87th Cong., 1st sess. [August 29, 1961], p. 16318) and second, because the *Time* reporter's source for the quote told me that he had deliberately left ambiguous the identity of the congressman, and, while the event really happened, the *Time* reporter was misled about whom it happened to.

[11] Dexter, *op. cit.*, chap. viii, p. 4.

[12] *Ibid.*, pp. 4–5.

as their candidate for Speaker. Immediately following the conclusion of this business, Richard Bolling of Missouri asked that the
agenda of the caucus be expanded by unanimous consent to include
the selection of a Majority Leader, and Carl Albert of Oklahoma,
his party's whip and the only congressman put in nomination, was
elected to that post. Thus ended a period of skirmishing for the
majority leadership that had principally engaged Bolling and Albert
from the time of Speaker Rayburn's death on November 16 of the
previous year.

Most newspaper coverage of this event gave the impression that
the battle between these two men was drawn on liberal-conservative
lines. In Bolling's press conference on January 3 announcing his
withdrawal from the race, newsmen repeatedly suggested that the
contrast between them was predominantly ideological. A newspaper-
woman asked, rhetorically, "Don't the liberals *ever* win around here,
Mr. Bolling?" Another widely quoted colloquy went:

Reporter: "Mr. Bolling, do you regard your withdrawal . . . as a
defeat for liberalism?"

Bolling: "Well, I consider myself a liberal, and at the moment I
certainly feel defeated."[13]

Close observation suggests that the liberal-conservative distinction
has only a limited kind of utility for understanding the Bolling-
Albert fight for the majority leadership.[14] It is not necessary to base
this conclusion on a *Congressional Quarterly* tabulation showing
that Albert supported the Kennedy program 91 per cent of the time
in the first session of the Eighty-seventh Congress and Bolling 94
per cent—a fact continually cited by liberal supporters of Mr.
Albert.[15] Equally significant are the facts, first, that Albert indeed

---

[13] The best news coverage by far of this press conference that I saw occurred
in the *Baltimore Sun*, January 4, 1962. See Rodney Crowther, "House Race
Dropped by Bolling."

[14] Pursuit of this line of thinking at a McCormack-Albert press conference,
January 9, visibly irked Mr. McCormack. "A reporter . . . caught [Mr. Mc-
Cormack] at the door of the Speaker's lobby and asked him if he had asked
for complete support of President Kennedy's program. The new Speaker drew
back indignantly. 'I'm not trying to put words in your mouth,' said the reporter. 'Yes you are,' said Mr. McCormack, 'I've been voting for progressive
legislation for 30 years. I'm not a one-year man. Why don't you wake up?' "
Mary McGrory, "McCormack Speaks as His Own Master," *Washington Star*,
January 10, 1962.

[15] *Congressional Quarterly*, XIX (November 24, 1961), 1893–94. This tabulation also shows that throughout their careers in Congress, the voting records
of these men were quite close by several criteria.

had a great deal of support among members with impeccably liberal records of long standing and, second, that he was regarded at the White House as a genuine friend of the Kennedy program.[16]

If, then, the outcome of the Bolling-Albert contest cannot be explained by the usual ideological arithmetic one uses in analyzing the House, how can one explain what happened? In part, an explanation can be based on the strategies each of the main actors pursued. These strategies were in turn largely dictated by their respective positions and roles in the House during the final years of the Rayburn speakership.

Often great differences in resources between political actors are largely nullified by the fact that resources are generally employed at low levels of intensity and with indifferent skill. In this case, however, resources on both sides were employed with considerable skill and finesse, and hence the outcome comes closer to reflecting a common-sense notion of the logic of the situation than might otherwise have been the case. It makes sense to describe the "cards" that each man held because, in this instance, the man who held the better cards made no more mistakes than his opponent, and, in the end, he won.

It is worth stressing that only part of the explanation can be given by referring to the roles and strategies of the main participants and to the different ways in which their demands were communicated to other House members. Two other significant variables can be sketched in only very crudely. This battle took place in the very core of an institution about whose habits and practices precious little is known, and, second, it engaged the participation of a great many more facets of the human personality than political decisions in the House normally do. The mysteries of how men interact with one another, of what leads people into enmity, jealousy, friendship, all seem to me to have played a very significant part in this contest.

---

[16] These statements, and many others throughout this paper, are based on interviews and observations gathered during the summer of 1961 and from December to February, 1961–62, in Washington. During these months I spoke on matters connected with the subject of this paper to over 100 congressmen, congressional aides, newspapermen, and others, and during the latter period, I conducted interviews with twenty-six Democratic congressmen from all sections of the country on the leadership selection process then going on. Quotations are from notes taken during these interviews, and are occasionally slightly altered so as to preserve the anonymity of the respondent. My work in the summer of 1961 was supported by a grant-in-aid from the Social Science Research Council, whose assistance is gratefully acknowledged.

Obviously, the extent to which the outside observer can detect and extract meaning from these relationships is extremely limited, and this must inevitably weaken the plausibility and also the generality of the case I am about to construct, using, for the most part, more readily accessible materials.

II

The realization that Speaker Rayburn's health was failing seriously dawned on different members of the House at different times during the summer of 1961. That summer happened to have been an extremely hot and humid one in Washington. The House stayed in session continuously through the summer, one of the longest, bitterest, and most grueling sessions in the memory of veterans on Capitol Hill.[17] Over the course of this period, many members and observers, especially those who were close to the Speaker, could not help but notice the wasting of Mr. Rayburn's solid, imposing figure, the occasional, uncharacteristic wandering of his attention from the business of the House, his increased susceptibility to bouts of fatigue and irritability, the slowing of his gait.

The House is, in the words of one of its members, a "Council of Elders." It honors age and places much power and trust in the hands of its most senior and oldest men. One consequence of this fact is the necessary, calm preoccupation of members—especially those just below the top rungs of power—with the inevitable occurrence of death. To that large fraction of members for whom the House is a career and a vocation, the longevity of members above them in the many hierarchies of the House—not the entirely predictable congressional election returns in their home districts—is the key to the political future. This is not to say that members habitually rub their hands ghoulishly or enjoy the prospect of losing valued friends, but only that the norms and the rules of the House bring due rewards to men who accept the world as it is, who prudently make their plans and bide their time.

On the other hand, informal norms of the House also put constraints on members based on commonly accepted notions of decent

---

[17] The session lasted 277 days, the longest in ten years. Late one especially debilitating August afternoon, an elderly southern congressman shuffled over to where I was standing just outside the Speaker's lobby, and confided that he was going to sponsor a bill that would abolish the final month of each session of Congress.

behavior, decorum, and good taste. Hence it is impossible for an outsider to say when Mr. Albert and Mr. Bolling began thinking in any concrete way about the next step in their careers within the House. However, it seems safe to make two assumptions: First, that they each had entertained some general thoughts on the question of the majority leadership well in advance of the occurence of an actual vacancy (on January 9) or probable vacancy (on November 16) in the position. Second, both men knew Speaker Rayburn well, and both undoubtedly guessed earlier than most members that his health had permanently disintegrated.

III

On Saturday, November 18, Sam Rayburn was buried in Bonham, Texas. Mr. Albert reports that he had planned to wait until the following Wednesday to begin his campaign for Majority Leader. "I was in my office in McAlester on Sunday night," Mr. Albert said, "when Charlie Ward [his assistant] came in and said, 'Bolling has announced for Majority Leader.' I heard it on the radio that night and saw a copy of the press release from my hometown paper before I announced myself. It was an Associated Press report, and Bill Arbogast [who covers the House for AP] wrote the story."

As a result of this turn of events, Mr. Albert got into the race sooner than he had intended. Mr. Bolling had thrown down a challenge which he could ignore only at his peril. In addition, Mr. Bolling's action offered Mr. Albert an opportunity to run a campaign against him, rather than against any of the more popular or more senior members who had been mentioned for leadership positions.

To each side it appeared that the other had begun to make plans well before Mr. Rayburn's death. Observers partial to Mr. Albert noted that as long before as the previous spring, Mr. Bolling was being referred to in public as a prominent contender for a leadership post.[18] It was easy to infer that, at least in part, these references had been suggested or "inspired" by Mr. Bolling. On the other hand, observers partial to Mr. Bolling thought an alliance between Mr. Albert and the Speaker-to-be, John McCormack, was being announced

---

[18] For example, Mr. Bolling was introduced to a large public meeting at the Midwest Conference of Political Scientists on May 11, 1961, as "the next Speaker of the House of Representatives."

when Mr. Albert, as his chief deputy, led the tributes on September 26, 1961, in honor of Mr. McCormack's twenty-one years as Majority Leader.[19]

It seems plausible to suggest that the signs and portents friends of both men were reading did not reflect concious efforts by either man to organize a premature campaign for the majority leadership. Rather, each man appealed particularly to slightly different publics: Bolling to the press corps, Albert to various groups within the House itself. These groups may, without encouragement from either man, have initiated activity designed to facilitate their chances of advancement. "After Mr. Rayburn went home to Texas," Mr. Albert reported, "I had fifty or sixty members pull me aside and say to me, 'He's not coming back. Don't sit there and be done out of what you're entitled to.' But I refused to discuss the matter with them." Several members mentioned that they had volunteered their support to Mr. Albert, and some, apparently, had attempted to persuade him to run for Speaker. "I would never do that against John McCormack," Mr. Albert said. "Mr. Rayburn and Mr. McCormack picked me and made me whip, and to run against Mr. McCormack would have been the act of an ingrate."

Two groups were especially partial to Mr. Albert: his deputy whip organization and colleagues in the Oklahoma delegation. "We make a fetish of the fact that if you scratch one Okie you've scratched all of 'em," one member told me. As soon as Mr. Albert announced that he would run for Majority Leader, the members of the delegation did whatever they could to help his candidacy. The deputy whips gave Mr. Albert a party after Mr. Rayburn had gone to Texas, and attempted, without success, to induce Mr. Albert to begin work on his candidacy at that time.

Mr. Albert's announcement to the press followed the report of Mr. Bolling's by several hours. As soon as the announcement was made, Mr. Albert sent off a telegram to all members asking for their support and began telephoning each of them individually. "I bet you he was on the phone four days running," one member said.

Mr. Albert's intensive telephone campaign began with the west coast members. "James Roosevelt [congressman from Los Angeles] was the first man I called outside my own delegation," he said. By

---

[19] Mr. Albert's tribute on this occasion was much more elaborate than that tendered by any other member—save by Mr. McCormack's Massachusetts colleagues. See the *Congressional Record,* 87th Cong., 1st sess. (September 26, 1961), pp. 20084–96.

the end of the first day of telephoning, Mr. Albert thought he had all but five westerners committed to him. "If I wasn't sure of a senior man in a delegation," Mr. Albert said, "I started with the most junior men and asked them directly to support me. Then I'd work my way up the line so that when the senior man said, 'I'll have to check with my delegation,' I would have something to report to him. Of course on a thing like this, you call your friends first, but I had no set, written-out plan. I don't work that way."

The reasons members gave for supporting Mr. Albert are quite illuminating. They reflect two dominant themes, both of which illustrate the "inside" quality of his influence. On the one hand, Mr. Albert was his party's whip. Although there is no tradition which dictates that the whip shall be advanced to the majority leadership (as there is in promoting the Majority Leader to Speaker) many members felt that Mr. Albert nonetheless was "entitled" to the job by virtue of his six years service in the leadership hierarchy of the House. Some of them said:

[From a liberal leader:] I made a commitment to Carl based on his years of service as whip and the fact that he was in line for this job from the standpoint of his long service as whip.

[From a southwesterner:] Because I feel that he was entitled to it by reason of his effective part in the leadership of the House along with the Speaker and Mr. McCormack, I promised him my support.

[From the elderly dean of a large delegation:] I am a firm believer in the rule that has governed the House for over 100 years, and that is that of seniority. If Congressman McCormack is to be promoted to the Speakership of the House on the premise of his seniority and being in line position, then obviously the majority leader and whip should pursue the same course.[20] I have had the honor of being a member of this great body for [many years] . . . and while I would be reluctant to

---

[20] Mr. Albert entered the House in 1947, Mr. Bolling in 1949, making them thirtieth (tied with nine others) and thirty-ninth (tied with nineteen others) in seniority respectively in the Democratic party in the House—not a very great difference. Mr. McCormack, on the other hand, was the beneficiary of a long tradition of advancement from Majority Leader to Speaker, and, in addition, after the death of Speaker Rayburn, was third in seniority. He had never served as whip, incidentally, nor had Speaker Rayburn. Both Mr. McCormack and Mr. Rayburn had held office for so many years it is highly probable that most members were unaware of the differences in the customs pertaining to the advancement of the Majority Leader and the whip.

say that the seniority process does not have some imperfections, nevertheless if any other procedure were to be applied, I am inclined to believe that rather a chaotic situation would immediately be evident.

A second theme illustrates Mr. Albert's personal popularity in the House. Many members could cite warm personal ties they had developed with Mr. Albert. The late John Riley of South Carolina said, "Carl Albert married a girl from Columbia, you know, and so he is practically a constituent of mine."

A northern liberal: "I'm in something of a special situation with Carl, since we're the only two members of the House who [belong to an exclusive, honorary organization]."

A congressman from a border state said, "In all good conscience, I had to agree to support Carl because of his great help and encouragement to me [on a pet bill]."

A southwesterner said, "As one of his deputy whips, I feel committed to Carl Albert."

A southerner: "I committed myself to Carl Albert, who is my neighbor in the House Office Building."

Another southerner: "My association with Carl Albert has been extremely intimate."

Three men who served with Mr. Albert on committees:

"Carl and I have sat side by side on [our] committee for fifteen years."

"Carl has been very kind to me in the committee work and has done several things for me which have been very important for my people. . . ."

"I sit right next to Carl Albert. . . . We have been close personal friends due to our connection on the committee. . . ."

Another member said, "Ordinarily I'm slow to make commitments, but due to a friendship with Carl which began when we were in the . . . Army together, I told him quite a while back that should he seek the position of Democratic leader, I would support him."

And some members, not unexpectedly, combined the themes. For example: "He is not only my neighbor but a member of my committee, and with it all a fine, able, conscientious man who has been doing the dirty work for the leadership for a long time. . . ."

It was characteristic of Mr. Albert's "inside" strategy of influence that he used the telephone energetically and extensively himself to make personal contacts with members as quickly as possible. As whip, he was the custodian of a complete set of home, office, and district telephone numbers for each member.[21] One member said:

> Albert got on the phone and tracked me down in the frozen wastes of northern Rockystate the first day after the Speaker was buried. You wouldn't think politicians would fall for that, but many of them did. They were impressed by the fact that he'd called them first. As a result he was able to line up a lot of the members, including many northern bleeding-heart liberals, in the first few days.

The principal argument which Mr. Albert used in asking the support of almost all the members I spoke with was the fact that he had already received a large number of commitments. This is instructive, because it evokes the almost obsessive preoccupation of congressmen with "getting along" and not sticking their necks out unnecessarily. "This House gives out no medals for individual bravery," said one congressman, "except posthumously."

Mr. Albert had an important further asset—the apparent backing of John McCormack. "I have heard McCormack say again and again that we have got to have a team player," one congressman said. "I guess he means by that a member of his team, and I suppose he favors Carl Albert." I asked a newspaperman who was following the situation closely to tell me who the most important congressman on Mr. Albert's side was, and he replied, "John McCormack." However, I could find no evidence that Mr. McCormack gave Mr. Albert any public endorsement.

Describing his campaign, Mr. Albert said:

> I didn't want to hurt Mr. Bolling's feelings. I never once threw knives or wrote mean things, although plenty of knives got thrown at me. I never once got on television. The sum total of my national publicity was a release when I got into the race and a release when I got up to Washington saying I thought I had enough votes to win. I refused to go on television although I was invited to go on most of the news and panel shows. I never mentioned Bolling's name at all. I never mentioned issues or anything. . . .

---

[21] Mr. Albert's administrative assistant said that this list happened to be in the Washington office while the telephoning was being done from McAlester, Oklahoma, where only the House telephone directory issued to all members was readily available.

IV

Mr. Bolling's campaign, in contrast, followed an "outside" strategy of influence. As in the Rules Committee fight at the opening of the Eighty-seventh Congress and on numerous other occasions where he had planned legislative strategy and tactics, he held aloof from direct contact with most members. "I seldom try to persuade people directly," he said. "Our districts persuade us—if we are going to be persuaded at all."

Bolling had an uphill battle on his hands. He was severely handicapped at the start by his unwillingness to do anything in his own behalf until well after the Speaker had died. "It's a funny thing that Dick was so dilatory," a friend said. Although he leaked an announcement of his candidacy for the majority leadership to the press on November 19, the day after the Speaker's funeral, it was not until November 28 that he sent a strikingly diffident letter to each of the Democrats in the House. This letter said:

> Just a note to confirm that I am running for Democratic floor leader and am seeking the support of my Democratic colleagues for that position. Reports during the past week have been encouraging and I am in this contest all the way.
> I am running on my legislative record and experience and hope that you will give my candidacy your consideration on that basis.

Several of his supporters expressed surprise at the mildness of this approach. The letter asked for "consideration," not support, and was not followed up by an energetic telephone campaign. Furthermore, Bolling had waited twelve precious days after the Speaker's death before making his move. Why?

Answers to a question of motive such as this one—even the answers given by Mr. Bolling himself—are bound to verge on speculation. My guess is that Mr. Bolling's hesitancy had something to do with the relationship he had had with Speaker Rayburn. According to the reports of numerous observers who had no axes to grind, Mr. Bolling and the Speaker had built a bond of affection between them that went well beyond the usual political alliance.[22] Mr. Sam, who

---

[22] Friends of Mr. Albert note that Mr. Albert was Speaker Rayburn's personal choice for whip in 1954 and further suggest that Mr. Albert was also a close personal friend of Mr. Rayburn's. One influential congressman said, "Mr. Sam thought the world of Carl Albert." But this same congressman indicated that he thought Mr. Bolling's relationship with the Speaker was unique. Without excluding the strong probability that Mr. Rayburn had a

had no immediate family, was well known for his habit of adopting political protégés with whom he could develop a relationship of warmth and trust similar to that found in the family situation. This was, apparently, Mr. Rayburn's way of overcoming the loneliness that otherwise might well have overtaken any elderly bachelor.

The need to overcome loneliness was strongly ingrained in Mr. Rayburn from childhood. Mr. Rayburn is quoted as saying:

> Many a time when I was a child and lived way out in the country, I'd sit on the fence and wish to God that somebody would ride by on a horse or drive by in a buggy—just anything to relieve my loneliness. Loneliness consumes people. It kills 'em eventually. God help the lonely. . . .[23]

Mr. Rayburn's advice to Presidents Truman, Eisenhower, and Kennedy reflect the same theme. As he reported afterward, on a conversation with Mr. Truman just after the latter had become President:

> "You've got many hazards," I said. "One of your great hazards is in this White House," I said. "I've been watching things around here a long time, and I've seen people in the White House try to build a fence around the White House and keep the various people away from the President that he should see. . . ."[24]

His biographer and research assistant, D. B. Hardeman says, "Mr. Sam was . . . annoyed by inactivity. When he could think of nothing else to do at home in Bonham he would get out all his shoes and polish them. He dreaded holidays and Sundays because visitors were few."[25]

Mr. Rayburn found it particularly congenial to work with younger men. D. B. Hardeman says, "Lyndon Johnson once con-

---

high personal regard for Mr. Albert (and, one supposes, several other members as well), the testimony of several knowledgeable and apparently unbiased observers was quite unanimous in indicating that for several years preceding his death Mr. Rayburn was particularly close to Mr. Bolling.

[23] David Cohn, "Mr. Speaker: An Atlantic Portrait," *Atlantic Monthly* (October, 1942), pp. 73–78. The quoted portion appears on p. 76. Mr. Cohn was a personal friend of the Speaker's. He comments on the quoted passage, "As he spoke, Rayburn relived the long, lean, lonely years of his childhood, and it was clear that he wished other children might be spared the bleakness of his youth."

[24] CBS News, "Mr. Sam: A Personal and Political Biography," telecast, November 16, 1961.

[25] D. B. Hardeman, "The Unseen Side of the Man They Called Mr. Speaker," *Life*, LI (December 1, 1961), 21.

fessed, 'The Speaker and I have always been very close but if we are not as close as we were once, it is because I'm almost 50. If you notice, he never has older men around him.' "[26]

"I always liked the House the best," Mr. Rayburn said. "There're more people there, usually they're younger people, and as I've advanced in years, I've stepped back in my associations, boys, young people ten, twenty years younger than I. Their bodies are not only resilient but their minds are too. They can learn faster than the fellow advanced in years."[27]

One of the things which no doubt drew Mr. Rayburn to Mr. Bolling was the exceptional resiliency and quickness of the latter's mind. On this quality, friends and political enemies of Mr. Bolling agreed. He is an extremely "quick study," and had several other things in common with the Speaker:

"Bolling loves the House," a judicious, slow spoken southern congressman who knows him rather well told me. "He loves it and has studied it. He has read everything that has been written about the House and has studied its power structure. He has a brilliant mind."

Although nearly thirty-five years separated them, both Mr. Rayburn and Mr. Bolling were strongly committed emotionally to many liberal programs. Bolling refers to himself quite frankly as a "gut liberal"; *Time* magazine has aptly characterized Rayburn as a "liberal of the heart."[28] In addition, both men shared a high sense of rectitude in their work, treating the majority of their colleagues with reserve and judging them rather severely. This social distance which both men maintained was no doubt related in some complex way to the intensity of their feelings about political issues. It is instructive in this connection to note the tendency of both men to become laconic in public when dealing with problems with which they had great personal involvement. Compare Bolling's prepared statement of withdrawal from the majority leadership race in 1962 with Rayburn's statement of withdrawal in 1934 from an unsuccessful race for the speakership.[29]

---

[26] *Ibid.*

[27] CBS News, "Mr. Sam . . .," *op. cit.*

[28] *Time,* LXXVII (February 10, 1961), p. 12. What is significant here, I think, is not the placement of either man on an ideological spectrum so much as the high degree of personal engagement which the references to parts of the body suggest.

[29] I was a witness to the events surrounding the composition of Bolling's statement of withdrawal, and am quite convinced that Bolling had no knowledge of Rayburn's statement. Rather, the striking resemblance between the two seems

In 1934 Rayburn said, "I am no longer a candidate for Speaker. There are no alibis. Under the circumstances, I cannot be elected."[30] In 1962 Bolling said, "I am withdrawing from the race for leadership of the House. Developments of the last few days have convinced me that I don't have a chance to win."[31] Bolling privately expressed an unwillingness amounting to an incapacity either to "do anything" until after a "decent" time had elapsed after the Speaker's death[32] or to canvass for votes in his own behalf. The major portion of this burden within the House was carried by Representative Frank Thompson of New Jersey and a group of four or five others. The brunt of Bolling's campaign was, however, carried on from outside the House.[33] Initially, he had to

---

to me to illustrate a remarkable similarity in the styles of the two men, not conscious imitation.

[30] Bascom N. Timmons, "Rayburn" (ditto, n.d.), part 4, p. 1. This series was supplied to certain newspapers at the time of Speaker Rayburn's death. Mr. Timmons is a newspaperman accredited to the House Press Galleries from a string of newspapers in the southwest. He is a Texan and was a friend and contemporary of Mr. Rayburn's.

[31] Rodney Crowther, *Baltimore Sun, loc. cit.* The psychologically-minded would also no doubt find it relevant that Mr. Bolling's father died when he was in his early teens. However, anyone concluding from data such as have been presented here that either Mr. Bolling or Mr. Rayburn gave indications in their behavior of being emotionally crippled or lacking in control could not possibly be further from the mark. The point here is simply that certain easily verified events and patterns in the lives of each man may well have predisposed him to like the other.

[32] Mr. Bolling's imputation of indecorousness (the news of which was communicated in such places as "Bitter Withdrawal," *Time,* LXXIX [January 12, 1962, 12]) was resented in the Albert camp. In their view, Mr. Bolling had himself precipitated the battle by first permitting word to leak to the newspapers that he was a candidate for Majority Leader.

[33] One index of this is the apparent fact that Mr. Thompson is generally not too popular in the House (a fact of which both he and Mr. Bolling are aware). Mr. Thompson is an able and gifted man with extremely good political connections outside the House, both "downtown" and in his home state. (See Richard L. Lyons, "Thompson Decision to Retain Seat Gives House Liberals Needed Lift," *Washington Post,* January 31, 1961.) But inside the House, he has a reputation for being sharp-tongued, supercilious, and too witty for his own good. He has a way of hanging nicknames that "stick" on friend and foe alike—to the delight of the former, the great chagrin of the latter. One political ally of Mr. Thompson's said, "He has got the reputation that whenever he is in favor of a bill, it is bound to lose. . . . Thompson is one of Bolling's major liabilities. I hear how the guys talk at the back of the room there [in the aisle behind the seats in the Hall of the House]. They say, 'Whose amendment is that? Thompson's? That guy? To hell with that!' And they vote it down." Another ally of Thompson's said, "Frank's always trying to talk silly with you when you're talking serious, and trying to talk serious when you're talking silly."

decide whether to run for Speaker or Majority Leader—which no doubt also contributed to the quality of hesitancy in his campaign.

Factors pointing to the speakership included the relative unpopularity of Mr. McCormack (1) with members, and (2) at the White House; but against this had to be weighed (1) Mr. McCormack's generally blameless voting record (from the standpoint of a pro-administration Democrat), (2) his long service in the second position, (3) the weight of a tradition which strongly favored the elevation of a Majority Leader, (4) Mr. Bolling's own relatively junior position, (5) the fact that Mr. McCormack, if he lost the speakership, would remain as a Majority Leader not especially favorably disposed toward the program of an administration that had just done him in politically, and, (6) the fact that opposing Mr. McCormack would unavoidably exacerbate the religious cleavage in the House and the country which the fight over school aid in the last session had revealed.[34]

And so, Mr. Bolling decided to run for Majority Leader against the extremely popular Mr. Albert. In a straight popularity contest, Mr. Bolling knew he was "born dead." His role in the House had been quite unlike Mr. Albert's; indeed, several congressmen contrasted them starkly.

A close friend described Mr. Albert's approach to the job of whip:

> The whip is more the eyes and ears of the leadership than anything. On controversial matters, they like to know what the chances of success are. . . . So the deputy whips count noses, and the whip's job is to evaluate the count—especially to assess the doubtfuls. . . . Albert developed quite a genius for knowing what people would do. . . .
> Another service he performed endears him to people. Carl's the kind of a guy everybody could find. He would talk to the leadership for [rank-and-file congressmen].
> A lot of these eastern guys have a Tuesday through Thursday club. The whip takes the duty on of telling them if the signals change so they can get back here if they're needed.
> He's done so many things for people. They trust him. They think of him, "Here's a man I can talk to when I need help." When the members go about picking a leader, they want personal services, not intellectuals.[35]

---

[34] See H. Douglas Price, "Race, Religion and the Rules Committee" in Alan Westin (ed.), *The Uses of Power* (New York: Harcourt, Brace & World, 1962), pp. 1–71.

[35] Mr. Albert's friend may, in reflecting unfavorably on Mr. Bolling, have done Mr. Albert a slight injustice. Mr. Albert was an honor graduate of the University of Oklahoma and a Rhodes Scholar—neither of which makes him an intellectual, but they clearly don't disqualify him either.

I dare you to find a member of Congress who said Bolling had lifted a finger for him.

A supporter of Mr. Bolling's (for whom Bolling had, according to this member's testimony, lifted many a finger) saw the roles of the two principals in much the same light, although his evaluation of their roles was quite different:

> Albert's approach to legislative matters is, well, everybody ought to vote his own district. . . . He brings his friends and his enemies in [to vote] both. . . . Why the hell get [a certain southern congressman] out [to vote]? He doesn't vote with us on anything. And he's a deputy whip! It's ridiculous. . . . The function of the whip [under Mr. Albert] is room service to members.
> Albert was the whip, but Bolling was doing the whipping. . . . When the heat was being put on in the Rules Committee and all the other fights, it was Bolling putting it on, and he wasn't making any friends doing it.[36]

Mr. Bolling was, as a friend of his described it, a "hatchet man" for Speaker Rayburn. This entailed a variety of activities on the Rules Committee, including monitoring the attendance of friends and foes, arranging for the disposition of bills, and keeping track of the intentions of the various (and numerous) factions in the House with respect to important legislation, in behalf of the Speaker. Occasionally, Mr. Bolling's job included putting the finger on members who were open to (or vulnerable to) persuasion, and he often had a crucial part in the process of persuading them—not always a pleasant task.[37]

Although Mr. Bolling is entirely in sympathy with policies espoused by liberals in the House, his position close to the Speaker precluded his joining in any formal way in the activities of the Democratic Study Group, the House liberal organization. As a friend of his put it, "Dick was aloof from the uprisings of the peasants."

---

[36] There are now several accounts of the 1961 battle over the Rules Committee in print, including a treatment of the episode in Price, *op. cit.;* the analysis of the vote by Cummings and Peabody in Chapter VII of this volume; a long chapter by Neil MacNeil in *Forge of Democracy* (New York: McKay, 1963), pp. 410–88; and a forthcoming case study in the Eagleton series by William MacKaye.

[37] See *Time,* LXXVII (February 10, 1961); William S. White, "The Invisible Gentleman from Kansas City," *Harper's* (May, 1961); Neil MacNeil, "The House Confronts Mr. Kennedy," *Fortune,* LXV (January 1962), 70–73.

"Bolling's got a sort of a chip on his shoulder," another member said.

"The thing you have to realize about Bolling," said an Albert backer, "is that he never bothers to speak to anyone else. I don't think Bolling understands politics."

Mr. Bolling's aloofness was, as I have suggested, probably something more than simply a reflection of his peculiar institutional position. A second friend of Bolling's said, "Despite a good deal of charm, Bolling just does not have a personality that inspires loyalty and friendship among men.[38] He's not a backslapping, how-the-hell-are-you type of guy. Bolling is personally quite pleasant, but reticent."

The late Clem Miller of California said, "Congress is a World War I rather than a World War II operation. You have to move huge bodies of men a few feet at a time. . . . Dick's spent the last few years divorcing himself from a base of fire. His job was right-hand man to the Speaker. He came to Democratic Study Group meetings but always identified himself as an observer, not as a participant. He came in a sense to lecture us like small children rather than lead us in our councils. There was a good deal of hostility toward him in the Study Group as a result of that. The Study Group was set up as a foil for the leadership. You can't have your foot in both camps, and so Dick alienated the base of support that he needed in the House."

Another member, often allied with Mr. Bolling, characterized him as "totally unfriendly."

Mr. Bolling's personal situation within the House was further complicated by a common enough phenomenon. As a relative newcomer, as an extremely able member performing difficult tasks well, and as an intimate of the Speaker, Mr. Bolling was, in the opinion of several observers, the victim of a certain amount of jealous resentment.

"Jealousy is a big factor," one congressman said. "Liberals have several characteristics that tend to make them ineffective, and vanity is one of them. They tend to be prima donnas."[39] Another said,

---

[38] Statements such as this one obviously are not intended to be taken with strict literalness. Most social scientists are agreed that the personal "qualities" of leaders vary according to the situation.

[39] Cf. a similar comment on Senate liberals by Tristam Coffin, "The Well Tempered Politician," *Holiday* (April, 1962), p. 107.

"Dick is not a popular man in the House, no doubt a surprise to newsmen. For one thing, he's resented because of his ability."

Liberals were clearly not the only group of congressmen susceptible to jealous feelings toward Mr. Bolling. His relative youth was offensive to some of his seniors. Mr. Bolling had risen very fast in the House and had been given many advantages by his friend, the Speaker. The record he had made thus far also suggested that, if elected, he would take many more initiatives than Mr. Albert and would more decisively challenge the powers of committee and subcommittee chairmen to control the flow and content of legislation—in behalf of programs for which many of these leaders had no particular liking.

Even to the superficial observer, Mr. Albert and Mr. Bolling are quite contrasting figures. Mr. Albert was fifty-three years old, exactly on the House median; Mr. Bolling was only forty-five. Albert is physically probably the shortest man in the House and looks nothing like the collegiate wrestler he once was. He has a softly lined, friendly, gentle face which, says a colleague, "always looks faintly worried." Bolling is a tall, husky, quite handsome and imposing-looking man who gives the appearance of great self-confidence and looks very much like the collegiate football player he was. Mr. Albert in conversation is homespun, soft-spoken, emotionally unengaged, and low-pressure. A colleague says, "You could vote impeachment of the President, and it wouldn't bother Carl." Mr. Bolling in conversation is articulate, expansive, sophisticated, intense; in short, one would surmise, a rather more threatening figure to someone of average inclinations than Mr. Albert.

Mr. Bolling has far greater acceptance in the higher echelons of the "downtown" bureaucracies and surely in the press corps than almost any other congressman, including Mr. Albert. Mr. Bolling is far more likely to spend his leisure hours among pundits, diplomats, and subcabinet officials than with congressmen, a pattern which Mr. Albert reverses. Mr. Albert prides himself, in fact, in spending a greater proportion of his time on the floor of the House than any other member, where he is continually accessible to his colleagues.[40]

---

[40] See John M. Virden, "Little Giant from Bug Tussle," *Saturday Evening Post*, CCXXXV (March 24, 1962), 94–97; Paul Duke, "Albert's Soft Sell," *Wall Street Journal*, March 6, 1962; "Carl Albert, Nose-Counter from Bug Tussle," *Time*, LXXIX (January 12, 1962), 13.

[Footnote continued on page 258.]

To a great extent, Mr. Bolling understood that a variety of institutional and personal "inside" factors were working against him, and so he launched an "outside" campaign.

V

Bolling's task, as he saw it, was divided into several phases of activity. First, he had to stall the Albert bandwagon. Then he had to receive enough commitments to win himself. His primary targets were the big state delegations of New York, California, Illinois, and Pennsylvania. Secondary targets included getting a firm grip on his home state delegation and going after younger, liberal congressmen and congressmen who had substantial labor and civil-rights-minded constituencies.

His strategy for accomplishing these ends had two major features. First, he intended to draw as sharp a contrast as he could between himself and Mr. Albert on issues and sell the contrast as hard as he could through the mass media. Second, he set about "pulling strings" on members, a process which he had practiced before in legislative battles.[41] This entailed identifying the men and interest groups favorable to his candidacy who for various reasons could reach and persuade members of Congress. Naturally, the foremost among these

---

Certain other characteristics place Mr. Albert closer to the rank and file of congressmen than Mr. Bolling. Mr. Albert was a small town boy, the son of a farmer and laborer, educated in public schools, and is a Methodist. Mr. Bolling was born in New York City, the son of a well-to-do physician. He grew up in comfortable circumstances and socially prominent circles in Huntsville, Alabama, after his father's death went to Exeter and the University of the South, has a Master's degree from Sewanee, and did further graduate work at Vanderbilt, and is an Episcopalian. If the script for this contest had been written by C. Wright Mills or one of his followers, Mr. Albert would have been the more "liberal" candidate and wouldn't have had a chance. (See Mills, *The Power Elite* [New York: Oxford University Press, 1956]). Mr. Mills carefully excludes Congress from his discussion of "the power elite" for reasons which seem to this reader designed to protect his thesis from evidence which would reject it.

[41] An example of this process was given in *Time*, Vol. LXXVII (February 10, 1961) at the time of the Rules Committee fight: "*Time* Correspondent Neil MacNeil listened as two Rayburn lieutenants were running down the list of doubtful members. On one: 'The General Services Administration ought to be able to get him.' On another: 'The Air Force can take care of him.' A third? 'If you can get the Post Office to issue that special stamp for him, you've got him.' And a fourth? 'The United Mine Workers can get him.' And a fifth? 'Hell, if we can't get him we might as well quit. Go talk to him.' A sixth? 'No, but I'll fix that bastard.' " *Time* gives the strong impression that the two lieutenants are Bolling and Thompson.

would have been the President, but at no time was presidential aid offered, and none was requested by Mr. Bolling.

The position of the White House in this battle was a complex one. While the mass media, on the whole, bought Mr. Bolling's contention that substantial differences in public policy separated him and Mr. Albert, the White House never did. It regarded both men as good friends of the Kennedy program, each having personal and political strengths and weaknesses. To intervene in behalf of one friend would have meant sacrificing another. For the White House to intervene and lose would have been disastrous for its prestige and legislative program. To intervene and win would have been more satisfactory but still would have involved (aside from the making of enemies) great exertion, the distribution of indulgences and the "cashing in" on favors owed, all of which could otherwise be employed to improve the chances for passage of controversial reciprocal trade, medical aid, tax reform, and education bills. Several members of the President's official family were close to Mr. Bolling and were almost certainly partial to him, but none participated in the fight.

Mr. Bolling and his backers in the House concurred in the White House policy of non-intervention and in the reasoning behind it. The major inside advantage of their side, as they saw it, was a professional ability to predict outcomes accurately and to recommend appropriate strategies. They understood fully that the risks to the White House were great, the probabilities of success dubious. If they could come close to winning on their own, within perhaps five or ten votes, then their recommendation might change, since the White House could then probably put them over the top. But it is not at all certain that even then the White House would have been ready to move.

If the administration was inactive, other keenly interested bystanders were not. The AFL-CIO backed Mr. Bolling strongly and performed several notable services in behalf of his candidacy. Labor lobbyists made a complete canvass of possible supporters in the House and, in several cases, made representations in Mr. Bolling's behalf with members. The NAACP was also active. Roy Wilkins, national chairman, telegraphed 153 selected branches of his organization, "Bolling right on 26 civil rights votes, Albert wrong. Wire, write or call your Congressman. This could affect civil rights legislation for years to come." The Democratic Reform Clubs of New York City were also interested in Bolling's candidacy, as were some local and national political leaders around the country and at least one farm organization.

An example of indirect influence in Mr. Bolling's behalf was described by an Albert supporter, "I heard that President Truman, a neighbor of Bolling's and a loyal Missourian, called Mayor Wagner of New York to try and get the New York delegation to support Bolling."

Mr. Bolling was especially successful in enlisting the aid of the mass media. Since the civil rights battle of 1957, when he anonymously kept newsmen briefed on the confusing tactical situation within the House, Mr. Bolling has been extremely popular with the Washington press corps.[42] He is asked to appear on broadcasts and telecasts much more often than the average member. He counts many Washington correspondents, including several famous ones, as close personal friends.

Hence, it is not altogether surprising that he was able to gain the endorsement of the *New York Times* as early as December 11. On Sunday, December 24, the *Times* reiterated its stand, saying, "The conservative coalition of Southern Democrats and Northern Republicans would find it much more difficult to exercise its suffocating veto over forward-looking legislation with the imaginative and hard-driving Mr. Bolling as majority floor chief."[43]

Five days previously, on December 19, James Wechsler, editor of the *New York Post,* gave a strong endorsement to Mr. Bolling, in which he printed a long verbatim extract of a letter endorsing Carl Albert which Bolling had received from Judge Howard W. Smith, leader of conservative southerners in the House.[44] Wechsler commented, "This is not to say Albert has faithfully followed Smith's gospel. He is a moderate, pleasant man whose voting record might be far more impressive if he came from a state more congenial to the advance of civil rights and less dominated by the natural gas interests. Despite their differences on a variety of matters, Smith is

---

[42] A Washington correspondent commented: "[Bolling] was a good news source and popular among newsmen from the time he first got on the House Banking Committee and became even more popular when he was moved to Rules as Rayburn's obvious protégé."
[43] *New York Times,* December 24, 1961.
[44] This letter was sent in response to Mr. Bolling's November 28 request for "consideration" from each Democrat. Supporters of Mr. Albert were dismayed by the fact that while they had not solicited Judge Smith's support and Mr. Bolling had, the Smith endorsement was being used by Mr. Bolling against Mr. Albert with the press.

plainly confident that he can handle Albert; he is equally convinced that Bolling spells trouble. . . ."[45]

On December 29, Marquis Childs[46] and Edward P. Morgan both urged the selection of Mr. Bolling, referring once again to the Smith letter and to issues separating the two candidates. Mr. Morgan was especially vigorous in his commentary:

> . . . where Bolling has been consistently for them, Albert has been basically against civil rights legislation, federal aid to education, full foreign aid and regulation of the oil and gas industry. It is reliably reported that one Texas congressman told a southern colleague that "with Albert in there, oil will be safe for twenty years. . . ."[47]

What of the outcomes of these activities? The relations between outside "pressures" and congressmen have been variously described in popular and academic literature. There is an old tradition which regards these relations as essentially nefarious.[48] Descriptively, the congressman is sometimes thought to be a relatively passive creature who is pulled and hauled about according to the play of pressures

---

[45] James Wechsler, "Hill Battle," *New York Post,* December 19, 1961. Mr. Bolling's constituency is the Fifth District of Missouri, which includes most of Kansas City. Mr. Albert represents the thirteen counties of Oklahoma's Third District, an area known as "Little Dixie." This district is predominantly rural and is somewhat depressed economically. Its major products are timber, peanuts, cotton, and livestock. Several Albert supporters suggested that a generally liberal record such as Mr. Albert had made in the House was in some ways a more creditable performance for a man from a district of this kind than for a man from a big city. Although this argument has some plausibility, it should also be noted that several of the most respected southern liberals and moderates in the House have come from districts very similar to Mr. Albert's. Sam Rayburn himself was one such example. Others would be Carl Elliott of Alabama, Frank Smith of Mississippi, and James Trimble of Arkansas. This argument may, in other words, be an attempt to appeal to a popular stereotype which automatically classifies big-city districts as "liberal" and rural southern districts as "conservative." But it may be that on the vast majority of issues coming to a vote in Congress, representatives from southern, rural, economically depressed areas have constituencies as liberal as any in the country.

[46] Marquis Childs, "The High Stakes in House Battle," *Washington Post* December 29, 1961—and elsewhere.

[47] "Edward P. Morgan and the News," American Broadcasting Company, December 29, 1961. The documentation of this case has never, to my knowledge, been made. I suggest that at the least the reference to Mr. Albert's position on federal aid to education would be difficult to defend.

[48] See, for examples of this tradition, H. H. Wilson, *Congress: Corruption and Compromise* (New York: Rinehart, 1951), Karl Schriftgiesser, *The Lobbyists* (Boston: Little, Brown, 1951).

upon him and whose final decision is determined by the relative strength of outside forces.[49] More recently, political scientists have become preoccupied with the qualities of reciprocity in the relations of interest groups and politicians. This literature calls attention to mutually beneficial aspects of the relationship and lays stress on the ways in which politicians may act to govern the outside pressures placed on them.[50]

My information on the impact of Bolling's outside campaign is necessarily incomplete. It is apparent at a minimum that a sufficient number of congressmen were never reached by this campaign. One congressman said:

> Bolling's best hope was forces outside the House—labor and civil rights groups. But I received not one communication in his behalf from anybody. There was nobody campaigning for him. Nobody knew if he was serious or not. Where was the heat?

Another congressman, from a heavily populated area, said:

> Our delegation was never put on the spot. Bolling never tried to wage a campaign in our delegation. Apparently he tried to get labor leaders to pressure Cautious [the state party leader] to put pressure on our congressmen. This is OK, but you really have to put the pressure on because if you know Cautious, he won't ever move unless he's really in a box.

In other cases, congressmen were able quite easily to *resist* pressure. "The word got around," one liberal congressman said, "that this wasn't like the Rules Committee fight, where there was a legitimate issue. Rather, it was all in the family, and any outside interference, even from the White House, would be resented."

---

[49] An excellent example of this mode of thinking is contained in Max Lerner, *America as a Civilization* (New York: Simon & Schuster, 1957), pp. 415 ff. and especially p. 424. More generally, see Arthur F. Bentley, *The Process of Government* (Evanston: Principia, 1949), Earl Latham, *The Group Basis of Politics* (Ithaca: Cornell University Press, 1952), Oliver Garceau, "Interest Group Theory in Political Research," *The Annals,* CCCXIX (September, 1958), and David B. Truman, *The Governmental Process* (New York: Knopf, 1955). Truman explicitly rejects the notion that congressmen are wholly passive.

[50] Lewis A. Dexter, *op. cit.,* and Dexter, "The Representative and His District," *Human Organization,* XVI (Summer, 1947), 2–13, reprinted as Chapter I of the present volume; Dexter, "What Do Congressmen Hear: The Mail," *Public Opinion Quarterly,* XX (Spring, 1956), 16–26. See also Donald R. Matthews, *U.S. Senators and Their World* (Chapel Hill: University of North Carolina Press, 1960), esp. chaps. viii, ix.

Harlem's Representative Adam Clayton Powell, announcing his support of Albert, charged that some organized labor representatives were putting pressure on some Democratic members of his committee. He added, "I can't understand why labor union leaders would do this. Frankly, this is Democratic party business, not labor business."[51]

On the other hand, Bolling's campaign from the outside made several converts. Representative Leonard Farbstein of New York City, for example, announced that he would vote for Mr. Bolling on the basis of Mr. Wechsler's column.[52]

Another congressman, a conservative veteran, wrote Bolling and detailed the substantial political disagreements between them, concluding, "But Famous Farmer tells me he is supporting you, and if he is supporting you, I am supporting you."

A leader of another interest group, in another part of the country, wrote, "I have just been informed by Congressman Dean Delegation's home secretary that Dean will be supporting you for majority leader. If there are any particular targets in [this state], I'm still available to apply whatever other pressures I can."

In aggregate, however, the impact of this campaign was not sufficient to accomplish Mr. Bolling's major goal. Edward Morgan commented with some asperity on the failure of Mr. Bolling to consolidate his support on an ideological basis, and at the same time he renewed the plea that the battle be defined in ideological terms:

> If they voted . . . in support of their constituencies' needs for protection on gas prices, housing, civil rights and the like, the big city and industrial area representatives would have to come down almost unanimously for Bolling over Albert on their voting records alone and the man from Missouri would have it cinched. But he doesn't have it cinched. . . . At least one Massachusetts congressman has already committed himself to Albert in writing . . . Adam Clayton Powell is looking south . . . So are a couple of New Jersey Representatives. . . . Most surprisingly, perhaps, two leading California Congressmen, Holifield and Roosevelt, have not dashed to Bolling's aid. . . .[53]

---

[51] Robert C. Albright, "Powell Backs Albert for House Post," *Washington Post*, December 1, 1961. Powell, unlike the congressman just quoted, checked with the White House before he made his announcement, obviously taking the position that the President had a legitimate interest in the outcome.
[52] *New York Post*, December 21, 1961.
[53] "Edward P. Morgan and the News," American Broadcasting Company, December 29, 1961. This account may be contrasted with a column put out by

Over the long New Year's weekend, Bolling, Thompson, and Andrew Biemiller of the AFL-CIO met and assessed Bolling's "hard" strength at between sixty-five and seventy votes. Perhaps fifty more would have joined them if Bolling were going to win, but otherwise, they faded. A Bolling lieutenant said, "Everybody wanted to know, 'What's his chances?' The typical response was, 'I'll lie low. I'm with you if you've got a chance; otherwise, nix.' "

By the most realistic calculations, however, Mr. Bolling fell short of the 130 or more votes that he needed. He decided to withdraw his candidacy rather than embarrass his supporters in their state delegations and possibly jeopardize their future effectiveness in Congress.

VI

It is possible to identify at least four reasons why Mr. Bolling's attempt to win from the outside failed. The first two have already been mentioned: Mr. Albert's extreme popularity and Bolling's relative isolation provided little incentive for individual members to seek outside excuses of their own accord to do what they could more conveniently do for inside reasons. Second, the hands-off policy of the White House deprived Mr. Bolling's campaign of what would have been a major outside weapon had the President chosen to come in on Mr. Bolling's side.

The third major obstacle to the success of the outside campaign was the fact that, through no fault of Mr. Bolling's, a few of his supporters unwittingly blunted one of his principal weapons, the ideological contrast between himself and Mr. Albert. Just before the opening of the second session of the Eighty-seventh Congress, and at the same time the struggle over the majority leadership was going on, a group of liberal congressmen proposed that a policy committee be created in the Democratic party to be elected by the members

William S. White, a former Capitol Hill reporter. White's explanation of what happened is: "Whatever chance [Bolling] might have had, however, was sunk without a trace by the ultra-liberals themselves. They rushed forward to gather him into their arms, through zealous indorsements by such too-gooder groups as Americans for Democratic Action. No man in a House which—like the country itself—is essentially moderate could possibly have survived such embarrassing public embraces. So Mr. Bolling had to withdraw his candidacy. . . ." *Washington Star*, January 5, 1962—and elsewhere. I could discover little evidence which would lend credibility to this analysis. Regrettably, Mr. White offers none.

from each of the eighteen whip zones. This committee was to advise and counsel with the leadership, and it was contemplated that it would be "more representative" (and presumably more liberal) than the leadership, unaided, would be.

Congressmen favoring this proposal circulated it among their Democratic colleagues in an attempt to get the fifty signatures necessary to place it on the agenda of the caucus which was to elect a new Speaker. Several liberals favoring Mr. Albert promptly signed, thus furnishing themselves with an excellent alibi, if they were challenged on ideological grounds by constituents and interest groups. They could claim that the fight over the majority leadership was not really significant since Bolling and Albert were, in their voting records, so close. But on the basic issue, on the institutional structure of leadership in the House, they were, as always, for liberalization.

This proposal went through several stages. At one point, it was seriously proposed that Mr. Bolling accept the chairmanship of this committee as the price for withdrawing his candidacy for the majority leadership. This proposal implied that the new Speaker had accepted the policy committee in principle.[54] Mr. Bolling was him-

---

[54] The rate at which tentative proposals and counterproposals of this sort fly around Washington is perfectly phenomenal. Theodore H. White rhapsodizes about the kinds of people who often act in the capacity of carrier pigeon: "Washington holds perhaps fifty or a hundred . . . men, lawyers all, successful all, who in their dark-paneled law chambers nurse an amateur's love for politics and dabble in it whenever their practices permit. Where, in the regions, cities and states of the country, provincial lawyers love to counsel local politicians, promote names for the local judiciary, arrange the candidacies of lesser men, in Washington lawyers dabble in national politics, in appointments to places of high political destiny. Their influence, collectively, can never be ignored, because, collectively, they possess a larger fund of wisdom, experience, contacts, memories, running back over thirty years of national politics, than most candidates on the national scene can ever hope to acquire on their own . . . ." *The Making of the President, 1960* (New York: Atheneum, 1961), p. 33.

Newspaper people also quite often undertake this sort of activity, and occasionally lobbyists do, too.

Fortuitously, much of the activity described in this paper took place during the Christmas-Debutante-New Year's social season in Washington. As a result, many of the participants in these events kept running into each other at parties. Political science may some day catch up with the slick magazines and novels in comprehending the true significance of Washington parties. In this case, it appears that much of the negotiating on whether or not Mr. Bolling would join the leadership group as head of the policy committee took place on an informal basis, through intermediaries and without any soul-stirring confrontations of rivals such as are found in Allen Drury's *Advise and Consent.*

self dubious about the chances that such a committee could perform the tasks its supporters envisaged for it. Counterproposals and negotiations buzzed back and forth about the possibility of putting "teeth" into the committee and about prior agreements as to its membership. At another level, Mr. Bolling and Mr. Thompson had to avoid being mousetrapped by the petition to put the policy committee on the agenda. To have signed the petition might have looked to Albert-McCormack forces like a proposal of terms and an acknowledgment of defeat. The fact that supporters of the Bolling candidacy were leading the fight for the policy committee was compromising enough as it was.

In the end, the whole idea came to nothing.[55] The proposal never received enough signatures to gain a place on the agenda, and at John McCormack's first press conference upon his nomination for the speakership, he said, "A policy committee is out."[56] But the policy committee plan served one significant purpose. It softened and blurred Bolling's attempt to define the issue between himself and Mr. Albert in such a way as to embarrass liberals who were not supporting him.

The fourth reason for the failure of the outside campaign is probably the most important. It has to do with the conditions under which the actual choice was going to be made. Normally, a congressman has considerable leeway in the casting of his vote because the issues are complex and technical, because the ways in which they are framed sometimes inspires no sharp cleavages of opinion, because interest groups are often disinterested and inattentive. But when an issue heats up and reaches the final stages of the legislative process,

---

[55] That is, it came to almost nothing. In mid-March, 1962, three months after the events described here took place, the Democrats reactivated a "steering" committee along the lines of the "policy" committee proposed at the opening of the session. Mr. Bolling did not become a member. A leading Democrat in the House observed to me that the members of this committee, including James Davis of Georgia, William Colmer of Mississippi, Paul Kitchin of North Carolina, Clarence Cannon of Missouri, were likely, if anything, to be *less* liberal than the leadership they were supposed to advise. This was an outcome exactly opposite to the one envisaged by proponents of the policy committee idea.
[56] For the story at various stages, see: Robert C. Albright, "Drive is Begun for Democratic Steering Group," *Washington Post,* December 30, 1961; Mary McGrory, "McCormack Silent on Liberals Plan," *Washington Star,* December 31, 1961; Robert K. Walsh, "Party Harmony Setup Seen by House Liberals," *Washington Star,* January 5, 1962; Richard L. Lyons, "Liberal Democrats Defer Demands," *Washington Post,* January 9, 1962; Rowland Evans, Jr., "Democrats Unanimous," *New York Herald Tribune,* January 10, 1962.

leeway dissipates. Interest groups become active. The mail begins to pour in.[57] Newsmen appear on the scene. Congressmen stick close to the Floor, listen to debate, mill around, stand ready to answer quorum calls or to vote on amendments.

There are four procedures for voting in the House: voices, standing, tellers, and roll call, in the order in which they expose members to public view. In the Committee on the Whole House, only the first three types of votes are taken. A diligent reporter or lobbyist can, however, even without benefit of a roll call, usually find out how a given member votes. The procedure is not foolproof, but, from the gallery, an outsider can always keep his eye fixed on one or a few congressmen whose votes are of interest to him. Corroboration, if any is needed, can be obtained by asking around among other congressmen.

The caucus at which voting for Majority Leader was to have taken place provided no such opportunities for outside surveillance. No spectators were admitted. Congressmen were even protected from the scrutiny of their colleagues; Representative Francis Walter, chairman of the caucus, sent word that the balloting for Majority Leader, when the time came, would be secret. The rules of the caucus say nothing about a secret ballot; rather, general parliamentary law governs the caucus meetings, and there is a special provision that "the yeas and nays on any question shall, at the desire of one fifth of those present, be entered on the journal"—all of which did not alter the fact that the balloting would be secret.

In spite of the interest which Mr. Bolling had stirred up among outside groups, these groups were operating under an insuperable handicap. The voting procedure maximized the chances that a congressman cross-pressured between the demands of "local agency" and his own personal feelings could vote his private preferences with impunity.

VII

What does this case suggest about the general relations between inside and outside influences in the decision-making processes of

---

[57] Lewis Dexter makes the point that the mail usually comes too late to affect the substance of legislation. However mail is used here only as an index of attentiveness to issues on the part of publics. See Dexter, "What Do Congressmen Hear . . . ," *op. cit.*

the House?[58] Several things. First, it shows the extent to which inside and outside strategies tend to encourage different modes of communication among members and to evoke different definitions of the decision-making situation. The inside strategy is likely to define situations as "family matters," and to feature face-to-face interaction among members. The outside strategy is likely to evoke a more ideological, issue-oriented definition of the situation. Interaction among members is more likely to take place through third persons, lobbyists, and the press. Second, this case suggests conditions tending to promote the success of each strategy of influence. Inside strategies are favored when: (1) the matter to be decided can be rationalized as in some sense procedural rather than substantive; (2) there are great differences in the inside strengths of the two sides, but their outside strengths approach equality; (3) members are protected from surveillance by outsiders. Outside strategies are favored, presumably, when these conditions are reversed.

Additional conditions bearing on the effectiveness of inside and outside strategies may be imagined. Presumably, the autonomy of a representative from constituent pressures diminishes as his constituency approaches unanimity in its preferences *or* as the intensity of preference for a given alternative by any substantial portion of his constituency increases. We know that few decisions before Congress are likely to unite constituencies in this way or to inflame their passions to such a great extent. In addition, Congress takes routine steps to insulate its decision-making from certain kinds of outside influences.

One such device is the consideration of business in the Committee of the Whole, where substantial revisions of legislation can be made on the Floor without binding congressmen to a record vote. The committees—whose composition and behavior sometimes reflect outside interests[59] and sometimes inside distributions of influence[60]—

---

[58] Obviously, no real-world case will fit a typology perfectly. It may be well to remind the reader that the predominant strategies of the major actors were as I have indicated, but that Mr. Albert had some support from outside the House (such as from Senators Kerr and Monroney and Governor Edmondson of Oklahoma), and many of Bolling's supporters within the House backed him for reasons other than outside "pressures" which he might have been able to bring to bear on them. These included some members from the South whose position on civil rights was more accurately reflected by Mr. Albert.

[59] As for example, the Agriculture Committee. See Charles O. Jones, "Representation in Congress: The Case of the House Agriculture Committee," *American Political Science Review*, LV (June, 1961), 358–67. Reprinted as Chapter V of the present volume.

[60] There are numerous examples of this—e.g., the operation of the seniority

mark up bills and vote on them in executive sessions only. A third device favoring inside distributions of influence in the House is the Rules Committee. One of the prerequisites for appointment to service on this committee is ability to "take the heat" and resist constituency pressures to report out bills which the House leadership wants killed.[61]

The enumeration of these devices hints at some of the problems facing two significant groups of outsiders: Presidents of the United States and political scientists. The President has a never-ending battle of converting decisions in the House choices from inside ones to outside ones. Most of his attempts to influence decisions are direct, but his efforts to dramatize issues before relevant publics may also be interpreted as attempts to activate interest groups and unify constituencies so as to make the employment of inside strategies of influence in the House difficult.

For political scientists, the lesson is clear. In order to understand the context within which decisions in the House are being made sufficiently well so that we can identify the goals in terms of which outcomes may be seen as "rational," it will be necessary to study the House at close range. On the whole, political scientists have taken a somewhat Olympian view of congressional behavior. We have tended to organize our conceptions of rationality and legitimacy around presidential goals and presidential party platforms.[62] This has operated to obscure the constraints on the behavior of those in the House who share the policy preferences these political theories imply. It has also, I think, bred a kind of impatience with the study of strategies

system. See George Goodwin, "The Seniority System in Congress," *American Political Science Review,* LIII (June 1959), 412–36. On the influence of state delegations on committee assignments and the force of tradition in determining the allocation of seats, see in general, Nicholas Masters, "Committee Assignments in the House of Representatives," *American Political Science Review,* LV (June, 1961), 345–57. Reprinted as Chapter II of the present volume.

[61] On the Rules Committee, see Robert L. Peabody, "The Enlarged Rules Committee," Chapter VII of the present volume, and the following articles by James A. Robinson, "Organizational and Constituency Backgrounds of the House Rules Committee" in Joseph R. Fiszman (ed.), *The American Political Arena* (Boston: Little, Brown, 1962); "The Role of the Rules Committee in Regulating Debate in the U.S. House of Representatives," *Midwest Journal of Political Science,* V (February, 1961), 59–69; "Decision Making in the House Rules Committee," *Administrative Science Quarterly,* III (June, 1958), 73–86; "The Role of the Rules Committee in Arranging the Program of the U.S. House of Representatives," *Western Political Quarterly,* XII (September, 1959), 653–69.

[62] This comment may be anachronistic, judging from much of the recent work on the House. It agrees with Ralph K. Huitt's similar judgment in "Democratic Party Leadership in the Senate," *American Political Science Review,* LV (June, 1961), 333 f.

and tactics of House decision-making, which study, I believe, is a necessary step in understanding why the House operates as it does.

PART FOUR

The House and the Executive

X

INNOVATION AND INTERVENTION
IN DEFENSE POLICY*

Raymond H. Dawson

STUDENTS OF congressional-executive relations have long recognized the weakness of legislative oversight of the Executive, and in few areas of public policy has this weakness been more pronounced than in national defense. A recent and significant change in this relationship was made when the 86th Congress in 1959 imposed upon a reluctant executive and military establishment a major innovation in the established processes of making defense policy. The innovation was deliberately intended to alter the balance in executive-congressional controls over some strategic decisions, and was in the form of a new requirement for legislative authorization of the principal weapons programs of the military services. Designated the Russell amendment, it was incorporated into the Military Construction Authorization Act for Fiscal 1960 as Section 412 (b) and directed that

> No funds may be appropriated after December 31, 1960, to or for the use of any armed force of the United States for the procurement of aircraft, missiles, or naval vessels unless the appropriation of such funds has been authorized *by legislation enacted after such date*.[1]

This terse stipulation served to break the monopoly long held by the annual Department of Defense Appropriations Act as the single regular confrontation of Congress, as a decision-making participant

* Reprinted from "Congressional Innovation and Intervention in Defense Policy: Legislative Authorization of Weapons Systems," *American Political Science Review*, LVI (March, 1962), 42–57, by permission of the author and the American Political Science Association. This is a part of a research project begun as a postdoctoral fellow of the Mershon National Security Program at Ohio State University. The project has also had assistance from the University Research Council, University of North Carolina.
[1] Public Law 86–149. 73 *Stat*. 322. Italics added.

through its appropriations committees, with the complex of strategic issues and choices contained in defense policy. In adopting the practice that has—notwithstanding objections—governed its foreign aid policy determination since the war, Congress reversed the long-standing custom of generalized authorization on a continuing basis for major procurement by the armed forces. It made a substantial and critical proportion of the defense budget subject to review by the legislative committees, by means of the requirement of a prior legislative authorization intended to operate on an annual basis.[2] Section 412, in effect, represents an attempt by key legislative spokesmen in the defense area to reorder the formal process of policy-making in a manner which, by broadening the span of control and jurisdiction of the Committees on the Armed Services, will enhance the power of Congress.

Students of military affairs have paid relatively little attention to the role of Congress and the legislative functions in defense policy-making.[3] There is a general assumption that Congress must be involved at some level in certain kinds of military decisions, but rarely as a constructive or significant participant. Its negativism, its preoccupation with detail and with marginal concerns, are duly noted,[4] and attention then turns to the executive and the military. Certainly the tendencies toward negativism, and the fixation with incidentals rather than with the major questions of policy choices, are real enough. However, such studies as those of Hilsman and Huntington[5] have pointed the way to a more explicit recognition of the legislative functions in the political processes of defense, and to the fact that the role of Congress, although subordinate, adds an important and distinctive element. An analysis of the origins and

---

[2] For fiscal 1962, when it requested $43,794,345,000 in new obligational authority in the Defense Appropriation Bill, the administration was required under Section 412 to seek new legislative authorization for $11,974,800,000 for major weapons procurement.

[3] See the discussion of Richard C. Snyder and James A. Robinson in *National and International Decision-Making: A Report to the Commmittee on Research for Peace* (New York: Institute for International Order, 1961), pp. 84–85, 145–148.

[4] Not unusual in this respect is the treatment of Congress vis à vis the military by Morris Janowitz in *The Professional Soldier: A Social and Political Portrait* (Glencoe, 1960), pp. 354–360, which he entitles "Congressional Negativism."

[5] Roger Hilsman, "Congressional-Executive Relations and the Foreign Policy Consensus," *American Political Science Review*, Vol. 52 (September, 1958), pp. 725 ff.; and Samuel P. Huntington, "Strategic Planning and the Political Process," *Foreign Affairs*, Vol. 38 (January, 1960), pp. 285 ff.

initial experience under Section 412 provides some additional insights into this role, and into the conditions of an active and effective legislative intervention in strategic decisions.[5a]

I. THE ROLE OF CONGRESS IN STRATEGIC DECISIONS: HYPOTHESES SUGGESTED BY THE AUTHORIZATION REQUIREMENT

A significant aspect of this episode was that, contrary to the more usual practice of expanding delegations of authority to the armed forces in a time of military danger and an atmosphere of "preparedness," Section 412 had the effect of rescinding or delimiting their authority simultaneously with a growing anxiety over such a danger. It could be argued from the timing of the move—coming from a Democratic Congress in the late stages of the second term of a Republican President whose judgment in military matters seemed invincibly popular—that Section 412 was the result of a temporary excess of partisanship. But the determined implementation of the device by a Democratic Congress in 1961, in the face of a world crisis and expanding military programs, is evidence of more than a cyclical zeal.

Also, the factor of inter-committee rivalry—the resentment by some Armed Forces Committee members of the preeminence of Appropriations—could be adduced as an important factor behind the adoption of Section 412. But though this element was certainly present, the fact remains that the leadership of what we may call the "412 movement" came from a group of senators who served on both committees in that chamber.

Partisanship and committee competition thus cannot adequately account for this departure from well established methods and procedures. This study will attempt to show that Section 412 is the product, basically, of a sense of restiveness among congressional leaders in the area of defense policy, particularly in the Senate. This restiveness has grown out of their dissatisfaction with the course of

---

[5a] Since the completion of this paper, Bernard K. Gordon has published a study of Section 412: "The Military Budget: Congressional Phase," *Journal of Politics,* Vol. 23 (November, 1961), pp. 689 ff. He ascribes much greater weight to committee rivalries, particularly in the House, as a factor in the origins of Section 412, and is more dubious of its benefits. He observes that Section 412 may have a "salutary effect," but he concludes that the goal of "effective congressional—and civilian—control of the military establishment" is more likely to be achieved through "a single locus of the appropriations power . . ." (p. 710).

events in the military establishment, the evident inability or disinclination of the administration to order matters more to their liking, and their own sense of helplessness in the legislative branch to influence military policy decisions, except by negative restraints that are of little significance in a period of international tension. Dissatisfaction, gradually accumulating over a period of years, created among these leaders a frame of mind receptive to a search for new techniques and devices which could redress in some measure the disparity in executive-congressional powers over military affairs, provide Congress with a more effective means of evaluating executive policy, and supply methods by which correctives sought by Congress might be applied.

Besides this general hypothesis of mood, the series of events leading to the imposition of the weapons authorization requirement also suggests that the likelihood of Congressional intervention in strategic policy questions in any specific instance is maximized under these circumstances:

(1) When technology and doctrine are in flux so that there is no standard orthodoxy, and, as a result, many important decisions must be reached on the basis of political as well as technical criteria;

(2) When the military services advance opposing doctrines, and thereby divulge derogatory information about rival programs, or, in the interests of mutually protective harmony, pursue such evidently duplicating programs that members of Congress are enabled to raise embarrassing questions and gain a foothold for action;

(3) When forceful committee chairmen in Congress, and senior members of these bodies, can match the administration's political executives at the Pentagon in span of experience, familiarity with specific details of policy and program development, and political standing.

These conditions all point to the obvious fact that evidence of executive indecision is an invitation to congressional intervention. In this connection, the origins of Section 412 demonstrate that hard-pressed executive officials will sometimes deliberately create an environment for legislative intervention. Pressed by rival programs or doctrines within their own agencies, and unwilling to assume the penalties of choice themselves, they may allow a "crisis" to bring an issue to a head knowing that Congress will compel some resolution of the conflict, transferring to itself the onus of ensuing deprivations. But Section 412 also demonstrates that the nature of such invited congressional arbitration is neither controllable nor predictable.

II. OTHER TYPES OF CONGRESSIONAL CONTROL

To put the Russell amendment—Section 412—in perspective, it will be useful to recall that, over the last decade, Congress has resorted to a variety of techniques to exert control over military policy. It has tried to interpose in the deployment and use of forces; it has engaged in direct attacks upon the military leadership; it has worked to structure the defense establishment and component agencies to facilitate its lines of access into the military departments; and it has conducted investigations and inquiries about various phases of military programs. All of this has availed it little, however, in the sense of tangible and direct influence upon policy.

Primarily, Congress has focused its efforts to reshape or modify policy through its control over appropriations. This too has been a disappointing instrumentality. Year after year, the defense budget represents the only consistent, regular, and systematic point of contact between Congress and the substantive policy issues of defense. The task confronting Congress in acting upon this budget is overwhelming. Its members have, and can have, no adequate facilities for formulating alternative programs in any systematic fashion; for this they must rely on military dissent. They must accept in the main what is submitted, grappling with thousands of items and reams of documentary exhibits. They will try to ferret out some evidence of waste and mismanagement, and usually succeed, but this bogs them down in a morass of detail and diverts their attention frequently from underlying strategic issues. In a time of military danger, with the attendant "preparedness" climate, they are naturally inhibited from making any major attack upon the budget proposals or from forcing significant reductions. And they have also been thwarted in attempts to alter policy by providing additional funds over the amounts requested by the President's agents. A legislative majority could not compel President Truman to increase aircraft procurement in 1948, nor could it compel President Eisenhower to accelerate the Nike-Zeus program, by the expedient of voting additional funds. When the President refuses to use the money, when he—in Charles Wilson's phrase—"puts it in the bank," Congress has no practicable recourse. In short, the totals involved in the defense budget have become so great, the lump-sums and carry-overs so large, the discretion to shift funds from one category to another so extensive, that budgetary controls have actually provided Congress with little leverage over policy.

The important positive decisions about defense and strategy have therefore not been made by Congress, though anticipations of congressional opposition have no doubt operated as inhibitions against some policy choices. In a degree not paralleled in any other field of public policy, the position of the executive in this sphere has been definitely ascendant, and Congress has not been able to reverse that fact. It has maintained its lines of access into the defense establishment, and it has rejected such proposals as UMT, which seemed to draft manpower unnecessarily and provoked strong dissent from many influential groups in American society. In the main, however, a degree of "inviolability"—as Samuel P. Huntington has phrased it—has attended the strategic policy proposals embodied in executive requests, an inviolability which stands in sharp contrast to the record of congressional action on presidential programs in domestic policy, or even in foreign policy.[6]

Section 412—the new authorizing requirement—does not mean that this executive primacy has been, or can be, overthrown. As a result of the very nature of defense policy, its substantive problems and issues, and of the qualities inherent in the nature of the legislative and executive branches as political institutions, this primacy will continue. But Congress has now put itself in a position to introduce its voice and its will through another channel of regular and systematic contact with basic strategic programs. Through resurrecting the device of substantive authorizing legislation, adapting it to previous experience and to some salient characteristics of contemporary defense planning, it has provided itself with one more means of leverage.

III. AUTHORIZING LEGISLATION AND THE MILITARY ESTABLISHMENT

Though the primary instrumentality of congressional action on defense policy has been through appropriations, certainly the involvement of Congress in the affairs of the armed forces is much more extensive than the voting of money. Year after year a vast

---

[6] Huntington, *op. cit.*, pp. 286–88.

amount of detailed legislation must be acted upon to insure the proper functioning of the military establishment. This legislation encompasses, *e.g.,* reserve affairs, military pay, retirement and other career incentives, contract negotiation, and a wide range of other problems. Legislative activities here are vital to the management and operation of the armed forces and essential to their effective functioning. For the most part, however, such matters as these are not the determinants of basic defense policy. They are, in the main, incidental to or in support of it.

This points up the extent to which defense affairs have not been closely related to substantive legislation that defines the operating framework of policy and the supporting programs. The authorization legislation for the military departments has characteristically only established ceilings—and these very high ones, so that the same authorizing statutes could support a defense budget of $15 billion, or $40 billion. Hence the unusual degree to which defense policy has been insulated from substantive, authorizing legislation and limited chiefly by budgetary action. The exceptions to this have been military pay, military assistance programs, and military public works. In these three categories the appropriations are determined in a framework of detailed substantive statutes, and the latter two are subject to annual legislative action. Military pay, however, falls into the category of legislation previously referred to, while military assistance is a part of the mutual security program and is within the jurisdiction of the Committee on Foreign Affairs and the Committee on Foreign Relations—not the Armed Services Committees. Of public works more will be said in a moment.[7]

The distinction made by Congress between authorization and appropriation, and their separation in the legislative process, is certainly not one to be overemphasized. The requirement that authorization precede appropriation gives rise to "friction" and is applied with "irregularity."[8] Yet it is a distinction to which Congress usually

---

[7] See Samuel P. Huntington, *The Soldier and the State: The Theory and Politics of Civil-Military Relations* (Cambridge, 1957), pp. 407–409.

[8] For a detailed analysis, see Arthur W. Macmahon, "Congressional Oversight of Administration: The Power of the Purse—I," *Political Science Quarterly,* Vol. 57 (June, 1943), p. 174 [Reprinted as the first part of Chapter XII of the present volume]. Macmahon comments: "The risk of friction is inherent in the existence of two partly parallel sets of committees. Much irregularity attends the fact that the whole distinction rests on provisions in the rules of the chamber, enforced by points of order. Through inattention or comity, points of order that would be sustained are often not made. Sometimes a special

gives due consideration, and the broadly drawn character of the military authorizing statutes, as contrasted with those affecting most domestic policy undertakings, and the sheer size of the military budget as contrasted with those of most other government agencies, have placed the military in an unusually favorable legislative position. No one, and Congress least of all, seems to know how to go about the task of a long-range, comprehensive revision of permanent force levels in the present fluid environment of international conflict. Confronted with massive military procurement programs each year, however, some members of Congress—and especially several members of the Senate Armed Services Committee—have become increasingly impressed over the last few years with the extent to which basic questions about strategy and policy have tended to form around a nexus of specific programs of the three services for the development and procurement of weapons. This led to a re-examination of the legal warrant held by the services to pursue the programs, a re-examination prompted by policy disputes in the field of missiles development, particularly with reference to continental air defense.

IV. ARMY-AIR FORCE AUTHORIZATION ACT OF 1950

The basic substantive legislation pertaining to the Army and the Air Force in these categories was the Army and Air Force Authorization and Composition Act of 1950. For the Air Force, it authorized "24,000 serviceable aircraft or 225,000 airframe tons aggregate of serviceable aircraft, whichever amount the Secretary of the Air Force may determine is more appropriate to fulfill the requirements of the Air Force. . . ." The Secretary was also empowered to procure "guided missiles" without any specified limitation, and the statute stated that these were not to be included in "the number of aircraft or airframe tons authorized"; and to procure "spares, spare parts, equipment and facilities necessary for the maintenance and opera-

---

rule is adopted at the request of the Committee on Appropriations which gives blanket protection against points of order. Much authorization is implied rather than expressed, furthermore, and in many situations there is a wide range for the judgment of presiding officers in applying the rules when points of order are made."

With specific reference to this parallel structure in military affairs, see Elias Huzar, *The Purse and the Sword: Control of the Army by Congress through Appropriations, 1933–1950* (Ithaca: Cornell University Press, 1950), pp. 40–46.

tion of the Air Force." The Secretary of the Army, in turn, was authorized to "procure materials and facilities, including guided missiles, necessary for the maintenance and support of the Army . . . and its divisions and other military organizations, and their installations and supporting and auxiliary elements. . . ." For the Army, Air Force and the Navy, the act also provided that money appropriated for these purposes, and for research and development programs, was to "remain available until expended, unless otherwise provided in the appropriations act concerned."[9]

The mood and the intent of Congress in making these liberal provisions were underscored in a parenthetical observation of the Senate Armed Services Committee when it first reported out the bill in 1949. Remarking on their belief that the House version of the bill permitted an excessive number of commissioned officers for the Regular Army, the senators reasoned:

> In the hearings on this bill, and by later investigation, it was found that the Army will not reach its present authorized strength [of 30,600 commissioned officers] for approximately 9 years. The committee feels that the size of the regular Military Establishment is far in excess of that which will be required in the event world conditions are stabilized, and it anticipates that such will be the case before 9 years have passed.[10]

Simultaneously with the final passage of this act, the nation became involved in the Korean war. As a result all personnel ceilings imposed in the act, and in the 1946 Navy personnel act, were

[9] 64 *Stat.* 321. For an analysis of the legislation, and the expressed intent of Congress in the authority voted, see Senate Committee on Armed Services, *Authorizing the Composition of the Army . . . and the Air Force of the United States,* S. Rept. 933, 81st Cong. (August 18, 1949); and House Committee on Armed Services, *Personnel and Composition of the Army and Air Force,* H. Rept. 64, 81st Cong. (February 10, 1949).
[10] *Authorizing the Composition of the Army . . . and the Air Force . . . ,* S. Rept. 933, p. 2. The Act authorized a troop strength of 837,000 for the Army, plus 110,000 inducted trainees in service at any given time; and the Air Force was authorized 502,000 regulars plus 15,000 trainees. Appropriations then being sought by the National Military Establishment were considerably under these levels. "Obviously," said General Omar Bradley in his testimony, "Congress cannot—and indeed will not—appropriate from year to year sufficient funds for the maintenance of this authorized force." House Committee on Armed Services, *Hearings on H. R. 1437* . . . (81st Cong., 1st sess., Committee Paper No. 12), pp. 105–106.

suspended for four years, and Congress has continued periodically to renew the suspension.[11] Generous provision was meanwhile made for the Navy's air power, in legislation authorizing an active force of up to 15,000 aircraft, with added admonition that if, "in the judgment of the Secretary of the Navy the number of airplanes authorized is insufficient to meet the needs of the national defense, the Secretary may, with the approval of the President, make such plans for procurement as the situation demands."[12]

The fleet, of course, had been provided for much earlier, in legislation dating back to the 1930s. Chairman Carl Vinson of the House Armed Services Committee in 1959 summarized the status of the Navy in this respect in these words:

> In the field of ship procurement, the situation is so broad today that the Armed Services Committees consider only a small fraction of the total shipbuilding program each year. . . . It [the Vinson-Trammell Act], with its subsequent amendments, provided enough tonnage for the Navy to build ships for an untold number of years without any further authorization. All the Navy has needed, and all it needs today is appropriations.[13]

This same statement could also have been made about the missile programs of all the services, and the aircraft procurement of both the Air Force and the Navy. Necessarily, then, legislative participation in policy decisions was localized around the appropriations function.

**V. REAL ESTATE, PUBLIC WORKS,
AND CONTINENTAL AIR DEFENSE**

A major exception to the exemption of the armed services from the practice of detailed substantive legislation in authorizing their principal programs, as noted already, embraced the area of real

---

[11] *Congressional Record,* Vol. 96 (81st Cong., 2d sess.), pp. 10998–11006, and 11083–85. The most recent suspension of the personnel limitations was voted in March, 1959. *Ibid.,* Vol. 105 (86th Cong., 1st sess.), pp. 1663–90, 3402–8.

[12] 10 U.S.C. §7341.

[13] *Cong. Rec.,* Vol. 105 (86th Cong., 1st sess., 1959), p. 13477. A useful history of the Vinson-Trammell Act, and subsequent Navy legislation, related in the context of executive-legislative relations, is in Lawrence H. Chamberlin, *The President, Congress and Legislation* (New York: Columbia University Press, 1946), pp. 235 ff.

estate acquisition and public works construction. Developments in weapons, and especially in missiles, have recently had the effect of imparting a new strategic significance to these public works.

Congress has always had a very pronounced interest in the real estate transactions and public works projects of the military departments, and kept them under close surveillance, although for reasons that historically have had far more to do with constituency politics than with strategy. Emergency legislation suspended the process of annual authorization for military public works after 1940,[14] but this traditional practice, on a detailed line-item basis, was resumed in 1947.[15] Even during the Second World War, however, a watchful eye was maintained over many real estate matters, especially by Chairman Vinson's House Committee on Naval Affairs. When cold war rearmament again led to vast military public works projects throughout the nation, the Congressmen were disposed to expand their supervision of real estate transactions, and in so doing they collided with the Budget Bureau and the President.

A climax was reached in 1951 when a bill was enacted which required the military departments to "come into agreement" with the Armed Services Committees on the great majority of all real estate transactions to which they were a party, as a condition precedent to the necessary legislative approval of such transactions. To the disgust of Chairman Vinson, the author of the bill, President Truman vetoed it, but the resourceful and influential Georgian thereafter attached the identical proviso to the Military Construction Bill that was before his committee. Retained by the Senate, despite administration protests, and made applicable to virtually all real estate transactions in excess of $25,000, the bill passed with the "coming into agreement" proviso securely ensconced in a construction authorization bill that was too pressing to be delayed by another exercise of the veto.[16]

---

[14] The first suspension was in an act of July 2, 1940, and it was subsequently extended for the "duration plus six months" under the First War Powers Act. 54 *Stat.* 712 and 56 *Stat.* 312.

[15] House Committee on Armed Services, *Hearings on H. R. 4122, Authorizing Military Construction* (80th Cong., 1st sess., 1947).

[16] President Eisenhower asked repeal of the proviso in his budget message in 1959, and in the fiscal 1961 budget message he stated that "the Attorney General has advised me that this section violates fundamental constitutional principles. Accordingly, if it is not repealed by the Congress at its present session, I shall have no alternative thereafter but to direct the Secretary of

Real Estate Controls and Air Defense Weapons

This "coming into agreement" clause, which was operative throughout the 1950s, and the long-established practice of annually passing legislation authorizing military public works, had the unintended result of involving the Armed Services Committees very deeply in the development of Army and Air Force programs for continental air defense and, more recently, in a variety of other missile site construction projects. Indeed, the involvement was more intensive than in any other strategic policy area, because of the close relationship of substantive legislation to policy development. Air defense was, moreover, throughout the 1950s, characterized by vigorously contested interservice disputes over doctrine and roles and missions, and marked by intense competition for funds in support of particular weapons programs. The experience made a deep and lasting impression upon the Armed Services Committees, particularly in the Senate.

This experience grew out of the fact that the air defense programs of both the Army and the Air Force entailed annual action by the Armed Services Committees on legislation authorizing the hundreds of construction projects required, and their approval of hundreds of separate real estate transactions to provide the sites for the projects. Radar networks had to be authorized, combat control centers approved for construction, and defensive weapons deployed. Some statistics on one Army program alone will illustrate the range of committee action that was entailed. Beginning in the summer of 1953 the Army began deploying its Nike-Ajax surface-to-air missile. The range of the missile was approximately twenty-five miles, and the Army had elaborate plans to site it around urban complexes and defense installations throughout the United States. Obviously the missile sites had to be located in immediate proximity to the point defended. Each Nike battery required, first, an area of about eight acres for radars and computers, a launching area consisting of some forty-three acres, and ten additional acres for equipment and as a safety zone. In each of the launcher areas it was necessary to construct three underground magazines with four launchers in each,

---

Defense to disregard the section unless a court of competent jurisdiction determines otherwise."

As a result of this demand, the proviso was removed and a clause inserted in the Military Construction Authorization Act of 1960, which requires instead that real property transactions be "reported" to the Committees in most instances thirty days prior to the completion of the transaction. 74 *Stat.* 186.

and the site had also to include a missile assembly and test building, a missile fueling facility, troop housing, mess hall, and troop support facilities.[17] From the start, the committee was necessarily and regularly involved in a detailed analysis and review of the program, approving the real estate acquisition and authorizing the construction of facilities on a line-item basis.

The Nike network was only a minor part of the total continental air defense programs. Including the radar warning systems, the SAGE control centers, the aircraft and bases of the NORAD fighter-interceptor units, the various Army and Air Force missiles systems that were deployed, the Secretary of Defense stated in 1958 that the total capital investment made in continental air defense in a period of four and a half years had exceeded $13 billion, and that operating costs were $2 billion annually.[18] A House Appropriations Committee report in 1959 stated that over a ten-year period the nation had spent $29 billion on these programs—warning, control, and weapons—that had been designed to meet the threats of manned-bombers and air-breathing missiles.[19]

The details of the various conflicts over doctrine, roles and missions, or weapons, which have arisen between the services in connection with air defense do not need to be noted here, except to say that they have been subjects of serious dispute. Both the Army and Air Force have questioned the other's proper function and mission, and cast doubts on the effectiveness of the other's weapons. Nor have such disputes been peculiar to the problem of air defense. They have been the common currency of Pentagon politics. What is important here is that members of Congress through the Armed Services Committees have consistently had a different kind of relationship to the developments in air defense than they had in any other strategic program throughout the 1950s, and that these Committees found that by participating at a stage closer to operations than appropriations they were able to state criticisms on the basis of a greater knowledge of problems and issues, knowledge gained from annual and detailed review of legislative programs. As a result, they

---

[17] Senate Armed Services Subcommittee, *Hearings on S. 1765, Military Public Works Construction* (84th Cong., 1st sess.), pp. 273 ff.

[18] A detailed analysis of air defense costs was in Senate Committee on Armed Services, *Military Construction Authorization, Fiscal Year 1959*, S. Rept. 1982, 85th Cong., 2d sess. (July 28, 1958).

[19] House Committee on Appropriations, *Department of Defense Appropriation Bill for 1960*, H. Rept. 408, 86th Cong., 1st sess. (May 28, 1959), pp. 15–16.

were able to exert a more effective leverage on policy decisions. The necessity for legislation prior to or complementary with the annual appropriations bills placed Congress in a more advantageous position, when it had a complaint or recommendation to enter.

The Nike-Talos Dispute

This was first brought out in 1956 when the Armed Services Committees were confronted with a request to authorize the Air Force to establish installations for a land-based version of the Talos surface-to-air missile. The Air Force wanted to begin deploying the missile to protect four bases of the Strategic Air Command. The Senate military construction subcommittee had been somewhat skeptical about the Nike program, and it was also concerned with the skyrocketing costs of air defense. It wanted to know why both the Nike and Talos were needed. If the Talos were the better weapon, why was it not used to defend cities? Otherwise, why would the Nike not suffice as the defender of SAC bases as well as cities? In any event, the Senators could see no purpose in having rival missile systems on site for the defense of overlapping areas.[20]

This expression of doubt and concern by the Senators naturally led the two services to fear action adverse to their interests. Each hurriedly came forward to defend its program. Army Chief of Staff General Maxwell Taylor bluntly told the Senate defense appropriations subcommittee that the Air Force decision to install the Talos was "an invasion of the Army antiaircraft role."[21] Other Army spokesmen asserted that the Air Force proposal was premature, since the Talos was not yet operational and would not be for some time. As for the Nike, the Army never retreated from its "unqualified assurance" that "Nike can be relied on" as a weapon "capable of operating against any known aircraft or any aircraft projected

---

[20] Senator Stennis referred to committee concern about the "effectiveness" of Nike and "its range or lack of range," and to the great expense incurred on air defense. He concluded: ". . . I certainly have always steered away from the idea that this subcommittee was a policy making committee on missiles for defense installations except we do approve this when we keep recommending these sites and this money. . . . " Senator Jackson maintained that for Congress to agree to finance both Nike and Talos was simply to compromise service rivalries. *Hearings on S. 3122, Military Public Works Construction* (84th Cong., 2d sess.), pp. 395–96.

[21] *Hearings, Department of Defense Appropriations Bill for 1957* (84th Cong., 2d sess.), p. 87.

into the future of the next five years or so."[22] The Air Force profoundly disagreed. An air staff analysis was leaked to the press at this juncture, dismissing the Nike as an ineffective weapon incapable of meeting the threat posed by high altitude jet bombers.[23]

The Senate subcommittee, after making some inquiries of its own, reacted to this by striking out the Talos in the military construction authorization bill. It said this was being done until "the relative merits of both systems have been positively tested and roles and missions clarified." While Congress ought not "to be placed in the position of defining roles and missions," or of passing on the merits of weapons, it continued, "unless concise responsibilities are assigned, duplication of weapons systems costing in the multi-billion range might result. . . ."[24] The House Armed Services Committee was reluctant to veto a military program, fearing that this was trespassing in the domain of professional decision. It was therefore agreed in conference that the Talos authorization would be conditionally restored, on the understanding that it would not be utilized until the Secretary of Defense had "come into agreement" with both Armed Services Committees on the subject, following an impartial study of the relative capabilities of both the Nike and Talos.[25] On this ground, and also because of an objectionable provision in the bill relating to military housing construction, the President returned it with a veto. He declared: "If the committees should fail or decline to agree with the plans prepared by the Secretary of Defense, the practical effect of this provision would be to lodge in the committees the authority to nullify congressional authorization."[26] With this, the Senate committee insisted upon striking out again all authorization for Talos installation construction, and both houses then agreed.[27]

Later that year the Secretary of Defense issued a memorandum

[22] Lt. Gen. S. R. Mickelsen, in House Appropriations Subcommittee, *Hearings, Department of Defense Appropriations for 1956* (84th Cong., 2d sess.), pt. 1, p. 396.
[23] On the air staff analysis "leak," see Anthony Leviero, *New York Times,* May 21, 1956, p. 1. This was but one of a deluge of leaks from the military departments during that spring and summer.
[24] *Authorizing Construction for Military Departments,* S. Rept. 2364, 84th Cong., 2d sess. (June 26, 1956), pp. 10–11.
[25] *Cong. Rec.,* Vol. 102 (84th Cong., 2d sess.), pp. 12167–77.
[26] *Ibid.,* p. 12959.
[27] *Ibid.,* pp. 14634, 14884.

clarifying roles and missions, in which he assigned to the Army the
development and deployment of surface-to-air missiles up to the
100-mile range, removing the previous limit of fifty miles. This
automatically put the development of the land-based version of the
Talos into the Army's hands. During 1958 the Army announced
discontinuance of the Talos program. Chairman John C. Stennis
of the Senate military construction subcommittee commented in
the upper house that, although enthusiastic claims had been made
before this group about the need for the Talos and the important
contributions it would make to air defense, since the 1956 action
nothing further was ever heard about it until word was received
that the Army had cancelled the program. The Senator was personally convinced, and his colleagues agreed, that if the 1956 request
had been given legislative approval additional Talos sites would
have been installed to cover areas already under the guard of Nike,
and that by this action Congress had forestalled a needless and costly
duplication that the Defense Department was either unable or
unwilling to prevent.[28]

It seems important to note, with reference to the Nike-Talos
imbroglio, that the issue was identified and brought to a decision
by the deliberations and actions of the Armed Services Committee
in the Senate—specifically, by the military construction subcommittee. The Nike program had been before the Appropriations Committees for several years, and annual presentations about its deployment and performance had been made by the Army. Yet, not until
the probings of the military construction subcommittee had obviously struck at some vulnerable and sensitive nerve ends in the
Pentagon did the appropriations committees join the fray. The
strong presumption must be that, immersed as they were in the
complexities of the total defense budget, the span of attention of
the appropriations committee members was too diffuse to permit
the isolation of concrete issues, despite widespread dissatisfaction
with missile programs generally.

Little more than a year after the Talos incident, the military
construction subcommittee found what it believed to be another
and more costly duplication in the air defense programs submitted
through the Defense Department. The Air Force in 1958 began
seeking authorization for installations for its Bomarc A missile, an
"area-defense" weapon as distinguished from the Army's point-

---

[28] *Ibid.*, Vol. 104 (85th Cong., 2d sess.), p. 15543.

defense missiles. Neither service had any hesitation in voicing its unbounded confidence in the superiority of its own defensive system, while looking with great skepticism upon that of its rival. Again the subcommittee made a detailed and critical review of what it considered to be duplicating programs, in this instance the Bomarc and the Nike-Hercules, and in the authorization bill made a twenty percent reduction in the total funding sought for the two systems.

> In taking this action [explained Senator Stennis], the committee does not attempt to set itself up as military experts. These are decisions that must be made by the Secretary of Defense supported by qualified technicians. The committee took this action as a matter of focusing attention on the problem and in underlining its beliefs that Congress should not be called upon to determine the merits of competing weapons systems.

The reduction, he stated, would still permit the Secretary to proceed with construction of essential missile sites, but it would bring pressure to bear to compel a needed decision upon a well ordered surface-to-air missile program that would eliminate unnecessary overlapping between the two services.[29]

Although legislative intervention of this nature in missile programs was primarily confined to the air defense area, these Senate actions on Talos, Hercules and Bomarc coincided with more general expressions of anxiety and dissatisfaction about all aspects of missile developments. The situation in air defense, congressional sources complained, was not unique but was, in fact, symptomatic of basic defects in the decision-making processes in the Department of Defense that were having an adverse effect in all areas of weapons development. Congressmen found confirmation of their views in the resignation, early in 1956, of Trevor Gardner and his public protest against what he called an "administrative nightmare" and "intolerable rivalry" between the services which were obstructing progress in missile development.[30] The congressional viewpoint was succinctly put in the statement of the House Appropriations Commit-

---

[29] Senate Committee on Armed Services, *Military Construction Authorization, Fiscal Year 1959*, S. Rept. 1982, 85th Cong., 2d sess. (July 28, 1958). See also the military construction subcommittee *Hearings on S. 3756, S. 3863, and H. R. 13015, Military Construction Authorization, Fiscal Year 1959*.

[30] See his article, "Our Guided Missile Crisis," *Look*, Vol. 20 (May 15, 1956), pp. 46–52. Gardner had been special assistant for research and development to the Secretary of the Air Force.

tee on May 21, 1957, pointing to "an apparent lack of timely, effective, and decisive action on the part of the Office of the Secretary of Defense in achieving a well-rounded, coordinated guided missile program at a minimum cost commensurate with an adequate system." Echoing Gardner's allegations, the congressmen criticised "an increasing degree of rivalry among the services for roles and missions," which had reached such proportions as "to jeopardize and delay the rate of build-up of our military power." Each service was "striving to acquire an arsenal of weapons complete in itself to carry out any and all possible missions."[31] Clearly the mood of Congress was one leaning toward further intervention, if it could isolate additional concrete controversies such as the Nike *vs.* Talos.

VI. REORGANIZATION AND THE GENESIS OF A LEGISLATIVE INNOVATION

At this juncture, the Soviet Union put Sputnik I into orbit, in October of 1957. This event immediately provided a focus for a theretofore unstructured political debate over missiles and U.S. defense posture. It produced a flurry of investigations in Congress and provided a powerful talking point for the legislative critics of administration policy. In this context—with Congress increasingly disposed to intervene in defense policy matters—the President advanced a series of proposals calling for a reorganization of the Department of Defense. In the spring of 1958 his proposals were embodied in specific legislative requests, and the immediate origins of the 1959 authorizing amendment are to be found in the resulting debate on defense organization.

As these debates progressed, Democratic spokesmen especially came to voice the notion that the administration was attaching to defects in organization the major shortcomings in defense policy, and that the onus of these defects was being placed upon the congressional doorstep. Chairman Russell of the Senate Armed Services Committee observed that many statements made in support of the President's proposals carried the implication that "the Secretary of Defense is powerless—that he is a mere figurehead—and that the Congress has made no provision for the unified strategic direction of the military services." This, he asserted, was "an impression that

---

[31] *Department of Defense Appropriations Bill, 1958,* H. Rept. 471, 85th Cong., 1st sess., pp. 19–20.

is without factual foundation."[32] Thus, there was a contest between
the two branches of government to fix responsibility for policy
failings, each holding the other accountable for serious organizational defects as a source of the trouble. Armed Services Committee
members in both houses repeatedly insisted that many weaknesses
in the decision-making structure could specifically be attributed to
a failure of officials to use powers already provided, more than to
any failure of Congress to endow the executive with needed authority. As evidence they cited the Talos dispute, and the Nike-Bomarc
dispute, and the Thor-Jupiter dispute, all of which the Secretary
had authority to settle.

In this setting, Senator Ralph Flanders, Vermont Republican
and then a member of Armed Services, interrupted his questioning
of Secretary McElroy in the reorganization hearings to voice his
opinion that the Committee was "not informed," and its judgment
was "not asked . . . on overall defense plans. . . ." At the time he
became a member of the Committee, he continued, he was "sur-
prised" to discover that most military authorization was of a "per-
petual" nature, that "we had no contact with it," despite the fact
that the "authorization process exists almost completely, I think,
through all the rest of the area of Government operations." The
Senator then observed:

> My only means of getting any concept of what an overall
> program is, is due to the fact that you [Chairman Russell] have
> kindly assigned me as an ex officio member of the Appropria-
> tions Committee.
> Can they take little bits and pieces of the appropriations,
> glue them together with some imagination, and arrive at an
> overall defense program?
> . . . I think it [an overall program] ought to be presented to
> us for our authorization and so that is the main suggestion
> with regard to this [reorganization] undertaking which I have
> to make.[33]

Senator Russell took this criticism under careful consideration, once

[32] *Ibid.*, pp. 7–8. This point came up repeatedly, not only in the reorganization hearings but also in the special investigations launched after Sputnik. See
Senate Armed Services Subcommittee, *Hearings, Inquiry into Satellite and
Missile Programs* (85th Cong., 1st and 2d sess., 1957–58); and House, Committee on Armed Services, *Hearings, Investigations of National Defense Missiles . . .* (85th Cong., 2d sess., 1958).
[33] *Hearings, DOD Reorganization Act of 1958*, pp. 31–32.

the reorganization bill was disposed of, and directed the committee staff to make a study of the problem.

The staff recognized, of course, the total impracticability of any complete, periodic authorization of the military budget. It was immediately impressed, however, by the convergence of basic policy and strategy and certain major weapons programs. Recalling also the air defense experience to that date, it concluded that the focus should be upon weapons, and as initially drafted and approved by the Committee early in 1959 the amendment stipulated that annual authorization be required for the "design, development, and procurement" of aircraft and missiles. In this form the proviso was attached to the Military Construction Authorization Bill—for reasons both logical and expedient—when it was reported by the Committee on May 19. The report commented but briefly upon this proposed change, soon designated as the "Russell amendment," and seemed to be at pains, in fact, to say as little about it as possible. It did note that the fiscal 1960 budget contained over $9 billion in proposed appropriations for aircraft and missiles, that in addition to the large expenditures for procurement *per se* these generated "requirements for expenditures in other major budget categories, such as personnel, construction, and operations and maintenance"; and that the authorizations on which these appropriations were based were noteworthy for a "lack of specificity." Therefore:

> The committee has concluded that in the discharge of its legislative responsibilities an annual review of the aircraft and missile procurement programs is needed. A thorough examination of this area of activity may serve to reduce the enormous cost of defense and should assist the Committee on Appropriations in their consideration of the mammoth defense budget.[34]

Immediately the Department of Defense voiced its strong disapproval of such a change. At this juncture, however, the debate on the authorizing amendment became intertwined with another but related action of the Committee, one which precipitated another explosion in the long-standing dispute over air defense involving the Army, the Air Force, the Defense Department, and the Armed Services Committee. The military construction subcommittee deleted over 75 per cent of the Army requests for Nike-Hercules surface-to-air missile installations, and repealed previous authoriza-

---

[34] *Military Construction Authorization . . . , Fiscal Year 1960,* S. Rept. 296, 86th Cong., 1st sess., pp. 15–16.

tions of fifty Nike batteries in the continental United States and eight in Hawaii. The subcommittee asserted that the Nike system was "virtually obsolete," that further expenditure was unwarranted, that the Army was investing too great a proportion of its resources in purely defensive systems, and that greater emphasis should be placed upon "area" defensive systems.[35] It demanded that the Secretary of Defense come forward with a "master plan" for air defense, which would eliminate unnecessary duplications in weapons and facilities, before the adjournment of Congress.

The immediate circumstance prompting the Armed Services Committee to take this extreme action, virtually a veto of a weapons program and an ultimatum to the Defense Department, was in remarks made by the Secretary of Defense. Perhaps inadvertently, the Secretary in effect invited drastic Senate action. Appearing before the Senate defense appropriations subcommittee on May 4, he remarked that air defense had been a problem "which has been, I suppose, more difficult than any I have touched—to resolve in a way that is at all satisfying." This led to an unusual colloquy:

> Senator STENNIS. . . . I am beginning to think that the Department of Defense would welcome a congressional decision on this matter and then you could move on into a more positive program.
>
> Secretary McELROY. You have certainly touched us in a place that I would call vulnerable.
>
> Senator STENNIS. I do not want to embarrass you.
>
> Secretary McELROY. You are not embarrassing us. This is one area where we have not done very well in making a decision.
> As far as I am concerned, it would not bother me if you held our feet to the fire and forced us in connection with this budget.
>
> Senator STENNIS. I appreciate your attitude tremendously, because I frankly think that is what has to be done, Mr. Secretary.
>
> Secretary McELROY. I think it is time.[36]

The Defense Department was distressed by these remarks, while the Army was staggered by the resulting blow inflicted by the Committee on its Nike-Hercules program. Each began attempting to undo the damage. The Army resorted to issuing a memorandum to every

---

[35] *Ibid.*, pp. 13–14. The Nike was defined as a "point" defense weapon.
[36] *Hearings, Department of Defense Appropriations*, 1960, p. 33.

member of Congress, which defended the Nike against the allegations made in the report and asked that the requested funds be restored and the Committee be overruled.[37] Before the week was out the confusion was compounded by steps taken in the House of Representatives. In reporting out the Department of Defense Appropriation Bill, the Appropriations Committee severely cut back funds for procurement of the Air Force surface-to-air missile system, the Bomarc. Mr. Mahon, chairman of the defense subcommittee, took note of the prolonged dispute over what most congressmen considered competing, not complementary weapons systems, and explained: "We proposed to help bring this controversy to a showdown through the utilization of the power of the purse."[38]

The Defense Department had no choice but to begin preparing at once a revised plan that reprogrammed both the Nike and Bomarc systems, insisting that both were needed.[39] Concurrently it urged the deletion of the authorizing amendment, Section 412, focusing its efforts on the House Armed Services Committee and its chairman. Mr. Vinson was variously reported as opposed, or, at best, lukewarm toward the Senate amendment. Three explanations were advanced: It was said that he feared such an action would violate the principle that "military men should make military decisions," a violation he allegedly believed already made in the Senate action on the Nike-Hercules.[40] Other observers felt that he might have inadvertently committed himself to the Pentagon in advance on the issue; still others believed that he was concerned that the additional work the amendment would demand might cause his then forty-three committee members to become bogged down in a morass of detail. Some significance might also be attached to the fact that the authorizing clause, at that point, did not include ships.

Pentagon chiefs were particularly worried about two issues raised by the Senate authorizing amendment. They feared that serious delay might result if an authorization process had to be gone through annually. Major complications might ensue from disagreements on programs within each of the Armed Services Committees, between these committees, and between Armed Services and Appro-

---

[37] The memorandum was reported in detail by Mark S. Watson, *Baltimore Sun,* May 23, 1959, p. 1.

[38] *Cong. Rec.,* Vol. 105 (86th Cong., 1st sess.), p. 8642.

[39] A revised bill, drawn on the basis of the "master plan," was reported to the Senate by the Stennis subcommittee on June 25 (S. Rept. 434, 86th Cong.).

[40] *Army Navy Air Force Journal,* May 23, 1959, pp. 1, 3.

priations in one or both houses. In the Senate, where there was an overlapping membership, this was less likely,[41] but it was a cause of considerable concern with respect to the lower chamber. Not only delay, but something approaching chaos, could be the outcome. Evidently the Nike-Bomarc experience also led some Defense officials to fear that there could easily be repetitions of this kind of encounter. One service organ, echoing these apprehensions, argued that Congress should exercise "close surveillance" over defense matters and that there should be the "closest possible liaison" between Congress and the Pentagon. But it warned that "this surveillance must not be broadened to an extent where Congress can dictate the weapons of defense."[42] The military commentator of the *New York Times* agreed that this was the clear implication in recent actions of the Senate. "Military decisions," he wrote, "properly can be made only by the Pentagon and the President." Otherwise, there was real "danger" that Congress would "choose a weapon or a system on the basis of political and economic factors rather than on objective military and technical ones."[43]

Against these objections the Senate Armed Services Committee stood firm. It felt that it had ample basis for its belief that something other than "objective" military factors were already involved in many weapons decisions, pointing as an example to a series of newspaper advertisements sponsored by defense contractors in support of rival Army and Air Force missiles (the Hercules and Bomarc), and released just as Congress was deliberating on the subject. It further pointed to numerous contradictions, expressed and implied, in statements released by the two military departments, and questioned whether only technical considerations were weighed in Pentagon deliberations. The Defense Department offered to submit procurement programs to the committees on an annual basis, with detailed explanations and support material; but to this Senators Russell, Stennis, and others countered that such an "information" procedure would place the burden of proof on Congress. If modifications were sought, if it were desired to effect any sort of change, legislation would have to be passed at the congressional initiative and it would be subject to a veto.

---

[41] In the 87th Congress, five members of Armed Services are also members of the defense subcommittee of Appropriations, and three members serve *ex officio* on the Appropriations subcommittee.

[42] *Army Navy Air Force Journal,* May 30, 1959, p. 12.

[43] Hanson W. Baldwin, *New York Times,* May 28, 1959, p. 13.

After prolonged conference consideration, the Senate and House came into agreement. Whatever his original view, Vinson now gave firm support to the revised amendment. Two reductions in scope, and one expansion, had been accepted by the Senate managers. First, it was agreed that specific mention of annual authorization would be deleted, so that more flexibility could be allowed if circumstances warranted it. The intent of annual action, however, was not dislodged. Second, the authorization of "design and development" was stricken out, and the requirement restricted to include only procurement of operational items. The Committee saw no feasible means of overseeing research. Finally, the amendment was altered to include "naval vessels" as well as aircraft and missiles—a move that no doubt quickened Vinson's interest. The provision was not to take effect until December 31, 1960. A trial run was to be made during 1960, with complete information to be submitted to the Committees on all ship, missile and aircraft procurement programs by January 31, 1960, including "cost," and the "number of each type and kind" to be procured, but this was for the Committees' study only and would not, in the first year, necessitate legislation.[44]

VII. THE 1961 PROCUREMENT AUTHORIZATION: PROCEDURES AND POLITICS

The full coming into effect of Section 412 thus coincided with the arrival of the Kennedy administration. The mechanics of procedure were worked out in the 1960 trial run, and the first legislation authorizing the procurement of ships, aircraft and missiles was submitted to the 87th Congress. It was a one-year authorization. No action was taken pending anticipated program revisions from the new President, and these were submitted in a special message late in March. On April 4 hearings began before the Senate Armed Services Committee on S. 1852, authorizing a procurement program of $11,974,800,000, as already noted, for fiscal 1962. The new obligational authority being sought in the revised Defense Appropriation Bill was $43,794,345,000.[45]

---

[44] 73 *Stat.* 322. In addition to the Senate reports already cited, see Vinson's defense and explanation of the amendment to the House, *Cong. Rec.*, Vol. 105 (86th Cong., 1st sess.), pp. 13476–77.

[45] Senate Committee on Armed Services, *Hearings on Military Procurement Authorization Fiscal Year 1962* (87th Cong., 1st sess.), pp. 26–27. The original Eisenhower request under 412 had been for $10,572,181,000.

The circumstances surrounding this novel legislative proceeding were themselves unusual. A presidential transition had meant delay in final program determinations, so legislative action did not begin until relatively late in the session. More important, however, was the atmosphere of crisis which pervaded the deliberations—Laos, Cuba, the Geneva stalemate, and then Berlin. Indeed, little more than a month after the passage of S. 1852, the President made additional military requests on July 26 because of the Berlin threat, and a second weapons procurement authorization of $958,570,000 was immediately passed.[46]

In both a procedural and a political sense, the authorization process bore an impressive resemblance to the established pattern of military appropriations. Procedurally, this is first demonstrated in the framework of the legislation itself, and secondly, in the type of "compact" entered into by the Armed Services Committees and the Pentagon. As agreed during 1960, the Department's bill contained only eight categories: Army aircraft, Navy and Marine Corps aircraft, and Air Force aircraft; Army missiles, Navy missiles, Marine Corps missiles, and Air Force missiles; and Navy vessels. For each of these eight, a lump-sum authorization was provided. The military departments then supplied detailed back-up material as justification, and itemized, detailed information concerning numbers to be procured, operational characteristics, costs and schedules for each individual weapons system within all of the categories. The statute itself was confined to a listing of the broad eight categories and the total amounts under each, as has been the practice in the defense appropriations acts for many years. And, as in the case of appropriations, changes in the numbers and costs of a given weapon, or in the "mix" of various weapons in a category or in two or more categories, may be made by "reprogramming." That is, the committees are consulted, but no additional legislation is necessary for the changes to be made. Specifically, the Defense Department agreed to submit regular quarterly reprogramming reports to Armed Services along with such special interim reports as changes warranted.[47]

---

[46] The supplemental procurement bill—S. 2311—passed the Senate on July 28 and the House on August 2, in both instances without dissent and after perfunctory debate. *Cong. Rec.* Vol. 107 (87th Cong., 1st sess.), daily ed., pp. 12905–12919, and 13312–13322.

[47] See especially the testimony of Major General R. F. Friedman, Director of the Budget and Comptroller, USAF, in Senate, *Procurement Hearings*, pp.

Some in the House professed a desire to use a line-item procedure, and the House Committee report took pains to point out that the lump-sum method was instituted only on a "trial basis for one year."[48] One has difficulty, however, envisaging a line-item approach to this area.

The lump sums, it should be pointed out further, are not confined to the "hardware"—*i.e.*, to the missiles, etc., *per se*. "Below the line" items essential to the weapon itself are included. In the case of aircraft, for example, not only the aircraft and all airborne equipment, but the spare engines, initial spares, peculiar ground support equipment and training items are all included. Inclusion only of the "hardware" would have reduced the authorization almost in half, and would have created also major accounting and budgeting problems.[49]

Even more notable, however, was the extent to which the political quality of the authorization process adhered to the appropriations pattern. Although crisis restraints were increasingly operative (and fully so on the supplemental authorization bill), and a spirit of cooperativeness incidental to the launching of a new administration was evident, the hearings demonstrated, first, a search for dissent within the military as a basis of criticism, evaluation and revision. After the style of Secretaries of Defense in the appropriations hearings over recent years, Mr. McNamara commented in his comprehensive statement to the committees that the

---

457 ff.; and the discussion between Congressman Kilday and Secretary of the Air Force Zuckert:

"Mr. KILDAY. . . . Now under 412, we will have in our backup here, but not in the law, the individual planes, missiles and ships which are authorized.

"As I understand it, the Comptroller General has held that this is binding on the Department [in appropriations procedure], even though it is not in the law, but that with the concurrence of the committee you could transfer the funds to another purpose.

"So here you have so much money authorized for airplanes, but we have a detailed justification. Then you are going to put in a detailed justification for Appropriations, but you are going to get your money in a lump-sum. You are going to be required by law to abide by the commitments made to the committees. But by concurrence of the committees, you can transfer it to different types of airplanes, missiles and ships, or change the priorities to which you have committed yourself. . . .

"Secretary ZUCKERT. That is an excellent statement of my understanding."
See House Committee on Armed Services, *Hearings on H. R. 6151, Authorizing Appropriations for Aircraft, Missiles, and Naval Vessels for the Armed Forces* (87th Cong., 1st sess., Committee Paper No. 10), p. 1533.

[48] *Authorizing Appropriations for Aircraft, Missiles and Naval Vessels*, H. Rept. 380 (87th Cong., 1st sess.), p. 10.

[49] Senate, *Procurement Hearings*, p. 462.

requests did "not provide everything that everyone would like to have."[50] Accordingly, a considerable part of the hearing revolved around congressional inquiries as to the nature of the items the military departments would have "liked," but which were denied by the office of the Secretary of Defense. The Navy was disappointed that its Eagle Missileer project had not been provided for.[51] The Army was displeased that it had again—after a strenuous campaign—failed to obtain authorization for funds to put into production certain components of its Nike-Zeus antiballistic missile. Senator Thurmond attempted to persuade the committee to add $169 million authorization in the Army missiles category for this purpose, but the committee accepted the Defense Department's ruling and defeated the amendment by a "decisive" vote.[52] Representative Gubser sought a $697.5 million addition to the bill to provide authorization for six more Polaris submarines. When the House committee, again accepting Defense Department recommendations, defeated this proposal by a vote of 3–25, Mr. Gubser carried it to the floor with the endorsement of the Republican Policy Committee. There the amendment was defeated 58–105.[53]

In one important respect only did the committees, and the two houses, reach a consensus at variance with the administration's program of major weapons procurement. The defense establishment did not include a request for authorization of further procurement of the B-52 or the B-58 bombers. The Secretary of Defense indicated that under existing plans B-52 production would end in August, 1962, and B-58 production in October, 1962. Pending further study of the role of the manned bomber, therefore, he saw no need for procurement authority during fiscal 1962. Further, in connection with the Department of Defense Appropriation Bill, the administration reduced the development funds for the B-70 by $138 million.[54]

The committees took strong issue with this evident downgrading

[50] *Ibid.*, p. 3.
[51] See *ibid.*, pp. 290–291.
[52] *Cong. Rec.*, Vol. 107 (87th Cong., 1st sess.), daily ed., p. 7412. The Army's drive for Nike-Zeus production was "kicked off" by the February issue of *Army* magazine, published by the Association for the United States Army. Speeches were made on the floor on behalf of the Zeus by Congressmen Daniel Flood, George P. Miller, and John McCormack; and by Senators Thurmond and Mundt. See *ibid.*, pp. 1580, 1727, 2022, 2439, 3560, 4425.
[53] *Ibid.*, p. 8321.
[54] House Committee on Armed Services, *Authorizing Appropriations for Aircraft, Missiles and Naval Vessels*, pp. 4, 6.

of the manned bomber. During the hearings, according to the House committee report, a "perceptible hesitancy in placing sole reliance and dependence on the ICBM for now or the near future" appeared. It noted that the bomber concept was still under study and emphasized the untried nature of the ballistic missile:

> . . . Also—and this is a thought which to the knowledge of the committee has not been stressed in the past—who knows whether an intercontinental ballistic missile with a nuclear warhead will actually work? Each of the constituent elements has been tested, it is true. Each of them, however, has not been tested under circumstances which would be attendant upon the firing of the missile in anger.
>
> By this the committee means an intercontinental ballistic missile will carry its nuclear warhead to great heights, subjecting it to intense cold. It then will arch down and upon reentering the earth's atmosphere subject the nuclear warhead to intense heat. Who knows what will happen to the delicate mechanisms involved in the nuclear warhead as it is subjected to these two extremes of temperature?
>
> The scientists may say that all of these things are determinable by extrapolation. Perhaps this is so. To the committee, however, it seems that our only knowledge of the actual workability of an ICBM fired in anger is in textbooks and in laboratories. The committee is unwilling to place the safety of this country in a purely academic attitude, and for this reason has added to the bill authorization for bombers.[55]

The committees not only sounded the trumpet against the academicians but also observed that (1) the bomber possesses a "utility and flexibility in application" not obtainable in missiles; (2) if a stable strategic deterrence were achieved the manned bomber would be able to respond to "other forms of warfare"; and (3) the availability of the Hound Dog air-to-ground missile and the development of the Skybolt enhanced the effectiveness of the manned bomber as a strategic weapon.[56]

The upshot of all this was, in the Senate, an amendment authorizing $525 million for B-52 procurement, and evidence of serious misgivings about the cuts made in the B-70 development. The House reduced and altered this, adding $393 million authorization for B-52 and B-58 procurement. The conferees agreed to restore the

---

[55] *Ibid.*, p. 3.
[56] Senate Committee on Armed Services, *Authorizing Appropriations for Aircraft, Missiles and Naval Vessels,* S. Rept. 253 (87th Cong., 1st sess.), p. 4.

Senate figure—$525 million—and specified only that it was for "pro-
curement of long-range manned aircraft for the Strategic Air Command."[57] The Appropriations Committees concurred in this
judgment on the need for manned bombers, noting the aerial
demonstrations during the year in Moscow. The appropriations
bill accepted by the conferees in August thus added $515 million
for purchase of B-52s or B-58s, and also added $400 million over
the administration requests for the B-70 program.[58]

Obviously, however, Congress can no more compel Defense
Department utilization of what it has authorized than it can compel
expenditure of funds which it has appropriated. Does the authorization process merely result in a situation identical with that of the
appropriations process? Has Section 412 altered the realities of the
decision-making process, or merely added a new procedural layer?

VIII. CONCLUSIONS

In three respects, Section 412 opens the way for an expansion of
the role of Congressional leaders in defense policy-making. First, it
strengthens the *access* of Congress to the processes of policy formulation. Strategy is an area of executive initiative and, in this basic
sense, Congress' role must be usually and essentially a negative one—
the role of critic, questioner, skeptic—though occasionally it can
be a prodder. With major strategic doctrines underlying policy
inherently focused in the procurement of major weapons systems,
the procedure of annually authorizing these systems (and the intent
to make this an annual process seems very firm) involves more Congressmen more immediately in the intellectual, technical and political processes from which policy and stategy emerge.

The authorization procedure lends itself to this function better
because it possesses, in turn, the *utility of focus.* Defense appropriations must roam across an immense terrain of policy decisions, from
the trivial to the momentous. The range of choices it too complex
for busy legislators to be able to extract and analyze systematically
the pertinent and the fundamental from the irrelevant and transitory. Moreover, important decisions not of a strategic nature become

[57] *Cong. Rec.*, Vol. 107 (87th Cong., 1st sess.), daily ed., pp. 9314–9315.
The Senate agreed to a House amendment for additional funds for new
engines for the C-135 and a compromise was reached on the procurement of
guided missile frigates by the Navy.
[58] *Ibid.*, pp. 14262–14265.

interlocked in the vast reaches of defense appropriations. A great deal of time was given in the debates on the Defense Appropriations Act for Fiscal 1960, for example, to the issue of federal subsidies to local educational resources in areas where large defense installations are located.[59] This is not an insignificant problem, and it falls into a category of constituency interests that demand legislative attention. But it is time-consuming and diverting from the central issues involved in national defense. Issues of this sort are always involved in the appropriations acts.

Such diversions are less likely to emerge in legislation wholly concerned with authorizing procurement of ships, aircraft and missiles. Strategic issues are not exhausted in the problems of weapons procurement, but S. 1852 clearly raised such questions as (1) the relative allocation of resources to preparations for limited and general war, (2) the relative utility of varying types of strategies of deterrence, (3) the mix of strategic weapons, and (4) the roles and missions of the services relative to these various policy objectives. Procurement hearings and debates may be sidetracked, but aside from the inevitable discussions about the mechanics of the novel procedure the 1961 record demonstrated an impressive degree of focus on the policy choices implicit in the legislation. Events dictated also a considerable concern in the hearings with intelligence programs and with the release of information on military programs, but these were questions deserving of legislative scrutiny and interest.

Finally, access and focus lead into one other important alteration in this executive-legislative dialogue. The authorization procedure creates an *expanded base of knowledge* in Congress for the critical analysis of defense issues. With decision-making in defense centralized around the budgetary process, the Committees on Appropriations—or, more specifically, the defense subcommittees—were in a peculiarly powerful position in setting the terms of debate and deliberation. Under Section 412, the subject-matter committees assume new importance. Chairman Vinson stated in the debates:

> . . . I am afraid . . . that members of the Appropriations Committees were the only ones in Congress who actually had very much knowledge of the tremendous programs and expenditures which the Congress was called upon to pass on each year.

[59] *Ibid.*, pp. 13624–13633.

It is my hope that section 412 has called a halt to this situation. If it did nothing else, it brought 37 members of the House [*i.e.*, those on Armed Services] into the heretofore exclusive area of knowledge of these very large programs.[60]

The Appropriations Committees have understandably refrained from expressing enthusiastic support for Section 412 and its implications. Privately some of the members agreed with the Defense Department in 1959 that it was an unwise and unnecessary procedure. But 412 certainly does not displace Appropriations from an important position in debate.[61] It does add, however, to that reservoir of information and knowledge available in Congress which is the prerequisite of effective and intelligent debate. While this may represent Congressional "negativism," the role of serious debate is fundamental.[62]

The authorization requirement poses some hazards to a rational political process. It may create delay and more troublesome complications if disputes arise between the two houses and the Armed Services and Appropriations Committees. It invites additional pressure tactics from weapons contractors. It imposes added burdens on overworked civilian and military officers by requiring that they spend more time on the Hill giving duplicating testimony before different committees. If these become the real legacy of Section 412 in fact, and if the "preparedness" atmosphere continues, a strong President and Secretary of Defense can probably even dislodge the requirement, ultimately.

Nevertheless, the innovation embodied in Section 412 opens the door to the fulfillment of a vital need in the processes of defense policy-making in the United States: effective searching debate of strategic issues and choices. Confinement of legislative review of policy to the appropriations process has not met this need. The enactment of 412 is thus not only suggestive of the circumstances in which Congress is prone to intervene in strategic decisions. Properly utilized, it provides an improved basis upon which such intervention can be informed and effective.

---

[60] *Ibid.*, p. 8218.
[61] On the preeminence of the appropriations committees, an interesting comment will be found in Douglas Cater, "The Lonely Men on Capitol Hill," *The Reporter*, Vol. 21 (October 15, 1959), pp. 23–26.
[62] See the remarks of Henry Kissinger in *The Necessity for Choice: Prospects of American Foreign Policy* (New York, 1961), p. 3.

XI

CONGRESSMEN AND THE MAKING
OF MILITARY POLICY*

Lewis Anthony Dexter

ROLE CONCEPTIONS OF CONGRESSMEN

This report is concerned with the way in which congressmen, especially those assigned to committees dealing with military matters, interpret their role and status, and what they assert and affirm about their exercise of influence over military policy and military men.

The conceptions held by a group of men about their role, status, responsibility, and influence presumably have some sort of relationship to what they actually do—but there is no reason for supposing that the relationship is direct and unequivocal.[1] Men may, con-

---

* This paper was based upon 100 interviews, chiefly with members of congressional committees having military responsibility and other leading congressmen, and with a few committee staff members, administrative assistants, and legislative liaison personnel from the Department of Defense. The majority of these interviews were undertaken under contract with the Center for International Studies, Massachusetts Institute of Technology, under a Carnegie Corporation grant; others were for the Advisory Committee on Civil Defense, National Research Council. The writer had previously conducted 400 interviews with congressmen, lobbyists, and prominent constituents on foreign trade issues, often touching on "defense essentiality." This other study appears in part in R. Bauer, I. Pool, and L. Dexter, *American Business and Public Policy* (New York: Atherton Press, 1963). See also, "The Representative and His District," reprinted as Chapter I of this volume. An emphatic disclaimer must be made of any responsibility of anyone but myself for any views or findings stated or implied herein.

[1] This point probably ought to be a perfectly obvious one, but I was delayed in interpreting the results of interviews conducted in 1955–57 because it took me five years fully to see that I was not reporting on how congressmen affect military policy but simply on *how congressmen define* their role and responsibility in regard to military policy.

Were this simply a personal error of my own, it would hardly be worth commenting upon, but I suspect that whether relying upon documents or interviews, a good many reports about politics, especially about Congress, fall into a similar error—role definition, attitude, or orientation, is interpreted as though

sciously or unconsciously,[2] emphasize or underemphasize their influence and importance; they may emphasize one aspect of their activity and underemphasize another. Tentatively, it seems reasonable to suppose that the way in which men define situations has some effect on how they behave in those situations; this point (that men's definitions of situations tend to have real and significant consequences) presumably is just as important in studying the congressional work-roles as in studying any other social behavior.

MILITARY POLICY IS NOT CONSIDERED

Congressmen interviewed generally indicate that they have little tendency to raise or consider questions of military policy *in terms of its meaning for some national or international political objective or goal.* By military policy is meant specific decisions about interpreting or handling weapons, personnel, appropriations, missions, organization, administration. In fact, during the 1946–57 period, few examples could be found where congressional committees created any impression of seriously evaluating decisions about weapons, appropriations, personnel, missions, organization, or administration in terms of national or international goals or objectives. The great difficulty in making this statement is the obvious fact that here, as elsewhere in politics, there is a rhetoric of justification which purports to explain what was decided in terms of high and serious considerations quite regardless of the relevance of these considera-

---

it threw *direct* light on the substantive exercise of influence or formation of policy. An extreme, but obvious, parallel is this: a whole series of interviews with quarrelling husbands and wives would not necessarily tell us what happens when spouses disagree. What it would tell us—and an extremely important thing to know—is how husbands and wives of certain sorts interpret their roles, responsibilities, etc. But it is important to know, too, what such sources do not *by themselves* yield.

[2] I am certain that all the congressmen (not necessarily all the staff assistants or Department of Defense personnel) I interviewed were "sincere" in expressing the definition of their stated role—of course a different situation or a different interviewing technique might have stimulated other, contradictory, but equally sincere definitions of role. There has been so little experimentation on the conscious modification of interview technique in the interviewing of elite personnel that one simply has to guess as to how "representative" of the range of alternative roles which an individual may assume the particular responses in a given interview are. I would guess—partly on the basis of other interviews on other subjects with some of the same informants, partly on the basis of direct personal acquaintance with some of them and personal acquaintance with many who have worked with a number of them, and partly on "intuition"—that the responses I use are representative.

tions to the decision-making process. I have not come across any major example where the rhetoric of justification seems to reflect much predecision policy analysis; nor have I found any other evidence during the 1946–57 period where there seems to have been much congressional concern with the over-all policy implications of military decisions.

On the other hand, instances where Congress has *appeared* to concern itself with over-all military policy seem generally to fall into one of the following categories: (1) Those where Congress feels it is able to judge between clamoring claimants—usually different military services—and give one or another of them a larger slice of the available pie. (2) Where congressmen are concerned with some local situation, usually an employment situation. Congressional support, especially support in the House of Representatives, of what Huntington has called "strategic monism,"[3] consisted largely of the congressional assumption of a judicial role, tempered by the pressure of various local contractor and employment interests—all within a framework of verbal "toughness." This is stance rather than a policy.

Congressmen also occasionally wish to mollify widespread personnel complaints (*e.g.* those emanating from the National Guard mobilization in 1961). And, of course, congressmen have personal concerns of their own (*e.g.*, personal loyalty to the Marine Corps). And, naturally, they always have straight constituent interests to defend (*e.g.*, preserving specific military installations in local areas).[4]

---

[3] Samuel P. Huntington, "Radicalism and Conservatism in National Defense Policy," *Journal of International Affairs*, VIII (1954), 206–33. This exceptionally brilliant analysis of the politics of national defense differs from the present report in one significant respect—it works back from the consequences of significant decisions to presumed ideologies and therefore takes seriously the justifications given in more or less formal statements for the record as to the reasons why a position has been taken. This may be a perfectly valid approach to political behavior, but in the instant case, at least, it seems to the writer that it misleads, much as the effort to categorize office-holders in terms of what they happen on some particular issue to say about "home rule" would mislead. Unfortunately, in terms of the available data and the present state of political science knowledge, there is no clear reason for choosing between Huntington's approach and others.

[4] R. H. Dawson, "Congressional Innovation and Intervention in Defense Policy: Legislative Authorization of Weapons Systems," *American Political Science Review*, LXVI (1962), 42–57 (reprinted as Chapter X of the present volume), reports a congressional effort (in 1959 and following years) to assume more systematic responsibility. Unfortunately, my study and interviews were entirely confined to the pre-1959 period; however, I strongly suspect that what Dawson reports could be interpreted more precisely in terms of the role which [Footnote continued on page 308.]

POLICY ANALYSIS: MILITARY VERSUS CIVILIAN

The attitudes and responses to military policy-making of members of the congressional committees concerned with military policy contrasted with those of members of committees concerned with foreign economic policy. Also, members not on key committees in either field showed a similar difference between these fields. In general, the broad aspects of military policy are not considered. In the tax field, members of Ways and Means often consider the presumptive effect of particular tax legislation upon national economic policy, but military decisions are generally treated by the relevant committees as independent of broader policy decisions.

This need not be the case, for it has not always been the case. In the 1930's, available evidence suggests, Ross Collins of Mississippi, for many years a member, sometime chairman, of the Subcommittee on Military Appropriations of the House Appropriations Committee, did in fact stimulate research and development in tank warfare—and he did a great deal to keep the possibilities of tank warfare before the informed public.[5] In fact, Collins' impact in the United States may be compared with that of the military

---

Congress from time to time does assume as an arbiter between technologists, discussed below; in the absence of such arbitrament and of such local pressures (as to which congressmen typically do regard themselves as experts) the episode would not have occurred.

I suspect, also, that Dawson in a sense is dealing with the congressmen's public and overt picture of themselves—the kind of picture which is likely to be presented in reports and speeches—whereas I am dealing with the private picture (the covert culture) of Congress. There is nothing which of necessity makes a man's private picture of himself or a covert culture "truer" than the public picture; both must be taken into account, and, if they are different, may suggest further investigation.

However, it is possibly relevant that in 1955–56, a distinguished scholar, familiar with congressional action on military matters in recent years, initially challenged emphatically my point that Congress in fact had very little influence on military policy. He stated that he had a list of some fourteen areas in which Congress had been influential. But after he reconsidered the point, he stated he had to agree that Congress had either given a little more or a little less than the Department of Defense asked or decided between competing technologists, but had not, in fact, undertaken any initiative.

[5] On Collins, see Frank C. Hanaghen, "The U.S. Army," *Harper's Magazine* (December, 1940), esp. pp. 9–13, and Ross A. Collins, "Do We Want a Mass Army?" *Reader's Digest* (June, 1941), pp. 1–9. It is greatly to be hoped that, with the present emphasis on oral history and on congressional behavior, some foundation will have the imagination and initiative, while some of the participants are still alive, to undertake interviews which would permit testing more accurately such matters as the assertions made in the text about Collins.

critics Fuller and Liddell-Hart in Britain and the military officer, de Gaulle, in France. (It may now be largely forgotten that de Gaulle's first claim to fame was a theorist of mobile warfare.)

In addition, in two particular areas, the Subcommittee on Military Operations of the House Government Operations Committee during the 1950's played a similar part. For a number of years, serious thinking about *civil* defense, its mission, purpose, and meaning, has been kept alive by that subcommittee, especially by its chairman, Chet Holifield (D.-Calif.); it is probably no exaggeration to say that if it were not for the pressure of the Holifield subcommittee on the administration, the whole subject of civil defense would have lapsed into a patronage "boondoggle." Despite the word "civil," "civil defense" is in fact an item in military policy[6]—but it is quite possible that it was very psychologically important for congressional activity that civil defense was called "civil" and until 1961 had a "civil" administration. If so, this would be crucial in terms of the rest of our argument.[7] Other congressmen were probably more willing to accept Congressman Holifield's leadership here because civil defense seemed civilian; they did not think that they were infringing on military technology.[8]

Particularly under the chairmanship of Congressman Riehlman (R.-N.Y.), but during the entire decade of the fifties, the same subcommittee has also been actively concerned with, and has probably stimulated, intelligent action about the optimal use of scientists in defense research, a matter which is at least on the fringes of military policy.

---

[6] The well-known writings of Herman Kahn make this point from one standpoint. From another—emphasis on "Defense Means Protection"—I make the same point in an article by that title, published in the *American Scholar*, XXIV (Summer, 1955), 299–308.

[7] The argument that congressmen are timid about invading the area of the military specialist; see below.

[8] Of course, this fact has been by no means an unalloyed benefit to civil defense. Some of those who advocated the action which actually took place in 1961—the transfer of civil defense to the Department of Defense—supported it partly because they thought a military identification would provide it with more prestige. However, part of the objective which advocates of the transfer had in mind was not achieved when the Thomas Subcommittee of the House Appropriations Committee, the subcommittee dealing with independent offices, which was accustomed to deal very harshly with civil defense budget requests, succeeded in keeping responsibility for the civil defense budget. Supporters of civil defense had hoped that the responsibility would be transferred to the Military Appropriations Subcommittee which is inclined to be much more generous and less critical.

Congress has in the past and perhaps has now some influence on military policy. But it is purely negative, probably as a consequence of dogmatic doctrines. Probably Congress made the adequate fortification of Guam by the Franklin Roosevelt Administration impossible, and perhaps that failure to fortify Guam encouraged Japanese militarists.[9]

THE ARMED SERVICES COMMITTEE "IS PRIMARILY A REAL ESTATE COMMITTEE"

In general, it was necessary to avoid the phrase "policy" in interviews on military policy; it was too ambiguous, although it was not too ambiguous in 1953–56 interviews with congressmen on foreign economic "policy." At that time, it was rarely necessary to explain to congressmen what was meant when we came to discuss policy implications; congressional thinking about the tariff and reciprocal trade have been structured in terms of policy by a history of discussion and communications within and outside Congress.[10]

One congressman, who was probably more concerned about the apparent absence of concern with military policy in the Congress than any other member of a relevant committee with whom I talked, said:

If I were talking to a new member of [my committee], I'd say that the main problem is to pinpoint responsibility at the White House and the boards [the various councils and committees concerned with national security] for policy determination. You can't really tell who does determine it; it moves into DOD [Department of Defense] and each of the three services, and you have a feeling [that], as relates to appropriations, there is not any unity. The capable men in each area are just trying to push for more for their services which is natural, but it means they think more in terms of how to spend more and more money than they do in terms of really thinking out a strategy that would more successfully justify these great appropriations.

In our hearings, I tried for purposes of communication to do some research to determine this matter of policy. What were

[9] Similarly, it is possible that the efforts of a congressman like Kastenmeier (D.-Wis.) to have the Congress, as a national policy, renounce chemical warfare, may indirectly have inhibiting effects upon support for chemical warfare.

[10] In fact, in these interviews, because I was chiefly (though not exclusively) interested in communications, I often found it necessary to steer informants away (sometimes quite sharply as with the late Senator George of Georgia) from discussion of policy toward consideration of communications.

they thinking of? Did they anticipate [this or that] . . . ? What had they in mind to accomplish?

Then, of course, you wonder about what actually the policy of the Congress is. . . . It's never been clear to me what direction there is in the matter. . . . Policy is supposed to be wrapped up [by the Joint Chiefs] under certain restrictions, but you wonder sometimes if the chairman of the Joint Chiefs knows what is going on in the minds of other chiefs . . . .

After our lengthy hearings, I wonder to what extent members of Congress . . . bring together sufficient staff to get a real perspective. *Most questions even in what are called policy hearings are directed really towards production. This is true equally of off-the-record hearings.* People are asked questions about specific manpower requirements, et cetera, not about general policy.

It does look as though the congressional committees operate in a vacuum. It comes right back to the tragic lack of time for reflection and study on the part of members of the Congress. *So maybe they don't get clear in their minds what policy is.*
. . . I believe there should be some serious policy thinking on the ideological side. It should relate the military to State and USIA . . . .

So far as I know you are the only person in my [more than eight years of] *service in Congress, or outside, who has been making any effort to delve into these problems.* I called on several people in various government departments, DOD, the committee staff, et cetera, to try to help me to frame questions to get at these policy issues [but did not get much help]. Symington's subcommittee is concerned with program and production—not too much with big policy issues.

I can see enormous possibilities in a very careful study of the problem. Could we move into new types of weapons and a future type of defense? How can we become more potent ideologically? [The military] lack direction. We [the Congress] must assume responsibility for policy determination.

More typical was the response of a much more influential member of the House Committee on Armed Services—who, when I tried to explain that I was trying to find out what Congress did do or could do on policy said:

What the hell is the point of that? What would you do with it? I don't see that any public service could be performed by it. You can't find anything particular to say. In fact, how do we [members] know what should be considered? We mostly reflect what the military people recommend; military policy is made by the Department of Defense.

Our committee is a real estate committee.

How do we check the military recommendations? I don't know. We just ask a lot of questions—questions that are not resolved. It's most difficult to make inquiries. Take bases. DOD says we need such-and-such bases. Well, we want to know why such-and-such a size. But we don't mostly know how to evaluate the answers; we aren't equipped to do so. So 95 per cent of the legislation is what DOD recommends. It's only when you come to personnel problems, size of army, that sort of thing, that you find us doing more—and that's naturally because that affects the lives of every voter.

And perhaps the most experienced staff man on military matters on the Hill, when I told him I was studying the Armed Services Committee, repeated again and again, to be sure the idea was properly communicated, "Our committee is a real estate committee. Don't forget that. *If you study our committee, you are studying real estate transactions.*" By that, he meant that the *location of installations and related transfer, purchase, and sale of properties is the main concern of the House Armed Services Committee.*

One of the major reasons why the congressional committees involved concern themselves with accountable and avoidable waste marginal issues in the appropriations field, personnel problems, and other such peripheral matters is the fear of lack of competence.[10a]

THE TYRANNY OF INFORMATION AND IDEAS: "WHO ARE WE TO SAY 'NO'?"

Congress is today better equipped to evaluate, assay, and sometimes develop and integrate ideas than it is to invent them or stimulate their invention. But if Congress is to function smoothly, there must *somewhere* be people who invent and transmit competing ideas. That is to say, generally speaking, Congress can readily check and balance when there are within the politically alert public, sets of ideas and interests which check and balance each other, thus creating a situation within which the Congress is able to *sift, winnow, and judge.*

But if there is no check and balance *outside* the Congress, then the Congress will find it difficult to perform the legislative functions

---

[10a] I discuss the general phenomenon of the increasing fear by the non-expert of the expert as a function of our schooling and university systems in my book, tentatively titled, "On the Sociology of Stupidity," to be published by Basic Books, 1964.

of investigation, inquiry, check, and balance. So far as congressmen are aware (or were aware in 1955–57), there is no such climate of controversy, opinion, and interest pertaining to military policy as such—outside the armed services themselves. The people for the most part certainly believe in a "strong National Defense," but beyond that, the members of Congress receive little or no articulate information on military policy from them. Most congressmen on relevant committees reported in interviews that, so far as constituent views and attitudes on military policy are concerned, there were none! This situation contrasts more or less sharply with other policy fields regarding which congressmen may hear a good deal from constituents; the members are well aware of the difference.

In regard to other matters of legislative concern, there are persons known to congressmen who have articulate views and to whom the congressmen can turn for ideas, suggestions, ammunition, and moral backing. The latter point is very important; few congressmen want to challenge the experts in a highly specialized field without first having their own experts to back them.[11]

In any case, members of Congress share the views which they generally attribute to their constituents: they hesitate to question the *basic* proposals of the military; that is, they regard the military as *experts,* not only on matters of organization and command, but on types of war plans, etc. Said one member of a relevant committee, better prepared by previous experience than most committee members, "The whole problem is that we are not military experts, and we have to rely upon what the military people tell us. We try to get them to cut out the window dressing, but it's hard."[12] He repeated

---

[11] The point is not so much to be guided by the specific advice of a particular expert; it is, rather, not to stick one's neck out by finding oneself opposed to all those who are "respectable" and "informed." A few seeming experts who take a minority view are all that are sometimes needed to embolden those who latently sympathize with them.

[12] Significantly, in the course of these interviews, no member said anything (except for reference to civil defense theorists) which indicated an awareness that there is within the scientific community considerable controversy about war plans. However, I know that three or four of the members I talked with do have some knowledge of the sort of argument one would find in the *Bulletin of Atomic Scientists,* but only one of them mentioned the matter in the framework of our interviews. In terms of the orientation of this article—*the social psychology of the occupational interfaces between* congressmen and military specialists—the omission did not need to be challenged; it would be interesting to replicate my interviews today to see if there is more spontaneous mention of the scientific discussion.

several times in the course of our talks the rhetorical question: "Who are we to say 'no' to the military people?" Members do not feel this respect for foreign policy experts from the State Department or for tax experts from the Treasury or for economists from relevant agencies.

MILITARY SPECIALISTS EXERCISE A MONOPOLY ON THE PRESENTATION OF ALTERNATIVES

In terms of the feeling just described, most congressmen and members of the relevant committees usually, if not always, *do* follow the recommendations of the military when these are clearly and explicitly propounded. However, members of Congress do not, in fact, want to know the military's specific war plans for security reasons,[13] and in many cases, they are not at all concerned with the nature of the war plans. In general, they seemed to be assuming that there are only two possible kinds of war—either (1) a thermonuclear war, or (2) a Korean-type war. They appear to have no idea that other possibilities (of other kinds of war) are worth investigating.

The military exercises a monopoly or quasi-monopoly on presentation of alternatives, with the result that congressmen have no reason to be aware of the gamut of possibilities open to them. When the generals very largely determine the explanations they hear, and the choices they are forced to make, congressmen have little opportunity to move into an area of reflection broader than that of the generals—unless they have the time and ability to innovate.[14]

The problem for congressmen is, then, to get alternatives posed for them. The issue is not confined to the military field; it is, impressionistically speaking, probably true in all areas in which the legislative branch is faced with specialists whose occupational prestige is such that members of the legislature are apt to feel that they are sticking their necks out by contradicting them. In other words, military men often belong to a category of technological specialists who can to a considerable degree get their own way by

---

[13] That is, they are afraid they will be inhibited and restrained and embarrassed by having access to more confidential security information than they desire to know.

[14] In an area not one of military policy as we have defined the term, but closely related thereto, Congressman John W. McCormack (D.-Mass.) has, according to members of his staff, manifested such innovative tendencies: He has, they report, played a creative part in pressuring the Department of Defense to rationalize purchasing procedures.

posing the questions for the legislature; public health specialists are another such category.[15]

"How the Hell Do We Know What Should Be Considered?"

How do the members of the relevant committees reach their decisions and evaluate the proposals made by the military? The answer seems to be that usually no such evaluation is made. In answer to the question, "Aside from your common sense and whatever help the staff can supply you, is there any way to check on the military experts?" members said:

> No. The most effective way is for a congressman to have a good knowledge of the installations in his district which unfortunately I do not have.
>
> * * *
>
> The problem as I see it is that even if we put into effect policy legislation, the executive department can circumvent it if it wants to. [This member stated that he probably attends more committee and subcommittee meetings than any other member; he was referred to by several committee colleagues as "an expert."]
>
> * * *
>
> Lord knows we need some help; I hope you can find something which tells us what to listen to.
>
> * * *
>
> How the hell do we know what should be considered anyway? We mostly reflect what the military men tell us. [This was from a member widely regarded as one of the two or three ablest men on relevant committees.]

Such acceptance of the leadership of the military, so far as the House is concerned, seems to be more characteristic of the Armed Services Committee than of the Appropriations Subcommittee on Defense. Almost all members agreed with the following point:

> We don't have a hell of a lot before our [Armed Services] committee. There's really much scarcity of policy legislation. . . . Maybe we have given to much authority to the

[15] Of course, this is a report from the standpoint of the legislature; most military men and public health experts will probably feel that they do not get their own way; and sometimes the legislature may say "no" to them, or say more often "a little less" or "a little later," but generally the legislature does concede to them the formulation of the issues.

Secretary of Defense and the Joint Chiefs of Staff. Congress
itself has promulgated legislation which says to them "use
your own judgment." . . . So policy is found in Appropriations
more than anywhere else. Yes, the question of jurisdiction on
these matters keeps people sore. Vinson stays at loggerheads
with Cannon about it [Vinson (D.-Ga.), Chairman, Armed
Services, Cannon (D.-Mo.), Chairman, Appropriations]

And, from another member of Armed Services:

Our committee accepts reports of the Department of Defense
more completely than does Appropriations. We never question opinions about personnel, et cetera. [This is not absolutely
correct, but more or less so.] We kid Appropriations members
about this, say we aren't military experts, but they are, et
cetera.

The foregoing comments apply to the House rather than the
Senate. Although there are differences in the personalities of the
members of the two House committees, the significant contrast seems
to arise out of the functional differences between them. Armed Services is a *legislative* committee, and, as such, deals chiefly with the
basic issues only once—when they are enacted into legislation. The
Appropriations Committee, on the other hand, considers issues
annually, and, as one member of Armed Services said:

Right. Appropriations *is* more important. We are over-all
men and deal with the over-all things. Now, you must qualify
that to this extent; this may not be true from the standpoint of
the armed services themselves. We do deal with things that
might not seem very important to civilians but are tremendously important to the military—like how many general officers can there be? [A Senate committee staff member indicated
that they have more personal visits on personnel matters, promotions, pensions, etc., than on any other matter.][16]

But in the conventional course of events, the Appropriations
Committee is concerned mainly not so much with *legislation* as
with avoiding *accountable waste*. As to getting into the *policy* field,
there its members have no clear viewpoint of whether they should
or should not. Thus, by and large, when Appropriations Committee
members do get into a policy question, it is either by accident or

---

[16] The parallel with school committees in cities and towns—which in some
instances spend more time discussing routes and who is entitled to bus rides
than considering educational matters—is interesting.

because some external event has attracted attention to it, or because of the personal interest of particular members.[17]

"We Need More Interservice Squabbling"

Several fairly senior members, when asked, "What are the major characteristics of a good committee member?" replied, in effect, "Be suspicious of the military! We need guys who won't let them put anything over on us."

For instance, one member said:

> Well, now, I'm sure you can supply [better] words to what I'm saying. . . . There's no way on earth to prevent military leaders from pulling the wool over our eyes. But we should keep check. . . . You have to watch their requests; many times they're made for political expedience. You've got to trust what military leaders tell you, but you can't turn them loose on things. . . . I'm not one of those who think the military are all bad, but we need a close check on them. Unfortunately you cannot have such a check unless you have well-staffed standing committees with tremendous expenditure.

Another [one of the two most impressive members of the relevant committees in 1956]:

> Congress can preserve a republican form of government and avoid a dictator by this sort of control [which Appropriations supplies]. . . . They frequently forget man is a human being; [yet] they're always talking about morale until I'm sick of the word. . . . A very important ability [on Appropriations] is to resist the blandishments and glitter of stars and rank. I make a rule never to accept any social invitation involving a top-ranking military man. . . . [Then you have] to be thick-skinned. It's hard to say "no." The services may not attack you directly, but indirectly. . . .

But since the military is supposed to be "trying to put something over on us" [the Congress and the people], what then? Again and again, the members said, in effect: "What we need is more inter-

---

[17] But the tremendous workload of the committee, plus the quite inadequate staff assistance, means that, at present, its most conscientious and penetrating members would have to make a very conscious decision to let millions of dollars of avoidable, accountable, or quasi-accountable, waste go unchecked, if they were to allow themselves the time to think through military policy problems! For anyone, and particularly for the kind of man who is likely to gravitate to the Appropriations Committee, this would be a most difficult decision.

service squabbling. *When the military falls out, then and only then can the Congress find out."*

One of the more influential staff men, a trusted advisor of one of the most influential men on the Hill, said, for example:

> Looking at these things, as I must, from the big end of the funnel, it seems to me that if everything goes smoothly, nobody ever knows what's going on, neither Congress nor anybody else. But when some one of the forces gets into trouble or gets riled up, then we hear about it and learn a lot. [Of course] we don't know whether the roots are in the military services themselves or start with the DOD civilians or with the military contractors; I just don't know and I wouldn't want to be [identifiably] quoted, but I'd like to know whether Boeing has stirred things up chiefly on these B-52s. Naturally, Senator Jackson [D.-Wash.] openly says . . . he'd like to see some more jobs there.
>
> I would say there is no secret that [in 1956] SAC has priority in people and things—*all over*. And the big squabbles arise when it [or somebody else] gets hurt. . . . But if nobody gets badly hurt, all the services will sit there as calm as can be, and Congress will hear nothing about it. . . .
>
> This old stuff of roles and missions is the central thing in our investigations, and always there you're cutting or threatening to cut flesh, nerve, muscle; and everybody wants to be seated at the table where such a threat is made. The reason for all the sensitivity is the simple possibility of a change in roles and missions.
>
> Fights get to Congress and lead Congress to know what's going on. . . .
>
> If somebody comes to you and wants you to investigate such-and-such a condition, you'll learn only what they in the services want you to learn, *unless there is interservice rivalry.* Then you can find out from the Air Force or vice versa and from Strategic Air Command about Air Defense or vice versa. That is, each service, then [when there's a fight], is ready to say "those dirty dogs are doing so-and-so" and you learn something.

A staff member is quoted here because he expressed, as it happened, more articulately and systematically what many members clearly indicated or implied. Said a member who had actually campaigned on the basis of membership on a committee related to the armed services:

> The thing I was least aware of before my service [here on the committee] was the interservice rivalry. Or course, my community tends towards one particular service; I'm not objecting to this [interservice rivalry]. I think a spirited competition is a very healthy thing.

This emphasis on competition and on the healthiness of it seems to imply what the staff member just quoted actually said; in a couple of instances, it came very close to the old saying, "When thieves fall out, honest men have their day." The atmosphere of not trusting the armed services was widespread in the Congress. Not that they think the military witnesses and leaders are thieves, of course, but in the words of another member:

> I suppose I'm unique among congressmen; I have a strong native bias against the military, as witness that word "garbage" which I just used as applied to what I hear from the Pentagon, but for refined intellectual reasons I'm more convinced than most that we have to have an intelligent defense policy and defend it, so I refrain from criticism except on special points. I find myself, that is, a strong supporter of an institution which I distrust profoundly.[18]

The belief that other members have a higher opinion than oneself has of the military seems fairly common, so I raised the question, "Do you really think that's unique? It seems to me to be standard."

> Oh, well, I think a lot of 'em would say "We've got to have the——s but we hate 'em"; mine is a more refined, permanent, philosophical distrust!

"The Military Is the Real Corruptor of Congress"

Another sophisticated member, recalling the then current excitement about the efforts by oil and gas interests to bribe a senator, said:

> Relatively, if they were really to study "corruption," all that [oil business] is peanuts in my judgment; the people who are really trying to bribe and pressure Congress are from the Department of Defense. They learn you want to go somewhere, and they call you up and say, "How about travelling on one of our planes?" And it just so happens there is riding along with you a pleasant, agreeable officer from the service which gives you the ride; he does not argue with you at all, but he does call your attention to things from their standpoint.

The member then pointed out that this kind of contact is designed to give the armed services the opportunity to determine what issues

---

[18] This member shared with several others the illusion that this was a unique point of view; in fact, it was the commonest one.

the congressman thinks about. He averred that, collectively, such contacts are far more "corrupting" than oil industry efforts because they do more to shape the way Congress looks at military questions than any mere bribe. His kind of awareness, however—that all the military services *may share* a common set of assumptions or views which it would be profitable to question, or *may omit* from consideration some important point which, in terms of over-all national interest, should be taken into account—is not commonly found among members of the committees directly concerned with military issues.

In fact, congressmen frequently assume the validity of the terms in which interservice disputes are raised because they know of no other way of getting at the issues. In any event, it is a common enough human tendency to accept the framework within which an argument is conducted; but in the Congress this tendency is considerably enhanced by the feeling that the Armed Services Committee is a *"quasi-judicial* committee."[19] Perhaps the judicial role is often a desirable model for congressmen to adopt; it might in fact increase impartiality and a readiness to change one's mind on due cause being presented. On the Armed Services Committee, it leads to the notion that that committee has two chief responsibilities: (1) to listen to the requests of the various services and say "yes" or "no"; or (2) in more complex issues, to decide which of the "litigants"—Army, Navy, Air Force, Marines, or subservices—shall get the most of what is wanted in the way of missions, money, prestige, and power.[20]

---

[19] This notion of being engaged in a judicial process is common enough on congressional committees, naturally so in a body which contains many lawyers, some would-be judges, and some would-be members of regulatory commissions. Committee chairmen may operate on the notion that they conduct hearings with the neutrality which a judge shows in court. At the time of this investigation such chairmen as former Senator Millikin (R.-Colo., Senate Finance) or the former chairman of the House Interior Committee, now Senator Engle (D.-Calif.), who had clearly-known views on controversial legislation, endeavored to portray themselves as impartially engaged in a judicial activity while conducting hearings on such legislation.

[20] Of course, on many matters, the committees could have great importance because of their latent power (the degree to which the executive branch calculates upon their acceptance or rejection of proposals may be as important as the actual approval or disapproval they articulate) rather than because of what they actually do. Hypothetically, it should be pointed out that committees would "rubber-stamp" all suggestions from a department if the department always guessed correctly what the committees would approve and submitted no other suggestions.

But this notion appears to have the grave weakness that it assumes that through the operation of some form of invisible hand, the "litigants" will necessarily present the basic issues of public policy with which the Congress ought to be concerned. It also assumes that the interservice hostility, thus not diminished, will not interfere with genuine cooperation between the armed forces where this is desirable.

WHAT IS "TECHNICAL" AND WHAT IS "NON-TECHNICAL"?

"You Have to Gnaw and Gnaw to Get Anything Out of the Service"

Even more basic, possibly, than the points already made in explaining or "justifying" congressional reluctance to tackle military policy problems is the little word technical. Congressmen tend to regard as "technical" such questions for "professional" military men as the nature of war plans. But they regard as "non-technical" and fit subjects for their consideration such matters as the way in which oil is stored at overseas installations or how service credit shall be allocated for ROTC or military academy training—problems of the type which at some universities would be thankfully left as a "technical" matter for registrars to decide.[21] Similarly, Congress will evaluate or try to evaluate the efficiency of given types of rifles or waste in the procurement of military overcoats. However—with the partial exceptions of the Subcommittee on Military Operations when Riehlman (R.-N.Y.) was chairman and the Senate Foreign Relations Committee in 1959–60—they have recently shown little interest in stimulating the invention and development of newer types of weapons or innovations in "grand strategy."[22] The historic distinction between *grand* strategy—war plans involving, for instance, such

---

[21] Officers might or might not receive longevity pay credit for their years in the military academies or in the ROTC; Congress in this case has tended to support reservists against the claims to special considerations from West Pointers, etc.

[22] The Foreign Relations Committee may seem an unlikely candidate here, but the truth was well-expressed by a sophisticated and experienced staff member of another committee who said, "I think you'll find out that jurisdiction is nine-tenths assertion" among congressional committees. If several influential members of the Interior Committee desired to do so, no doubt they could study basic military policy because of their responsibilities for public lands, conservation, etc., which provides an entering wedge; the only difficulty would be that, if they did this, they would not have time to do something else which they might wish to do.

matters as the desirability and feasibility of *massive* retaliation versus *measured* retaliation—and *specific* strategies is quite unfamiliar in the Congress. This explains in part why questions about military policy are often regarded as suggesting that congressmen concern themselves with *technical* military issues. In other words, many congressmen assume that there is some sort of over-all approach to military policy which need not be questioned, or which is axiomatic. In any case, questions of over-all policy are not raised by many witnesses or "litigants" (in general, it would be against the interest of *most* of the vociferous litigants who approach Congress to query prevailing assumptions). But a contrast is provided by congressmen who have recently been able and eager to consider basic policy in fields such as full employment or international trade.

A number of members made the point that the Constitution gives the President special authority over military matters because he is designated as Commander-in-Chief. This, again, seems to assume that questions about military policy must necessarily deal with specific war plans and to ignore the area of grand strategy. In any case, it might equally well be argued that the American constitutional system is supposed to operate through competition between the branches of government, that is to say, check-and-balance, and that there is also constitutional warrant for assumption by Congress of responsibility in military matters.

One reason cited by several congressmen for hesitation about "interfering" with the executive branch on military matters is that efforts to do so during the Civil War resulted (actually or supposedly) in difficulty and trouble. Southern members, who are, of course, in senior positions when the Democratic party is in the majority, seem to be particularly influenced by this contention. Perhaps Senator Truman of Missouri, through his establishment of and leadership in a committee concerned with investigating defense mobilization, contracting difficulties, etc., and because of his own intense historical sense, called attention to or enhanced the importance of this point of view.

The question is, could Congress learn to think about military policy without getting into the war plans area? This is, of course, a standard problem of legislative-executive relationship, generalist-specialist tension, and, for that matter, top administrator-middle administrator difficulty. The president of a university, and the board of trustees under some circumstances, may properly be concerned with the curriculum but not with the content of the comprehensive examination; they may set policy within which future comprehensive examinations may be established, but they should never handle complaints about current comprehensives. Senator Truman's position (which he probably saw no reason to change when he became President) was that the Congress could not, psychologically, make the judicious sort of distinction here described, and therefore should stay out of the field altogether.[23]

Under present practice, it is probably true to say, as one active and influential congressman did, that "On these matters, you have to be a——bulldog and gnaw and gnaw and gnaw to get any [information out] of the services." (He added, "the whole damn trouble with Congress is they let people file things.") "You've got to be a policeman and keep hounding and hounding ... to get a job done."

POWER-SEEKING POLITICIANS VERSUS TECHNOLOGISTS?

One commonly held conception about politics is that politicians seek power actively and aggressively. Whatever other conclusions may be derived from the present report, it seems apparent that congressmen on relevant committees could readily enough strive for greater power in military affairs with a reasonable chance of obtaining it. *In fact, they think that the satisfactions they obtain by not seeking power are greater than those they would get by trying to maximize it.* Among the factors which may explain such "restraint" are (1) traditions of institutional organization including "separation of powers"; and (2) the notion in Congress that professional and technical matters should be left to professional and technical men. On the basis of the present study we cannot say whether these traditions and notions are "rationalizations" of some other motivation (such as the discomfort conceivably involved in systematic thinking about the potentialities of modern war—former Civil Defense Administrator Petersen, also a politician, spoke of himself as one "who [has] been looking into hell for three years") or are independent causal factors. The writer's best guess is that they are, to a considerable extent, causal factors, the weight and

---

[23] The Congress does not ordinarily get into specific administration; however, I have several times heard the assertion that under Senator McCarran's chairmanship, the Judiciary Committee did get into specifics of immigration administration. In some state legislatures, ways and means committees deal on a continuing basis with administrative matters, although of course state governments do not anticipate the same military crises the Congress must envisage.

significance of which are very much increased by other motivations, such as the one just mentioned, and by simple fear that a civilian who fights a technical man will be made to look ridiculous before his public.[24]

---

[24] For another discussion of self-restraint where some interpretations would predict an aggressive seeking of power, see Lewis A. Dexter, "Where the Elephant Fears to Dance Among the Chickens. Business in Politics? The Case of Dupont," *Human Organization,* XIX (1960–61), 188–94, republished with some modifications in Bauer, Pool, and Dexter, *op. cit.*

XII

CONGRESSIONAL OVERSIGHT OF ADMINISTRATION: THE POWER OF THE PURSE*

Arthur W. Macmahon

LEGISLATIVE OVERSIGHT of administration is a familiar and well-grounded assumption of responsible government. Accepted, too, is the corollary that the need for such oversight increases with executive initiative in policy and the delegation of discretion under the broad terms of statutes. But the actualities of legislative oversight have been insufficiently examined and its hazards and proper limits have received too little attention. The moods and methods of the new Congress sharpen an old question to a pressing issue.[1]

Congress shows novel zest for staffs of its own. In various ways, it seeks to attach strings to action. How far can this double tendency be pushed under the presidential form of government without creating ambiguities of administrative responsibility? There is a related and deeper difficulty. Can a legislative body—the institutional virtue of which lies in the decentralized choice and diffused responsiveness of its individual members—act on details otherwise than through small groups within itself which, by their special biases, may distort the application of public policy and even destroy its integrity? Public policy must be fused from the localisms inherent in popular representative bodies; it must then be carried out with as much wholeness as possible. Mighty issues appear in the present assertive-

* Reprinted from the *Political Science Quarterly*, Vol. LVIII, Nos. 2 and 3, pp. 161–190, 380–414, by permission of the author and publisher. Copyright (1943) by the Editors of the Political Science Quarterly.

[1] The present article—concerned especially with supervision through the appropriations committees of Congress—is the first of a series in which various aspects of legislative oversight of administration will be considered. The assistance that the author has derived from conversations for background purposes with two score members of Congress, among others, is not less appreciated because their help must remain anonymous.

ness of Congress. Welcome as are the stirrings from the lethargy of its own institutional tradition, its restlessness holds at least as much portent as promise.

I

There has been a significant change of emphasis in the Congressional attitude toward administrative discretion and its control. Originally, legislative suspicion and reluctance were reflected in the detailed character of statute law. But, especially in dealing with the flux of economic relations, leeway for administrative determinations was inevitable. The disposition then was to seek checks through the courts; in Congress this reaction reached a climax in the bill vetoed by the President late in 1940. A new stress is rising in crescendo in the Congress of 1943. The weight is no longer on the initial insertion of statutory detail or upon judicial review. Rather, the legislative body itself seeks to be continuously a participant in guiding administrative conduct and the exercise of discretion. The cords that Congress now seeks to attach to administrative action are not merely the pre-drawn "leading-strings of statutes" of which Woodrow Wilson wrote in *Congressional Government*. The novel feature of the attempted relationship is its immediacy.

The shift of emphasis just described affects one's perspective on the purposes of legislative oversight of administration. In the theory of the matter, four types of objective have been recognized. First, the objective of legislative oversight may be to check dishonesty or waste. Especially is this important when the stream of supervision within the administrative system is poisoned near its source. Apart from checking malfeasance, moreover, legislators have opportunities to see the results of governmental programs; at times they can serve administration almost as a supplementary inspectorate. Second, the objective of legislative oversight may be to guard against unsympathetic or perhaps merely over-zealous attitudes among officials which produce harsh or callous administration. Third, the ideal of legislative oversight has assumed that the non-special minds of legislators, brought to bear upon the administrative routines, may challenge the means in terms of a broad and realistic sense of ends. It may freshen inventiveness as to the means themselves; at least it may rebuke stupidity. Fourth, the objective of legislative oversight may be to see that there is compliance with the legislative intent as embodied in law. This is the face of the theory that is high-lighted by the events of the hour.

Within the notion of enforcing compliance with legislative intent a shift is discernible. Formerly compliance meant legality and this was enforced by methods which were essentially external to Congress; the courts, the General Accounting Office as a vast routinized bureau, the Department of Justice, the Treasury controls, and the departmental fiscal offices. Now the legislative intent that is conceived is one of incompletely resolved policy. Without withdrawing power, the Congress seeks in sundry ways to claim what it gave; it asserts the right of continuous intervention.

It is worth pausing to review in baldest fashion some of the methods by which continuous intervention is now essayed.[2] Clues may be drawn from measures or proposals in Congress since January 1943. (1) The amendment of statutes is a method of oversight; as Dr. Elias Huzar has very cogently shown, there is no sharp borderline between legislation and supervision.[3] Recently amendments to wartime laws have been provoked by particular incidents and have cracked like warning whips. (2) Meanwhile Congressional investigations multiply. There is no novelty in this safeguard of free government, but some persons are agitating for a unification of inquiries into the conduct of the war. The thought now is less the convenience of administrators harassed by multiple hearings than the possibility of creating a single instrument of potent influence.[4] (3) The standing legislative committees summon administrators to explain and justify decisions, past and pending. A special House committee investigates the extent to which administrative directives

---

[2] The listing deliberately omits reference to the growing use of the concurrent resolution, especially as an alternative method provided in wartime statutes for their own termination, since this device does not assert active intervention in details of administration. See John D. Millett and Lindsay Rogers, "The Legislative Veto and the Reorganization Act of 1939," *Public Administration Review,* Winter 1941, vol. I, pp. 176–89. Likewise, for somewhat similar reasons, the enumeration in the text does not mention requirements for the submission of reports, although interesting developments in this regard have taken place.

[3] "Legislative Control over Administration: Congress and the W.P.A.," *American Political Science Review,* February 1942, vol. 36, pp. 51–67.

[4] H. Res. 19, 78th Cong., 1st Sess., introduced by Representative Dirksen on January 6, 1943, proposes to explore this theme, among others. No attempt is made to mention here numerous resolutions for inquiry into post-war conditions and policies, international and domestic; for their purpose is to assert legislative initiative in planning, not control of administration directly.

have been inconsistent with law, or arbitrary.[5] Some members of Congress are urging that the standing committees should be permanently empowered to watch and perhaps censor the exercise of administrative discretion in their respective fields of jurisdiction.[6] Others, however, propose more inclusive organs for the exercise of continuous scrutiny.[7] (4) Related in spirit, being a likely opening for intervention in administration, is the preposterous but formidable move to broaden senatorial confirmation of appointments.[8] (5) Meanwhile Congress begins to talk of staffing,[9] but with many shades of opinion about its nature and nexus: whether the personnel should be permanent or transitory and how appointed, whether the attachment should be to committees, and if so to which committees, or should be to the chambers as wholes but singly, or to joint agencies of House and Senate.[10] (6) But outstanding as practical developments have been steps actually taken to enlarge the facilities and duties of the committees on appropriations.

On February 11, 1943, the House authorized the employment of staff by the Committee on Appropriations and subsequently made

---

[5] A special House committee of seven, headed by Howard Smith of Virginia, was authorized on February 11, 1943 by H. Res. 102, adopted by a vote of 294 to 50. *Congressional Record*, 78th Cong., 1st Sess., vol. 89, p. 925 (daily edition). The resolution states: "The said committee shall report to the Congress from time to time the results of such investigations and such recommendations as they see fit with respect to the personnel of those administering any such department or independent agency, or shall recommend such legislation or amendments to existing legislation as they may deem desirable."

[6] See especially Jerry Voorhis' H. Res. 27, introduced in the 78th Congress on January 6, 1943, *Congressional Record*, p. 931 (daily edition). See also H. Res. 186 (Lewis) and H. Res. 93 (Fulmer), the latter applying only to the Agricultural Committee; also, as an example of committee censure, House Report No. 208.

[7] H. J. Res. 66, introduced by Representative Dirksen on January 25, 1943, proposing a "Joint Committee on Administrative Review."

[8] Already imposed for all positions paid $4,500 or over in the Manpower Commission by Public No. 763, 77th Cong., 2nd Sess., approved by the President with a protest, October 26, 1942. Senator McKellar's general bill in the 78th Congress, S. 375, was reported favorably by the Senate Committee on Judiciary, March 3, 1943, nine to five.

[9] See Lindsay Rogers, "The Staffing of Congress," *Political Science Quarterly*, March 1941, vol. 56, pp. 1–22.

[10] Among other proposals in the 78th Congress, see H. R. 83 (Lanham), for an "Office of Fiscal Investigation"; H. R. 30 (Dirksen), for a "Federal Efficiency Service" in the GAO; H. J. Res. 57 (Dirksen), for "research secretaries" to committees through the Legislative Reference Service; S. 764 (Tydings), for a "Joint Committee on Appropriations"; and H. Conc. Res. 8 (Dirksen), for a "Joint Committee on Economy and Efficiency."

$100,000 available for the purpose.[11] The investigations, it was said, were to be "pre-appropriation," conducted through studies without hearings, and "limited strictly to matters within the jurisdiction of the Committee on Appropriations." The staff was to be essentially a rotating one, consisting of persons drawn temporarily from various governmental agencies. "While the committee will have authority to employ personnel without restriction," said the chairman, "under the plan agreed upon all auditors and examiners will be appointed from those now serving in civil-service positions."[12] Such an improvised group of investigators was soon looking into the affairs of the hapless Farm Security Administration and the Rural Electrification Administration.

Even more pregnant with the spirit of detailed intervention in administration was the power vested in the House Committee on Appropriations by a resolution of February 9, 1943. It directed:

> That the Committee on Appropriations, acting through a special subcommittee thereof appointed by the chairman of such committee for the purposes of this resolution, is authorized and directed to examine into any and all allegations or charges that certain persons in the employ of the several executive departments and other executive agencies are unfit to continue in such employment by reason of their present association or membership or past association or membership in or with organizations whose aims or purposes are or have been subversive to the Government of the United States.[13]

As to the use of the information thus gained, the resolution was vague: "Such examination shall be pursued with the view of obtaining all available evidence bearing upon each particular case

---

[11] H. Res. 69, 78th Cong., 1st Sess., *Congressional Record*, vol. 89, p. 930 (daily edition), implemented by H. Res. 116, adopted February 18, p. 1143. Clarence Cannon, Chairman of the Appropriations Committee, after remarking that the better staffing of the committee had been long under consideration, said in explanation: "The delay in reaching some earlier solution of the matter has been largely occasioned by two major difficulties, the difficulty of building up an organization which through its intimate association with the members of the committee would slowly but surely increase its salaries, its personnel, and its jurisdiction until it became in effect a Frankenstein which could not be controlled or dislodged, and, second, the establishment of an organization amenable to political manipulation which could be used for partisan purposes," p. 928 (daily edition).
[12] *Congressional Record*, vol. 89, p. 1143 (daily edition).
[13] 78th Cong., 1st Sess., H. Res. 105, *Congressional Record*, vol. 89, p. 780. See also Chairman Cannon's explanation, p. 747.

and reporting to the House the conclusions of the committee with respect to each such case in the light of the factual evidence obtained." But there was the added ominous provision: "Any legislation approved by the committee as a result of this resolution may be incorporated in any general or special appropriation measure emanating from such committee or may be offered as a committee amendment to any such measure notwithstanding the provisions of clause 2 of rule XXI."[14]

Behind this organized action lay a series of sporadic incidents in which at least the attempt had been made to insert in general appropriation acts limitations that prevented the employment of specified individuals. In the relief appropriation act passed in 1941, the sally begun on the floor of the House had actually succeeded; and the mighty hand of Congress, in bestowing more than three quarters of a billion dollars, expressly forbade the employment of one named individual in its administration.[15] The various attempts to outlaw by name the employment of individuals are, of course, hardly distinguishable below the surface from uncounted instances in which appropriations for particular units have been trimmed or eliminated for reasons that were at least partly personal.[16] Often the pressures of the purse-power have been even more indirect.

It is not easy for the shamed observer of recent events to discuss this matter at all. He does not wish to spread injustice by echoing the names that have been so casually and cruelly bandied in stigmatizing debate. Representative Anderson of New Mexico has truly said "that the only thing that many of these people have in the world is a good name."[17] Indeed, there was understatement in

---

[14] The rule states: "Nor shall any provision changing existing law be in order in any general appropriation bill or in any amendment thereto."

[15] The act attached to the clause that carried $875,000,000 almost as one great fund the following: "Provided, that no part of any appropriation contained in this act shall be used to pay the compensation of ———— ————," naming the former head of the Workers' Alliance. Introduced by Representative Dirksen, the proviso was adopted on June 12, 1941 after considerable debate, by a vote of 131 to 88. *Congressional Record,* 77th Cong., 1st Sess., vol. 87, pp. 5110–13.

[16] For example, see the cut made by the House in the item for the research and power planning branch of the power division in the Interior Department appropriation bill for 1943. *Congressional Record,* 77th Cong., 2nd Sess., vol. 88, pp. 2890–97, 2926–33. For Secretary Ickes' very vigorous protest, see 77th Cong., 2nd Sess., Senate Committee on Appropriations, *Hearings before a subcommittee on the Department of the Interior appropriation bill for 1943,* p. 25.

[17] *Congressional Record,* 78th Cong., 1st Sess., vol. 89, p. 3088 (daily edition), April 7, 1943.

Representative Folger's comment that "It is not a little thing for this Congress to find by solemn vote that a man who is an American citizen . . . is unworthy to hold a position of trust or honor in the United States of America."[18] Quite apart from any constitutional question involved, the observer gags on the logic of the House member who, quite typically, said: "If a man is an employee of this Government and if some people have seen fit to question his loyalty, and knowing, as I do, that he has no property right in the job which he holds, why can I not, as a Member of this House, vote to have him taken from the payroll?"[19] Yet only by naming those who have been included in the 1943 attacks could the perspective and proportions of alarms in Congress be revealed. Wide indeed has become the net which, in the course of the expenditure of half a million dollars by the Dies committee, has been woven from such sleazy fabric as letterheads drawn from a period when decent and prescient men, alive to the mortal danger of the world, even then starkly to be seen in Spain, often had to choose between silence and taking a stand through improvised and shifting organizations. This does not deny that the active membership in a disciplined exotic party may create problems of crisscrossing loyalty which may genuinely embarrass an administrative hierarchy. But this important if limited aspect—involving issues in the relationship of ends and means—seems to be hopelessly lost in an undiscriminating Congressional recoil from critics, partial as well as complete, of what Representative John E. Rankin has called "our capitalist form of government." Ironically, the author of this curious constitutional phrase himself qualifies its political realism by standing as a foremost champion of the TVA and public power.

The unreckoning mood impending in the House was shown in the circumstance that led to the creation of the Appropriations subcommittee under the resolution of February 9. The House was then considering the Treasury and Post Office appropriation bill—the first of the regular money measures to reach the floor in the new Congress. On February 4 Representative Hendricks proposed an

---

[18] *Ibid.*, p. 3090 (daily edition).
[19] *Ibid.*, p. 693 (daily edition), February 5, 1943. This member had voted shortly before to bar 38 named persons from employment under the national government although he said, "I did not of necessity believe the charges that I have heard." For him, it was enough that they had been made; there were many worthy candidates for the public service about whom no question at all had been raised.

amendment "that no part of any appropriation in this act shall be used to pay the compensation of . . .," listing thirty-eight persons by name. They had been mentioned by Representative Dies in a speech a few days before. Only one was employed at the time in the departments covered by the bill. The others were included, it was said, "to prevent hedge-hopping." On the following day, after debate, the amendment failed by only seven votes.[20] Thereupon, by a margin of fifty-two, the committee of the whole inserted an amendment aimed specifically at the single person who was employed by the Treasury—a Negro leader in the war savings organization.[21] In the course of the discussion on the original amendment, the chairman of Appropriations said, "We are all in thorough sympathy with the purpose of this amendment."[22] But he added, "The question immediately before us is the penalizing of thirty-eight men of whom we have never heard before, and here for the first time called to our attention by this unexpected amendment." He promised a formula "in keeping with our American institutions," if one could be agreed upon with the ranking minority member of his committee.

The "orderly procedure" for which Chairman Cannon pleaded was offered to the House a few days later in the resolution already described. A subcommittee of five members, with Representative Kerr of North Carolina as chairman, undertook to examine masses of material assembled by the Dies committee, the Department of Justice, an interdepartmental committee, and the Civil Service Commission. On April 7, when the House was taking up another of the regular bills, and still the subcommittee had not reported, Representative Dirksen, hot and angry on the scented trail, wondered what the subcommittee had been doing about "names I propose to bring into this well unless some action is taken reasonably soon."[23] The chairman of the subcommittee confessed that it was "a great deal larger job than any of us thought we had to undertake." Another member said that "we had just one terrific time to get any attorney to act as counsel for this committee."[24]

---

[20] *Congressional Record,* 78th Cong., 1st Sess., vol. 89, p. 691 (daily edition). The first vote was 130 to 137; with tellers, it stood 146 to 153.

[21] *Ibid.,* p. 691 (daily edition). The vote was 163 to 111. This proviso was later dropped.

[22] *Ibid.,* p. 690 (daily edition).

[23] *Ibid.,* p. 3085 (daily edition).

[24] *Ibid.,* p. 3086 (daily edition). Representative Dies (whose committee meanwhile had begun to subpoena some of the individuals involved) said the

On April 21, the subcommittee reported on three employees of the Federal Communications Commission "named by the chairman of the special committee to investigate un-American activities in a speech on the floor of the House of Representatives, February 1, 1943."[25] Of two of these individuals it was declared that their "views and philosophies . . . constitute subversive activity as defined by the committee" and that each was therefore "unfit to continue in Government employment." No specific steps were recommended. Of the third—a well-known historian—it was said that the committee "does not find sufficient evidence to support a recommendation of unfitness to serve in the employment of the Government at this time."

In the steps taken in 1943, the House seemed to overlook not only rebukes suffered earlier at the hands of the Senate, but even its own earlier repentance. The latter had been evidenced in regard to the provision aimed at the former head of the Workers' Alliance. Late in 1941 a repealing clause was inserted by the House committee in the third supplemental defense appropriation bill. The report remarked that "personal legislation of the character enacted . . . is rare"; and added, "It was taken, the committee feels, without suffi-

fact of membership in various organizations (other than the Communist Party) was seldom denied; it all depended on what conclusions one drew from such membership.

[25] 78th Cong., 1st Sess., House Report No. 448, April 21, 1943. The text is also given in the *Congressional Record* of that date, pp. A-2130–32. The subcommittee (consisting of Kerr of North Carolina, Gore of Tennessee, Anderson of New Mexico, Powers of New Jersey, and Keefe of Wisconsin) declared that "it is not hostile to what is known these days as liberalism." "Subversive activity," it said, "has not been defined by the courts or by Congress," so the subcommittee adopted the following definition to guide its examinations:

"Subversive activity in this country derives from conduct intentionally destructive of or inimical to the Government of the United States—that which seeks to undermine its institutions, or to distort its functions, or to impede its projects, or to lessen its efforts, the ultimate end being to overturn it all. Such activity may be open and direct as by effect to overthrow, or subtle and indirect as by sabotage."

As to the organizations, "front" or "questionable"—membership, present or past, in which counts heavily against the employee—it was said:

"These organizations have not been adjudged by the courts or by Congress as subversive. They have operated either without constitutions or bylaws, or when their aims and purposes have been brought into question the constitutions and bylaws have been withheld or destroyed. No witness can be found who will or can produce any record of these organizations. But the 'court of public opinion' of the United States has passed judgment upon them and has found them subversive and un-American."

cient consideration."[26] The report noted that in the case of the employee named "the legislation makes it difficult for him to obtain other employment." But the repealing language was knocked out on a point of order. Twice in the following year, however, the Senate vetoed House provisions directed against individuals. Thus the Senate committee followed the plea of the Secretary of the Interior and eliminated from the departmental appropriations a proviso that would have forbidden the further employment of a woman whose enthusiastic book on the Soviet arctic had made her seem useful to the publicity department of the Alaska railroad.[27] And again, in 1942 the Senate struck out a proviso in the independent offices appropriation bill aimed at the well-known educator who was to be one of the employees branded as unfit by the House subcommittee.[28] The Senate subcommittee in 1942 eliminated the hostile clause; the whole committee restored it. On the floor Senator Barkley was among the leaders of a sortie that got rid of the language.[29] In the debate much was made of the argument that barring an individual amounted to a bill of attainder.

The emerging issue of constitutionality is a double one. The ideal of legislation is generality; toward that ideal constitutional practice has struggled for centuries. Provisions aimed at particular individuals work an injury worse than the risk of personal injustice.

---

[26] 77th Cong., 1st Sess., House Report No. 1470, December 3, 1941, p. 39. On the question of "sufficient consideration," the Dies committee, in its report of January 3, 1941, had said of the Workers' Alliance that "its non-Communist element withdrew under the leadership" of the very man barred by the relief appropriation act. 77th Cong., 1st Sess., House Report No. 1.

[27] 77th Cong., 1st Sess., Senate Committee on Appropriations, *Hearings before a subcommittee on the Department of the Interior appropriation bill for 1942,* p. 89. For the House action on May 14, 1941, on Representative Taber's amendment, see *Congressional Record,* vol. 87, pp. 4072–73.

[28] The action was initiated in the House subcommittee on December 10, 1941. 77th Cong., 2nd Sess., House Committee on Appropriations, *Hearings before a subcommittee on the independent offices appropriation bill for 1943,* pp. 321–34. On the floor it was announced that "the full committee, although opposed in general to this type of amendment, adopted this morning an amendment denying funds for the payment of any salary" to the individual in question. It was added: "This seems to be the only recourse open to the committee in view of the apparent unwillingness of Mr. Fly and the Federal Communications Commission to take any action in the matter." *Congressional Record,* 77th Cong., 2nd Sess., vol. 88, pp. 552, January 22, 1942.

[29] *Congressional Record,* 77th Cong., 2nd Sess., vol. 88, p. 3997, May 6, 1942. Senator Barkley, in his argument, said: "The appointment of men to office is an executive function, not a legislative function, and the whole history of Congress, with one or two exceptions, indicates that it has frowned upon provisions of this kind which are, in fact, bills of attainder; that is what they amount to."

The tendencies they set in train handicap the realization of the noble dichotomy between an area of interests, agitation, compromise, and finally broad statements of prime policy—the distinctive concerns of legislative bodies—and the area of application, both administrative and adjudicative. It is a poor though understandable defense of trespassing legislatures to say that the methods of administrative recruiting are often haphazard or partial. To be effective, the application of policy must be relieved from distorting pressures and at the same time be flexible.

From the standpoint of both flexibility and integrity, is it not possible that protective corollaries will be drawn from the still nearly latent concept of constitutionally vested "executive power" as a field of administrative responsibility which "legislative power" cannot invade?[30] Legislative supremacy in determining major policy does not require that the dicta of Kendall v. U.S.[31] shall burgeon without limit. But the accommodation of legislative and executive relations to administration is not a matter in the main to be imposed and enforced by judicial decisions. Like the essence of constitutional government itself, such accommodation grows from mutual awareness and self-restraint.

In this connection, careful attention must be given to the far-reaching claims that are made for control incidentally to the appropriating process. The introducer of the amendment which in February 1943 sought at a stroke to bar nearly forty persons from being paid out of the funds carried by the bill said quite significantly: "Any other measure that we may pass could be considered by the courts as an infringement upon the powers and prerogatives of the executive branch but an appropriation bill originates in the House of Representatives, and the House is entitled to put any limitation that they so desire on these appropriations."[32] When a point of order was made against the proposed amendment, the chairman of the committee of the whole ruled that "the amendment simply limits the appropriation," and that "If Congress has the right to appropriate, Congress, by the same token, has the right to limit the appropriation."[33]

---

[30] It would be necessary to project an incipient doctrine considerably beyond such cases as Springer v. Philippine Islands, 277 U.S. 189 (1928), and People v. Tremaine, 252 N.Y. 27 (1929).

[31] 12 Peters 524 (1838).

[32] *Congressional Record*, 78th Cong., 1st Sess., vol. 89, p. 660 (daily edition), February 4, 1943.

[33] *Ibid.*, p. 682 (daily edition), February 5, 1943.

Claims like the foregoing give added point to a study of the supervisory role of the committees on appropriations. Through them is accomplished most of the oversight that Congress exercises over administration. In them the pressure for intervention finds its natural focus.

II

The committee structure of Congress reflects the distinction between authorization and appropriation—between the passage of acts which define purposes, convey power, and authorize appropriations, on the one hand, and the year by year provision of money, on the other. The standing committee system has two elements: the legislative committees and the appropriating committees.[34] The separation of authorization and appropriation has the advantage, among others, that it accommodates itself to the technique of planning, for programs may be laid out broadly, to be implemented annually at a tempo suited to conditions.

The separation of authorization and appropriation, with the requirement that the former must precede the latter, is subject to some friction and irregularity. The risk of friction is inherent in the existence of two partly parallel sets of committees. Much irregularity attends the fact that the whole distinction rests on provisions in the rules of the chambers, enforced by points of order.[35] Through inattention or comity, points of order that would be sustained are often not made.[36] Sometimes a special rule is adopted at the request

---

[34] A third element exists in rudimentary form in the committees on expenditures in the executive departments, to the failures of which as organs of oversight attention will be given in a later [section of this chapter].

[35] House of Representatives, Rule XXI, 2, states: "No appropriation shall be reported in any general appropriation bill, or be in order as an amendment thereto, for any expenditure not previously authorized by law, unless in continuation of appropriations for such public works and objects as are already in progress." The rule also provides: "Nor shall any provision in any such bill or amendment thereto changing existing law be in order." The last is subject to a qualifying provision—the "Holman rule"—which permits new material of a legislative character which is germane to the bill and will result in retrenchment. This sub-rule may actually invite the very kind of detail in an appropriation bill which interferes with the flexibility of administration.

[36] In wartime, especially, appropriations are sometimes allowed to run ahead of authorizations. "I would have no objection," said the chairman of the House Committee on Naval Affairs in January 1941, "to allowing the Appropriations Committee, since we have acted on the matter, to incorporate it in their bill in the House, and have the legislative authority passed later." 77th Cong., 1st Sess., House Committee on Naval Affairs, *Hearings on H. R. 1437*, p. 30.

of the Committee on Appropriations which gives blanket protection against points of order. Much authorization is implied rather than express, furthermore, and in many situations there is a wide range for the judgment of presiding officers in applying the rules when points of order are made.

The problem of the adjustment of responsibilities between the standing legislative and appropriating committees was increased in both houses after 1921 by the attempt to centralize jurisdiction over appropriations. In the House the select committee on the budget recommended a single committee of thirty-five members. "Without the adoption of this resolution," it was said in the report, "true budgetary reform is impossible."[37] Changes in the rules of both House and Senate within a few years corrected the effects of the centrifugal forces which, especially strong in the case of the House between 1877 and 1885, had scattered jurisdiction over many of the regular appropriation bills in the hands of the legislative committees. When the Senate reorganized its Committee on Appropriations in 1922 it compromised with the spirit of the old arrangement to the extent of allowing the chairman and ranking members of certain legislative committees to participate in appropriations subcommittees, when funds for agencies within their jurisdiction were being considered. This liaison has been retained and extended. It is logical in the face of the double committee system. For the observer, the absence of any positively favorable comment suggests that at the best it can be concluded that the device has done no harm.

What has been said raises questions about committee jurisdictions which are beyond the scope of the present inquiry. A bare indication of viewpoint will suffice. If the committees of Congress are conceived of as existing primarily for the oversight of management, there should not be a dual system of standing legislative committees and appropriating committees with their subgroups. Instead, as W. F. Willoughby has long advocated,[38] the whole committee structure should be recast so that there will be as close correspondence as possible between the scope of the standing committees and the administrative departments. To the present writer this view seems

---

[37] 66th Cong., 1st Sess., House Report No. 373, October 11, 1919.

[38] See, for example, his *Principles of Legislative Organization and Administration* (Washington, 1934), pp. 358–59. But note his underlying assumption: "As has been repeatedly emphasized, much the most important continuing task of our legislatures is that of acting as a board of directors of the government corporation."

profoundly misconceived. The emphasis in committee reorganization, so far as it is possible at all, should be to enable the legislature
to handle prime policy, not the supervision of management. As
things stand, legislative attention is splintered. The revised pattern
of a standing committee system should rest upon the identification
of the broad zones of public policy within which a comprehensive
consideration of measures would be possible. Each zone would cut
across the jurisdiction of many administrative agencies; this fact
would be an advantage, for it would be more likely to result legislatively in a detached and synthesizing viewpoint. It would be in
the appropriations committees that close correspondence between
administrative and legislative divisions would fittingly develop.

The appropriations committees of House and Senate work separately. House members, especially, shy away from formalized joint
action; experience, they say, shows that it is likely to subordinate
them to the Senators. Custom concedes to the House the right to
initiate the appropriation bills. The Senate committee is smaller
than that in the House; its members serve upon many subcommittees; the staff has less responsibility. In a sense, the Senate Committee on Appropriations sits in an appellate capacity. It circularizes
the departments to find out if they have particular items to present
in its hearings. Often the agencies choose to take their small cuts
at the hands of the House and let well enough alone. But administrators value the opportunity for appeal that the Senate committee
affords. The House members, for their part, regard the Senate
group as undisciplined and irresponsible. Institutionally, the weight
rests heavily on the side of the House. This explains why (despite
a few outstanding bits of wartime supervision attempted by the
Senate committee) the emphasis in the pages that follow is so generally on the methods of the House Committee on Appropriations.

III

The realities of the appropriations committees are in subcommittees,[39] in the chief clerk, and in the clerks assigned to the subcom-

---

[39] The House Appropriations Committee has eleven subcommittees: Deficiencies (11 members); Interior (7); Agriculture (7); Independent Offices
(7); Treasury and Post Office (7); State, Commerce, and Justice (7); War
(7); Navy (7); Labor-Federal Security (7); Legislative and Judiciary (5); and
District of Columbia (7). The Senate Appropriations subcommittees, ten in
number, duplicate the foregoing except for one subcommittee for the Departments of State, Commerce, Justice, and Labor-Federal Security.

mittees. The ideal of a concerted consideration of expenditures has not been attained. The committee as a whole sometimes considers what are called questions of policy common to all appropriation bills, as in recent stipulations about promotions and about subversive affiliations inserted in identic language in all bills. But on the appropriation bills themselves, the main committee can hardly be said to act. Bills typically come before the committee an hour or so before they are to be brought on the floor in charge of a subcommittee chairman and his associates. The printed bill and the committee report are ready. Indeed, the report (though still without a number) has been given out bearing the notice that it is "subject to release when consideration of the bill which it accompanies has been completed by the whole committee" and with the request that, before it is released, there be a check "in order to be advised of any changes." Alterations in the full committee are rare. Nevertheless, in addition to the continuity of its small and well-knit staff, the committee is united by a body of procedures and an atmosphere, by the influence of the chairman, and by the constant direct association of the subcommittee chairmen in the subcommittee on deficiencies.

It used to be said that there was an "appropriations type": hardworking, hard-bitten. Certainly the committee is a place for men who like long hours and a sense of power. In recent years some members of the House have deplored an alleged laxness in the making of committee assignments, reflected (they say) in members of weaker fiber on the appropriations group. The inundation on the Democratic side after 1930 did indeed bring on the committee relatively untried material of uncertain quality. The charges of committee deterioration must be viewed in the light of changing views of general fiscal policy, which the committee inevitably reflects. But the dour tradition still lives.

Since the actualities of the House committee's work lie so largely in its eleven subcommittees, great importance attaches to the assignments of committee members among these groups. The value of the standing committee device is the combination it affords of some specialization in subject matter with a degree of detachment not likely to be found among administrators. But how much emphasis should be placed upon detachment in the choice of the subcommittees that will deal with particular subjects and departments? The selection is made by the chairman of the whole committee, conditioned by the total play of forces in the House. Committee chairmen have followed two courses. Chairmen such as Martin B. Madden (1921–28) and James P. Buchanan (1933–37) asserted the belief that members should not go on subcommittees touching matters in which conditions in their districts gave them an especially vital interest. Edward T. Taylor, chairman from 1937 until his death in 1941 at the age of 83, avowed as well as practiced a more indulgent view.[40]

Whatever the chairman's view, experience shows that the gravitation of special preoccupations can be delayed but hardly resisted. Given time, men will achieve the subcommittee they especially desire and, once on it, they rise by seniority and may thus achieve the chairmanship. Nor is it always necessary to wait long. An incident from the past is still revealing. A few years ago a new western member of the Appropriations Committee, when asked his preference as to a subcommittee, said that he wished to serve on the subcommittee on the Interior Department bill. I thought so, said the chairman, in effect, but you can't have it; you'll be after money for that dam. The member's second choice was Agriculture. I thought so, said the chairman; you have all those forest reservations on your mind. He said that he would give the member—a former judge—a chance to use his judicial talents on the District of Columbia subcommittee.[41] But the member said he had not come to Congress to be judicial. He said flatly he might be appointed to, but would not serve on, the District of Columbia subcommittee and he won his point; for he soon was a member of both the Interior and Agriculture subcommittees.

The problem of contact and bias is a complicated one. Was it undesirable that all of the House subcommittee on agricultural appropriations in 1941 should come from essentially agricultural

---

[40] Mr. Taylor, who represented a Colorado district, said in 1938 that he intended to remain a member of the subcommittee on appropriations for the Department of the Interior and that he would be present at least when the subcommittee was "marking up" the bill, "because this Department and the matters that come before this subcommittee are tremendously vital to all of the arid states of the West and especially to Colorado." 75th Cong., 3rd Sess., House Committee on Appropriations, *Hearings before a subcommittee on the Interior Department appropriation bill for 1939*, p. 1.

[41] Long the purgatory of new members on the Appropriations Committee, the District of Columbia subcommittee is now recruited on a virtually volunteer basis. Its tasks may be lightened by allowing the District government greater responsibility in the preparation of its own budget.

constituencies, fairly well distributed sectionally? On the Interior subcommittee all the members could be called western, except one on the majority and two on the minority sides. Did this sacrifice detachment to knowledge? A little knowledge may be a dangerous thing. Ross Collins, former Representative from Mississippi, popularizer of the idea of mechanized armies, has remarked that, in the face of the changing technology of war, military service in early life followed by long participation in the National Guard does not fit a member of Congress for incisive and imaginative criticism of military routines.

In seeking detachment, repulsion may be as risky as attraction. Distorted viewpoints may come from a little contact in one's district with a problem that is still largely foreign. The recent chairman of the subcommittee on Labor-Federal Security, Malcolm C. Tarver of Georgia—one of the most industrious and generally effective subcommittee heads—has a little manufacturing in his district. Some of Mr. Tarver's prepossessions were perhaps shadowed in his remark in recent hearings before the subcommittee on agriculture, of which he was a ranking member and has since become chairman.[42] "I am not one of those," he said, "who supported the passage of the wages and hours law for workers in industry nor am I in agreement with statements which have been made concerning alleged benefits received by workers in industry through the passage of that and similar legislation."[43]

The stake of a member of a naval appropriations group in a navy yard in his district is obvious, whether it matters to him or

---

[42] Mr. Tarver resigned the chairmanship of the Labor-Federal Security subcommittee in order to succeed Clarence Cannon as head of the Agriculture subcommittee, when Mr. Cannon became the general chairman late in 1941. Incidentally, those who have thought of the latter as a fruit-grower have been intrigued by the proviso regularly carried in the agricultural appropriation act against the conduct of investigations into the allegedly deleterious effect of sprays.

[43] 77th Cong., 1st Sess., House Committee on Appropriations, *Hearings before a subcommittee on the Department of Agriculture appropriation bill for 1942,* p. 23, January 7, 1941. An innocent enough bit of committee benevolence, and additionally understandable when one considers that an outstanding industry in the subcommittee chairman's Georgia district is said to be a bedspread mill, was reflected in the 1940 report on the Labor Department appropriation: "The only change effected by the committee other than the elimination of sums for administrative promotions was to add $3,000 to the Budget estimate in order that a survey might be made of the candlewick-bedspread industry in the South." 76th Cong., 3rd Sess., House Report No. 1822, p. 13.

not. Many stakes are smaller, hardly to be seen, and difficult to provide against. Yet it may be necessary for the departmental budget officer, surveying the battlefield on which the bureau cohorts must defend their requests, to know that a particular committee member's district is touched by the rivalry between Remington-Rand and International Business Machines or to take account of the location in another member's district of a plant that makes patented safety locks. In the vast range and polyglot character of most of the appropriation acts and consequent jurisdictions of the subcommittees, most biases are relatively insignificant. Yet members may be all the more attentive to them because the appropriation bills as wholes are so overwhelming and baffling.

In the case of at least two subcommittees—Interior and Naval Appropriations—it has been customary to assign individual members to the scrutiny of items for particular administrative units. This practice risks the further splintering of the main committee, with attendant hazards of individual predilection. It used to be considered undesirable from a practical standpoint, because in the end the chairman of the subcommittee must be prepared to handle the bill as a whole on the floor. Recently there have been instances where each subcommittee member has presented and defended his part of the bill.[44] In general, individual fixed assignments do not seem desirable. But one subcommittee chairman who makes them says that unless members are given something to do they become bored.

Whatever group specialization is afforded by the subcommittee is undermined by the presently increasing importance of the subcommittee on deficiencies. At one time or another through the year it covers the whole range of the government. This subcommittee is normally presided over by the chairman of the main committee and consists of the heads of the other subcommittees, with several ranking minority members.[45] With the rush of defense and war, the tail has come to wag the dog, so mammoth and constant has become the flow of deficiency and especially supplemental appropriation

---

[44] The subcommittee on agricultural appropriations was congratulated in 1942 for dividing the task of defense of the bill on the floor among its members. This step, it was said, "should have been done long ago . . . and will add to the interest in the debate." *Congressional Record*, 77th Cong., 2nd Sess., vol 88, p. 1886, March 3, 1942.

[45] In 1941, however, two chairmen of subcommittees declined to serve, preferring to be members of another group in addition to the one over which they presided.

bills handled by the deficiencies subcommittee.[46] The scheme of the deficiencies subcommittee is indeed illogical. The strain of divided jurisdictions in 1941 was lessened somewhat by allowing the members of the subcommittees on Navy and War Departments appropriations to sit at appropriate times with the deficiencies group.

It is not Congress, not the House or Senate, not even the appropriations committee as a whole that should be thought of as abstractions, set against administration. The reality is a handful of men from particular states or districts, working with a particular committee clerk on a multitude of details.

IV

The importance of the staff of the appropriations committees can hardly be exaggerated. The modesty of its scale has been truly amazing. Yet here has been the only point (the other exception being the Joint Committee on Internal Revenue Taxation) at which Congress has for many years provided an expert, stable personnel for committee work.[47]

In the case of appropriations, the smallness of the staff has been offset by its continuity and experience. The House committee has had only three clerks since its establishment in 1865: Robert J. Stevens (1865–1884), James C. Courts (1884–1916), and Marcellus C. Sheild. At the time of Mr. Sheild's appointment in 1916 as head of the committee's staff (though with the unpretentious title of "clerk") he had already been an assistant clerk for eight years. He had entered on the duties at the age of twenty-three after two years of college and a little training in law school. One can hardly state too strongly the respect in which Mr. Sheild is held not only in Congressional circles but also throughout the government.

---

[46] In the calendar year 1941 Congress passed nine deficiency and supplemental appropriation acts; in 1942, eight—in all, seventeen in the life of the 77th Congress.

[47] Of the situation in the states it is said: "New York is probably unique in providing its appropriation committees with expense funds, with stenographic assistance, and in furthering committee operations. Even this state, however, with a daily cost of government of over one million dollars, does not provide its committees with sufficient funds to provide staffs to check and to study estimates." Jacob W. Sundelson, *Budgetary Methods in National and State Governments* (State of New York Special Report of the State Tax Commission, No. 14, 1938), p. 453.

In addition to Marcellus Sheild, the House committee has been served in recent years by six or seven assistant clerks.[48] Counting Mr. Sheild, those who are assigned regularly to the subcommittees have averaged slightly more than twenty years of continuous work for the committee. Despite the tremendous growth of governmental operations in recent years, this staff has grown hardly at all. In nine years down to 1941, only one assistant clerk and a page were added.[49] The servicing of the subcommittees is parcelled among six of the senior members, including the clerk himself. Mr. Sheild has been serving the groups on deficiencies and on Legislative-Judiciary. The subcommittee on Agriculture has been assisted by Arthur Orr, who had one year of college and one year of law training, nine years of business experience, and who had been a statistical agent in the Bureau of Fisheries for five years before coming to the Committee on Appropriations in 1920. Robert P. Williams has been put on the District of Columbia subcommittee. William A. Duvall has been assigned to the Interior and Independent Offices subcommittees. Prior to his appointment as assistant clerk in 1927, he had been a clerk in a senator's office, and assistant clerk and clerk of the Senate Military Affairs Committee for a decade. John C. Pugh, twenty-one years with the committee, has assisted the two subcommittees on appropriations for the defense departments.[50] Before that he was

[48] The appropriation act for the legislative branch in the fiscal year 1943 (77th Cong., 2nd Sess., Public Law 600) made provision specifically for a clerk at $8,000; for six assistant clerks (one at $7,500, one at $4,900, two at $4,500, one at $4,200, and one at $3,900); for a messenger; and for "additional clerical assistance at rates to be fixed by the chairman of the Committee on Appropriations," $15,960; for four clerk-stenographers at $1,800, assigned to certain subcommittees and appointed by their chairmen with the approval of the chairman of the main committee. The 1944 estimates asked for no change. The investigative staffing provided in 1943 under H. Res. 69 is in addition to the regular committee personnel. See *supra*, p. 165.

[49] The House committee report in 1938 on appropriations for the legislative branch spoke of the fact that "the enormous increase in governmental activities and units during the past several years has placed a considerable burden on the subcommittees." It referred to "a constant stream of letters and callers seeking information on matters of appropriation and administration." The very terms in which the problem was stated were emblems of the tradition. 75th Cong., 3rd Sess., House Report No. 2128, April 11, 1938.

[50] The usually caustic Mr. Ditter, ranking minority member of the subcommittee on naval appropriations, remarked to the House on March 4, 1943: "Some of you may feel that it is your intellectual approach to the problems of legislating and appropriating which ultimately brings order out of chaos. May I say in a humble way, after long years of service, that were it not for the work of one John Pugh, than whom there is no better clerk on the hill, I can hardly imagine what an appropriation bill for either the Army or the Navy

a civil service employee on the "budget desk" in the Navy Department. Jack K. McFall, who worked regularly for the subcommittees on the State, Commerce, Justice, and Judiciary, and the Labor-Federal Security appropriations until his resignation to enter naval service in 1941, was an assistant secretary to a senator prior to his appointment to the appropriations staff in 1928. In addition to the degree of "bachelor of foreign service" he had also taken a law degree. His place has been filled in part by C. D. Orescan, college trained, employed for a time in the regular departments, and more recently budget officer of the OWI. Meanwhile the substitute assistant clerk, George Harvey, has advanced to a regular assignment to the subcommittees, on the Treasury and Post Office and Labor-Federal Security appropriations. He originally came to the appropriations staff from Clarence Cannon's office.

In the Senate committee continuity of staff has been nearly as marked as in the House. Six different clerks have served the committee in the span of seventy-five years, but Thomas P. Cleaves was in office from 1873 to 1910, Kennedy F. Rea from 1910 to 1913 and again from 1913 until 1939, when he was replaced by the veteran assistant clerk, E. H. Smith. Thus the combined service of two clerks covered sixty-six years. More than in the House, the clerk of the Senate committee himself, rather than the assistants (who are younger than in the case of the lower chamber), directly serves all the subcommittees.[51] But, it should be remembered, the Senate's relation to the appropriating process is more appellate, less continuous, less exhaustively detailed, and in a sense less responsible from a fiscal point of view than is that of the House.

It is the clerk assigned to a subcommitte who takes the proof of the budget (for hearings may begin on some of the bills before its formal presentation) and draws off its material on the wide-margined committee print of the bill, with the supporting material of the estimates run small below each textual item. It is the clerk who

---

would look like." *Congressional Record,* 78th Cong., 1st Sess., vol. 89, p. 1577 (daily edition). It may be said generally that a word of tribute to the assistant clerk from both sides of the aisle is now a customary feature of the opening of debate on a regular appropriation bill. See also the floor "celebration" of the twenty-fifth anniversary of the association with the Committee on Appropriations of James F. Scanlon ("Uncle Jim") who edits the hearings. *Ibid.,* p. 1040 (daily edition), February 16, 1943.

[51] The appropriation act for 1943 provides for a clerk at $8,000 and seven assistant clerks (one at $4,800, one at $3,900, three at $3,000, and two at $2,200).

prepares many of the questions to be put at the hearings. Sometimes a dependent chairman follows down his list, virtually reading the questions to the departmental representatives. Perhaps the technical question arises whether a given item contains "legislative" matter ordinarily inadmissible in an appropriation bill. "I will ask the clerk to look into that matter." Or, from another chairman: "I am wondering if it is agreeable to postpone the hearing until tomorrow, as Mr. Sheild and I want an opportunity to go over some of these items." It is the subcommittee clerk who works with the chairman in preparing for the crucial process of "marking up the bill" in executive session. He is a consultant in this process; he must keep track of and embody the changes. Then, under very great pressure, he may be almost wholly responsible for writing the report that will accompany the bill—a document with probably growing importance in legislative oversight of administration, as will be illustrated later. The clerk's judgment shapes what goes into the printed hearings.[52] Through all this it is at once the strength and weakness of the committee aides that they remain "clerks," even "assistant clerks."[53] Some of the staff's relative self-effacement may reflect personal limitations and the protective convenience of routine. Some of it, as will be said again (for the point is crucial), reflects Marcellus Sheild's awareness of the ticklish problem of duplicating leadership under separation of powers. Meanwhile the staff's esprit de corps and cheerful procedural competence has perhaps offset and even delayed the movement for increased staffing around the focus of appropriations.

It is not that the idea of heavier staffing has lacked advocates.[54]

---

[52] A departmental budget officer, after telling of the tables and exhibits at hand, added: "We will work that out with the Clerk and see what his judgment is. He would know what the committee would want." 77th Cong., 2nd Sess., House Committee on Appropriations, *Hearings before a subcommittee on agricultural appropriation bill for 1943*, p. 149.

[53] In the debate on the State, Commerce, Justice, and Judiciary appropriation bill for 1942, a member of the subcommittee in charge said: "Why would it not be in order for the gentleman or the rest of us in this committee to suggest to the legislative subcommittee of the Committee on Appropriations that we change the title of clerks of the Appropriations Committee to advisers, or counselors, or some similar name?" *Congressional Record,* 77th Cong., 1st Sess., vol. 87, p. 2931, April 2, 1941.

[54] Speaking in the House on October 4, 1940, a minority member of the Committee on Appropriations echoed a suggestion by Representative Woodrum, the ranking majority member: "I believe that the greatest recommendation to the Appropriations Committee was made by the gentleman from Virginia [Mr. Woodrum] that each subdivision of the Appropriations Committee should have a

Sporadic suggestions have been voiced, probably increasingly. "I think we all agree," said a minority member recently, "that we are rather inartfully going through these items without the advice of specialized counsel on these various projects and the only counsel is from the departments which are getting the funds."[55] He added: "We have to get such suggestions as we can from the clerk of the committee, and dig it out as best we can, because we are not specialists in these fields." Members of Congress often deplore, as did the late Senator Adams, that "we provide endless equipment for the executive and administrative agencies to take care of themselves; but we are not provided with the machinery to do those things that we ought to do."[56]

Not all committee members who have expressed discontent with existing methods of getting information have favored an increased permanent staff for the appropriations committees. The new chairman of the House Committee on Appropriations, Clarence Cannon, has been skeptical about fixed committee assistants. "The committee," he remarked while chairman of the subcommittee on agriculture, "is at a great disadvantage in hearing the witnesses who appear before us."[57] But Mr. Cannon has feared that permanent members of an increased committee staff might become too intimate with the departments to which they are assigned. This viewpoint, as has been noted, was reflected in the flexible scheme of assistance for the House Appropriations Committee adopted early in 1943.[58]

The really momentous issue is the extent of the staffing under

<hr />

man, to be paid $10,000 a year, to keep the Appropriations Committee informed of just what was going on." *Congressional Record,* 76th Cong., 3rd Sess., vol. 86, p. 13239.

[55] Frank B. Keefe of Wisconsin, in hearings on the Treasury and Post Office appropriation bill for 1942. Subsequently, in debate on the floor, he expanded on his views, exclaiming: "We have no expert auditors to challenge the testimony of the people who come before the committee."

[56] 77th Cong., 1st Sess., Senate Committee on Appropriations, *Hearings before a subcommittee on the legislative branch appropriation bill for 1942,* p. 12.

[57] 77th Cong., 1st Sess., House Committee on Appropriations, *Hearing before a subcommittee on the agricultural appropriation bill for 1942,* February 1941, p. 519. Mr. Cannon continued: "We are busy men. We come from offices crowded with work. We go back to our offices crowded with work. All we know is what they tell us. And it goes without saying that all the testimony adduced here by those seeking appropriations is consciously or unconsciously biased by personal interest. Much of it on even cursory examination is of doubtful value." Mr. Cannon's comment was elicited by the Farm Bureau Federation criticism of the department's field organization.

[58] See *supra,* p. 165.

the Committee on Appropriations which would be consistent with good budgetary relations and an integrated responsibility in administration generally. Staffing might easily be pushed to a point where it would bring a legislative budget method into existence in rivalry with the executive budget. An ambiguous responsibility might develop in the departments. There is need for the most careful consideration, not glib endorsement of the idea of staff and more staff.

V

There is another reason for caution in staffing in addition to the risk of doubling the lines of authority within administration. The peculiar virtue of the lay element in legislative thinking may be sacrificed. The legislator is immediately in touch with his constituents and this gives him an awareness of government from the side of the public. In wielding oversight of administration, it is his duty to bring this practical public sense to bear. How far must this be personal and immediate, not vicarious? In addition, and quite as important, is the criticism which a robust, imaginative lay mind can bring to bear on technical operations. Something of the value of the mingling of special and non-special minds might be lost if the politician-legislator dealt with administration only through an intermediate legislative bureaucracy.

This viewpoint is sometimes heard in Congress. Often it merely echoes the general distrust of experts, which is an extension of distrust of government itself.[59] But sometimes it is more soundly rationalized in terms of the inherent duties of the legislator as an individual. When this is the case, and the member of Congress acts on his own precepts, he is usually a person of outstanding energy, curiosity, more than a trace of self-dramatization, and at least the possibility of danger. In recent years Albert Engel of Michigan has been a conspicuous example. In 1939 he found himself on the subcommittee newly charged with responsibility for both Labor and Federal Security. Confronting the ramified social security operations still novel to nearly everyone, Mr. Engel undertook to inform himself about all the agencies covered by the bill. He went to some of

---

[59] Representative Lambertson, Republican, of Kansas: "I am fearful of these scientific investigations. The brain trust has cost us money every time it went into action. In my opinion, it will take some farmers from county seats to do it." *Congressional Record,* 77th Cong., 1st Sess., vol. 87, p. 932, February 12, 1941.

the units in the Department of Labor. A veteran official in this department said at the time that Mr. Engel was the first member of Congress who had made such a visitation, in such a manner and mood, in the course of nearly three decades. It was in the Federal Security Agency that Mr. Engel made his more extended and intensive visits. The administrators who accompanied him say they learned a good deal. Mr. Engel insisted on knowing what was being done in each room; he pulled half-written letters from typewriters; on occasion he was caustic. But he emerged as a defender of the relative efficiency of the Social Security Board, particularly in the mass operations of the old age insurance system. In 1940 Mr. Engel shifted his attention to defense matters and especially camp construction, this time by solitary inspection in his own car.

Mr. Engel's feats of visitation have been an extreme case. Few men have his type of kinetics. Nor is such first-hand contact without risks: for a man who lacked Mr. Engel's saving sympathy for governmental responsibility and the administrative processes, zeal might be a nuisance. Besides, even with the best of will and unusual gifts for observation and understanding, the individual is limited; his personal contacts are spasmodic and sporadic. Such contacts provide a background; they do not supply continuous and effective analysis. Nevertheless, if legislative oversight is to have the freshening influence that is assumed to be one of its virtues, individual members of committees must enjoy considerable first-hand observation of the procedures for which they are appropriating money.

Travel by committee members and clerks brings some information to the aid of the committees on appropriations. Such travel is made possible by items usually present in the appropriation acts which permit funds to be used during the ensuing year for travel in the consideration of estimates. There is much difference of opinion about its usefulness. The reputation of junketing has not been outlived. Hard-driving members of Congress, caught in its routines or in the political perplexities of their own districts, justify their reluctance to visit the departmental field organizations by treating the trips of others as pleasure jaunts. Nearly everyone agrees that the chief obstacle is time—it is hard to get away from the incessant preoccupations of one's office and one's district, not to mention the now nearly continuous sessions of the chambers.

Outstanding illustrations of subcommittee field inspection have been afforded by the group handling appropriations for the departments of State, Commerce and Justice and for the Judiciary. In 1939

a number of members of the subcommittee and the clerk assigned
to it visited embassies and legations in Europe, primarily to inspect
the quarters, interview the personnel, and gain a background on
the housekeeping aspects of the foreign service. A report was printed
in the hearings. It was noted in the following year that "with one
exception all of the recommendations made by the committee have
either been carried out in their entirety or are in course of attainment."[60] Again, between August and October 1941, five of the nine
members of the subcommittee, accompanied by the clerk as secretary, visited the missions in Central and South America. The
observations and findings of the group, with some specific recommendations, were embodied in a printed report of more than forty
pages, prepared by the clerk and published on December 4, 1941
for the use of the Committee on Appropriations.[61]

Another recent illustration of field visitation may be drawn from
the work of the same subcommittee. In reporting in 1941 on appropriations for the Bureau of Prisons, the committee remarked that
"during the past two or three years practically every institution of
the Bureau—numbering 29—has been visited by one or more members of the subcommittee or by the subcommittee clerk."[62] The
committee was perhaps justified in a self-righteous comment. "It is
surprising," stated the report, "to note that in only one instance was
it disclosed that a judge had visited a Federal penal institution
and in that case it developed that he was a personal friend of the
warden."

Few other subcommittees have been so active in travel. But
abstractly, at least, most chairmen would probably agree with the

---

[60] 77th Cong., 1st Sess., House Report No. 360, p. 4.

[61] *Official Trip of Examination of Federal Activities in South and Central
America. Report of a subcommittee of the Committee on Appropriations, House
of Representatives,* 77th Cong., 1st Sess. For the follow-up, see 77th Cong., 2nd
Sess., House Committee on Appropriations, *Hearing before a subcommittee on
the State Department appropriations for 1943,* pp. 15–17, 417–47. The committee relied heavily on the method of interviewing individually all the personnel
in the United States foreign service at each point of thirty points of call. The
report remarked: "As far as the committee has been able to ascertain this trip
was the first ever taken to either South or Central America by a committee of
Congress visiting the Latin-American countries as an official congressional committee."

[62] 77th Cong., 1st Sess., House Report No. 360, p. 43. See also comment in
1942 on personal visits to observe the probation system. 77th Cong., 2nd Sess.,
House Committee on Appropriations, *Hearings before a subcommittee on judiciary appropriations for 1943,* p. 87.

head of the subcommittee on naval appropriations when he said in a 1943 hearing: "I can learn more in a few hours of physical application than I can by sitting around this table for several days."[63] Needless to say, the department in question can make travel easy and impressive.

VI

The committees on appropriations have been identified as the outstanding instruments of Congressional oversight. It is timely to conclude an analysis of their influence by comment on their hearings, reports, interim contacts with administrators, and interaction with the organs of administrative supervision.

The formal Congressional hearings on the estimates begin, for some of the bills, before the session opens and before the budget has been presented.[64] Hearings on a routine major bill may run for six weeks of nearly daily sessions. Swelled on the one hand by matter prepared in advance (like the justifications) and by information worked up later at the request of committee members during the hearings (usually inserted at the point where the question appears), the printed hearings have become monumental—more than twenty thousand printed pages of material annually.[65] The bulk has not fallen off noticeably in wartime despite the amount of discussion "off the record."[66]

---

[63] 78th Cong., 1st Sess., House Committee on Appropriations, *Hearings before a subcommittee on the supplemental Naval Department appropriation bill for 1943*, p. 25.

[64] Thus the hearings on the 1944 appropriation bill for the Treasury and Post Office Departments began on December 10, 1942.

[65] In the 77th Cong., 1st Sess., 1941, the hearings on 26 appropriation bills (which included supplemental and deficiency and some special measures) aggregated 18,129 pages in the House and 4,592 in the Senate—not counting indices—in all 22,721. In 1942 the new chairman of the House Appropriations Committee complained, "The tendency of all of our subcommittees is to go very far afield in our examinations." 77th Cong., 2nd Sess., House Committee on Appropriations, *Hearings before a subcommittee on the Department of Commerce appropriation bill for 1943*, January 8, 1942, p. 2. But the 1943 hearings gave no evidence of a change.

[66] In answer to a complaint in the Senate that a supplemental defense appropriation was being considered on the basis of 62 pages of hearings in the House and before the Senate hearings had been published, Senator McKellar said, "About nine-tenths, or probably fifteen-sixteenths, of the testimony that was heard was off the records."*Congressional Record*, 77th Cong., 2nd Sess., vol.

The volume of the hearings is increased by the practice of going around the table, giving each member an opportunity to ask questions about a broad segment of the bill. This is at best a clumsy method of insuring innings for the minority members. The result is duplication and often superficiality, for points are not explored as fully as they might be if all the questions they excite were raised and answered at the same time.

The usefulness of the printed hearings is real but limited. Their great but largely unexplored value for the study of administration is another matter; these records are one of the main outcroppings of administrative methods. Some committee members say privately that the appropriations hearings are "junk." They doubt both whether the mass can be read and whether, if read, it enlightens the legislator. At the time a bill is being finally rewritten in the House committee, moreover, the printed hearings are not easy to use, for the index is not ready. The hearings are not released to the House members generally until the bill is reported; despite some grumbling, this practice is inveterate.[67] In the Senate committee, the House hearings are available for reference. The clerk, in editing the committee print of the bill (wherein he inserts under each item the Budget figure, the sum set in the House, as well as the appropriation for the previous year), gives the page citation to the House hearings.[68]

As an exact record of what is said, the printed hearings are deficient in more respects than the amount of "off the record" material, so identified. The actual proceedings are informal, often rapid;

88, p. 789, January 28, 1942. In connection with the State, Commerce, Justice, and Judiciary appropriation bill for 1942, a member of the committee said on the floor, with reference to the hearings, "More than seventy per cent of what was said in the hearings was off the record for obvious reasons." *Congressional Record,* 77th Cong., 1st Sess., vol. 87, p. 2920, April 2, 1941. Yet the subcommittee chairman pointed out that, in the course of nine weeks of hearings, more than two thousand pages of printed record had been built up. *Ibid.,* p. 2908.

[67] See the defense by Clarence Cannon, who said that the refusal to release appropriations hearings until the bill had been reported has existed "for fifty years." *Congressional Record,* 77th Cong., 1st Sess., vol. 87, p. 7916, October 8, 1941.

[68] In a hearing before a Senate subcommittee, however, when a departmental witness said, "I doubt very much whether I can add anything to the hearings on the House side," the chairman remarked, "We have the House hearings, but I imagine most of us have not read them." 77th Cong., 1st Sess., Senate Committee on Appropriations, *Hearings before a subcommittee on emergency cargo ship construction* (H.J. Res. 77), January 29, 1941.

several persons may be talking at once and even the efficient stenographer cannot get all of the remarks. The transcript is submitted to the participants for editing. The effect is usually to clarify the statements and to add to their informational value. But the practice may wipe out some of the color or blur inadvertent admissions.

In editing the transcript, administrators must make close judgments in keeping within the spirit of the custom. Especially they must avoid changing the wording of questions. In commenting on the practice of the Senate Committee on Appropriations in submitting the transcript to the agency spokesmen, Senator Truman said, "The reason that is done is to be sure that the facts are correct and the record shows what is said." Malcolm Kerlin, reflecting caution learned in twelve years as virtual manager of the Department of Commerce, said that the rule of his associates was never to "change the testimony so far as the facts are concerned," adding, "If there is anything to be considered in that connection we always come up and talk with the committee chairman. . . ."[69]

Occasionally administrators are rebuked for the liberties they take with the transcript of their remarks. Thus Senator Adams broke in on a hearing in 1941 to say:[70]

> Gentlemen, for the second time we have had an unfortunate experience in connection with the record of proceedings. It is our custom, as you gentlemen know, to have the stenographic records submitted to witnesses, where convenient, so that they may make corrections. The purpose of the record is that we may have printed for our use and the use of members not present a correct transcript of what took place before the committee. Their testimony is submitted to the witnesses in order that they may correct it to show just what took place before the committee—not for the purpose of editing or revision. Unfortunately, the record of our previous meeting has been so

---

[69] 77th Cong., 2nd Sess., Senate Committee on Appropriations, *Hearing before a subcommittee on the State, Justice, Commerce, and Judiciary appropriation bill for 1943*, p. 131.

[70] 77th Cong., 1st Sess., Senate Committee on Appropriations, *Hearing before a subcommittee on additional appropriations for the TVA*, pp. 39–40. The occasional exercise of discipline may be illustrated further by noting the insistence of a subcommittee chairman in 1937 that the hearings of that year should set forth in full some testimony about visas for visiting lecturers with allegedly radical views—testimony which had been deleted from the printed version of hearings in the previous year. 75th Cong., 3rd Sess., House Committee on Appropriations, *Hearings before a subcommittee on the Labor Department appropriation bill for 1939*, p. 273, December 10, 1937.

extensively edited and revised, I had to send word to print it
as it came from the stenographer.

Defense and then war brought additional grounds for conceding
leeway to administrators in striking out confidential material. Thus
a subcommittee chairman said to the head of the Public Health
Service in 1941, after a discussion that impinged on the work of
the medical corps of the Army: "Doctor, when your remarks
come back to you, you may feel perfectly free to eliminate anything you think might best be left out, and, in some cases, if the
situation justifies, you can elaborate on what you have said."[71] But
there was possible portent in a statement by a minority member to
the Secretary of the Navy in a hearing on appropriations early in
1943: "We are going to ask—at least some of us are—that the resort
which has been had in times past by some witnesses to a privilege
of deleting the record at their own discretion will have our supervisory action."[72]

The limitations of hearings on appropriations as a method of
getting at the facts are admitted by Congressmen who participate
in the process. Some of the members who are outspoken about the
restricted usefulness of impromptu cross-examination have been lawyers with trial experience and successful prosecuting attorneys. Often
a broad answer blunts a leading question that is not pressed home.
"General," asked former Representative Ross Collins of the Chief
of Staff, "have you made any study of the elimination of branches in
the Army?" The answer was, "Yes, sir"; and with that the matter
was dropped. The interrogation shifted to the average age of en-
listed men.[73] Sometimes committee members reveal a kind of defeat-
ism, for they neither fully trust the professional administrator nor
know how to challenge him. Thus in the hearings in 1941 on some
supplemental national defense items, Senator Adams said to the
witness: "Of course, I know that you regard those fields as essential
and it would be a perfectly foolish question to ask if you did not
think so, but I still have in my own mind a wonderment about it;
that is, I just have difficulty in convincing myself that we need this

[71] 77th Cong., 1st Sess., House Committee on Appropriations, *Hearings before
a subcommittee on the first deficiency appropriation bill for 1942,* p. 303.
[72] 78th Cong., 1st Sess., House Committee on Appropriations, *Hearings before
a subcommittee on the supplemental Navy Department appropriation bill for
1943,* p. 32.
[73] 77th Cong., 1st Sess., House Committee on Appropriations, *Hearings before
a subcommittee on the military establishment appropriation bill for 1942,* p. 32,
April 28, 1941.

extensive air development in Alaska." But the Senator added, before the discussion went "off the record," "I know that there is no use in asking a fellow who is advocating it whether it is sound or not."[74] There is a temptation to focus on occasional details. An item such as army saddles at $90 apiece is a tempting mark. The amount seems high; the equipment smacks of privilege; and everyone knows something about saddles.[75]

The foregoing comments do not deny the expository value of the hearings. Some of the best interchanges are sheerly explanatory. When a subcommittee has recently acquired jurisdiction over an agency, it may consciously go to school in the agency's methods.[76]

Nor do the shortcomings of the method of question and answer deny the galvanizing effect that the mere fear of embarrassing questions may have on the conduct of administration. Inept though it is, and easy though it usually is to parry questions, the annual cross-examination is an ordeal for administrators. On the whole, it is good for them. Some officials at departmental headquarters say that an experience of bureau representatives before a committee teaches more to careless heads of units than lecturing within the department on administrative proprieties. The risk, of course, is that the reflex makes for caution rather than courage. This danger could be lessened by more stress in the hearings on essential results, rather than on methods, provided legislators would make allowance for the extent to which the fruits of governmental action are long-run and indirect.

Sometimes, as with a chairman like Tarver of Georgia, the questioning is insistent. In 1942 he was asking the head of the Division of Labor Standards about safety and health work in industrial establishments. "Can you point out any particular plant, or any particular industry," he queried, "where the work you have done under this appropriation has been beneficial in character? General

---

[74] 77th Cong., 1st Sess., House Committee on Appropriations, *Hearings before a subcommittee on the first supplemental defense appropriation bill for 1942,* p. 258, August 9, 1941.

[75] 77th Cong., 1st Sess., House Committee on Appropriations, *Hearings before a subcommittee on the fifth supplemental national defense appropriation bill for 1941,* p. 99.

[76] See, for example, the protracted explanation of weather forecasting in the hearings before the subcommittee in charge of the appropriations for the Commerce Department, to which the Weather Service had recently been transferred. 77th Cong., 1st Sess., House Committee on Appropriations, *Hearings before a subcommittee on the State, Commerce, Justice, and Judiciary appropriation bill for 1942,* pp. 235–46, February 13, 1941.

statements that good has been accomplished do not weigh very much with me."[77] Nor was he satisfied with reports from the field agents themselves.

The effect that the hearings might have in forcing the heads of large units to master their affairs is weakened by permitting, even expecting, subordinates to be present and to testify on their respective bailiwicks. Yet the subcommittees resent the failure of the head of a bureau or like unit to appear.[78]

Consideration of bills in the whole Committee on Appropriations—customarily an affair of an hour or so—is virtually telescoped with the floor debate.[79] A vast majority of the measures—perhaps ninety per cent—are taken up in the House on the same day on which they are considered by the main committee. The "general debate" on appropriation bills has been customarily a vehicle of widely ranging comment, often wholly unrelated to the bill. Such

---

[77] 77th Cong., 2nd Sess., House Committee on Appropriations, *Hearings before a subcommittee on the Labor-Federal Security appropriation bill for 1943*, p. 164. The aftermath was reflected in the committee report on June 3, 1942. In speaking of a reduction of $50,000 in the appropriation for a safety and health program, the committee conceded its importance in the war effort but added: "The committee sought to secure some tangible evidence that real gains have been made and that the expenditure of the appropriation has been worth while. The representatives of the Department were unable to produce any statistical evidence on the subject which was to any degree conclusive." But $150,000 was allowed "in the hope that the departmental officials will restudy their methods and revamp their program in such fashion as to be able to present a record of accomplishment." 77th Cong., 2nd Sess., House Report No. 2200, June 3, 1942, p. 4. The effect of the foregoing could be seen in the care with which the bureau bolstered its testimony on the point in the 1943 hearings. 78th Cong., 1st Sess., House Committee on Appropriations, *Hearings before a subcommittee on the Labor-Federal Security appropriation bill for 1944*, pp. 53–66. But the committee comment was still disparaging and the appropriation was not increased.

[78] Thus, unfavorable notice was taken in 1942 of the fact that a departmental solicitor had not appeared personally for several years. A member remarked: "It is a matter of record that the Commander in Chief of the United States Fleet and the Chief of Naval Operations are glad to come up and give half a day of their time to us. They are never too busy. The Secretary of the Navy and the Secretary of War also appear before us. It would not be strange if an official could not appear one year, but if he did not appear for many years, it would be difficult to understand." 77th Cong., 2nd Sess., House Committee on Appropriations, *Hearings before a subcommittee on the Interior Department appropriation bill for 1943*, pp. 99–100.

[79] In the 77th Cong., 1st Sess., 1941, on 26 appropriation measures (carrying a total of 55 billion dollars) the House discussion occupied 1,017 pages in the *Congressional Record*, with 100 pages more on the conference reports; the Senate discussion occupied 400 pages, with 38 additional on the conference reports.

discussion, of course, may be valuable because of its irrelevancy, which serves the informing role of Congress. When, in the past, members have complained that the documents on the bill itself—the text of the measure, the report thereon, and the hearings—have not been available to the members before the beginning of the "general debate," the leaders of the House have explained (in the words of a majority leader about an appropriation bill some years ago) that "general debate on a bill of this sort means a very wide discussion upon things that do not pertain directly to the bill which is supposed to be before the House."[80] Certainly the ideal of a broad congressional consideration of major measures—to say nothing of a whole budgetary program—has not been realized. While the bills individually move in fragmentary fashion through the committee of the whole, the subcommittees are in charge; the chances favor their amendments.[81]

Under the conditions, attendance is slight. It does not follow from this one fact, of course, that the bills are not receiving consideration; for government by discussion may proceed largely through the printed word. In the debate on a recent defense appropriation measure, when a caustic minority member took note of the small number on the floor, a member of the majority rebuked him with the statement that "we should be cautious about statements that may lead the public to believe that the Congress is not at work unless they are all on the floor." He added: "Can we not study this bill, both Democrats and Republicans, in our offices, by consulting the departments, and in the library studying measures over, just as well as here?"[82] The caveat was well said; for confidence in the legislative process should not rest upon a forensic fantasy. In this instance, however, the picture of cloistered documentary research was likewise unreal. Said the minority member, resuming his taunt:

This bill did not come to the Committee on Appropriations until 11 o'clock. They did not have a chance to get the bill

---

[80] *Congressional Record,* 70th Cong., 1st Sess., vol. 69, p. 2204, January 30, 1928.

[81] On 26 appropriation bills in the 77th Cong., 1st Sess., 1941, 263 amendments were offered in the House, 25 being committee amendments; 94 were adopted, including all of the committee amendments. In the Senate, 1,067 amendments were offered, 967 being committee amendments; 1,016 were adopted, including 959 committee amendments.

[82] *Congressional Record,* 77th Cong., 1st Sess., vol. 87, p. 2474, March 21, 1941.

here on the floor until 12 o'clock. The gentleman did not get a chance to see the bill after 12 o'clock. It is now 2:35 o'clock, p.m. How much time did the members have to look at it? I will wager the gentleman never has read the bill.

From the standpoint of legislative oversight of administration, one of the most vital features of the floor action on appropriations is the way it may strengthen or qualify the directive force of the committee reports as guides to administration through the year.

VII

The reports of the committees on appropriations, especially of the House, are prime instruments of legislative control. These reports command increasing notice by administrators, while they raise problems of responsibility that deserve more analysis than they have yet received.

Each bill is accompanied to the floor by a report. This is a pamphlet which, in the case of the regular appropriation bills in the House, runs from twenty-five to fifty pages, including tables.[83] The report is the work of the subcommittee. The full Committee on Appropriations seldom alters a document which, indeed, has already been printed provisionally. More particularly, the report is the handiwork of the subcommittee chairman and of the assistant clerk regularly assigned to the group. Their respective parts in the actual preparation of a report vary with personalities and circumstances. The role of the clerk is necessarily heavy; the writing is apt to fall to him. The product must be appraised in the light of the fact that, in the exigent rhythm of appropriations, an assistant clerk (who often covers two subcommittees, each with jurisdiction over many agencies) has at the most a week of day-and-night work in which to frame the report after the subcommittee has "marked up" the bill in executive session.

In drafting the report, the departmental officers are sometimes consulted. In at least one case in recent years, the departmental budget officer sat through a week-end with the committee clerk in framing many parts of the report. Under these circumstances, naturally, the report is likely to contain remarks that later will provide fulcrums whereby the department can exercise leverage upon its

---

[83] In the 77th Cong., 1st Sess., 1941, the House reports on 26 appropriation bills totaled 726 pages; the Senate reports, 140 pages.

self-assertive parts. Such a nexus of departmental leaders and committee clerks is more than interesting. It is highly significant, for it illustrates two things: first, that the disciplinary strains in government are not a simple alignment of administration as a whole against the legislative body; second, that the pressure of the legislative body may be exerted in fortifying the central machinery within the administration itself. But reciprocal centripetalism is not simple; organs of over-all supervision like the Bureau of the Budget must be considered. Sometimes legislative pressure may strengthen the independent position of favored agencies. To the fundamental problem of the interaction of the several sources of discipline—legislative, over-all executive, and departmental—it will be necessary to return in later paragraphs.

The sanctions of the reports are extralegal. Here is an uncertain field of custom. Strictly speaking, what is said in the report does not enter into the law that must be followed by the Treasury and the General Accounting Office. But when the National Labor Relations Board once so argued, one of the oldest and most respected of departmental budget officers submitted an informal opinion that he knew of no instance where an agency had asserted the right to disregard a mandate in a report from the Appropriations Committee. The difficulty lies in determining what is a mandate. In the reports are mingled many shades of suggestions, of precise recommendations, of doubts, of warnings, of commendations, and of rebukes. It is the difficult task of administrators to construe the reports and to identify the commands and interdictions which the committee intends to have an intrinsic force, not merely advisory value.

The efficacy of committee reports is the fact that disregard of them may lead to a cut in appropriations in the following year. A follow-through is the more likely because, amid the vastness of the governmental operations as presented in the estimates, committees are repetitive; members repeat old questions and pursue old strictures. An illustration shows one type of situation. A recent committee comment on a phase of the work of the Social Security Board stated:

> The reduction in the estimate is made because of a dissatisfaction of the committee with the administrative cost of carrying on the unemployment compensation program of the various states during the past year. The committee called attention in its report last year to the great disparity that existed in the administrative costs in the various states of car-

rying out the program of providing compensation for the un-
employed. In that report the committee enjoined the Board "to
give this matter immediate consideration with a view of reducing the variables that enter into the picture." If anything has
been done in the connection, it is not readily evident. . . . The
committee expects the Board to exercise this discretion in cases
where it is evident the states are spending too much money
in administering this program. The committee again emphatically suggests that the Board devote its earnest attention to
bringing about some element of uniformity in the matter of
these administrative costs.[84]

In the Senate subcommittee hearings a year later the foregoing
language was recalled and the departmental witness was asked,
"What did you do with reference to that admonition?[85]

A warning in the report is likely to lead to a question of some
sort in the following year, perhaps a second complaint. The very
fact that the matter can come up again reveals the limited compulsion of committee verbiage. For example, the report on the
Social Security appropriations in 1941 quoted from the committee's
report for the preceding year, which criticized the standards of the
Children's Bureau regarding medical practitioners entitled to participate in services administered under federal grants-in-aid. The
committee had found itself "unable to endorse the wisdom of such
a policy of exclusion"[86] and had suggested that the bureau reconsider its requirements. But the report in the following year declared
that no consideration had thus far been given to the suggestion.
Accordingly, it was said, "the committee desires again to call attention to the matter and to request emphatically that the responsible
officials of the Department of Labor give immediate and objective
consideration to the proposal."[87]

Some of the ambiguities that attend the application of language
in committee reports were notably illustrated in several years of
wrangling over the affairs of the National Labor Relations Board.
A butt of attack in 1940 was its Division of Economic Research. In

---

[84] 77th Cong., 1st Sess., House Report No. 688, p. 33.

[85] 77th Cong., 2nd Sess., Senate Committee on Appropriations, *Hearings before
a subcommittee on the Labor-Federal Security appropriation bill for 1942*, p.
124.

[86] 77th Cong., 1st Sess., House Report No. 688, p. 11.

[87] 77th Cong., 2nd Sess., House Report No. 2200, p. 7. In 1943, despite continuing bureau protests, an express proviso on the matter in question was inserted
in the appropriation act for 1944.

the administration of the act the head of this unit was often brought to the firing line when testifying in cases; besides, in the rifts of leftward factionalism, he seems to have been under some cross fire from his own associates. The original grounds of assault on the Division in the appropriations subcommittee did not, however, purport to be personal; it was argued that the law did not authorize the Board to engage in "research" which in any case could be done by the Bureau of Labor Statistics. The committee, in its report on the Labor-Federal Security appropriation bill for 1941, reduced the Board's appropriation for the fiscal year 1941 by $337,000. The report carried a table "as a guide to the committee's general attitude." The report added, "It is felt, however, that no need exists for a Division of Economic Research and it is expected that this section will be entirely eliminated."[88] The committee felt itself fortified by the fact that on the floor an amendment to restore the deleted amount was defeated, 160 to 92. The Senate committee undertook to cancel the proposed cut; its report indicated a desire to continue the Division of Economic Research. But in conference the figure set by the House prevailed. Two days before the new fiscal year began the Board abolished the Division and transferred most of its personnel to a new unit called the Division of Technical Service. In mid-summer the House group on Labor-Federal Security appropriations—at the time outstanding among the subcommittees for parental and disciplinary zeal under the chairmanship of "Judge" Tarver of Georgia—was stirred to action by newspaper comment and by information from the special committee then investigating the National Labor Relations Board.[89] The subcommittee was convened in a supplemental hearing. Late in August Mr. Tarver spoke before the subcommittee on deficiencies. It was his belief

that directions given in the reports of the Appropriations Committee as to the purposes for which the funds carried in

---

[88] 76th Cong., 3rd Sess., House Report No. 1822, p. 36. The report said: "The committee does not desire it to be understood that in effecting these reductions indicated the Board must necessarily make decreases in the exact amounts indicated in this table as it is probable that many variations will essentially have to be made from this pattern for the purpose of serving good administration. . . . If good administration demands that variations be made in the amounts shown above, the committee will entertain no objection."

[89] The personal angle given to the affair was illustrated in the headline of the item in the *New York Times*, August 2, 1940: "Assert NLRB Defied Congress on Saposs."

an appropriation bill should or should not be used, when those
directions have been expressly approved by action thereafter
of the Congress itself, have been universally accorded consideration by departmental authorities as constituting man-
dates by Congress as to the uses to which the funds carried in
the appropriation bill, to which the report related, might be
put.

The representative of the Board defended its action partly on the
ground that "we have an opinion of the Comptroller General on the
subject of the legality of the Board's action in retaining those
people."[90] He added:

> . . . the Board, in taking the action that they did take, were
> confronted with a serious and very painful dilemma . . . the
> Board concluded that a certain amount of the activities then
> being carried on by the division were absolutely essential to
> the proper conduct of our work. . . . We made sure that as
> far as we could determine what activities then carried on by
> the division seemed utterly objectionable to the subcommittee
> were to be eliminated.

Mr. Tarver, for his part, did "not think that any other department
has even undertaken so flagrantly to disregard a direction of the
Congress."[91] The report prepared by the subcommittee on deficiencies was severe. "The committee," it stated, "feels that the action
of the board is contrary to the intent of Congress as expressed in
the report of the committee . . . ."[92] A provision was inserted in
the bill, as follows: "After the date of the enactment of this Act,
none of the appropriation 'Salaries, National Labor Relations
Board, 1941,' shall be obligated for the Division of Economic Research or for the Division of Technical Service."[93]

A little later the subcommittee on Labor-Federal Security appropriations seemed friendlier toward the National Labor Relations
Board, which meanwhile had been altered in membership.[94] But

[90] 76th Cong., 3rd Sess., House Committee on Appropriations, *Hearing before
a subcommittee on the supplemental civil functions appropriations for 1941*, p.
486, August 27, 1940.
[91] *Ibid.*, p. 475.
[92] 76th Cong., 3rd Sess., House Report No. 2966, p. 14.
[93] 76th Cong., 3rd Sess., Public No. 812, ch. 780.
[94] The committee report on the regular appropriations for the fiscal year 1942
remarked: "Since the committee had occasion during the past fiscal year to deal
with the appropriations for the National Labor Relations Board, the Board has
undergone a reorganization, and it appears from the evidence given the committee that there is a genuine cooperative spirit now existing. . . ." 77th Cong.,
1st Sess., House Report No. 688, June 2, 1941, p. 40.

within a year scolding was resumed. Again the grievance was alleged disregard of language in a committee report, although now the particular ground was a technical matter of salary increases. In the hearing on April 23, 1942, Mr. Tarver declared:

> It makes no difference whether there might have been a legal obligation on the part of the Government to pay these increased salaries, and I understand that it is admitted that there was not, so far as the salaries of field employees are concerned, but even if there were such a legal obligation, the National Labor Relations Board could not properly spend money . . . for uses which are expressly negatived in the report of the committee in connection with the bill making available to it such funds. In other words, Congress said, in approving this report, that you should not use any of this money to raise the salaries of field employees.[95]

The subcommittee would not condone the action even though the Board had explained the matter to the Bureau of the Budget and to the deficiencies subcommittee. The subsequent committee report sharpened the rebuke. "This is the second occasion within two years," it ran, "in which the National Labor Relations Board has expended funds for a purpose denied by action of Congress."[96] The appropriation was reduced by $46,000—the amount of the allegedly illegal salary increases. The committee expressed the hope "that it will not again be confronted with disregard of the direct mandate of Congress by this agency." Incidentally, the report deplored what is believed to be the Board's practice in leaving a large part of its administrative responsibility to subordinate officials.

A committee report can be a means of chastisement by which errors are set forth for other departments to see and to shun. An unusual but revealing instance of such censure was found in the

---

[95] 77th Cong., 2nd Sess., House Committee on Appropriations, *Hearings before a subcommittee on the Labor-Federal Security appropriation bill for 1943*, p. 550, April 23, 1942. The Board had taken the position that the reallocation of certain field positions was mandatory under the Comptroller General's rulings and accordingly had effected it at an annual cost of $46,000.

[96] 77th Cong., 2nd Sess., House Report No. 2200, June 3, 1942, p. 23. For echoes of the controversy, see also the hearings and report on the second supplemental national defense appropriation bill for 1943. 77th Cong., 2nd Sess., House Report No. 2519, October 8, 1942, p. 20. In the hearing on September 30, G. D. Reilly, member of the Board, stated that the subcommittee leaders had told him the "action was not taken because they wanted the Board to have salaries lower than those prevailing in the field staffs of other agencies but because the subcommittee felt the Board had disregarded the intent of Congress."

1941 report that accompanied the agricultural appropriation bill.[97] Under the heading, "integrity of sources of information of committees of Congress," the following comment was made:

> Since Congress and its committees are not armed with facilities to make personal and field investigations, it must rely upon the accuracy of data and facts which are from time to time submitted by the executive agencies of the Government. During the hearings on the agricultural appropriation bill the committee was confronted with a situation involving a basic question which, although related to a relatively minor matter, not only eclipses the matter itself, but transcends in importance the activities of the agency and its relations with the Committee on Appropriations or its subcommittee and goes to the very vitals of the relationship between the committees of the House and Senate and the executive agencies of the Government. The committee was furnished, by the Rural Electrification Administration, on request, certain information in regard to promotions which, it now develops, was not wholly accurate. The matter is presented to the House in this report on account of the importance of absolute good faith on the part of the officers and employees of the executive branch in dealing with the Congress.[98]

The situation immediately at issue did involve administrative carelessness at the intermediate level in a thoroughly well-intentioned, unusually energetic, imaginative, truly efficient, but new organization. In late years the subcommittees on appropriations have been suspicious of within-grade promotions. In 1940 an alert and persistent member of the minority, Mr. Dirksen of Illinois, began to pluck at the REA's raveled sleeve.[99] Statements were obtained from the REA itself, from the personnel office of the Department, and

---

[97] The censure did not extend to the central machinery of the Department of Agriculture, within which the REA had been placed in 1939. It is apposite to remark that the value to administrators of the confidence of the subcommittees on appropriations can hardly be overstated. The ability to earn and retain such confidence is perhaps the most useful single quality in a departmental budget officer. Like a good deal that belongs under the head of honesty, the trait rests in part on an outward eye and a scrupulous and retentive memory. Of William A. Jump, veteran director of finance in the Department of Agriculture, it is said that he is one man from whom the subcommittee is prepared to accept at its face value and without detailed substantiation any statement that he makes.

[98] 77th Cong., 1st Sess., House Report No. 176, p. 5.

[99] As part of the punishment, the appropriation for REA salaries for the fiscal year 1941 prohibited the use of funds "to pay the salary of any person who received as many as three steps of administrative within-grade promotion" under certain conditions, which were specified.

from the General Accounting Office. When once Mr. Dirksen had found discrepancies he would not let go; 1942 found him still engaged in a punitive quest. Meanwhile, the committee, in alluding to "this regrettable series of incidents" in its 1941 report, added the admonition: "The attention of other agencies of the Government is also invited to the matter and a reading of the hearings, appearing on pages 232–261, volume 2, is suggested." To the observer there was in all this more than a touch of the selectively persecutive tenacity that at times seems to mar Mr. Dirksen's admirable energy. The observer wonders why it is so often agencies like the Rural Electrification Administration and the National Labor Relations Board that stay in trouble. At all events, the misdeeds of the REA were dealt with once again in the report on the appropriations for 1943. The Secretary of Agriculture was quoted as having told the committee on November 15, 1941 that his investigation "fully supported Mr. Dirksen's contention that the promotion figures submitted by the Rural Electrification Administration" were inaccurate. The Secretary informed the committee that the assistant administrator of the REA had been reprimanded, the chief of information removed, and the budget officer of the agency suspended for thirty days. "The Secretary," concluded the committee's comment, "is to be commended for this expeditious, forthright, and resolute disposition of this regrettable matter."[100]

The foregoing instances have at least ostensibly concerned oversight of administration in its narrower sense. More important is the leverage exerted by the appropriations committees upon administrative policy. An illustration may be drawn from the field of rural electrification. A recent committee report remarked that "during the hearings some difference of opinion developed between members of the committee and officials of the Rural Electrification Administration as to the extent to which the Administration should go in aiding the cooperatives after they have completed their construction programs and are operating." The report conceded that a degree of continuing supervision was necessary to protect the government's interest in its loans. "The committee," it declared, "is not opposed to this educational program in its entirety but is of the opinion that intensive work of this character should be confined to the period of a year or two immediately after a new line goes into operation and that thereafter a much less extensive program would suffice."[101]

---

[100] 77th Cong., 2nd Sess., House Report No. 1848, March 2, 1942, pp. 11–12.
[101] 77th Cong., 1st Sess., House Report No. 176, p. 20.

A significant example of a committee judgment on administrative policy concerned inspections under the Fair Labor Standards Act. The issue was one of method but it involved the efficient enforcement of the act as a whole. In 1941 the subcommittee declined to allow funds to increase the inspectors from 930 to 1,070.[102] At the rate of fifteen inspections per month per inspector, the larger force could "inspect every one of the 300,000 firms covered by the provisions of the act on the average of about once every 18 months."[103] "As a matter of policy," declared the report, "the committee is unable to find any justification for placing the inspection on a basis of inspecting each and every plant that might be covered by the act." The committee believed that inspections should be confined to following up complaints or sample checking of industries. The 1942 report of the committee quoted its statement of policy in the preceding year. It noted, further, that an amendment to increase the amount for inspection had been defeated on the House floor, thus directly approving the committee's position. "It now develops," ran the 1942 report, "that the officials of the Department charged with enforcement of the law have failed to adopt the spot-checking system approved by the Congress."[104] The report continued:

The Congress cannot pursue these matters into the administrative branch of the Government and enforce its own direc-

---

[102] The head of the Wage and Hour Division stated in a letter placed in the hearings: "I am convinced that nothing short of an inspection of every one of the more than 300,000 establishments in which employees subject to the act are employed will give assurance of fair and uniform compliance with the act in every one of the states and territories." 77th Cong., 1st Sess., House Committee on Appropriations, *Hearings before a subcommittee on the Labor-Federal Security appropriation bill for 1942*, p. 3.

[103] 77th Cong., 1st Sess., House Report No. 688, June 2, 1941, p. 13.

[104] 77th Cong., 2nd Sess., House Report No. 2200, pp. 8–9. On the other side, the Department did claim that it had regretfully altered its methods after the rebuff in 1941. In the hearings in 1942, the Secretary of Labor said to the subcommittee: "You made it pretty clear to us in your report that the idea of working toward total routine inspection technique was beyond the likelihood that Congress would ever appropriate sufficient funds to support such routine inspection. Therefore, we revised our program. . . ." 77th Cong., 2nd Sess., House Committee on Appropriations, *Hearings before a subcommittee on the Labor-Federal Security appropriation bill for 1943*, p. 24. In 1943, the new head of the Wage and Hour Division, when asked before the subcommittee whether its judgment in insisting upon the spot-check method had not been shown to be wise, answered, "I am grateful to be able to join you in the judgment of the committee." 78th Cong., 1st Sess., House Committee on Appropriations, *Hearings before a subcommittee on the Labor-Federal Security appropriation bill for 1944*, p. 161.

tions, and must of necessity rely upon officials of the various departments to carry out faithfully the policies established and the directives given to them by the Congress, but adequate methods for securing compliance are available to the Congress if administrative officers do not heed congressional intent as expressed in reports and debates.

The appropriation was reduced, while the attention of the Wage and Hour Division was called to "the desire of Congress that the enforcement of the law be carried out on a spot-checking basis" and that there was "no intention of abandoning an effort to see that the recommended procedure is followed."

Sometimes the strictures in the reports merely put administrators under notice that certain results are expected and that information on them must be submitted in the future. There is endless variation, of course, in the nature of the compulsion applied, the response expected, and the time allowed. Thus notice is often served that, as a condition to the approval of funds for the year beyond that for which appropriations are being made, specified information must be presented to the subcommittee.[105] The span of appraisal may be longer than a year. In the report a few years ago on agricultural appropriations the committee said of the four regional laboratories set up especially for the discovery of new outlets for farm products: "At the hearings the Department representatives were challenged to achieve results within ten years which will consume sufficient surpluses and be of sufficient commercial advantage to justify the expenditures under this head and if not to discontinue the laboratories. This challenge was accepted both by the Bureau chief in charge of the work and by Dr. Jardine, Director of Research for the Department."[106] In reporting the agricultural appropriation bill in April 1943, the committee recalled the original challenge,

---

[105] For example, the report of February 17, 1938 on Commerce appropriations for the fiscal year 1939 said of certain air navigation facilities: "Before approving the estimate for the fiscal year 1940, in any amount for this item, the committee will require of the Department of Commerce a full report on this subject, showing not only the results that will accrue by the employment of the ultra-high frequencies on radio ranges, but, in addition, a long-term program that will effect the change-over, without impairment of safety, from the present system to the 'last word' in proved technical design." 75th Cong., 3rd Sess., House Report No. 1830, p. 19.

[106] 76th Cong., 3rd Sess., House Report No. 1540, p. 12. In the report in the following year the challenge was renewed. 77th Cong., 1st Sess., House Report No. 126, p. 13.

adding: "Annually, thereafter, the committee has closely examined the work of these laboratories in the light of the ten year pledge quoted above."[107]

Illustrative of a type of warning that is strengthened by the intimation of a later question was the following in a 1940 report: "The committee in calling attention to these violations of an express inhibition in the statute desires to serve notice that the practice of using official cars for private business must be stopped at once. An appropriate inquiry will be made in the future to determine whether this admonition has been heeded."[108] Even more pointed was the complaint in 1943 about civilian contract employees in the Navy Department. The report stated that "the committee is not satisfied with the manner in which such authority has been exercised." It added a warning:

> There should be a curtailment of not less than 25 per cent in numbers as early as separations, with proper notification, may be effected. It is the purpose of the committee, in connection with the regular 1944 naval appropriation bill either (1) to pursue this matter further itself, based upon a presentation already called for in harmony with the letter and spirit of existing authority, or (2) to undertake a special inquiry under the investigative powers with which the committee recently has been clothed.[109]

Enough has been said to show the range of intervention in administration through language in reports of the appropriations committees. Much ambiguity attends this method of oversight. Several factors affect the degree to which an administrator must regard any particular bit of verbiage as mandatory. How precise is it? Was the point raised in the hearings and, if so, was it dwelt upon? Did the administrator himself make any admission or commitment? Did the legislative body give any especial attention to the item in question? Especially, was there a vote upon it, as in the rejection of an amendment not desired by the subcommittee? The foregoing are some of the circumstances which the administrator

---

[107] 78th Cong., 1st Sess., House Report No. 354, p. 12.
[108] 76th Cong., 3rd Sess., House Report No. 1822, March 21, 1940, p. 4.
[109] 78th Cong., 1st Sess., House Report No. 202, p. 5. As to investigative methods under H. Res. 69, down to the middle of 1943, about fifteen different persons had been borrowed from other agencies on a reimbursable basis for assignments of several days or weeks. Meanwhile 200 employees had been interviewed in building a "pool" of available temporary investigators.

must consider. His exercise of judgment is apt to be harder because he must reckon with two chambers.[110]

VIII

The discussion thus far has mainly concerned direct relations between subcommittees and administrators when appropriations are being made. It is appropriate to consider interim contacts during the year. As a background, it is necessary first to comment on the nature of appropriations in the national government of the United States.

The form and content of appropriating legislation in the national government have received very little analysis, official or academic. It has been the accretion of practice, for the most part stubbornly repetitive, but shaped in the past by countless forgotten situations. The result is highly uneven; there is no standard unit. Within the Department of Agriculture, as Verne Lewis has pointed out, some of the items "were as small as $5,000; other items were as large as $500,000,000."[111]

Once a breakdown of appropriation items has become customary, the tendency is to perpetuate it. Comparison from year to year is aided by repetition, which indeed is encouraged by the law and by

---

[110] A minor example of the ambiguities of bicameralism was found in a colloquy over Post Office appropriations before a Senate subcommittee. The House report had stated that twenty additional inspectors for national defense work were "allowed by the committee with the definite understanding that they are provided for the emergency and are temporary." A departmental spokesman told the Senate subcommittee that it would be embarrassing to train men and then to let them go. Thereupon the following interchange occurred:
"Senator Hayden. Well, I was wondering whether you had given the House committee assurances to that effect.
Mr. Aldrich. We did not.
Senator Hayden. This is dictum on their part.
Mr. Aldrich. This is their own restriction.
Senator Hayden. You do not agree with the House?
Mr. Aldrich. No, sir; we do not agree with it."
77th Cong., 1st Sess., Senate Committee on Appropriations, *Hearings before a subcommittee on the Treasury and Post Office appropriation bill for the fiscal year 1942*, p. 22, March 7, 1941.

[111] John M. Gaus and Leon O. Wolcott, *Public Administration and the United States Department of Agriculture* (Chicago, Public Administration Service, 1940), Appendix A, by Verne Lewis, p. 410. Verne Lewis adds: "Of the 175 items for the fiscal year 1939–1940, 145 or about 80 per cent, ranged from $5,000 to $900,000, yet they equaled only 2.5 per cent of the total appropriation for the Department.

the Budget Bureau's instructions.[112] Sometimes, where appropriations have been segregated, efforts at simplification are defeated by outraged subcommittee members who cling to items that have a local habitation and a name. If space allows, it would be instructive to trace a decade of largely frustrated attempts to consolidate the relatively numerous items for such matters as Indian hospitals and schools.[113] But Congress does not always insist upon retaining a stereotyped itemization. In 1939, for example, the subcommittee in charge of funds for penal institutions favored a consolidation of appropriations in order to provide flexibility "and bring about a uniformity in working conditions which is not possible when each institution is appropriated for separately."[114]

The prevailing type of breakdown in national appropriations truly evades definition. "Lump sum" is hardly the term for it, apart from some emergency appropriations. But the usual categories are broad. Because of the scope of the ordinary item, the appropriation language itself leaves wide administrative leeway. A crucial question, therefore, is the continuing force of the highly detailed preparatory material: the estimates, the justifications, and remarks made by the administrators in the hearings.[115]

Here is an uncertain area of administration upon which administrators themselves are hesitant to generalize. So far as the "law" goes, the preparatory materials have no effect; only the language

---

[112] Circular No. 391, June 10, 1942, in giving instructions for the submission of estimates for fiscal 1944, stated: "The arrangement of estimates of annual appropriations will follow that of the corresponding appropriations in the appropriation act for the fiscal year 1943."

[113] See 72nd Cong., Senate Report No. 25, and 73rd Cong., House Document No. 206, for the early stages of an effort at reform which was again defeated in 1942. Said members then: "Now this committee has always insisted since the days of old Bill Hastings that the appropriations for these schools be made in separate items. . . . If the subcommittees and the Congress yield the power of making specific appropriations, not only in this bill but in the other bills in which it has been urged, we will destroy the power of the people over the purse." 77th Cong., 2nd Sess., House Committee on Appropriations, *Hearings before a subcommittee on the Interior Department appropriation bill for 1943*, Part 2, pp. 577, 582.

[114] 76th Cong., 1st Sess., House Report No. 658, p. 20. On the assumption of savings through "greater administrative elasticity," the appropriation was cut by $50,000.

[115] Under exceptional circumstances, the schedules of the Budget may be incorporated by reference in an appropriation act. For example, see 77th Cong., 1st Sess., Public Law 144, approved July 1, 1941.

of the appropriation acts and of the permanent legislation counts. Of course everyone assumes that the money will be spent in about the manner that the departments have stated. But hardly exactly. For the estimates are so highly detailed that they could not be made literally binding without inconvenience. The practical need, therefore, is to distinguish allowable from improper types and degrees of deviation. The distinction is crucial in the relation of law to administration. Its enforcement is one of the most difficult questions in the exercise of legislative oversight.

The prepared material that goes to the appropriations committees comprises three elements. First, the estimate for the appropriation item in question gives the exact phraseology which, if all goes well, will be incorporated in the law. Attendant notations show what was actually spent for the corresponding item in the last completed fiscal year, what was appropriated for the year in progress, set beside the amount asked for the new year. Second, the so-called "green sheets" break the estimate down by "objects" and sometimes (though this is still an innovation) by purposes also. Under "personal services," for example, the "green sheets," carried in revised form into the printed budget, show the grade, title, number employed, and salary, for the three years that are compared as an expenditure, as an appropriation, and as an estimate, respectively. Finally, the justification is an elaborate explanation and argument which seeks especially to show the reasons for any proposed changes from previous years. The justifications are not printed in the budget. They remain in typed or mimeographed form unless they are incorporated in the printed hearings. In any case they are supplemented by the oral testimony in the hearings, bolstered in turn by information submitted on questions raised therein. All of these elements may enter into the problem of the binding force of the estimate, but the issue turns mainly on two classes of information: first, the material in the "green sheets" as carried into the budget; and, second, statements in the hearings which may be construed as promises.

This is a difficult, highly empirical field for practical judgments by administrators on the nature of their obligation. The agencies differ in the degree to which they seek to stick literally to the estimates. Some find it easier than others; much depends on the tempo and the need for adjustment. The "green sheet" schedules on proposed personnel, for example, are too detailed to be rigor-

ously binding on any agency.[116] The attitude of different units
varies with their experience. The head of a bureau which has been
caught and chastised is jumpy and watchful. Some years ago the
estimates meant less than they do now, but recently enough administrators have been in trouble to put all on guard. Sometimes, when
consultation seems necessary in the face of a need to disregard the
plan of expenditure in the estimates, the Bureau of the Budget is
visited. But on occasion it is deemed advisable to clear with a
House appropriations subcommittee.[117]

Discipline may follow a departure from the estimates without
prior consultation with the subcommittee. An instance of such
punishment involved the administrative division in the Department
of Justice. A report in 1940 stated that in the previous year the
committee had approved certain additions to personnel "on the
basis of testimony presented the committee indicating that a genuine
need existed for the positions requested."[118] The report continued:

> It appears, however, that instead of filling positions, the
> justification for which had been established to the satisfaction
> of the committee, the Department set up two new positions—
> one at $6,500 and one at $4,600—without securing previous con-
> gressional approval for such use of funds. Appropriations made
> in good faith for particular purposes must be used in good
> faith for such purposes and the tables of expenditures and
> estimates in the Budget must present a true picture with
> respect to each position authorized. The committee is elimi-
> nating the $11,100 from the appropriation which represents
> the sum used for the purpose of filling these two positions.

---

[116] Even Senator McKellar implied approximation, not absolute compliance,
when he grumbled to a departmental witness, "I think you ought to stick right
close to what the Budget estimate provides." 78th Cong., 1st Sess., Senate Committee on Appropriations, *Hearings before a subcommittee on the Treasury and
Post Office appropriation bill for 1944*, p. 82.

[117] Thus in 1941 the Bureau of the Census faced a heavy emergency task in
providing information germane to proof of citizenship. The subcommittee, duly
convened and consulted, said it would be all right under the circumstances to
spend money appropriated for a somewhat different purpose. The deputy head
of another bureau, who had consulted the subcommittee on Labor-Federal
Security about an adjustment during the year, was asked by the observer whether
he had taken it up also with the Bureau of the Budget. "No," he replied, "we
went where our friends are."

[118] 76th Cong., 3rd Sess., House Report No. 1575, February 6, 1940, p. 24.
The Department of Justice was attempting to provide for a new personnel officer
in accordance with the executive order of June 1938.

The degree to which the estimates are binding must be construed in the context of remarks made in the hearings. Much depends upon whether the subcommittee expressly raised a point that led the administrative officer to make a pledge. Sometimes the officer declines to make a promise. Thus in the 1941 hearings on appropriations for the Civil Aeronautics Authority, a senator asked: "There is $25,000,000 in this bill, then, for pilot training?" The agency representative replied: "Yes, sir; but as to how is the best way to spend that I would rather not commit myself, because what I say here would bind us."[119]

The subcommittees sometimes expressly say that there is room for administrative leeway. This may be done when the Budget figure has been cut and the tables from the "green sheets" no longer fit. A committee report in 1940, when discussing the appropriations for forest protection and management which the subcommittee had reduced by more than two million dollars, remarked: "The committee's action is predicated on the further consideration that the Forest Service will have, by an understanding with the committee, discretion to allocate the appropriation to the several subprojects under this head irrespective of any earmarking that may have been set up in the Budget."[120] Similarly, after trimming an appropriation for the Bureau of Immigration and Naturalization, the committee reported: "It is the intention of the committee that the reduction of $298,000 in the Budget estimates should be applied to such phases of the expansion program as the dictates of effective administration demand."[121]

Subcommittees on appropriations have sometimes required that quarterly or other periodical reports should be filed with them. This may be offered as a substitute for details in appropriations. Following a trip of inspection in 1941 through the foreign posts of the United States in Latin American countries, the subcommittee in charge of State Department appropriations favored increased funds

---

[119] 77th Cong., 1st Sess., Senate Committee on Appropriations, *Hearings before a subcommittee on the State, Commerce, Justice, and Judiciary appropriations.*

[120] 76th Cong., 3rd Sess., House Report No. 1540, January 30, 1940, p. 7.

[121] 77th Cong., 1st Sess., House Report No. 360, p. 37. See also the remark in connection with a cut of $236,000 in a fourteen million dollar estimate for air navigation facilities: ". . . the committee did not feel that it was sufficiently conversant with all of the detailed needs of this unit to endeavor to make specifications as to which positions should be allowed and which disapproved." *Ibid.*, p. 19.

for the improvement of the posts as well as for a program of friendly relations. In reporting the bill, the committee said: "The committee was at first disposed to earmark each of the projects in the bill in order that controls might be exercised over the expenditure of the money, but on reconsideration it was the thought of the committee that the relative need of the different South and Central American nations for the various services proposed under this heading must change with the passage of time."[122] Therefore a lump sum was granted with the understanding that "in general, the expenditures under the appropriation will follow the projects explained in detail before the committee." The report added:

> In order that the committee might be fully informed as to the direction in which the Department is moving with the use of these funds, it is suggested that a brief quarterly progress report be filed with the chairman of the subcommittee during the next fiscal year, giving the amount of expenditure during the preceding quarter under each project, and setting forth changes that have taken place in the complexion of the project as originally projected at the time of the hearings on this bill.

On occasion the mildly disciplinary prerogative of exacting current reports has been shared by the legislative committees with the committees on appropriations.[123]

What is impressive, in tendency if not as matured fact, is the extent to which administrators meet with appropriations subcommittees in *ad hoc* sessions during the year. Sometimes the administrators themselves seek the contact as a safeguard; sometimes they are summoned for admonition or worse. The subcommittees vary in the degree to which they engage in such activity. Much depends upon the chairman. But generally speaking, interim supervisory relationships are increasing.

IX

What has been said about continuous control leads directly to the relations of the appropriating groups to the Budget Bureau and generally to the organs of administrative management.

---

[122] 77th Cong., 2nd Sess., House Report No. 1771, p. 15.

[123] A supplemental national defense appropriation act for 1941, for example, provided that the Secretary of War should submit monthly reports on all cost-plus-a-fixed-fee contracts to the respective chairmen of the Senate and House committees on appropriations as well as military affairs. See 76th Cong., 3rd Sess., House Report No. 2866, September 26, 1940, pp. 9–10.

The degree of exactness with which the amounts of the annual appropriations follow the Budget estimates is beside the point of the present inquiry.[124] Negatively, at least, a Budget recommendation is almost an absolute prerequisite of House action.[125] Indeed, members of the Senate appropriations group complain that House conferees frustrate the Senate's initiative by standing in conference against any item that has not been recommended by the Budget.[126] But this does not mean that the subcommittees are unwilling to go behind the Budget figure. Fairly typical was the question put by a subcommittee chairman to the representative of the Civil Aeronautics Authority: "We will start off by asking you how much you asked the Budget for."[127] Typical of many administrators, too, was the reply of a spokesman of the power division of the Interior Department when, having revealed in response to a direct question that his unit had suffered a cut, he was asked: "Will you be able to get along with this amount, do you think?"[128] He said, "I think we will." But not all bureau heads are so regardful of hierarchy. One of them declared flatly in a 1942 hearing:

---

[124] In 26 appropriation bills enacted in the 77th Cong., 1st Sess., 1941, the House reports showed 1,801 items, of which the House increased 103 above the Budget estimates while it decreased 542. The Senate then increased 453 items above the House figure and reduced 16. The enacted total was $55,325,771,373, against Budget estimates aggregating $53,133,772,689.

[125] In a hearing on September 13, 1940, a member of the deficiencies subcommittee said to a witness: "You know, Admiral, also, do you not, that on the basis of experience there is an understanding in the Appropriations deficiencies committee that no item shall be approved by the committee which has not been approved by the Budget?" Here the ranking majority member broke in with the remark, "That does not apply to defense items." 76th Cong., 3rd Sess., House Committee on Appropriations, *Hearings before a subcommittee on the third supplemental national defense appropriation bill for 1941*, p. 17.

[126] The late Senator Adams of Colorado, a wheel horse of the Senate committee, said in a hearing on April 15, 1941: "We have tried to put some items in the Senate thinking under our constitutional authority we have the right to amend an appropriation bill. However, we have been confronted with the very adamant mental attitude when we tried that because the particular items were not in the Budget and that seems to be the law and the gospel which they seek to apply to us." 77th Cong., 1st Sess., Senate Committee on Appropriations, *Hearings before a subcommittee on the War Department civil functions appropriation bill for 1942*, p. 49.

[127] 77th Cong., 1st Sess., House Committee on Appropriations, *Hearings before a subcommittee on the Department of Commerce appropriation bill for 1942*, p. 354. In this case the answer was, "We asked for $167,420,152, and the amount approved was $75,123,886 . . . a decrease of $92,296,266."

[128] 77th Cong., 2nd Sess., House Committee on Appropriations, *Hearings before a subcommittee on the Interior Department appropriation bill for 1943*, p. 78.

I believe that it is clearly my duty as Director of the Bureau of the Census to fully inform your committee regarding what is needed by the Census Bureau in order that it may properly perform the functions assigned to it by the Congress. Accordingly, in good conscience, I can do no less than urge with all of the earnestness at my command that this committee add back the sum of $908,746 which was slashed from our original estimates by the Bureau of the Budget without good reason. . . .[129]

One might suppose that the subcommittees would have little difficulty in persuading administrators to confess their sense of need. But the subcommittee in charge of agricultural appropriations for 1943 thought it had reason to complain. "The subcommittee has noticed, from time to time," it reported, "the reluctance of bureau chiefs to answer inquiries propounded by its members respecting the adequacy of amounts granted by the Budget . . . and the wisdom, in the light of the public interest as they view it, of Budget reductions in such amounts."[130] The committees (ran the argument) need the complete and first-hand knowledge possessed by the bureau chiefs. Since "under our Budget plan, the function of the Executive is to propose and that of the legislative branch is to dispose, . . . the right to interrogate any and all witnesses on any pending matter of legislation and that of having such witnesses give responsive answers thereto is fundamental and inherent in the legislative branch." All this was put down "to clarify the minds of those in the Department who may have been entertaining unfounded misapprehensions. . . ."

The direct impetus for the foregoing warning was an incident in the hearings on appropriations for the Bureau of Plant Industry.[131] "Whose idea was it," asked Mr. Tarver, chairman of the subcommittee, "to decrease this investigational work, and how is it proposed to justify it? Did you ask for a reduction in the amount of the funds you had before, or did the Bureau of the Budget through some plan of its own, or ideas of its own, as to reductions which

---

[129] 77th Cong., 2nd Sess., House Committee on Appropriations, *Hearings before a subcommittee on the Commerce Department appropriation bill for 1943*, p. 86. In a 1943 hearing Senator Lodge said he had been wondering for years, "When the Bureau of the Budget turns something down, why should not somebody from the Budget be up here to defend it?" 78th Cong., 1st Sess., Senate Committee on Appropriations, *Hearings before a subcommittee on the State, Justice, and Commerce appropriations for 1944*, p. 139.

[130] 77th Cong., 2nd Sess., House Report No. 1848, March 2, 1942, p. 11.

[131] 77th Cong., 2nd Sess., House Committee on Appropriations, *Hearings before a subcommittee on the agricultural appropriation bill for 1942*, pp. 448–49, 458–77, 497–500.

might be justified, bring them about insofar as their recommendations are concerned?" When the bureau representative loyally said, "This is in line with the Budget estimates," the committee members were not content, and drew from him the statement that he had originally asked for the "continuation of our appropriations as of the current fiscal year with an additional $20,000 for work with corn in the South." Later, when the same witness said of reductions that operations could be adjusted thereto and "I think we can carry our responsibility," his answer was treated as "not fully responsive." He was admonished that his understandable "inhibitions do not go to the extent of preventing him from giving the committee the benefit of his best judgment. . . ."

At this point, significantly, the subcommittee undertook to ask about the methods of the Bureau of the Budget. How long had the bureau head and his assistants been before the Budget representatives? From nine o'clock in the morning until two p.m., was the reply. Whom did the Budget Bureau assign to the hearing? What was their "general background . . . have they some special aptitude in the field of agriculture?" The discreet finance officer of the Department of Agriculture came to the rescue by giving some biographical details about the several Budget examiners. He was asked whether the Budget examiners had made field trips. Yes, he said; "the Budget Bureau staff has been able to visit much more of our work in the field than formerly was the case." The cross-examination went on to the question of how the Budget cuts were distributed. Apparently both the subcommittee chairman and the departmental representatives thought that the Budget Bureau should impose any reduction that was ordered upon a bureau as a whole, allowing the administrators to work out the distribution of the cut.[132] The interchange ended with sharp minority comment

---

[132] In the 1941 hearings on appropriations for the Bureau of the Budget, Director Smith said (in answer to a question about methods), "In the main, we indicate where the cut is to be made." 77th Cong., 1st Sess., House Committee on Appropriations, *Hearings before a subcommittee on the Independent Offices appropriation bill for 1942,* pp. 737–38. As confirmation, see 77th Cong., 2nd Sess., House Committee on Appropriations, *Hearings before a subcommitttee on the War Department civil functions appropriation bill for 1943,* p. 56. But practice varies. In the Indian Office appropriation for 1943, there was a double cut, the first detailed, the second coming after Pearl Harbor; and in the latter the bureau was allowed to recommend where it would be applied. 77th Cong., 2nd Sess., Senate Committee on Appropriations, *Hearings before a subcommittee on the Department of the Interior appropriation bill for 1943,* p. 83.

on the "captious and capricious" Budget and the intimation that in the future Budget Bureau examiners in charge of agricultural appropriations might be summoned before the committee. The same story was enacted with other witnesses.[133]

The subcommittees have also resented the attempt of the Budget Bureau to effect savings since 1940 by ordering the impounding of "reserves" under certain appropriations. What right, members asked, had the Budget Bureau to cut athwart the will of Congress? Were such appropriations not mandatory? This attitude was reflected in the remark of a subcommittee member to the representative of the Soil Conservation Service: "The action of the Budget in setting up a reserve of almost the entire amount of the money which was added by the committee seems, at least to some of us, to indicate that the Budget is seeking to superimpose its judgment on that of the committee and of the Congress. . . ."[134] In the later House debate, the spokesman of the committee said of the whole tactic of "freezing" appropriations by the Bureau of the Budget: "We resent such attempted supervision by the Budget of congressional discretion as unauthorized by law and an abuse of power."[135]

There has been not a little Congressional sniping at the Bureau of the Budget. The subcommittees have at times seemed to be

---

[133] *Ibid.*, p. 833, where the administrator said, "I do not think I ought to make a recommendation here which is contrary to what the Budget has decided," and the chairman explained, "If every witness before our committee took that position we would never be able to get any evidence whatever which varied in any way from the Budget recommendations." See also, in the same manner, 77th Cong., 2nd Sess., House Committee on Appropriations, *Hearings before a subcommittee on the Commerce Department appropriation bill for 1943*, p. 217, where the witness began, "I am not supposed . . .," and the chairman broke in, "You are supposed to answer any questions that the committee asks."

[134] 77th Cong., 2nd Sess., House Committee on Appropriations, *Hearings before a subcommittee on the agricultural appropriation bill for 1943*, p. 934. The increase referred to was mainly for technical services to soil conservation districts.

[135] *Congressional Record*, 77th Cong., 2nd Sess., vol. 88, p. 1891, March 3, 1942. And in a 1943 hearing the impounding of funds led to a threat to summon the Director of the Budget. "I think we will have to lock horns with the Budget," grumbled a member, ". . . to decide who will make the appropriations, the Budget or Congress." 78th Cong., 1st Sess., House Committee on Appropriations, *Hearings before a subcommittee on the Labor-Federal Security appropriation bill for 1944*, p. 13; see also p. 261. But, in contrast, note the discretion expressly vested in the "Director of the Bureau of the Budget, after a hearing thereon with representatives of the Department of Agriculture," to adjust certain parts of its appropriations during the fiscal year 1944. 78th Cong., 1st Sess., Public No. 129.

provoking the bureaus to revolt against Budget control. This attitude has not been as inconsistent as it seemed with the Congressional outcry against bureaucracy. The attack on administration is seldom really generalized; it is particular and selective. The attack on an Administration is specific. The managerial role of the Bureau of the Budget is a subject of criticism. Mr. Wigglesworth complained of "work which seems to me in large measure outside the normal scope of operations of the Bureau."[136] Mr. Taber exclaimed: "Worse than anything else, the Budget has begun to reach out."[137] But the committee reports generally commend the current activities of the Bureau of the Budget, including reorganization studies and field surveys.[138]

A paradox is seen in the contrasting attitudes toward centralization at the departmental level held respectively by the appropriations committees and the staff of the Budget Bureau. The committees wish to give departmental headquarters control over matters like travel and printing; they press for the concentration of legal services under the solicitors; only in the case of personnel administration and latterly of research have the Congressional groups shown marked hesitation in their integrative disposition. The motive, of course, is not confidence in the tools of management but rather the desire to put certain especially suspect fields of supposed waste beyond the reach of the operating agencies. The budget staff, from its side, favors strong and well-endowed, if not altogether self-sufficient, operating bureaus.

But collaboration is not absent between the Bureau of the Budget and the appropriations committees. An especially fruitful pattern of cooperation has been followed at times when the whole committee has become aware of a problem common to many of the appropriation bills and has requested the Bureau of the Budget to report on a solution. Thus in 1939 the question of a general policy about administrative promotions was handled in this way. The Bureau's study became the basis of a statute, reflected in turn in subsequent appropriation acts.[139] The Bureau of the Budget has made other inquiries at the instance of the appropriating groups. The act

---

[136] *Congressional Record,* 78th Cong., 1st Sess., vol. 89, p. 1024, February 15, 1943 (daily edition).
[137] *Ibid.,* p. 1080.
[138] 78th Cong., 1st Sess., House Report No. 109, pp. 5–6.
[139] 77th Cong., 1st Sess., Senate Report No. 503.

of 1921 provided a broad basis for such requests.[140] Recently, of course, Senator Byrd has revealed the embarrassing possibilities of this provision.[141] But its main potentialities are harmonious and complementary.

What about closer cooperation in the routine handling of the annual appropriations? Some informal contact already exists between the staffs of the Budget Bureau and the committees on appropriations. But further intimacy, especially if institutionalized, must be developed cautiously. A practicable minimum step would be to have the committee clerks attend the annual hearings before the estimates division of the Budget in the late summer and fall. The clerks, however, should not remain for the executive sessions in the afternoons wherein the Budget examiners discuss and decide tentatively upon revised figures for the units they have had before them in the morning. Even the first-mentioned step would require enlarged permanent staffs for the committees on appropriations. A reasonable minimum would be one experienced assistant clerk for each regular appropriation bill.

No amount of legislative staffing could take the place of executive supervision. Fitful legislative intervention is no substitute for controls within administration. The most valuable contribution of legislative oversight is to galvanize the disciplines of administration itself. It is significant that the reports of the appropriations committees abound in recommendations to administration that it investigate its procedures and organization, sometimes at the bureau or departmental level, sometimes above. The committees frequently disclaim competence for detailed constructive inquiry in these matters. The staff necessary for continuous inquiry could be main-

---

[140] "The bureau shall, at the request of any committee of either House of Congress having jurisdiction over revenue or appropriations, furnish the committee such aid and information as it may request." 42 Stat. L. 23, approved June 10, 1921; 31 U. S. C. 212.

[141] At the instigation of Senator Byrd, the Senate Committee on Finance, by resolution on August 28, 1941, requested the Director of the Budget to submit three detailed revisions of the estimates for the fiscal year 1942 "as he would make if instructed to prepare three budget estimates," lower by one, by one and a half, and by two billions than the appropriations actually made. The director's analysis of 15 printed pages, submitted October 15, stated: "It should be kept clearly in mind that it is the responsibility of the President alone to submit budgetary recommendations to Congress." The Director, along with the Secretary of the Treasury, was already a somewhat uncomfortable member of the Joint Committee on Reduction of Nonessential Federal Expenditures, set up pursuant to section 601 of the Revenue Act of 1941.

tained only at the risk of a harmful division of responsibility,[142] while such a staff would still lack a first-hand sense of operations. The hazard is that a body like Congress, when it gets into detail, ceases to be itself; it acts through a fraction which may be a faction. This, among other lessons, is a moral to be read in the work of the committees on appropriations.[143]

---

[142] In a press conference on July 13, 1943, the President indicated that he had in mind a message for later delivery to Congress in opposition to the policy of the rider to the urgent deficiency appropriation bill (H. R. 2714, 78th Cong., 1st Sess., which the President had reluctantly signed), preventing the civil employment under any existing or future appropriation of three named persons—the secretary of the Virgin Islands and two employees of the Federal Communications Commission—unless named to and confirmed by the Senate before November 15, 1943. This rider was the fruitage of the Kerr appropriations subcommittee under H. Res. 105, 78th Cong., 1st Sess. Having conducted hearings in April, of which 380 pages were printed, the Kerr group reported through the whole committee on April 21 and on May 14, House Report No. 448. In addition to the three employees who were stigmatized, three others from the number originally challenged were questioned and cleared. The House's insistence on the rider broke through the opposition of the Senate, except for the compromise about the continuance of the employees if confirmed. At the same time the House forced the dropping in conference of a Senate proviso which sought to require Senatorial confirmation of all employees in a score of war agencies who received $4,500 or more a year.

[143] No attempt is made in the present text to frame an over-all appraisal of the methods of legislative oversight of administration. The series of which the article here concluded is part will be resumed at a later time.

BIBLIOGRAPHY

From among the vast number of books on the Congress of the United States, we have limited our selection, in the main, to books which focus primarily on the House of Representatives—particularly empirical studies conducted since World War II. In addition, we have included a number of the most important official and semi-official reference works which all students of Congress find invaluable in their research. For more extended comment on the use of these reference works, the reader is directed to Roland Young's "Research Guide," *The American Congress* (New York: Harper, 1958), pp. 281–324. We have found the mimeographed bibliographies of Edward N. MacConomy and Walter Kravitz of considerable assistance in the preparation of this bibliography (Washington, D.C.: Legislative Reference Service, Library of Congress, 1959,1962).

Bailey, Stephen K. *Congress Makes a Law*. New York: Columbia University Press, 1950.

_____, and Samuel, Howard D. *Congress at Work*. New York: Holt, 1952.

Bauer, Raymond A., Pool, Ithiel de Sola, and Dexter, Lewis A. *American Business and Public Policy: Politics of Foreign Trade*. New York: Atherton, 1963.

Clapp, Charles L. *The Congressman: His Perceptions and Problems*. Washington, D.C.: The Brookings Institution, 1963.

Congressional Quarterly Almanac. Washington, D.C.: Congressional Quarterly, Inc., 1945–, Vols. I–.

Congressional Quarterly Weekly Report. Washington, Congressional Quarterly, Inc., 1945–, Vols. I–.

Carroll, Holbert N. *The House of Representatives and Foreign Affairs*. Pittsburgh: University of Pittsburgh Press, 1958.

Ewing, C. A. M. *Congressional Elections, 1896–1944*. Norman: University of Oklahoma Press, 1947.

Fenno, Richard F., Jr. *The House Appropriations Committee*. Boston: Little, Brown, forthcoming.

Galloway, George B. *History of the U.S. House of Representatives.* New York: Thomas Y. Crowell, 1962.

————. *The Legislative Process in Congress.* New York: Thomas Y. Crowell, 1953.

Green, Harold P., and Rosenthal, Alan. *Government of the Atom: The Integration of Powers.* New York: Atherton, 1963.

Griffith, Ernest. *Congress, Its Contemporary Role.* 3rd rev. ed.; New York: New York University Press, 1961.

Gross, Bertram. *The Legislative Struggle.* New York: McGraw-Hill, 1953.

Kofmehl, Kenneth. *Professional Staffs of Congress.* West Lafayette, Ind.: Purdue University Press, 1961.

MacNeil, Neil. *Forge of Democracy: The House of Representatives.* New York: McKay, 1963.

MacRae, Duncan. *Dimensions of Congressional Voting.* Berkeley: University of California Press, 1958.

Martin, Joe. *My First Fifty Years in Politics.* New York: McGraw-Hill, 1960.

Miller, Clem. *Member of the House: Letters of a Congressman,* ed. John W. Baker. New York: Scribner, 1962.

Munger, Frank, and Fenno, Richard F., Jr. *National Politics and Federal Aid-to-Education.* Syracuse: Syracuse University Press, 1963.

Price, H. Douglas. "Race, Religion, and the Rules Committee: The Kennedy Aid-to-Education Bills," in Alan F. Westin (ed.). *The Uses of Power.* New York: Harcourt, 1962.

Riddick, Floyd Millard. *The United States Congress: Organization and Procedure.* Manassas, Va.: National Capitol Publishers, 1949.

Robinson, James A. *The House Rules Committee.* Indianapolis: Bobbs-Merrill, 1963.

Scammon, Richard (ed.). *American Votes.* Vols. I–IV. New York: Macmillan, 1956, 1957. Pittsburgh: University of Pittsburgh Press, 1958–.

Truman, David B. *The Congressional Party*. New York: Wiley, 1959.

Turner, Julius. *Party and Constituency: Pressures on Congress.* Baltimore: The Johns Hopkins Press, 1951.

U.S. Bureau of the Census. *Congressional District Data Book.* Washington, D.C.: Government Printing Office, 1961.

U.S. Congress. *Biographical Directory of the American Congress, 1774–1961.* Washington, D.C.: Government Printing Office, 1961.

————. *Congressional Record.* Washington, D.C.: Government Printing Office, 1873–, Vols. I–. (Begins with 43rd Cong.)

———— ——. *Congressional Directory.* Washington, D.C.: Government Printing Office, 1807–. (Begins with 10th Cong.)

Voorhis, Jerry. *Confessions of a Congressman.* Garden City, N.Y.: Doubleday, 1947.

Wilson, Woodrow. *Congressional Government.* New York: Meridian, 1956. (Originally published 1885.)

Young, Roland. *The American Congress.* New York: Harper, 1958.

INDEX

ADA (Americans for Democratic Action), 183, 185, 188
Adams, Alva, 353
Administration, see Executive
AFL-CIO, 230, 259
Agricultural Adjustment Act (1938), 112
Agriculture, House Committee on, 45, 50, 55; commodity interests, 112 14, 115, 118–20; constituency interests, 112–14, 115, 118–25; geographical distribution, 112; "omnibus" legislation, 114 ff; organization, 111-14; party interests, 112–14, 115, 117–20
Air Force, U.S., 280 ff
Albert, Carl, 177, 242, 245–49, 254, 257, 259, 260 ff
Alexander, Hugh, 22
Alford, Dale, 54
Anderson, Clinton, 330
Apprenticeship, 96–97, 99 ff, 206
Appropriations: and authorization, 279 ff, 336; estimates, accuracy of, 371–75; jurisdiction over, 337–38; nature of, 369–71
Appropriations, House Committee on, 38, 44 ff, 53, 55; and administrative policy, 365–69; and Budget Bureau, 374–80; chairmen, 340; Deficiencies, 342–43; membership, 339–42; supervisory, 374

Appropriations, House subcommittees on: and administrative policy, 365–69; and Budget Bureau, 374–80; chairmen, 340; Deficiencies, 342–43; membership, 339–42; supervisory, 374

Appropriations, Senate Committee on, 337, 338
Armed forces: authority, 275, 312 ff; funds for, 273 ff, 277–78, 284 ff; rivalry, interservice, 317–19
Armed Services, House Committee on, 45, 55, 282, 283, 284 ff, 310–12, 315–16
Armed Services, Senate Committee on, 280, 281, 283, 284 ff, 288–89, 292
Army, U.S., 281 ff
Army and Air Force Authorization and Composition Act (1950), 280–82
Authorization, 279 ff, 296–301, 336
Ayres, William, 220

Bailey, Cleveland, 218
Baldwin, Hanson, 295 n
Banking and Currency, House Committee on, 45, 55
Barden, Graham, 207, 209–16, 219
Barkley, Alban, 334
Bass, Ross, 161
Biemiller, Andrew, 264
Bloc-voting, 72–74
Bolling, Richard, 177, 242, 245–46, 250 ff
Bomarc A missile, 288–89
Bombers, manned, 299–300
Bowles, Chester, 38
Buchanan, James P., 340
Budget Bureau, 283, 370, 374–80
Budget, defense, see Military policy: appropriations
Burke, Edmund, 238–39
Burke, Thomas, 215
Byrd, Harry, 380

Calendar Wednesday, 173
Cannon, Clarence, 329 n, 347
Cannon, Joseph, 169
CBS Reports, 177
Census, Bureau of, 372 n, 376
Children's Bureau, 360
Childs, Marquis, 261
Civil Aeronautics Authority, 373 n, 375
Civil defense, 309
Civil Rights Act (1960), 173
Civil Service Commission, 332
Cleaves, Thomas P., 345
Cohn, David, 251 n

[387]